Red States

SERIES EDITOR

Riché Richardson, Cornell University

FOUNDING EDITOR

Jon Smith, Simon Fraser University

ADVISORY BOARD

Houston A. Baker Jr., Vanderbilt University

Leigh Anne Duck, The University of Mississippi

Jennifer Greeson, The University of Virginia

Trudier Harris, The University of Alabama

John T. Matthews, Boston University

Tara McPherson, The University of Southern California

Claudia Milian, Duke University

Red States

INDIGENEITY, SETTLER COLONIALISM, AND SOUTHERN STUDIES

Gina Caison

The University of
Georgia Press
ATHENS

Parts of chapter 1 appeared, in somewhat different form, as "Looking for Loss, Anticipating Absence: Imagining Indians in the Archives and Depictions of Roanoke's Lost Colony," in *Indography: Writing the "Indian" in Early Modern England*, edited by Jonathan Gil Harris (London: Palgrave Macmillan, 2012). Parts of chapter 2 appeared, in somewhat different form, as "Romantic Sympathy and Land Claim in William Gilmore Simms's Native South" in the *Simms Review* 23.6 (2015): 5–17. Parts of chapter 5 appeared, in somewhat different form, as "'Land! Hold on! Just hold on!': Flood Waters, Hard Times, and Sacred Land in 'Old Man' and *My Louisiana Love*" in *Faulkner and the Native South*, edited by Jay Watson and Annette Trefzer (Jackson: University Press of Mississippi, 2018).

Paperback edition, 2020
© 2018 by the University of Georgia Press
Athens, Georgia 30602
www.ugapress.org
All rights reserved
Set in 10/13 Kepler Std by Graphic Composition, Inc., Bogart, Georgia.

Most University of Georgia Press titles are
available from popular e-book vendors.

Printed digitally

The Library of Congress has cataloged the hardcover edition of this book as follows:

Names: Caison, Gina, 1980– author.
Title: Red states : indigeneity, settler colonialism, and southern studies / Gina Caison.
Description: Athens : The University of Georgia Press, [2018]
| Includes bibliographical references and index.
Identifiers: LCCN 2018003974| ISBN 9780820353357 (hardcover : alk. paper) |
ISBN 9780820353340 (ebook)
Subjects: LCSH: Indians of North America—Southern States—History. |
Indians of North America—Southern States—Government relations. |
Southern States—Politics and government.
Classification: LCC E78.S65 C35 2018 | DDC 975.004/97—dc23
LC record available at https://lccn.loc.gov/2018003974

Paperback ISBN 978-0-8203-5879-6

For Mother Caison

CONTENTS

ACKNOWLEDGMENTS ix

A NOTE ON TERMINOLOGY xiii

Red States: An Introduction 1

CHAPTER ONE Recovery 29

CHAPTER TWO Revolution 65

CHAPTER THREE Removal 109

CHAPTER FOUR Resistance 159

CHAPTER FIVE Resilience 194

Rights and Returns: A Coda 217

NOTES 223

BIBLIOGRAPHY 243

INDEX 263

ACKNOWLEDGMENTS

It seems nearly impossible to thank everyone who has contributed to my writing of this book. All of the best parts of this monograph are owed to the following institutions and people; the shortcomings of this project are mine alone.

First and foremost, I am eternally grateful for the support of my dissertation committee, Mark Jerng, Michael Wilson, and Julia Coates, as well as the intellectual support I received from the Departments of English and Native American Studies at UC Davis and the Department of English at the University of Wisconsin–Milwaukee. Mark Jerng continues to be a perfect mentor long beyond his duties as the director of my dissertation. Michael Wilson has proven unfailing in his support over the past sixteen years, and I cannot imagine my scholarly life without his steadfast advice. Julia Coates remains a source of constant encouragement, and much of this project emerges from our conversations about the U.S. South. My intellectual life has also been shaped by the undergraduate education I received from Auburn University: Paula Backscheider and Hilary Wyss taught me to love the earliest of archives, and Jim McKelly convinced me that I might have a future as an English major. Additionally, several members of the UC Davis community nurtured the development of the dissertation project that would become this book: Hsuan Hsu, Michael Ziser, Martha Macri, and Judy Alexander offered their feedback, support, and enthusiasm as I imagined what this work could become. This project also owes much of its early conception to conversations with Jack D. Forbes, and one of the treasures of my life is having had the opportunity to talk to him about these ideas before he passed on.

The Department of English at Georgia State University has offered me invaluable support over the last six years. I am especially grateful for the wonderful GSU graduate students and undergraduates who have shared their contagious enthusiasm for literature and history. In particular, David Gomez and the New Echota students have always challenged my thinking about what Native American history and literature means to the contemporary U.S. South; the best part of my job has been working with David and these students to improve the way Georgia accounts for its Removal legacy. Likewise, the Native undergraduate students I have had the pleasure to teach, including Molly Bowman, Olivia Cambern, Jessica Parker, and Lindsey Smith, are leading the way at GSU and in Atlanta for creating a better future for Indigenous peoples in the U.S. South. They leave me humbled and inspired to undertake this work. My department chairs, Randy Malamud and Lynée Gaillet, have supported my research. Harper Strom has consistently been the person there for me to help solve any crisis. My faculty mentor Matthew Roudané is possibly the world's most wonderful colleague. I am proud to consider him a friend. Fellow junior faculty members Emily Bloom and Ashley Holmes offered immensely helpful advice on the initial proposal for this book, and I am especially indebted to Emily for encouraging me to just go ahead and call the book *Red States* even though I was hesitant to own such a potentially provocative title. Likewise, Lindsey Eckert has listened to so many iterations, stops, and starts of this book's evolution that I am grateful that she still allows me to come into her office. Without a doubt, Scott Heath has been my closest intellectual companion over the last five years. If not for his generous ears and mind, this book would not exist.

Additionally, this book would not be possible without the material and financial support from several key institutions and individuals. I thank the American Antiquarian Society, the Davis Humanities Institute, the Southern Historical Collection at UNC–Chapel Hill, and the Georgia State University Research Initiation Grant for their generous support of my work. Likewise, two summer programs sponsored by the National Endowment for the Humanities allowed me to hone my ideas. Scott Manning Stevens of the D'Arcy McNickle Center at the Newberry Library offered early feedback during his 2010 Institute. Theda Perdue, Malinda Maynor Lowery, Clara Sue Kidwell, and Michael Green of the University of North Carolina's American Indian Center helped me refine my argument during their 2011 Seminar, and Malinda Maynor Lowery offered invaluable feedback about portions of the book in its final stage. This project also benefited from conversations at the 2010 Clinton Institute for American Studies Summer School at University College Dublin. Special thanks to Ashley Cataldo, Laura Clark Brown, Lara Cohen, Paul Erickson, Jack Larkin, Jaclyn Penny, and Laura E. Wasowicz for their archival guidance during my time at the American Antiquarian Society. I also wish to thank the reviewers and editors from the University of Georgia Press. Walter Biggins, Jon Smith, Riché Richardson, and Eric Gary Anderson as well as the anonymous readers of the manuscript have all worked to make this book so much better than my brain alone could have achieved. In addition to the libraries and research centers that have helped make this book possible, I also owe an enormous debt of gratitude to those who took the time to talk with me about their work: Lauren Adams, Margaret Bauer, Jim Clark, Brian Clowdus, Dacia Dick, Clyde Ellis, Jeff and Shannon Hatley, Willie French Lowery, Malinda Maynor Lowery, Robert Richmond, Eddie Swimmer, and Leah Wilhelm all shaped my thinking about outdoor drama in the U.S. South. I would also like to thank the Paul Green Foundation and the Roanoke Island Historical Association for their continued support of my work. I am fortunate to be a member of two of the best scholarly communities in academia: Native American studies and southern studies. None of my work would be possible without the generosity and rigor of the scholars in these fields. In particular, Ben Frey, Todd Hagstette, Lisa Hinrichsen, Jeff Rogers, and Kirstin Squint have offered direction, clarification, resources, and encouragement for parts of this research.

Writing a book also requires friends and family who act simultaneously as sounding boards and reservoirs of immense patience. The friendship of Ken and Rebekka Andersen, Dana Arter, Chris Bates, John Garrison, Christoph Gumb, Angel Hinzo, Patricia Killelea, John Mac Kilgore, Jenny Kaminer, Shanae Martinez, Melissa Leal, Karolyn Reddy, Sonja Schillings, Grace Tirapelle, Kaitlin Walker, and Bryan Yazell made graduate school worth the trouble. Brook Colley and Cutcha Risling Baldy continue to be the best teammates in the world; I cannot overstate their importance to my life. Sue Kim has provided emotional, intellectual, and psychological support for the past fourteen years, and I doubt I ever repay the debt. Boris Vormann read every word of this project in its inception, and it is much better for his careful attention. Similarly, Matthew Franks read much of this work in its late stages, and his feedback has been priceless. Since coming to Atlanta, Sheri Hall, Sally Hawkins, Kevin Hayden, Ashley Jehle, Erich Nunn, Lynette Rimmer, Stephanie Rountree, Gabe Sherry, Dustin Stewart, Kris Townsend, Reanna Ursin, and Kelly Vines have enriched my life with their humor and intelligence. Whether they know it or not, Jody Alexander, Amanda Blankenship, Julie Knowles, Isaac Slape, and Andrea Wolf helped make everything about my life—and by extension this work—possible. My parents, Ken and Becky Caison, built a world for me where I was free to learn without judgment. Their quick wit and laughter continue to inspire me. I do not know if my parents (both math education majors) have always understood their liberal arts–inclined daughter, but they have always trusted my decisions, and this is the greatest gift a child can receive. Together, the Caison and Byrd families created my love for a good story, and I hope they may see a bit of themselves in this project. Billie Caison and Jessica Burris also offered much-needed encouragement and laughter along the way, and Debbie Caison Kozuch remains the best big sister a person could ask for.

Lastly, I am certain I could not have written this book if I had not grown up in what we currently know as North Carolina. I also know that I could not have written this book without having had the privilege of learning from so many Native people from across the state during my lifetime. Academic books rarely make anyone money, and I doubt this book will prove any different. However, to my mind, allied, non-Native scholars such as myself should not profit from work that owes itself to the Indigenous communities that have offered them so much. To that end, and because this work could not have existed without my time at the UNC American Indian Center, all author proceeds from this book will be donated to that institution whose mission forwards the educational concerns of Native communities of present-day North Carolina.

A NOTE ON TERMINOLOGY

I have been fortunate in my educational and professional career to be exposed to numerous schools of thought in Native American/American Indian/First Nations/Indigenous studies. As such, I realize the weight that such terms carry in different parts of the academic and nonacademic worlds. I believe that first and foremost we all have the human right to be called as we wish, and because of this belief, I attempt to refer to the authors and figures in this study—if known—as they referred to themselves. After that, I believe in the inherent sovereignty of Native American/American Indian tribes and nations on this continent, and because of this, I make every effort to use the appropriate tribal designations for those Native peoples I write about. When not using specific personal or tribal/national designations, I largely use the terms Native American, American Indian, and Indigenous interchangeably to refer to the original inhabitants of the present-day Americas. The meaning of the term "South" is also under necessary debate. When speaking of the U.S. South, I refer largely to the states that participated in the Confederacy. Additionally, this project stays largely east of the Mississippi as it considers many of the legacies of Indian Removal in the nineteenth century; however, because of Removal, I also look toward present-day Oklahoma, east Texas, and points farther west. I also draw from intellectual traditions emerging from the circum-Caribbean. In other words, the very term "Native South" that this project uses as its organizing heuristic is, at best, contentious. This is a problem that I remain interested in examining but one that I do not pretend to solve. I look forward to more scholarship that continues to challenge what we might mean by these scholarly categories and how they affect those peoples and communities who we imagine are included in such inadequate rubrics of identity.

Red States

Red States
An Introduction

Perhaps it is unwise to title a book *Red States*. The folly of such a decision may seem all the more apparent given the 2016 presidential election, which saw the "red" spread even farther across the country, pushing into the northern Midwest and gaining momentum among traditionally "blue" strongholds of the Rust Belt. These election returns and the demographics they suggest left political pundits scratching their heads and spinning in their seats as they tried to understand what it meant that so many states went *red*. While numerous media outlets had predicted the "purpling" of key southern states including Georgia, North Carolina, and Virginia, none had seemingly given much thought to the fact that "purpling" can work both ways. Blue can bleed into red, but red can also bleed into blue. Rather than support an American progressive fantasy, for many the story of the 2016 election became a lesson in the American regressive movement. Though numerous people appeared dumbfounded, I noticed that a lot of my colleagues in Native American and southern studies seemed less surprised (albeit equally dismayed) by the results. This is not to claim that those of us in these fields are smarter or more informed (indeed, we have our own fantasies) but that we have long trafficked in histories that breed a certain cynicism, that evoke a distinct side eye at any narrative suggesting the United States has moved beyond its roots in settler colonialism and plantation economies.

Indeed, I began this project an entire presidential term (or two) ago. In 2009, when I started conceiving and writing the dissertation that would become this book, President Barack Obama was not far into his first term. The day after the 2009 Inauguration I sat in what would be one of my last and most treasured graduate school courses: Native American Studies 217 on Public Law 280 with the late professor Jack D. Forbes. My peers and I (several of whom would become my dearest and most trusted friends and colleagues) listened as Professor Forbes explained that while we were to enjoy the euphoria that came with such an important milestone, we were to stay aware that Native people remained absented from this show of American progressive patriotism, citing that the Inauguration had included few if any Native people or overt references to their political futures. In short, he tempered our enthusiasm. He reminded us that historically speaking, progressive fantasies are often sandcastles built on the dispossessed land of Native people while regressive moments frequently ask them to pay with their physical bodies. Importantly, he added, both progressive and regressive philosophies did so all while romanticizing a specious version of Native history, claiming it for their own logistical ends. Though he speculated that a "brown" president might very well prove more sympathetic to Native political claims, he instructed us that our job was to remain vigilant, to ask the hard questions, and to resolve ourselves to speak the toughest of answers about our own investments in settler colonialism.

The title of this book, then, signals both an interrogation of settler colonialism in the U.S. South and a certain youthful naïveté. When I began this project in a fit of wide-eyed enthusiasm, I wanted to turn the contemporary understanding of the region inside out, to render visible how every cubed inch of the U.S. South exists on top of Indigenous land and history. I wanted to push past the understanding of the region within a black/white and Old/New binary logic. My background in Native American studies led me to realize that neither the racial nor the temporal structures implied in these older approaches to the U.S. South did much to explain the long scope of the region. In each case it elided Native people, their land claims, and their understandings of temporality. Despite this elision, stories of Native history (real or imagined) pervaded southern literature. In every text I read for my work in southern literary studies there seemed to be some reference or plot concerning a Native person or their land. In much of the Native American literature and Native studies scholarship I read, there emerged thorough considerations of how to assert land claims and traditional Indigenous knowledges that challenged narratives and practices of settler colonialism. While I recognized some of the surface-level shared investments in southern and Native appeals to traditional values and cultural distinctions, what emerged more clearly was the way that these works diverged significantly in questions of material land claims and constructions of time. Thus, space and time seemed largely different in the (historically speaking) relatively recent U.S. South and the long presence of Native people and nations from the same geographic region. Though this project would take on many iterations, and it is largely different in form and content from its dissertation predecessor, I came to see that this was a book about, literally and figuratively, red states.

For this project, then, the red state represents a multivalent approach to understanding the intersection of Native American and southern studies. The term should be understood to call on geographical distinctions as well as states of being that depend on narrative order. In this way, the term "red state" links space and time. It is commonplace to assert that the U.S. South has been shaped by race relations, plantation economies, cultural blending, and a "sense of place." This book, however, interrogates the ways that all of these defining factors can be traced back to two of the most fundamental of issues for what will become the region: Indigenous land claims (space) and competing claims to narrative order (time). I term the intersection of these two issues, land claim and narrative order, the red state, signifying at once the spatial conception of the U.S. South as a profoundly Indigenous place and the narrative order of the region as dependent on a set of temporal fantasies that frequently rely on indigeneity to establish a coherent set of meanings for the region in the past and today. To clarify, by "land claim" I mean the material, legal, and/or physical occupation of the land. Indigenous peoples have original and primary land claim to all the lands of their territories. Settler colonialism attempts to mitigate if not destroy these claims through juridical and narratological maneuvers as well as physical violence. Additionally, narrative order suggests the way that fictional stories as well as historical events are organized via an understanding of time. For the audiences of these narratives, this organization of events frequently produces outcomes that engage power relationships of their lived reality. Together these two phenomena—land claim and narrative order—reveal the underlying assumptions that buttress the ongoing relationship of the U.S. South (and occasionally studies of the U.S. South) with settler colonialism. Indeed, settler colonialism takes many forms.[1] For the purposes of my investigation, I mean the European system of colonialism that relies on racialized violence, religious "conversion," and manipulations of the law to establish the settlement of its people at the expense of Indigenous nations and individuals.

Specifically, I argue that the red state represents the following: a geographic space that popular rhetoric encourages audiences to imagine as politically and socially conservative; a state of being where Indigenous history is used to undergird southern exceptionalism through articulations of white southern nativism and land claim; and a state fantasy where dynamic and sovereign Native nations exist as static referents for white southern feelings, including a sense of place, romances of the Lost Cause, and fervor around counternational rhetoric. However, one of the core goals of this book is to demonstrate how this relatively bleak formulation of the red state is not a given. Through their literature and other cultural productions, Native people of the U.S. South have used key articulations of land claim, conservation, and regional belonging to resist popular red state logics, demonstrating a much older, more complex region. They have maintained another version of the "red" that prefigures and proceeds from the traditions of the Red Power movements and their legacies.[2] The U.S. South is a relatively young creation, and an

Indigenous-centered understanding of the red state forces an understanding of the U.S. South as a set of narrative orders constructed to maintain land claims under more romantic notions of race, place, and economy. Furthermore, up until the Nixon administration, the U.S. South was not understood as particularly "red" at all. Therefore, I argue that the older and more meaningful red state might be the one called on by the region's long history of Indigenous resistance to colonization. Alongside of this, I argue that even as political parties change in scope, geographical home, and ideology, the Native presence within and resistance to settler colonialism subtends the formation of a "southern" identity. The red state, then, can be both a fantasy of settler colonialism *and* a site of resistance where Native people demonstrate their original claims to the region.

Therefore, *Red States* takes up both white southern nativism and Native responses to the phenomenon—two issues that have not been considered thoroughly within one place. This book, then, examines how the recurrent use of Indigenous history in cultural and literary texts produces ideas of regional belonging that have consequences for how present-day conservative political discourses resonate across the United States. I argue that notions of Native American identity in the U.S. South can be understood by tracing how audiences in the region came to imagine indigeneity through texts ranging from the nineteenth-century newspaper the *Cherokee Phoenix* to the twentieth-century Lumbee-produced regional outdoor drama, *Strike at the Wind!* Policy issues such as Indian Removal, biracial segregation, land claim, and federal Termination frequently correlate to the audience consumption of such texts, and therefore, the reception histories of this archive can be tied to shifts in the political claims of—and political possibilities for—Native people of the U.S. South. This continual appeal to the political issues of Indian Country ultimately generates what we see as persistent discourses about southern exceptionality and counternationalism. Using five core narratives—recovery, revolution, removal, resistance, and resilience—this project considers the importance of Indigenous literary traditions for shaping concepts of the region. This renewed understanding of region, I argue, affects larger national narratives of belonging particularly as it pertains to the concerns of Indigenous peoples. Ultimately, I conclude that the U.S. South is indeed made up of red states, but perhaps not in the way we initially imagine.

I propose, then, that southern studies adjust its thinking about the term "red." This proposal may not be modest and is certainly not new. Numerous activists and scholars before me have outlined the contours of the Red Power movement and the claiming of the "red" as a significant act of resistance against settler colonialism. Among the most foundational among this tradition includes the scholarship of Vine Deloria Jr., whose works ranging from *God Is Red: A Native View of Religion* (1972) to *Red Earth, White Lies: Native*

Americans and the Myth of Scientific Fact (1995) put forward the idea of "red" as the center of an Indigenous universe. The coalescing of Native identity in the Americas under the term "red" has allowed for pantribal alliances while maintaining national distinctions among sovereign tribes. At the same time, the very idea of "red" as a marker of indigeneity is one of the primary ways that narratives of the U.S. South have flourished via a received cultural legibility often at the expense of living Native people and their land claims. Just because Native people have been rendered invisible in this model, however, does not mean they have disappeared. Quite the contrary. They have remained, and they have fought. Through political campaigns, armed resistance, and narrative reordering of history, the Native people of the U.S. Southeast have kept their own red state alive, creating and re-creating a region in their own image.

Red States uses a regional focus in order to delineate both the tenets of white southern nativism and Indigenous resistance to colonial aggression. I contend that colonialism is indeed localized, flexible, and exploitative of particular material conditions that exist in specific places. It is supported by a complex network of cultural practices. In order to appreciate the focus on regionalism when we look at Native American literary and cultural productions, I argue that we must fully appreciate the machinations of power that Native people were and are working against in specific locations. This can be accomplished through a careful dissection of non-Native-authored texts that depend on versions of Native and regional history for their narrative goals. With this in view, we can better appreciate how Native people work within, around, and against colonialism to fight for and maintain sovereign land claim in their home spaces. However, Native people do not have to be physically in these locations in order to engage these issues. As Choctaw scholar Michael Wilson has posited about much Indigenous resistance fiction, Native works continue to "write home." Following his logic, we might consider that the narrative does not have to be *about home* to *write home* within an Indigenous tradition. This reading allows critics to loosen a "sense of place" from land claim and renegotiate the tensions that inform settler colonialism as occupying spaces in an attempt to undermine indigeneity as coterminous with land tenure. As Wilson articulates regarding modernist "homing in" narratives that represent Indigenous peoples returning to traditional centers of culture, "in contemporary fiction [...] 'homing in' narratives demand resolutions to culturally hybrid positions, for unresolved liminality remains thematically untenable and stylistically unsatisfactory" (M. Wilson xii).[3] Wilson asserts, and I agree, that "For the most part, Indigenous writers and activists have emphasized the fundamental importance of sovereign geographic spaces to the future of indigenous groups, indicating their commitment to a measure of independence within America's own grand narratives of national unity" (151). I extend this core idea in order to undo the critical logics that intellectually recapitulate Removal by neglecting southeastern tribal national diaspora across the continent.

Simply put, this book seeks to disarticulate the southern "sense of place" from land claim. Within this project, I attempt to pry apart an understanding of settler-colonial territorial occupation from landed Indigenous sovereignty. The affective realm of the "sense of place" can tend to move us all too easily into a material attachment to the physical land, without remembering as Eric Gary Anderson notes, "Native southern ground is not lost (or preliterate) ground, not simply a mistily nostalgic pre-southern place, situated in some other culture's bracingly chronological order and largely defined against the canonical non-Native South, the post-southern non-Native South, and the most recent manifesto-driven incarnation, the New (but still pretty much non-Native) South" ("On Native Ground"). Instead, the Native South is past, present, and future, and Indigenous land claims are not terminated when or just because non-Native southerners feel attached to their homes. This disjoining of a "sense of place" from a material land claim is important for then considering the geographic and temporal assertions that support concepts of the popularly held red state. It acknowledges that Native people exist as national citizens of their own spaces and that despite attempts at removal, Native people and nations still exist regardless of how much or how little they have in common culturally, politically, or individually. I think one of the main responsibilities of non-Native scholars is to undo continued structures of white supremacy and settler colonialism by educating their fields and fellow non-Native scholars about continued blind spots to Indigenous issues. In the case of this book, I spend a fair amount of time demonstrating how southern studies has continued to build itself on fantasies of settler colonialism that efface Indigenous people and politics from the region.

In many cases, the region becomes the site where individuals traffic in a more coherent nationhood even when that region may assert counternational belonging. In other words, the region becomes the vehicle for the nation by which citizens assert their sense of place. In so doing they reaffirm a land attachment that works to fulfill the settler-colonial logic of the nation disguised as their own individual ideas of place-based belonging.[4] What the acknowledgment of a southeastern diasporic tribal national population disrupts, then, is this easy glide from sense of place to a priori land tenure. Then, in terms of Native nations, rather than a pantribal melting pot, we suddenly see the landscape dotted with a complex network of distinct and interconnected sovereign nations beholden to one another as partners in a web. Such a formulation might allow us to hold in view a tribally focused approach as advocated by Craig Womack in his seminal study *Red on Red* (1999) while simultaneously recognizing the larger vectors of a multinational, multitribal

Native American literary tradition. This approach might help speak to Jodi Byrd's call in "A Return to the South" (2014) that we see how "such patterned intimacies request a willingness to be responsible to people and to land as well as to the geographies beyond nation-states and other such Norths" (619).

Territory has long been one of the most obvious markers of sovereignty. Next to that is story. Whether creation stories or sanctioned histories, the stories people tell about the lands they inhabit (and why they inhabit them) matter for the recognition of their sovereignty. Additionally, sovereignty remains necessarily and paradoxically both inherent and dialectic. Indigenous claims to sovereignty exist intrinsically. However, national sovereignty is often also dependent on recognition. The United States exists as a sovereign nation-state because other sovereign nation-states recognize it as such. While at present tribal nations must officially look to their colonial occupiers for legal recognition, this does not always and forever have to be the case. As sovereign nations, tribal governments might recognize other tribes—as they have done in the past and with a much longer history than the current standards from the Bureau of Indian Affairs. And indeed, one of the core tenets of the BIA recognition process is the tribe's maintaining of a historical narrative and documentation since before 1900, demonstrating the ways that the construction of histories matters for sovereignty.[5] Furthermore, for the purposes of this book, it would be good to remember that the Confederate States of America was never recognized as a sovereign nation by any other sovereign nation. This leads us to the necessary question: why do narratives dependent on Confederate land claims take up so much space in our present-day understanding of the red state? How have these narratives come to dominate considerations of the region over the other narratives of sovereign nations that exist in the region?

Keeping these questions in mind, I take up the issues of southern memory, performance, and stories in relationship to Native history and literature. To do so, I analyze the intersections among these complex ideas, and I explore how Native American literatures construct larger narratives of southern history and how non-Native authors from the U.S. South integrate their own versions of Indigenous history into narratives of southern exceptionalism. While the project engages numerous performance texts, it is not a performance studies project per se. I engage theories and methods from performance studies, but this book does not necessarily make an intervention into that field. Instead, each section of the project considers how discursive debates around the notion of an "authentic history" appeal to audiences' desires for a stable region in order to justify shifts in the political climate of the U.S. South. In other words, at times the shaped truth of history becomes irrelevant when the decontextualized historical artifact and the juridical construction of Native presence are conflated by the general public. By examining the discourse surrounding crucial historical moments alongside their later retellings, I trace how regional Native history has been constructed by both Native and non-Native people in their articulation of beliefs about appropriate Native policy. Through genres such as early travel narratives, antebellum periodicals and ephemera, twentieth-century performances, contemporary novels, and documentary film, I isolate recurrent themes in the public's understanding of Native identity and land claims in the U.S. South.

While the U.S. South has been popularly considered as a post-Removal space dating from the 1830s, I argue for the necessity of considering the continued presence of Native people in the U.S. South while foregrounding the realities of Native nations as sovereign entities with specific historical and legal claims to the region. Instead of simply "excavating" southern cultural history for an Indigenous presence, this project acknowledges and foregrounds the continued Native presence in the region, which includes ten federally recognized tribes and members of other recognized tribes who live in, work in, and write about the region. Additionally, one of the largest and best-known state tribes without complete federal recognition, the Lumbee Tribe of North Carolina, calls the region home. Their unique history in the region highlights the very problems of being Native in the U.S. South where racial classifications have long obscured Native national sovereignty. Foregrounding this Native presence helps this project undermine narratives of Removal as a complete and total process for the region, and it highlights the ways in which southeastern Native people in diaspora still have legal, intellectual, material, and moral land claims to their southeastern homes.

Although there have been numerous attempts over the last five centuries to physically and psychologically remove Indigenous peoples from the present-day U.S. Southeast, the fact is that they remain in both regards. As the editors of the journal *Native South* argue, "in order to write a comprehensive history of the American South, one must consider the Indian experience, that Indians mattered in the course of Southern history, and that scholars exclude them from the region's major narratives at their peril" (Carson et al. x). I agree, but I also argue that Indians continue to matter to the southern present and future and not simply its history. As Geary Hobson, Janet McAdams, and Kathryn Walkiewicz, the editors of the recent anthology *The People Who Stayed: Southeastern Indian Writing after Removal* (2010), echo Simon Ortiz in his poem "Travels in the South": "Indians are everywhere" (6). As the editors note, these histories point to acts of physical relocation, document genocide, and the rhetoric of disappearance as the primary ways that Native people were removed from the U.S. South. As many now realize, these are largely the culprits of the popular misconception of the U.S. South as a black/white racial binary space.[6]

In addition to narratives of Indigenous Removal, the U.S. South has also been largely conceived as a geography determined by narratives of the Lost Cause. I argue, however, that a reorientation of the region around much earlier moments such as the Roanoke voyages, the southern front of the American Revolution, and the issue of Indian Removal shows that the informing arguments of the Lost Cause predate the Civil War, allowing us to rethink southern narratives of identity that appeal to the region's "unique" history. Indeed, the continual focus on a uniform plantation economy and slavery in the U.S. South, as well as the foundational myth of the Lost Cause, have tended to obfuscate the histories of Native American people in the U.S. South as well as the region's—and the field of southern studies'—ongoing investment in settler colonialism. However, if we examine the themes that emerge in the region's literary and cultural texts, we can see that the oppression of Native American people, as well as the later memories of their land claims, was constitutive of narratives in which the U.S. South positioned itself vis-à-vis other imagined regions. This positioning emerges before the Confederate loss of the Civil War, and it challenges those critical readings that upstream relatively new southern identities back onto Indigenous histories.

To pursue this argument, I build on existing critical literature that emphasizes the importance of race and class for regional societies. This project situates itself within the New Southern Studies, and it takes inspiration from the work of scholars such as Deborah Cohn, Jon Smith, Jessica Adams, Michael Bibler, Cécile Accilien, and others who highlight the economic, racial, and political continuances across the Caribbean and the U.S. South. Much of New Southern Studies considers the global projections and influences both inside and outside of the region. Collections such as Smith and Cohn's *Look Away! The U.S. South in New World Studies* (2004) pose many of the same questions that interest me about the region such as how to locate, or perhaps dislocate, the U.S. South in a New World paradigm. In doing so, they highlight the difficulty in articulating a postcolonial "South." This difficulty arises from what they see as the U.S. South's uncanny hybridity, which they find present in the relationship between a U.S. South that imagines itself as oppressed by an imperial North and a South that continues to implicitly and explicitly oppress other souths. They assert that the U.S. South is "simultaneously (or alternately) center and margin, victor and defeated, empire and colony," and they argue for the increased work toward specification when dealing with the traditionally collective identity of "southern" (9). My project also answers their call that "we cease to speak of 'southern identities' except as contingent and performative" (15). However, despite this call for work that complicates our understanding of the U.S. South, the essays in this volume never fully turn toward considering the Native past and present of the area and how this might inform and complicate regional performativity alongside representations of plantation economies. In short, much of the best new work on the U.S. South never quite reaches a sustained investigation of how the region emerges from the logics and logistics of settler colonialism.

Because of the ways that this project interrogates the use of history within the region, I draw extensively from work in ethnohistory in order to demonstrate the complicated nexus between an archival past and a performed or narrated present. Within Native American studies, this project has numerous antecedents, primarily in the field of ethnohistory. Theda Perdue, Michael D. Green, and Clara Sue Kidwell's work in articulating the construction of race within southeastern tribes and within the larger region remains seminal to the field and central to this project.[7] Likewise, new work in southeastern ethnohistory such as that of Malinda Maynor Lowery, Angela Pulley Hudson, and Christina Snyder demonstrates the breadth and depth of scholarly possibility when the colonial, antebellum, Reconstruction, and Jim Crow Souths are put into dialogue with the region's complex Native histories.[8] While scholars such as Maynor Lowery, Pulley Hudson, and Snyder move across issues of race and economy to demonstrate the convergences and divergences of the strategies that Native people used to survive the changing realities of the region, critics such as Claudio Saunt seem to pay more attention to the questions of race as overdetermined by notions of static identity and the economies "adopted" by Native people, primarily those Native people he identifies as mixedbloods or "mestizo."[9] Despite their various perspectives on how to account for some of the region's complicated intersections of Native identity, racial logics, and the politics of land claim, I agree with all of these scholars working in ethnohistory that issues of race and economy mattered—and continue to matter—to people across the region when it comes to engaging the terrain of American Indian presence and participation in the U.S. South.[10]

While those of us in literary studies have been much slower to pursue questions of the Native South than our colleagues in ethnohistory, a small group of scholars are working now to pay attention to the nuances of both the U.S. South in Native American literature and the representations of Native people and history within southern literature. This project foregrounds the work of literary and cultural materials in order to think through the issues of received historical truths that begin to coalesce into material realities. While the work in ethnohistory remains critical to the field, a literary perspective of the Native South will help uncover the ways that stories from and about the region have material impact within the region. When writers imagine and tell about the U.S. South, they build ideas that at times collapse into anticipated and received historical truths. Though not the only approach, literary studies offers an important perspective on the construction of the region through (hi)stories, and I am indebted to several scholars who have already begun this endeavor. These include Eric Gary Anderson, Jodi Byrd, John

Lowe, Kirstin Squint, Melanie Benson Taylor, Annette Trefzer, Jace Weaver, and Craig Womack, among others. Anderson has worked extensively in the field, and I follow his argument that "American and Southern Studies [need to] reimagine their own provocative presences and absences within Native Studies, to rethink [...] the tenets and governing assumptions of these disciplinary 'regions'" ("Native Ground"). Likewise, while my work here has a different focus, Annette Trefzer's study, *Disturbing Indians: The Archaeology of Southern Fiction* (2006), represents a strong initial step toward exploring the ways that southern modernist writers imagined the Native past in an attempt to construct their own oppositional regional white identities. Whereas Trefzer focuses on a specific period of non-Native literature, I argue here for the benefits of thinking transhistorically and cross-culturally so that we can better understand how Native and non-Native people alike built and continue to build the U.S. South through the use of story.

In addition to those working explicitly within a Native South framework, there are numerous Native literary critics who have produced formative work about the literature from southeastern tribes. As I mention above, Craig Womack's *Red on Red: Native American Literary Separatism* (1999) is foundational as both an in-depth look at Creek literary productions and a methodological approach to Native literature that centers the tribal history, culture, and linguistic traditions from which that literature emerges. Additionally, in their *American Indian Literary Nationalism* (2006) Jace Weaver, Craig Womack, and Robert Warrior each rely on Native epistemologies that come from their Cherokee, Creek, and Osage intellectual traditions, respectively. Similarly, Daniel Heath Justice, in his incredibly important *Our Fires Survive the Storm: A Cherokee Literary History* (2006), uses a Cherokee epistemological heuristic of a Beloved Path and Chickamauga Consciousness to read a number of Cherokee literary texts. Likewise, while Jodi Byrd's *Transit of Empire: Indigenous Critiques of Colonialism* (2011) addresses numerous cultural and literary productions, her methodology emerges from a Chickasaw worldview that allows her to interrogate her assembled archive from a Native perspective. In other words, over and above their objects of study, these works forward the idea of Native American studies as a discipline that is grounded in method. For far too long, many have understood Native American studies as an object-focused discipline, as one that pursues Native people and culture as objects of study. What each of these significant works posits, however, is that Native American studies offers an epistemological approach to the world—as a discipline that draws from Indigenous knowledges to construct methods of analysis that can be applied to a diverse set of objects. Rather than taking concepts from the discipline of Eurocentric literary studies and then applying those standards to Native literature, Womack, Byrd, and others demonstrate how to take Native American studies as a methodological framework that allows us to reread beyond Native-authored texts. This distinction remains important for understanding how and why Native American studies is more than an amalgamation of traditional Western disciplines. In the case of these scholarly works, collectively these critics produce scholarship that forwards the Native South beyond the literary object and instead outlines new ways to approach literary criticism as a discipline.

Working within a Marxist literary studies framework, Taylor's *Reconstructing the Native South: American Indian Literature and the Lost Cause* (2011) has argued for the need to reread the construction of a post–Civil War southern identity that emerges within and alongside of Native identity in the region and the larger United States. My project echoes Taylor's contention that a Lost Cause ideology continually overdetermines how Native history is or is not seen in the region. However, my project takes a different direction as I ask the following questions: what existed before the Lost Cause, and how does thinking across the historically emphasized Civil War divide of the region illuminate a greater understanding of the formation of Native and non-Native identities in the U.S. South? These questions render visible the region's and southern studies' largely uninterrogated investments with settler colonialism. Indeed, an initial consideration of Native history and literature in the region may seem like it is related to other regional "Lost Cause" fantasies. Such a conclusion might initially appear to be true because so much of the initial "recovery" efforts of Native history in the region, including the reconstruction and protection of historic sites such as New Echota or the Chief Vann House in northern Georgia, emerged from a mid-century moment when white southerners turned a sympathetic eye toward Native history to mitigate the "bad press" from the civil rights movement where the racism of the white South toward black citizens received a national spotlight. Thus, if we attempt to find a relationship between southern and Native lost cause nostalgia, we have to be careful to historicize what stories about the Native South appear when in order to accomplish certain political ends for different people.

Taylor's work represents an important contribution to the field, but Taylor and I have points of difference in our temporal approach to the region. Whereas Taylor reads Native sovereignty within the region through the Marxist totality of the plantation economy, I focus on recurrent narratives of imagined colonial loss that far predate the white-invented Lost Cause of the Confederacy, and I outline a Native-studies approach in order to posit that stories do more than follow a teleology from plantation economy to neoliberalism. Narratives slither around corners, seep through crevices of received truth, and overflow containers of fact.[11] As California Coast Miwok/Southern Pomo critic and author Greg Sarris has succinctly offered, "Remember that when you hear and tell my stories, there is more to me and you and that *is* the story" (46, emphasis in original). While the method I outline may be ambitious in its attempt to hold both author and audience in view, I argue that it takes ambition to think ourselves out of the plantation economy that has seemingly dominated so many considerations of the region. This is not to say the economic structures of the U.S. South are irrelevant, but that they require interrogation as the only framework by which to understand the region's cultural and literary productions. Thus, my analyses incorporate, extend, and challenge Taylor's work. Whereas Taylor theorizes a U.S. South of the relatively recent Confederate Lost Cause, I historicize a *longue durée* of the red state.

Therefore, I offer an analysis that pays particular attention to transhistorical reception as a means by which to analyze how the U.S. South has or has not remembered the Native ground on which it stands. The focus of this project may indeed seem broad, particularly in terms of periodization. However, when one begins to examine something called the "Native South," the reified heuristics of periodization begin to break down. As I discuss later, even the two most prominent ways to talk about the region in temporal terms, the "New" and "Old" South, fail to take the long Native presence into account. Furthermore, even something such as the idea of literary periodization is bound up with a colonial enterprise, as several scholars note in the "Theories and Methodologies" section of the March 2012 *PMLA* titled "The Long and Short: Problems in Periodization." Following the lead established by Wai Chee Dimock, these scholars take on the questions of how the period and the archive change when we look past colonial formations of "measuring tape" time (Dimock 2).[12] As Ato Quayson notes in his *PMLA* contribution, "Periodization in postcolonial literary studies, then, cannot restrict itself to dates or periods, since the dates automatically imply historical epoch-making events *and* the inauguration of various spatial relations" (347). At times *Red States* examines items that may appear at once to be both vastly removed from one another and intensely recursive in their resonances. Given that the region in question seemingly deploys and redeploys various logics of indigeneity to account for its own formation, such a shuttling between historic events and texts alongside contemporary performances and politics may at once illuminate registers of meaning rarely accounted for in narratives preoccupied with clear distinctions between the Old and New Souths. Such a focus on the logics subtending the formation of one particular geographic region speaks to the question posed by Abenaki scholar Lisa Brooks in her contribution to the *PMLA* special section. She asks: "What would it mean to privilege place when discussing periodization, to consider, as the geographer Davis Wishart does, that 'period' and 'region' are deeply linked narratives? What different shape might literary history take if we account for distinct conceptions of time that arise simultaneously from particular places? How might Indigenous methodologies help answer some of the vexing questions that literary historians ponder in our present world?" (309). Like Dimock, Brooks sees possibility in the prevalence of the spiralic time associated with the Indigenous Americas. In thinking with this different temporal construction, our assembled archive may look messier, more incoherent, or even vaguely disjointed. However, this spiralic temporal construction may allow us to see new archives that emerge from the continually revised logics of the region we examine rather than from the teleology of their presupposed functions as pieces for national narrative-making. As such, I interrogate the uses and reuses of various new and old histories in cultural productions across the last five hundred years in order to illuminate the recurring ways that the U.S. South has attempted to understand the much longer temporal registers of Indigenous presence. Likewise, I examine how Native people in the region have used alternate temporal structures to resist the southern narratives that have been put upon them. As Barbara Harlow offers of resistance literature and its authors: "It is part of their historical challenge, their demand for an access to history which necessitates a radical rewriting of the historiographical version of the past which gives prominence of place to a western calendar of events" (86). My investigation of the region across traditional periods is meant to query the region's epoch-making across multiple moments and the resistance to such narratives. As Anderson argues, we can think through alternate temporal frameworks in order to understand the Native South. He writes: "Without abandoning linear history, Native studies and American studies scholars can learn to step outside of it in strategic ways and respect Native understandings of a host of genealogies and temporalities, including time immemorial" ("Presence" 257). While I would argue for more abandonment of linear history than Anderson might, I follow his lead that in stepping out of such linearity we gain new ways to see the interconnectedness of genres, times, texts, and objects that recur and evolve as different people take up these narratives in different moments. The spiralic time I advocate for across this project offers a heuristic to see recurrences that might not be as readily obvious with traditional literary periodization. This approach requires a recognition of the value of synchronic historicism as well as the foregrounding of a diachronic analysis that recognizes that narratives can move across deep time.

One way to register the shifting resonance within a different scope of periodization is through the close examination of reception histories and dynamics. Because audiences constitute a site where multiple genres intersect across time in the consumption of varying texts, this project turns occasionally toward reception as a place to query the recursive logics and uses of Indigenous identity and history in the region. As Katie Trumpener argues, audiences read in the "present tense," and the registers of their reading are bound up with both their individual memories and the collective logics of their own time alongside the texts' original moments. She proposes, "If we see time not as an inert, empty placeholder but as the agglomeration of individuals' subjective clocks, then period comes to seem a problematic concept" (350). In thinking through how we might take seriously this undoing of period and other heuristic "blocks," this project weaves together texts and periods through a careful analysis of the records of reception left by these texts' recursive temporal terrains. This is not simply an act of reader response where I privilege my own subjective responses to the works I examine, but rather a careful tracking of the numerous places where literary critics might follow a textual genealogy through various audiences' responses to the texts. In so doing, this project takes the power of the critical and popular texts' audiences seriously.

Through this methodological approach, this project foregrounds the power that audiences possess over what a text will mean for the political material world. This is not to say that meaning exists *purely* in the audience. However, through an examination of the discursive terrain of power circulating around a given text's reception, we can catch glimpses of how audiences understand material claims to indigeneity in the U.S. South through their consumption of a multifaceted archive of cultural materials. As Foucault reminds us, "power passes through individuals," and through these networks "they are in a position to both submit to and exercise this power" ("*Society*" 29). These networks can be examined as he suggests in their local contexts through the uses of truth to construct histories that materialize into an understanding of public rights. Therefore, in several instances, this project offers readings of the public and political policies that exist within the contemporaneous networks of a given work's reception. This is not to suggest a causal relationship between political outcomes and textual consumption, but instead to think through the assertion made by Ruth Wilson Gilmore in her 2012 presidential speech at the American Studies Association that "policy is the new theory" (263). She notes that this way of thinking constitutes "a script for enlivening some future possibility—an experiment" (263). It is in this spirit that occasionally I turn to the policy milieu surrounding reception. Such moments may help theorize what a given audience's reaction to a text at a particular historical moment might mean for why the study of literary texts matters for the lived conditions of Native people in and from the U.S. South. These conditions necessarily change over time as audiences' feelings regarding the "authentic" or "true" history expose genealogies of received thought that yield material consequences.[13] Specifically in the chapters that follow, I analyze this field of power through debates about and appeals to "authentic" history within the continued consumption of texts that build recursive narratives of the red state. In this way, this project takes up Scott Romine's work in *The Real South: Southern Narrative in the Age of Cultural Reproduction* (2008) as like Romine, I am "less interested in defining terms such as 'authentic' and 'real' as metaphysical or psychoanalytic categories than in understanding how individuals and groups *use* these concepts in a region and an age compelled by them" (10, emphasis in original). Also like Romine, I see this deployment of the "real" as a function of desire. However, this desire is complicated when we acknowledge that Native nations have claims to the land in the U.S. South that are more "real" than the invented narratives of settler-colonial southerners.

This structure of historical land claim plays on concepts of southern feelings, and frequently these feelings undermine Native sovereignty in the region in order to produce a coherent and troubling version of a red state. However, as this project hopes to demonstrate in numerous examples, Native people of the U.S. South have their own ways of feeling and seeing the region. These moments do not rest on loss. Instead they continue to foreground presence, and despite nineteenth-century Removal, Native people still have a significant material, psychological, and—might I add—constitutionally valid claim to the region. Although this project takes a hard look at the slippery nature of affect in the region, it also takes up the moments when feelings about Native identity and history seem to shift. Despite the long attempts to co-opt Native people and their history into the contemporaneous political and material feelings of other people in the region, Native people in the U.S. Southeast have long persisted on their own terms despite the toughest of odds. Even when this project engages non-Native authors and texts, it attempts to always hold this persistence in view. Additionally, I spend a fair amount of time investigating how audiences, both popular and critical, have seen or not seen the Native people and history of the region. In many ways, this project largely becomes about when, where, and how audiences, both Native and non-Native, see or fail to see Native presence in the U.S. South. Although above I mention that many conceive of the region as a post-Removal space, there also exists a constant obsession with the region's Indigenous history. While there remains a dearth of critical examinations of Native histories, themes, and characters in southern literature, when one looks closely, there are instances of Native American presence and representation everywhere in the literature itself. These instances repeatedly turn back to questions of perceived Indigenous absence in the early archives, as well as issues of removal, sovereignty, land claim, and lost causes. Thus, I contend *how* audiences see Native presence is as important as the representations themselves.

In terms of land claim, there has also long been a romantic link between the U.S. South's Indigenous history and the desire to indigenize whiteness to the region. As Richard Gray narrates in his foreword to *South to a New Place: Region, Nature, and Culture* (2002), one of the U.S. South's most famous authors, Margaret Mitchell, understood the realm of southern feelings for the land. He quotes Mitchell's recounting of the "southern curse": "The curse I refer to is loving land enough to give everything you've got to get it. Never would I own a foot of it, city or country land. If I had spare money it would stay in the bank or the stock market but never in red clay. Then about two years ago when I set out to write the great American novel I was confronted by the fact that whether I liked it or not, it was a story of the land and a woman who was determined not to part with it" (qtd. in Gray, "Inventing" xiv). As Gray analyzes, Mitchell's sentiment demonstrates great "emotional truth," as it "seems utterly southern in the sense that attachment to the southern land—or, as William Faulkner would have it, loving and hating that land—has always been taken as a determining feature of what it means to be southern" (xv). Such a conclusion probably rings true for many southerners. However, this pronouncement is complicated by the later observation by Gray that for Mitchell, along with Alice Walker, what remains important is "a feeling for the past that is part of *their* earth and therefore part of them" (xv; my emphasis). And as he argues, it comes forward in Eudora Welty's work that "To this extent, we can infer, inventing the South is a product of an *aboriginal* impulse we all share" (xxi; my emphasis). This "aboriginal impulse" may explain many of the specious claims to Indigenous identity in the region, and these statements call forth Anderson's warning against non-Natives in the U.S. South simply "assuming a southern sense of home but at the same time remaining, even today, far from home on living Native ground" ("Native Ground"). At the same time, these moments of feeling resonate with the broad temporal scope of the objects I examine, and in paying attention to the language of feeling in a text's continual reception, we may indeed demonstrate Trumpener's assertion that "layers of time, indeed, prove connected by memory, sensation, external stimuli, and above all, feeling" (350). In other words, because the language of feeling emerges time and again in audience reception, and because feelings can change in such ways as to register what Raymond Williams identifies as "in process" and "emergent," it represents a locus by which to gauge the shifting social dynamics that can affect the understanding of claims to Native identity and history in the U.S. South.[14]

As I outline throughout the book, Native people appear within the pages of southern literature with an extensive regularity. Sometimes the presences are submerged, but sometimes people cannot see what they are not looking for. Because of this, I take a primarily ethnohistorical viewpoint of the U.S. South where I look closely for the existence, traces, and representations of Native voices within each of the works I examine. Sometimes these voices are only there in representation, which is categorically not the same thing as the Native voice itself. However, instead of discounting these representational practices as merely false and disregarding them wholesale, I attempt to pay attention to what they can tell us about how non-Native people were imagining and receiving the Native voices in their midst. So while the Native South may be a region seldom seen by some, it is not a region removed or dissociated from its Indigenous past, present, or future. Furthermore, Native people have long been conscious of the need to engage in representational practices for their own interests. Frequently, these moments are rhetorically constructed in order to achieve a desired end, and they should not be dismissed as "inauthentic" simply because they are deployed for the purpose of affecting an outcome.[15]

In many ways, *Red States* engages the dialogue established in the concluding roundtable at the 2002 joint conference between the American Literature Association and the Society for the Study of Southern Literature on "Postcolonial Theory, the U.S. South, and New World Studies" where Annette Trefzer asked, "to what extent have we [...] excluded or elided a Native American presence in the traditional South?" ("Concluding Roundtable" 175–76). The responses included that of Suzanne Bost, who suggested that the "container" of southern studies might overflow if we add too much, including a turn to Native southern and Latino southern lines of inquiry, and even more interestingly Melanie Benson Taylor, who speculated: "for all our efforts here [at the conference] to be transnational, I think in lots of ways we still conceive the Native American population as another nation" (179, 192). Both of these comments illustrate the precise reasons why Native American and southern studies need a more productive dialogue. What Taylor's comments do not register, despite her certain awareness of this fact, is that Native American populations *are* members of separate sovereign nations and not to imagine or refer to them as such undermines significant political claims both inside and outside of the region.[16] Bost, too, worries about the container being too full, and she unwittingly establishes a removal metaphor suggesting that the U.S. South overflows and must push out anything that does not "fit." Instead, my project asks that we see the many nations—both past and present—within the U.S. South and that we abandon exclusive containers for more complex geographic terrain and temporal orders.

One such way to imagine a more productive red state is to hold into view Jace Weaver's concept of a Yoknapatawpha of "split earth." As he writes in *American Indian Literary Nationalism*, Faulkner's fictional landscape is a combination of the Choctaw and Chickasaw words of "yocona" and "petopha."[17] In addition to articulating a profound sentiment about how Faulkner may have imagined his literary landscape in relation to Indigenous peoples, it also leaves Weaver wanting to

> suggest that Yoknapatawpha is a kind of metaphor, indeed a powerful one, for Native existence in general and Native literature in particular. Not only have Natives been split from their lands [...] but since the arrival of Europeans, the land itself has been split, not only by the conqueror's plow, but by the conqueror's law. What was once home and family is now mere property, a commodity to be owned and possessed, bought and sold. The land that was once wholly

Natives' has been split from them. A physical, but also psychical, fissure has cleaved Native land from non-Native land. ("Splitting" 66–67)

He continues to argue that the concept of split earth also has resonance with the ways that critics attempt to split the "authentic" Native voices from the "inauthentic" and employ Western theoretical frameworks of "hybridity," failing to realize, regardless of their intentions, that to do so seems "paternalistic" and "part and parcel of continued attempts to define indigenes out of existence" (68). This measuring of authenticity remains one of the most powerful tools in the U.S. South to remove Native people from the region and to split them from their land. Taking Weaver's lead, I want to posit in this project that instead of reading the split earth as a way to define Native people out of existence, we as critics read the U.S. South in such a way that pays special attention to how the earth remains split with Native and non-Native stories existing simultaneously. This may mean that as with thinking through new ideas of periodization, we need to envision multiple concepts of the region at the same time. Or, as David Blackbourn writes of the need to reimagine the heuristics of period, "we must be able to hold two ideas in our heads simultaneously, one pointing to rupture, the other to continuity" (305).

As I describe below, each historical narrative I examine allows us to see the intersections of cultural artifact and audience response in varying ways. Rather than pretending that various textual forms do not exist in the same historical moments and then acquire different meanings as they continually intersect over time, this project places these forms in a direct dialogue through a careful attention to the ways that audiences have responded in strikingly similar ways to what might appear at first to be entirely separate textual or generic traditions. Tracking reader reception allows us to see the material implications of texts that might not otherwise be acknowledged as mutually informative through their coalescence into received knowledge. This analytical framework, then, allows me to track persistent narratives of indigeneity diachronically while paying attention to their synchronic effects.

Because so much of southern identity, particularly white southern identity, is founded on settler-colonial narratives of land connection, the historic and continued presence of Native people in the region represents a hurdle for this associative bond. To overcome this reality, Euro-American southerners have often mediated their racial identities through Native ones in order to feel appropriately and justifiably connected to their adopted and bellum-defended homeland. However, "playing Indian" in order to "feel southern" is not exclusively an affective act of white southerners who have continually manifested an anxiety about their recent inhabitation of the region. African American residents of the U.S. South have also continually appealed to Native identity for reasons ranging from land connection to an escape from a racially subordinated position in the region. As I began the project many years ago, I was spurred on by a sense of responsibility to account for the continued land and identity theft white people of the U.S. South have committed against Native people. As such, this book never adequately addresses the long history between Native American and African American literatures of the U.S. South. As this book addresses settler colonialism and southern studies, it is necessary to be clear about the fact that the vast majority of African American people in the U.S. South should not be understood as settlers. To categorize them as such undermines the significance of how settler colonialism enslaved African peoples as part of its larger mission in the Americas. This renders African American history as it relates to settler colonialism and Native American history a complicated terrain of diverging and converging interests and alliances. This is an area that needs its own book—several books, to be exact—and indeed, numerous scholars including LaRose Davis, Sharon Holland, Tiya Miles, and Ron Welburn have made significant inroads in this area. As Jack D. Forbes offers in his seminal study *Africans and Native Americans: The Language of Race and the Evolution of Red-Black Peoples* (1993), the language of race has been used routinely to decrease Indigenous land claims by diluting Native identity through an imagined lack of "authenticity" in mixed-blood peoples and increasing the number of people responsible for working the land under a racialized plantation economy by establishing blackness based on rules of "one-drop." This consideration is imperative for understanding the dynamics at work in the creation of the region. There is much more good work to be done, and I regret that I have not been able to address these issues here. Likewise, there is still more important and significant work to be done at the intersection between southern and African American literature, and the scholarship of Riché Richardson, Trudier Harris, R. Scott Heath, Jarvis McInnis, and Regina Bradley offers a solid foundation and promising future for investigating those convergences. Keith Cartwright and Sharon Holland have previously investigated the intersection between Native and African literatures of diaspora within their U.S. southern contexts, and I am excited to see what the future holds for the field. Without a doubt, the transatlantic slave trade and the land theft by settler colonialism are part of the exact same process, and the continued systemic racism against black citizens as well as the sustained aggression against Native sovereignty work together to maintain white supremacy. The fact that there is tension in Native nations around important issues such as the Freedmen cases results from the pressures of larger continued colonial apparatuses.[18] The vectors of these issues that emerge from and continue to play out in the U.S. South are some of the most important investigations that southern studies needs to take seriously. And the intersection of Native and African American literature and history will pose new compelling, difficult, and essential questions about the region that southern studies scholars will ignore at their own peril.

Furthermore, there are a number of significant literary contributions emerging from the Native South that I have not been able to consider here. For example, Robert Dale Parker's anthology of early Native poetry, *Changing Is Not Vanishing* (2010), offers numerous southeastern poets including John Rollin Ridge, whom many also consider to be the first Native American novelist. Likewise, the aforementioned anthology, *The People Who Stayed: Southeastern Indian Writing after Removal*, edited by Geary Hobson, Janet McAdams, and Kathryn Walkiewicz, offers the writing of numerous southeastern Native writers across the last two centuries. Cherokee playwright Lynn Riggs was one of the most successful Native writers of the mid-twentieth century, and Craig Womack has made significant contributions to understanding how the author understood his surrounding Native Oklahoma landscape. Louis Owens's creative and critical output has contributed greatly to many questions that Native South scholars ponder today, and Melanie Benson Taylor has done an excellent job of foregrounding his importance to the field. LeAnne Howe is among the most important writers working from the U.S. Southeast today, and Kirstin Squint's continued scholarship on Howe's career will prove essential in the coming years. In short, there are many, many excellent Native writers working within a southern framework, and I regret that I could not discuss all of them in this book. However, I am encouraged and excited by all of the compelling scholarship that my colleagues are creating across Native American and southern studies. In other words, the archive I use to investigate the relationship between southern studies and Native American studies is by no means the only archive that one might assemble. I have attempted to select literary and cultural texts that while not necessarily paradigmatic are also not exceptional. One could examine the same questions and concerns with a variety of texts from the region, and I am confident that many of the tenets of the red state I propose would prove useful to understand the way that land claim and narrative order work to forward issues of settler colonialism in the region.

Some readers may begin to recognize that this book is neither fish nor fowl. Indeed, it is not entirely a Native American studies project in terms of its objects of study, yet it always attempts to keep a productive Native-studies methodology at the forefront even when scrutinizing non-Native literary and cultural texts. At the same time, this project's fit within southern studies may be equally uncomfortable, as it draws from Native texts whose authors may have been born or currently live in diaspora from their southern homelands. As much as southern studies has recently turned toward productive inclusion, many in the field still default to the accident of geographic birth to construct an "authentic" canon. When it comes to Native literatures, this move seems especially troubling given the history of Indian Removal in the region. Throughout the book I pursue an analysis that holds disciplinary questions from both fields in view. However, I am not interested in the superficial convergences between Native and southern texts. Rather, I follow the discursive threads of specific historical moments and their later retellings in order to illustrate how the continued battle over red states continually returns to questions of land claim and narrative order. In this way, I hope those from both Native American studies and southern studies may find some value from this work even when my framework seems more in line with one field over another.

Throughout the project, whether analyzing the cultures and genres of performance, newsprint, or narrative, I examine the deep past of the region to offer ways of thinking about the region's possible futures as a continued Indigenous space. In what follows, I outline this prismatic approach to my objects of study, and I articulate the ways that we may see more of the spectrum of Native presence in the U.S. South. Each chapter takes up one core narrative across a slice of spiralic time. As Lisa Brooks explains: "This spiral is embedded in place(s) but revolves through layers of generations, renewing itself with each new birth. It cannot be fixed but is constantly moving in three-dimensional, multilayered space. It allows for recurrence and return but also for transformation. Its origins lie in ancient worlds, but it moves through our own bodies in the present, perhaps with a sense of irony" (309). This spiralic time works through much of Native American literature. Brooks, for example, points to the work of Muscogee poet Joy Harjo, and I would add to this list the work of LeAnne Howe, Allison Adelle Hedge Coke, and Janet McAdams among others who forward a spiralic time in their poetry. Although Howe's 2006 documentary *Spiral of Fire* does not directly offer a stated spiralic temporality, the recurring connections between generations of Cherokee and Choctaw women emerge as linked under the film's title and its scenes of counterclockwise Cherokee stomp dances. This spiralic time suggests a recurrence of events and narratives beyond the cliché of "history repeating itself." In the settler-colonial construction of the red state, I use spiralic time as a methodology for examining how narratives of supposed or invented Native history get told again and again in order to buttress the specious land claims of settlers. When examining texts that challenge settler colonialism, I examine how the work's internal logic forwards a temporality and narrative order that challenges a flat-line linearity of Western calendar time that would render Native people as vanished or totally removed from their homes. In this way, I employ an Indigenous idea of spiralic time as explained by Brooks in order to critique the narrative order established by settler colonialism, and I examine how Native authors continually appeal to time signatures that trouble any settler-colonial distinction of Old and New Souths. The idea of spiralic time appears in numerous Indigenous traditions from the Southeast as well as the circum-Caribbean and present-day Mexico and Central America where recurrence figures heavily in circular calendar forms as well as sacred texts such as the *Popol Vuh* and other surviving Mesoamerican codices. Rather than establishing the spiralic as a static heuristic, I want to posit that it offers a useful concept to think with in its privileging of pattern over exceptionality.

The jostling of periodization via the use of spiralic time within my inquiry may seem to create a somewhat abstract constellation of stories, but in pursuing these connections as they emerge from historical narratives, I hope to demonstrate the benefits of thinking transhistorically for enlivening future possibility. To borrow a term from Wai Chee Dimock, this alternate temporal order creates a "double threading" of how we might read southern literature under a rubric of a Native American studies methodology. As Dimock describes, "This double threading thickens time, lengthens it, shadowing in its midst the abiding traces of the planet's multitudinous life" (3). Calling this phenomenon "deep time," she explains how it "highlights [...] a set of longitudinal frames, at once projective and recessional, with input going both ways, and binding continents and millennia into many loops of relations, a densely interactive fabric" (3–4). Working from this idea of deep time alongside concepts of spiralic temporality, I attempt to reveal a large canvas of possibility when we loosen ourselves from the U.S. South as determined by temporal blocks of the "Old" and "New."

Perhaps many authors share the experience of having a book published just before their own that seems to address many of the ideas they have spent years grappling with. In my case, this work is Mark Rifkin's *Beyond Settler Time: Temporal Sovereignty and Indigenous Self-Determination* (2017). As he argues, "Rather than approaching time as an abstract, homogenous measure of universal movement along a singular axis, we can think of it as a plural, less as a temporality than temporalities" (2). He tackles questions of Indigenous temporal sovereignty, recognizing that settler colonialism attempts to control the measure, scale, and form of time for Indigenous peoples. I share his perspective that "Rather than marking an absolute distinction between Natives and non-Natives, suggesting that there are unbreachable barriers that generate utterly incommensurable and hermetically sealed Indian and white forms of experience, I am suggesting the presence of discrepant temporalities that can be understood as affecting each other, as all open to change, and yet not equivalent or mergeable into a neutral, common frame—call it time, modernity, history, or the present" (3). And within this I would like to make clear that I am not suggesting that the conception of spiralic time I follow as my method is in any way a universal or even prevalent "Native time." Instead, I am posing a question to southern studies about what happens when we acknowledge that our conceptions of region have long been built on fantasies of settler time. In order to outline an answer to this question, I allow a different temporal framework than the one that has long governed literary periodization to guide my analysis across the five chapters.

Each chapter begins with an analysis of the discursive terrain of a historical moment and then spirals out, following the narrative through time to examine how it buttresses contemporaneous discourse surrounding Native and southern political moments. Although I begin chapter 1 with an early moment of colonial contact, I do not mean to set up the English arrival as the "beginning" of this study or of the Americas. Rather, this opening may be understood as one point on a spiralic time frame, and the rest of the project will look forward and backward as it considers the intersection of land claim and historical narrative order. Chapter 1, "Recovery," takes up the first attempt of English settlement in the Americas through an examination of the Roanoke Island colony that will eventually become popularly known as the "Lost Colony." I begin with a detailed examination of the archives dealing with the initial English voyages, demonstrating how even the earliest colonial actors attempted to tie ideas of loss and absence to the figure of the Native. In executing this analysis, I attempt to elucidate the stakes of "recovery" work that must imagine a Native absence in order to justify Western positivistic claims. These two modes, loss and recovery, later become central tenets by which the U.S. South begins to imagine itself. Rather than regard these moments of "loss" as post–Civil War imaginings, the first half of this chapter outlines how from the earliest moments, the colonial project depended on the projection of "lostness" onto Native people. From there, I examine Paul Green's later retelling of the colony in his outdoor drama, *The Lost Colony*. Originally staged in 1937, for the colony's 350th "anniversary," the play managed to consolidate this original English loss with feelings resonant with a Confederate Lost Cause. This largely happened against Green's stated aims as the reception of the work fomented a white southern pride in loss over and above Green's likely intentions. I follow the spiralic scope of the Roanoke colony story through the contemporary staging of the play. As a dramatic work with a run over eighty seasons and counting, the play offers an opportunity to examine the synchronic context of the work across a diachronic analysis. When contemporary (and largely regional) white audiences of the play attempt to recover the history of the colony to make sense of their own southern attachments to loss and land claim, the larger stakes of the contemporary red state come forward.

From this early colonial history, my analysis then moves into narratives of the American Revolution. Chapter 2 takes the concept of "revolution" as its organizing heuristic, playing on the denotation and historical connotation of the word. In this examination of narratives across spiralic time, this chapter understands the American Revolution as a historical moment that later narratives repeatedly pass through in order to reassert settler-colonial land claim. As with the first chapter, I begin by reading the discourse surrounding a historical moment, in this case the American Revolution. Through the letters and writings of Thomas Jefferson, I outline how southern and Native identities come to be tied to one another as markers of both statelessness and state control. From there, I move into a sustained analysis of William Gilmore Simms's romances of the Revolution, particularly the novel *Mellichampe* (1836). Focusing on the mixedblood Catawba character, Blonay, I demonstrate how narratives of the American Revolution in the U.S. South came to stand in for contemporaneous arguments about southern approaches to American Indian policy. In order to contextualize this reading, I place Blonay within the historical context of the Catawba Nation's struggles against South Carolina. From there, I move into the twentieth century to an analysis of Kermit Hunter's outdoor drama, *Horn in the West* (1952), which deals with the onset of the American Revolution alongside Cherokee conflict in the Appalachian Mountains. Like *The Lost Colony*, the play's continued staging allows for a reading that holds both historical context and audience reception in view. I read its moment of inception during increased debates about racial segregation in the mid-twentieth century as well as its contemporary appeals to rights, economy, and land in the Appalachian South, thus demonstrating the revolving nature of red state logics. By way of closing, I consider our current red states as represented through political Tea Party rhetoric and Indigenous movements against the continued use of Native mascots.

Whereas the first two chapters only engage briefly with Native-authored materials, the next three chapters engage more Native-produced material, showing the long history of resistance of Native nations in the U.S. South. Chapter 3 centers the book with an extended consideration of Indian Removal in the U.S. South in both Native and non-Native works. I begin with a consideration of the Removal-era newspaper the *Cherokee Phoenix*, contextualizing it within the scope of the nineteenth-century print culture. Working from numerous archival sources, I outline the ways in which white southerners were articulating their identities as beleaguered and put upon by the federal government and their northeastern counterparts. From there, I offer an analysis of Simms's "The Broken Arrow. An Authentic Passage from an Unwritten History" (1844), which details the assassination of the Creek leader William McIntosh and the debate over Creek Removal. This analysis allows me to establish how land, race, and the plantation economy informed the construction of the narratives of Native people shortly after Removal but before the Civil War. From there, I offer an analysis of Charles Frazier's novel *Thirteen Moons* (2006) in order to demonstrate how public reception of a complicated Removal narrative fails to gain traction while the simplified narrative of the contemporary off-Broadway musical *Bloody Bloody Andrew Jackson* (2010) perhaps unwittingly re-creates a consolidation of the ever-popular—and populist—wages of whiteness in the U.S. South. As a counterexample, I address how Cherokee author Blake Hausman in his novel *Riding the Trail of Tears* (2011) has managed to complicate the continued consumption of these Removal narratives.

Chapter 4 explores the Henry Berry Lowry wars and Lumbee resistance in eastern North Carolina. I use a tribally centered approach in order to offer a reading of Lumbee cultural texts that speaks to their specific material concerns over generalized romantic conceptions of Native literature or the U.S. South. After contextualizing the historically and politically unique position of the Lumbee Tribe of North Carolina, I analyze the Lumbee's outdoor drama *Strike at the Wind!* (1971). I argue that the Lumbee people have continually challenged the recurrent narratives of Native disappearance, a biracial U.S. South, and a romanticized Lost Cause based on temporal understandings of Old and New Souths. This resistance grows throughout the region, and it challenges the cipher of the representational Native American as a figure of pathos. Rather, I argue, as evidenced by the form and content of the recently rereleased albums *Plant and See* (1969, 2012) and *Proud to Be a Lumbee* (1976) by Lumbee musician Willie French Lowery, Lumbee cultural productions challenge us to see a future of hope in the region where many have only seen a past marred and defined by loss.

The final chapter, "Resilience," focuses on three contemporary texts from southeastern Native artists. This chapter takes a slightly different approach in that instead of foregrounding a specific historical narrative, it examines a recurring narrative trope. Each of these texts features "natural" disasters ranging from hurricanes to earthquakes. Using recent critical work in Native studies, this chapter challenges the narrative of loss by showing how Native authors write through the presumed apocalypse of their own cultures in order to posit more productive futures. It challenges any traditional borders of the South whether spatial or temporal. I begin with a close reading of Linda Hogan's *Power* (1998), which features a fictional tribe that must survive environmental degradation along with a hurricane. I trace the novel's investment in sacred narratives of the circum-Caribbean and larger geographic southeast, bringing forward lexical investigations and sacred texts. From there, I offer a reading of Janet McAdams's novel *Red Weather* (2012), which features present-day linkages between a speculative South-South connection through its setting in the fictional country of Coatepeque. Like *Power*, it pulls the reader back through time, in this case to a moment of Muscogee Creek creation. Lastly, I look to Sharon Linezo Hong and Monique Verdin's documentary *My Louisiana Love* (2012), which examines the effects of Hurricane Katrina and the BP oil spill on the Houma community in southern Louisiana.

I examine the pacing and temporal dynamics of the film in order to delineate how present-day ecocritical concerns may require a serious consideration of Indigenous temporalities. Together, these texts outline an aesthetics of resilience that does more for understanding the Native South than do narratives of irrevocable loss.

Indeed, these chapters might seem large in their temporal scope. However, that is only true if we continue to privilege measuring-tape linear time. Working within a temporal methodology such as the one Brooks outlines, which privileges spiralic recurrences, we may see that this set of materials is tightly bound. Each chapter offers a slice of the spiral, tracking the recurrence of specific events in select narratives. By drawing these events together across traditional periodization, I hope that new insights might emerge. This is by no means a last word for understanding the Native South. Instead, it is my sincere wish that this book represents just one among a divergent set of opening gestures for reconsidering period, region, and the narratives that result from our constructions of those concepts.

Additionally, much of this project begins with a focus on the Carolinas, and the fourth chapter focused on Lumbee cultural productions also stays largely within this area of the U.S. South. Admittedly, part of this may result from the accident of my own birth in central North Carolina. It is the state that I continue to know best. One of the core benefits of the New Southern Studies is that it encourages scholars to "zoom in" on micro-areas of the region, and it demands specificity in our approach to "the South." This critical practice is somewhat congruent with the push in Native American studies to forward tribal specificity rather than homogeneous ideas of "Indian Country." I do not see North Carolina, in particular, as exceptional or wholly representative of the region. It has its own history, as do South Carolina, Georgia, Alabama, Florida, and so on. While this book constellates texts from across multiple time periods, I also foreground local vectors that matter to understanding how Native people resist settler colonialism within specific state contexts. It is my hope that in layering these specific state and tribal stories while respecting their nuances as well as their similarities, we may arrive at some initial understanding of how the region we might call the U.S. South has long depended on particular fantasies of settler colonialism to support its other (often spurious) claims to regional distinctiveness. Likewise, keeping tribal specificity in mind helps us understand the innovation and resistance of specific Native nations as they build their own regional networks to maintain their sovereignty.

In what follows I aim to demonstrate the contours of a more critically inflected and nuanced idea of the red state. I hope that readers will come to see the ways that much of southern studies could benefit from a strong injection of Native American studies methodology and an examination of the settler-colonial logic that subtends our preoccupation with the plantation economy. While we in southern studies have productively troubled our appeals to authenticity in the past twenty years, I think we have much work to do in divesting ourselves of narratives based on the implicit land and temporal claims of settler colonialism. Likewise, I hope that this regional focus will contribute to the ongoing discussion in Native American studies that examines the locally specific ways that settler colonialism operates and how Native communities continue to resist these forces. I also aim for my methodological approach in forwarding Native American studies as an epistemological framework rather than an object-focused discipline to continue the conversation about the exciting new directions for Native studies organizations, departments, and courses. It has not been easy to attempt to put so much material in conversation, and I admit that at times my reach may exceed my grasp, but I hope that my ambitious approach does not diminish the call to reevaluate the red state.

CHAPTER ONE

Recovery

> Recently been reading and planning "Lost Colony" play. Another trip to Roanoke Island to consider plans for the theatre, exhibits and celebration. Bothered a bit about the "authenticity" of material. But after all the "feeling" of the participant is important too.
>
> —Paul Green, March 29, 1937

In the fall of 2016, the popular FX series *American Horror Story* launched its sixth iteration, *Roanoke*. Set largely in rural eastern North Carolina (though filmed in Santa Clarita, California), the sixth season focuses on a house of horrors, ostensibly haunted by the ghosts of the 1590 Roanoke Lost Colony. The stories of the historical Lost Colony figure very little in the plot of the season, and the series imagines a landscape filled with rural abjection and death. Incidentally, there are very few, if any, appearances by Native characters as the show seems more preoccupied with supernatural violence at the hands of the fictional leader of the Lost Colony, Jon White's fictional wife, Thomasin White (Kathy Bates). White takes over the colony in her husband's absence and becomes known as "The Butcher" after becoming a follower of the original "Supreme" witch Scáthach (Lady Gaga), who had previously killed a group of soldiers. Notably, the English blame the local Native people, not Scáthach, for the massacre of the soldiers. The season is told in a set of frame tales. The first is a documentary format, which recounts the strange and horrific occurrences affecting an interracial couple, Matt and Shelby, after they purchase an eighteenth-century farmhouse in the woods. This documentary, *My Roanoke Nightmare*, intersperses narration from the real-life Matt and Shelby (André Holland and Lily Rabe) and reenactment scenes featuring a fictional Matt and Shelby played by Dominic Banks (Cuba Gooding Jr.) and Audrey Tindall (Sarah Paulson). *My Roanoke Nightmare* also features the story of Matt's sister Lee Harris (Adina Porter), played by the fic-

29

tional Monet Tumusiime (Angela Bassett). Then, after the success of that television "documentary," the season morphs into a "Return to Roanoke," where the reenactment cast of the first documentary moves back into the house with their "real-life" counterparts to have a "reality television" experience during the particularly dangerous time of the "Blood Moon," when the ghosts of the Roanoke colony are at their most vengeful. As a result of this foolhardy decision on behalf of the director, the entire cast—real and fictional—die with the exception of the real-life Lee Harris, who is put on trial for the death of her husband and several of her companions in the house. After she is acquitted, she ultimately returns to the site of the house and essentially sacrifices herself to appease the Roanoke ghosts and protect her daughter. In short, this 2016 Roanoke iteration recounts an all-consuming loss where every attempt at recovery begets more death.

I have attempted to outline the basic plot structure as simply as possible, but rest assured that the frame tale and found-footage style of the interlocking documentary worlds make the show almost inscrutable. While the intricacies of the season's form deserve their own space for analysis, I am most interested in how and why the Roanoke story found its traction again in 2016. Long a touchstone of regional apocryphal history and tourism, the Roanoke colony produces a certain type of mystery around the beginning of English colonization in the Americas, though nowhere near as gory or as sensational as the one that FX provides. However, perhaps in this revisionist approach, something about *American Horror Story: Roanoke* hits the mark in how the earliest English act of settler colonialism continues to resonate across the continent. Roanoke might very well be the first English American horror story, but it begs the consideration of whose horror. When placed in its southern landscape, on which *Roanoke* draws in the most offensively stereotypical of ways with an inbred, cannibalistic Polk family (toting guns and thick accents), the story of Roanoke becomes not just a tale of the horror wrought by English colonialism but also a projection of the dark fantasies of an abjected U.S. South, repressed from a larger national imaginary.

In this way, the show's relative absence of Native people reads as a practical relief (who could imagine how FX might employ those narrative and representational stereotypes) and a telling omission. Roanoke, historically speaking, cannot be considered without addressing the eastern Algonquian people who populated the region where the English settled. After all, it is their historical horror story. The show directly depicts the horrific actions of the early colonists and their later ghosts, but their violent acts are rendered into an abstract horror, a senseless routine of killing to maintain "their land." Perhaps these motives, however, are not so far off. The trouble is that in the depiction of the sacrificial destruction of contemporary bodies, the audience might imagine the Butcher and her colonists as aberrations, ghostly protagonists who only kill non-Natives, rather than their likely historical counterparts who enacted numerous terrors against living Algonquian people. Significantly, the Polk family, who seem to stand in for all rural southern whiteness, have had a long-standing deal with the Roanoke ghosts: they bring the Butcher someone to sacrifice each year during the Blood Moon so they too can stay on "their land." And in this way, the show becomes about the horror of settler colonialism where white southerners continue to offer tithe to the ghosts of Roanoke in order to maintain their own land claims. In some ways, settler colonialism has become so good at this narrative that, as *American Horror Story* demonstrates, it no longer needs Native people at all. Any body will do. And yet the recurrence of variations of the Roanoke story appear again and again, particularly when, as I will demonstrate in this chapter, anxieties about national and regional loss approach their own climaxes. Through a close reading of the Island's earliest archival presences and an interrogation of its resulting historical fictions, I examine how as a foundational signifier, Roanoke depends on Native history in order to establish settler-colonial land claims and narrative order for the region we now call the U.S. South.

The Long Loss

Through a sustained analysis of Paul Green's dramatic text *The Lost Colony* (1937), I demonstrate how these imaginings of the early U.S. South (indeed, before it was the United States) remain bound up with concerns over regional distinctiveness characterized by narratives of backwardness and exceptionalism grounded in scenes of Native history. Such narratives enforce the problematic idea that the U.S. South as a region remains exceptional to American exceptionalism. Green's *The Lost Colony* represents a particularly powerful illustration of this logic as it reaches back through time to a "founding moment" of southern exceptionalism in 1587 and carries through the present with its continued yearly staging on Roanoke Island. This instance of Green's historical imagining informs this chapter's consideration of how even the earliest records of the space that will eventually become the U.S. South are marked by the concurrent ideas of loss and archival absence. In other words, indigeneity in the region that will become the U.S. South traffics in the concept of loss long before the Confederate Lost Cause. To examine this, I trace texts from the late 1500s through the contemporary performance of Green's outdoor drama. Because these outdoor dramas are reperformed every year amid various political moments, they serve as an apt site to investigate how local imaginings of Native history enter the collective ether.

Paul Green's 1937 self-described symphonic drama depicts the events leading up to the historic disappearance of 115 men, women, and children from Roanoke Island. The outdoor drama continues to play six nights a week every summer in Manteo, North Carolina, and because of this text, many consider Green to be the father of the "outdoor drama," a genre characterized by its extensive production materials, use of local history, annual performances, and, of course, staging in large outdoor theaters. Although one could easily quibble with several of the textual details in Green's play, it is clear from his papers and extensive surviving archive that he conducted rigorous research when writing the script.[1] His grasp of the mood, tenor, and implications of the Roanoke voyages mirrors those of many of the extant texts relating to the sixteenth-century colonial expeditions, and his use of historical details and individuals have numerous archival antecedents. Of course, any staged events on Roanoke Island after John White leaves the 1587 colony stem entirely from Green's imagination. Despite this creative license, almost all of Green's characters correlate to some part of the archive. However, the only Native woman in the play, Agona, corresponds to no written historical record. In fact, she hardly even exists in Green's script as she offers only one line throughout the play: "Tee-hee." So while other Native characters, such as Manteo, Wanchese, and Wingina, and all of the English characters, Queen Elizabeth I, Walter Raleigh, John White, and Simon Fernando, are based on individuals who exist in the historical record, the Native Agona alone stands as the mark of a profound absence in the archive. The relationship between absence, presence, loss, and recovery becomes a preoccupation for ordering the earliest Roanoke interactions, and it is the circulation of these ideas around indigeneity that begins to accrue additional "lost" meanings across the deep time of the region.

As with many "Indians" in the historical record, only a lacunary trace of their presence remains. However, many times these individuals stand in absent spaces where their reconstruction depends on historical imagination. This is not to say that these Indigenous people did not exist as significant agents in the colonial history of the Americas but rather to suggest that being Indian in these contexts is often marked by archival sites of loss and recovery. In this way, this chapter engages the work of Anishinaabe critic Gerald Vizenor, who posits that "The Indian is the simulation of the absence" (*Manifest Manners* 14). Significantly, the historically absent Agona from Green's play is the very person who, along with her lover Tom, buoys the colony's hopes for survival. Arguably, the play's ending makes clear that many, if not all, of the colonists will perish. Agona and Tom appear to be the only two equipped to survive, and of all the characters, it seems that they will people the "New World" with their combination of Indigenous knowledge and resourceful Devon ethics. Certainly, the trope of racial mixing is not an original narrative in the Americas, as it constitutes a familiar narrative from Pocahontas to la Malinché.[2] However, in most cases there exists at least a recorded historical trace of the Native woman. At best, Green's Agona is modeled after a woman whom White's watercolors depict eating from a bowl.[3]

It might be easy to dismiss Green's representation of the Algonquian people as an instance of stereotypical Indian representation in the twentieth century. As Michael Harkin argues regarding renderings of the 1587 colony, the "trope of inevitable loss and change allowed modern readers and audiences to incorporate the events of the Lost Colony into their own individual and collective history" ("Performing Paradox" 109).[4] I agree with these sentiments; however, I argue that this feature of the Lost Colony is not simply an invention of modern authors and their audiences. The precise ways in which early moderns wrote about the Roanoke colony and its relationship with Native Algonquians expose how loss and absence operated alongside ideas of early ethnography as the English began to link their own identity with positive proof within the archive and the landscape. On the one hand, just as the prominent character Agona appears on the stage influencing the other characters' actions while remaining textually unrepresented in the script, the early English representations of Indian people render them absent in the written archive despite their likely enormous influence on the colony. On the other hand, in the visual archive Indians dominate the landscape where the English are rendered as conspicuously absent despite their obvious presence in the colonial venture. In other words, to be rendered "Indian" in these texts is to participate in an economy of strategic and simulated absence that informs much of the early modern writing on these expeditions and their later land claims on Virginia. While indeed numerous critics have noted the ways in which early moderns erased American Indians from the landscape, I examine a more conspicuous albeit less-cited creation of absence in the Roanoke archive: the created and absenting of the English and the material evidence of their presence.[5] This control of the absent body and/or item switches the terms by which we might understand lost items, and it applies pressure to the historiographic problems of reading an archive's absences for the loss of the Indian. Each of these concerns remains bound up with the power structures of a colonial gaze that informs not only the early modern actors but those of us who attempt to recover information from their written records.

It may seem anachronistic or even an act of historical "upstreaming" to use a twentieth-century play to help us reread the archive associated with the late sixteenth-century voyages. Despite these dangers, such a transhistorical comparative approach may reveal more than it conceals. For instance, Joyce E. Chaplin argues that White's drawings "introduced Virginia's natives to the English as if he were displaying them in a theatre. The spectators who had the front-row seats, meaning the English who colonized Roanoke, are invisible even though they were actually interacting with the natives whom White depicted" (51). This description of the staged depiction of Roanoke from the original visual documents resonates in many ways with the contemporary consumption of this history in its yearly staging as an outdoor drama in

North Carolina. Significantly, the absent body for Chaplin's argument is not the Indian but the English. The twentieth-century play replicates the power structure that informs the earliest documents in its mediation between an archive and a repertoire where some presences are noted while others are assumed.[6] The power to stage the Americas as a "New World" open for colonial conquest for European audiences creates a dynamic between objects and subjects, the viewed and the viewer. As Thomas Cartelli argues regarding the later Plymouth colony, there was a rhetorical effacement of Native people from the New England landscape that served to presage a physical removal.[7] With the Roanoke voyages, however, we have a slightly different set of factors and outcomes. It is not simply the representation of absence that causes settlers to feel as if they can take over Indigenous land claims. Instead, it is the power to control the absented body or item that ultimately justifies dispossession. Simply put, the fact of absence is not the only determining factor. In these early records of Virginia, it is the power to frame the loss of objects, others, or even oneself that ultimately matters. This framing of loss persists through present critical work in the field. To point out "loss" begs for the power of recovery, and the act of scholarly recovery is one to approach with caution as it can result in further uneven power dynamics between scholars and the communities their work affects. By interrogating the language of loss around the spiralic recurrence of Roanoke narratives, I hope to complicate the use of this language for continued narratives of Native history.

In *Reconstructing the Native South: American Indian Literature and the Lost Cause,* Melanie Benson Taylor attempts to synthesize elements of the Confederate Lost Cause with the region's Native American literature and history in order to make sense of the contemporary forces of global capitalism. Indeed, such work has value. It does, in Taylor's words, ask us to "confront difficult questions: in the aftermath of Removal and colonial devastation, what remains—for either group—to be recovered?" (21). While she asserts that she does not wish to "forge a false harmony between historically antagonistic groups" or "deny the necessity and the reality of tribal sovereignty and nationalism," much of her analysis may unintentionally do just that (21). To be clear, not much remains to be recovered for the South of the Confederate Lost Cause because it is impossible to recover what was never lost in the first place: namely, the continual possession of stolen lands and white racial supremacy in policy, policing, and practice. As for what remains to be recovered for the Native South, we might begin with the present-day state of Georgia. While I hear Taylor's assertion that "we have been swift to defuse the white South's most damaging myths and performances, we have been notably more hesitant to deconstruct Natives' similar and no less compensatory fictions" (21), I ask, what compensation? When there are still no federally recognized tribes in the state of Georgia, and when in 2017 I am ushering through the proposals for Georgia State University's first Native American literature course offerings, I wonder about the use of deconstructing that which is only beginning to be rebuilt.

Whereas Taylor looks to examine the convergence of multiple lost cause narratives across southern and Native contexts, I seek to pull them apart a bit—to show their vast dissimilarities. From a biological perspective, convergence is used to describe organisms that are wholly unrelated but only *appear* to have shared characteristics due to similar environmental conditions. As Taylor argues in her contribution to the recently reimagined *Southern Literary Journal, south*, when it comes to Native people and southerners, "The convergences are so obvious, ultimately, that they shouldn't be surprising—and yet they are, and often unpalatably so" ("In Deep" 70). I wonder, however, about this idea of convergence. Indeed, surrounding conditions have placed Native people and communities in predicaments similar to those of many other humans living on the planet, including non-Native southerners, during the time of late capitalism. However, the point of convergence is that two things—though appearing alike—are in fact *not the same*. So when Taylor quips regarding the uncanny linkage between images of Native people and the Confederate flag, "A lost cause is a lost cause," I cannot help but wonder about the assumptions embedded in such a claim (71). The cause of the Confederacy is not the cause of Native sovereignty on this continent. As I demonstrate throughout the first part of the book, to draw the equivalence and rest it on the idea of convergence is to attempt the same psychological leaps as early southern writers when they attempted to draw the image of the Indian into their own narratives of white southern identity. Furthermore, even the use of the word "loss" continually enforces the idea that Native people are responsible for the theft of their lands, suppression of their languages, and dismantling of their sovereign political organizations. My colleague Brook Colley has often suggested that we replace every instance of the word "lost" with a more accurate verb.

Much of my contention with Taylor's examination of lost cause convergences has to do with the presentist focus of her work. When Taylor asks, "Is it acceptable to identify an Indian 'Lost Cause,' much as we have acknowledged the futility of the white South's tribalism and nostalgia?" I am prompted to turn toward Robert Warrior's statements on the lost cause's currency in American Indian studies (21). Via previous work from Edward Said, Warrior points out, "a cause seeming lost or not is a matter of many things, including the juncture in history at which the determination is being made, the sort of narrative the determination is part of, and the perspective from which judgment on the cause is being pronounced" (218). And he reminds us that "American Indians have never lost some fundamental things, like the relationship to their homelands," and that for Said, "no cause is ever finally lost until its hope is extinguished in the last person who holds it in her or his consciousness" (219). I agree with these assertions, and I would like to extend this idea to zero in on the fact that these determinations are often based on a belief in a linear temporality, and that the benefit of thinking past and through the lost cause is exactly the type of new consciousness that emerges in the creativity of survival that sees a future beyond linear time. Taylor's analysis stays firmly within the twentieth century, and thus it might be difficult to examine the contours of the long discursive terrain of loss. She acknowledges this in proposing "the important thing is simply to keep digging deeper, and to try to locate both the awful and beautiful stories that unearth themselves along the way" (205). Despite her use of the problematic archeology metaphor, given the long history of non-Native archeologists literally digging into the ground and unearthing Native bodies and possessions without the consent of Native people, I agree with her call to look more closely at how southern and Native worlds have been constructed with one another in active mind, and in doing this, I argue that neither the temporality nor the language of loss has to be determined exclusively by the region's Confederate history. The later use of this discourse was not invented by but merely repackaged into the eventual Lost Cause narratives we identify today. Therefore, we might not put so much pressure on the *losses* as the *causes* behind such identifications. My interrogation in this chapter of the recurrent Lost Colony narratives attempts to empty the cache of the term "loss" for southern studies, as it manages to both undergird Confederate nostalgia and efface settler colonialism's active theft of Native land.

In attempting to think through a more productive methodological engagement between southern studies and Native American studies, Vizenor's theory of the archival Indian informs my consideration of the ways in which Virginia at the turn of the sixteenth century is framed by the concurrent ideas of loss and absence. For Vizenor, the lowercase, italicized *indian* represents an invention of the colonial dispossessor who covers over the presence of Native inhabitants by creating a simulated absence that can allow for later instances of colonial violence against the original inhabitants of the geographic space. These instances later become what he calls moments of "aesthetic victimry" that current scholars perpetuate when they mistake the Indian absence for narratives of inevitable defeat or lost causes (*Fugitive Poses* 21). These narratives are bound up precisely with early modern records as this simulated absence is for Vizenor, "an event created in discourse" that becomes a commodity (25). Following Derrida, Vizenor notes that "the *indian* is the simulation of a logocentric other" and an institutive archive (34). The loss that this chapter examines is an exercise in orientation as early modern English writers attempt to simulate absences that can situate their newfound land claims under the logic of a Eurocentric positivism.[8] These simulated absences, however, are not simply those of the absent Indians. As noted earlier, White simulates his own absence as well as the absence of his numerous fellow travelers, rendering them almost as naturalized as those who stage, frame, and control the events before them. Within the records, there also exist numerous other created absences that are rendered into positivistic proof used to justify English colonial and imperial actions.[9]

The power to disappear or to render items as "lost" pervades the discourse surrounding the Roanoke voyages. Beginning from a place of loss allows the continuation of deeply ahistorical narratives of southern, U.S., and hemispherically American history as it begs for speculation on "origins" and leaves romantic imaginings thoroughly intact. The story of the 1587 settlement on Roanoke Island constitutes an iconic, albeit fleeting, moment of historical significance given its place as the first intended permanent English settlement. Additionally, the birth of Virginia Dare, the first English child born in the Americas, remains as a familiar flashpoint in colonial history. Most enduring, however, is the powerful mystery of the colony. With the dramatic backdrop of England's confrontation with the Spanish Armada, John White's failed attempt in 1590 to find the colony, which included his own daughter and granddaughter, marks a point of familial and national loss in the "New World." Likewise, the cryptic messages of "CRO" and "Croatoan" inscribed on trees, as well as the ruined remnants of White's personal papers scattered about the abandoned site, establish a narrative of intrigue and chaos involving English settlers disappearing into the supposed "wilderness" of the American landscape.

What remains from this narrative of loss is collected in the extensive letters, journals, travel logs, and propaganda materials detailing the voyages along the present-day Carolina coast from 1584 to 1590. In addition to Thomas Harriot's *A Briefe and True Report of the New Found Land of Virginia* (1588 and the later illustrated Theodore De Bry edition of 1590), Richard Hakluyt collected numerous documents for his 1589 *Principal Navigations, Voyages, Traffiques and Discoveries of the English Nation*, which he updated in 1600.[10] These texts offer accounts ranging from Philip Amadas and Arthur Barlowe's early explorations along the coast to Harriot's own extensive descriptions of the islands. White's numerous watercolors of the people, flora, and fauna, which were edited by De Bry for the 1590 engravings, inform many of Harriot's categorizations.[11] Together, these documents represent the wealth of information that we know about the initial colonial efforts in early modern Virginia. However, despite this remarkable extant record, what we do *not* know about the Roanoke voyages looms larger: how the 1587 English colony was "lost" to the geographical space of the Algonquian people.[12]

As one traces this theme of loss and absence through the letters, journals, and travel logs of the Roanoke voyages, the colonists' disappearance emerges as a foreshadowed epistemological ordering of the New World where commodities and land attachment are negotiated through protoracial terms of othering. At first glance, it seems that the Algonquian people of the Eastern Seaboard figure relatively prominently in these materials. However, when one looks closer for an understanding of the Native coastal populations of this time, the records become harder to navigate as the Algonquian people are imagined primarily in relation to their English counterparts.[13] From these documents there emerges a narrative of loss where recording the Indian presence exposes the slippage of anticipating the preconceived textual absence in the historical archive. When we examine Roanoke and later colonial Virginia, and even later the U.S. South, we must consider how loss and the recorded Indian come to be tied to one another from even the earliest moments, and relatedly, what this might mean for the fact that many still consider this initial failed attempt at colonization a vanished colony rather than an English defeat.

Subsequently, the loss of the Algonquian agent and the anticipation of the absent Indian affects how people approach these texts today. This is evidenced from the assumptions about an inevitable destruction of Algonquian life to the fact that few scholars question John White's singular account of the colony's supposed safety. As critics we tend to orient ourselves by the end of the narrative, looking back for clues about a Native identity that supports the end of the colonial story. However, these archival absences are simulated by a scholarly forgetting that in the early modern Americas the narrative was by no means formed, and it was entirely indeterminable how the encounter between Europeans and Native people might proceed. In other words, the Native people appear as absent as much because of the way scholars read the archive as the way that it was written. When critics read the Confederate Lost Cause backward onto Native literatures of the U.S. South, they eschew the ways in which the concept loss serves as an organizing heuristic from the earliest moments of colonialism in the region. In this vein, critics may then elide the ways in which the European narratives of the region depended on a relationality of loss from the very beginning.

Of those documents written by men stationed at Roanoke, most records (when not using the term "savage") refer to the Algonquian inhabitants either by tribe or as "Virginians."[14] The idea that the Indigenous people of Roanoke could be understood as Virginian speaks to the ways in which identity came to be tied to a colonial place with a newly acquired name.[15] While the term "Indian" would seemingly orient Native bodies as periphery to an English center populated by English bodies, the renaming of the Algonquian people as Virginian ties them to the very center of English national sentiment in the body of the virgin queen. This centering of Algonquian people as inhabitants of the Virginian landscape links them to the well-understood idea of the Americas as an Edenic space.[16] This prelapsarian space's status can only be understood in retrospect. In other words, the material proof of the virgin would, for many, occur in the loss of that status. It, like the figure of Vizenor's *indian*, is conceived in its potential and relational absence.

This creation of absence reveals itself in many of the documents relating to the voyages. In the 1600 edition of "Principall Navigations," Hakluyt omits a line from Barlowe's description of the first voyage in 1584. Barlowe writes: "The earth bringeth foorth all things in abundance, as in the first creation, without toile or labour" (qtd. in Quinn 108). Quinn speculates that Hakluyt deleted this line because he saw it as "contributing nothing to the narrative" (108). However, given the later history of the colonists, Hakluyt would know that this prelapsarian space would become the site of numerous losses. Instead of imagining this line as contributing nothing to the narrative, it may be more useful to imagine it as contributing too much. At first, Virginia represented a found paradise, and the Roanoke colony's fate had already been imagined in a narrative that placed Englishmen back in the Edenic landscape. The loss of the single line that depicts Virginia as paradise suggests that over the course of the Roanoke voyages and the subsequent disappearance of the colony, Virginia as landscape can no longer be represented as Eden. This omission from Hakluyt marks a failed repossession of an imagined heavenly paradise. Hakluyt omits the line describing Virginia as a space free from original sin, and in so doing, he suggests that the colonial space either lost, or more likely never had, virgin status.

Perhaps this editorial decision by Hakluyt makes sense; after all, the space of Roanoke became a place of violent encounters almost immediately on Amadas and Barlowe's arrival. Many historians have noted the story of Amadas's men spending several days with the people of Secotan at Aquascococke, and even by their own record the soldiers "were well intertayned" (qtd. in Quinn 191). However, after departing from the village, the men seemed to think that the Secotans had stolen a silver cup.[17] After discovering the alleged theft, the men marched back to the village. In what reads as just a quick line entry in the journal, Amadas notes, "not receiving [the silver cup] according to his promise, we burnt, and spoyled their corne, and Towne, all the people being fledde" (ibid.). The loss of this cup and Amadas's subsequent reaction sets the stage for what becomes a quickly escalating violence between the Indigenous people and the colonists. The exhibition of such force over what must have seemed a rather inconsequential item demonstrated to the Algonquian people that the English had no reservations about punishing an entire town for the supposed actions—or nonactions—of a few individuals. Significantly, the silver cup was never recovered, and there is little evidence from the primary materials indicating why Amadas even believed that the cup was with the Secotans. From the records, it is unclear if the lost cup ever existed in the first place. An entire town is destroyed over what might have amounted to a simple misunderstanding between people from vastly different cultures. This excessive military reaction over the always-absent item then works to further remove the physical presence of the Indigenous person from the colonial landscape. As Cartelli argues regarding New England, the rhetorical desire for an empty landscape often resulted in emptying the space of the Native inhabitants through force. The response to the silver cup activates this determination as it provides an excuse to act on the likely wishes for an Edenic space free from the Algonquian people. However, instead of disappearing the Algonquian people through rhetorical wish, the Amadas and Barlowe accounts *create* a physical item to render as lost. In turn, they must conduct an aggressive and destructive search for the created item, and in so doing they use the lost item to justify imperial violence. This fleeting historical moment serves as a useful illustration to understand how such losses do not have to be the same in degree or kind to create colonial fantasies of recovery.

Like the textual omission by Hakluyt pertaining to Virginia's Edenic essence, the loss and search for this silver cup implies a fall from the spiritual purity needed to achieve its recovery. Before the cup's attempted recovery, we hear no mention of it. Admittedly, this would make sense as such a small item might not warrant an extended discussion in the record, but after its loss it becomes something much larger for the narrative. It becomes the never-recovered item that ultimately orders the behavior and knowledge of these two groups from opposite sides of the Atlantic. Consideration of this lost cup begs at least one important question: why would, facing the burning of their town and the destruction of their food stores, the Secotans not simply return the cup? Does it not seem possible that there was no cup to return? In coming to exist only in its marked absence, the cup represents the way that Virginia came to be figured as a space where things were irretrievably lost. Just as Virginia falls from its description as prelapsarian ground, the English soldiers are left searching for the remains of an item that may have never existed outside the textual representation of its search. The epistemology of the new geographical space then becomes one where items or people are most commonly represented through their absence and can appear precisely because they must disappear forever. The creation of an absence demonstrates an extra turn in the conceptual cog between rhetorical effacement and the ability to enact violence. Lee Miller proposes in her study of Roanoke that the "loss" of the 1587 colony was created and promoted by the later Jamestown colony in a precise effort to instigate and justify war with the Powhatan. Following her reading, in the early archive, Virginia becomes a space where loss justifies force. The written record produces strategic and simulated absences that put into motion a Eurocentric agenda of using negative proof as means of aggressive colonial actions.

While the first two examples of absence that I have outlined deal mainly with the absence of evidence, I now turn to consider the figure of Manteo, who arguably "became English" during his lifetime through his profound archival presence.[18] As one of the two young men brought back to England by Barlowe, Manteo has a significant place in the historical archive and afterlife of the Roanoke voyages. He and his companion, Wanchese, came to England where they toured the country, learned the language, and, according to some sources, served as human propaganda for future investments in Raleigh's enterprises.[19] On October 18, 1584, Lupold von Wedel described Manteo and Wanchese as "in countenance and stature like white Moors" and noted also that "[n]o one was able to understand them and they made a most childish and silly figure" (qtd. in Quinn 116). This description seems both protoracial in terms of a phenotypic classification and also denotes a geographical placement. It also implies that the two men are slightly less than fully human given that the term "silly" at this time could be applied to one "deserving of pity, compassion, or sympathy," "helpless or defenseless; especially of women or children," or "of animals."[20] The protoracial markers are allied with ideas of geography, gender, and relative humanity. Likewise, von Wedel's inability to "understand" the two men renders a polysemous moment. Indeed, he could have been speaking quite literally about the difficulty of communicating with the non-English-speaking Algonquians. However, his inability to understand Manteo and Wanchese also signals his incapacity to render meaning from the two men on the visual scale.

The description of Manteo and Wanchese as "white Moors" also provides a key to understanding the relationship between land claim and emergent racial paradigms in early Virginia. In their relative proximity to the English center and their advertised role as aides for a colonial venture that hoped to secure a commodities market, the two men are rendered by a term that stands in for the potentially, but never fully, mutable stranger. Von Wedel marks the two men as from a longer global tradition in England and in so doing demonstrates the conceptual proximity of the East and West Indies for the early modern English. This is all despite the very real fact that not only were the two men far different from their East Indian or African colonial counterparts, but also we know they were likely culturally different from one another with Manteo from the Croatan villages farther south and Wanchese as a kinsman to Wingina and likely from the area more immediate to Roanoke Island. However, von Wedel's analogy of them as "white Moors" demonstrates not simply a flattening of the global difference of those subsumed under the period's imperial logic, but rather his attempt to modify a previous category by calling on a phenotypic register of whiteness. In this we see how race, proximity, and loyalty begin to foment with regard to the Native people of Virginia.

According to the English accounts, Wanchese may have remained skeptical of English behavior throughout his life, but the writings about Manteo suggest that he more eagerly accepted many ideas resulting from his new experiences. Two entries from John White's account of the 1587 voyage suggest that not all processes of recording Indians point to the absent archive, and that in the case of Indians becoming English, positive presence marks the spot. In one sense, Manteo might be thought of as *going English*. On August 13, White recorded: "[O]ur Savage Manteo, by the commandement of Sir Walter Ralegh, was christened in Roanoak, and called Lord therof, and of Dasamongueponke, in reward of his faithfull service" (qtd. in Quinn 531). In this instance, Manteo becomes the first Indigenous person of North America to be admitted into the Church of England and further becomes a landed subtenant for Raleigh. While we cannot be certain that Manteo thought of himself any differently after these ceremonies, we also cannot simply assume that this instance meant nothing for either the English colonists or for the Indigenous Manteo. Notably, John White records Manteo's christening by noting that he is "Our Savage." It is impossible to know exactly what White meant by this collective possessive pronoun, but given von Wedel's image of the men as something silly, connoting women, children, or livestock, it puts pressure on the way that White may have conceived, or simply recorded, Manteo as going English through his belonging to the colonists rather than through his own agency. In either case, in this instance the English records suggest that "becoming English" leaves a positive archival mark. Manteo's christening generates an open passage between Englishness and Indianness that hinges on religious affiliation and English land claim. If it is possible to become English, then it might be just as likely to become Indian when one locates oneself within different linguistic, cultural, or geographic registers. However, this process is complicated by the fact that to become English means to become present in the written archive while the visual archive assumes an overt Indian presence in relation to the absence, but perhaps given omnipresence, of the English. As we have seen with the loss of a "New World" paradise from Hakluyt's records and from the loss of Amadas's silver cup, loss leaves its own mark in the archive. From the beginning, then, Virginia represents a space that can only cover over what never was: virgin soil. The positivistic presence of Manteo in the record around land claim represents one among the earliest ways that narratives of loss and land intersect with earliest archival records of what will become the U.S. South.

This shuttling between presence-and-absence and presence-through-absence haunts the archive of Roanoke in one more significant way. After writing a 1593 letter to Hakluyt from Ireland, White himself becomes lost, never to make another recoverable archival mark.[21] Although in his 1590 description of the attempt to locate the colony White seems assured that his countrymen were indeed safe with Manteo and his Croatan people farther south, the tone of this later epistle more profoundly communicates despair. In the documents of the 1590 voyage, he writes of the colonists: "I greatly joyed that I had safely found a certaine token of their safe being at Croatoan, which is the place where Manteo was borne, and the Savages of the Iland our friends" (qtd. in Quinn 616). Here White points toward the "certaine token" as the clear mark of the positive evidence of the colonists' continued existence. Strangely, this certain token worked in combination with the *absence* of a distress signal. As White writes, "thereof were curiously carved these faire Romane letters CRO: which letters presently we knew to signifie the place, where I should find the planters seated, according to a secret token agreed upon betweene them & me at my last departure from them" (qtd. in Quinn 613). This "secret token" of the letters was unaccompanied by a cross. White reinterprets this textual nonevidence of the colonists for his reader: "I willed them, that if they should happen to be distressed in any of those places, that then they should carve over the letters or name, a Crosse ✣ in this forme, but we found no such signe of distresse" (qtd. in Quinn 614). Like the silver cup, the cross is significant precisely because of its absence. White alleviates his worries seemingly because of something that he does not see; in other words, the assurance of the colonists' safety is confirmed by negative evidence. Furthermore, this absence is presaged by what he identifies as a secret token. The certain and secret token comes into being much like other simulated absences in the archive. White reads the signs of things that no one else could corroborate because they were previously unknown to anyone but himself and the colonists he left behind. Why should we, as readers, take White at his word that the absence of evidence stands in for the presence of a safe colony? He covers over two possibilities with his written record of the absent sign: one, that the colonists were indeed distressed as they had been defeated by the surrounding Native populations, or two, that they had decided to abandon Englishness and become Algonquian.

Unlike his relatively optimistic initial account of the colony, White's later 1593 letter to Hakluyt documents a 1590 journey filled with loss and disappointment. His later description of the voyage is marked by the loss of "one of our ship-boates; and 7 of our chiefest men: and also with losse of 3 ankers and cables, and most of our caskes with fresh water left on shore, not possible to be had aboord" (qtd. in Quinn 715). The 1593 document reads like a more private letter, and White describes a certain kind of despair: "Which evils and unfortunate events (as wel as their own losse as to the hinderance of the planters in Virginia) had not chanced, if the order set downe by Sir Walter Ralegh had been observed, or if my dayly & continuall petitions for the performance of the same might have taken place. Thus may you plainly perceive the successe of my fift & last voiage to Virginia, which was no less unfortunately ended then frowardly begun, and as lucklesse to many, as sinister to my selfe" (ibid.). After this correspondence, White disappears from the archive. White's final letter and following archival absence render him as an apt metaphor for the process of loss and becoming in the transatlantic contact between the English and the Indian. While portraits of Raleigh are ubiquitous in relation to the colonial Americas, and even Harriot's portrait is common enough alongside his *Briefe and True Report*, White's image has disappeared behind those of the Indigenous people he painstakingly recorded in pencil and watercolor. When we recall John White, we imagine his profound loss of English family, and we view the Indians and landscapes he left behind.

As have other historians, Ian Steele, in his book *Warpaths: Invasions of North America* (1995), has argued that scholars have too frequently imagined colonization of the Americas as a forgone conclusion, neglecting the fact that tribal nations of the Eastern Seaboard were politically and militarily complex groups that challenged European invasion and their accompanying ideas of "virgin soil." Although rarely thought of as such, it is probable that the Lost Colony of Roanoke might constitute a moment when the English were soundly defeated by tribes resistant to their colonial invasion and settlement. That is, it might do well to reformulate the colony not so much as a "loss" but perhaps as a profound "win" for the Algonquian people of early modern Virginia. Continuing to think of the colony as something mysteriously "lost," rather than as an English colonial defeat, obscures the early history of English colonialism in the present-day U.S. South, and it continually renders the Algonquians as passive victims rather than cultural negotiators of their own fates. This discourse informs much of the way that people continue to think about Native history even today. Recasting the very idea of "loss" in the Lost Colony reinserts a likely history of Native success against early colonial invaders, and it pushes against the legacy of aesthetic victimry that Vizenor pinpoints as a preoccupation of contemporary scholars who deal in loss and lost causes. To return to Hakluyt's deletion of the prelapsarian imagery from his 1600 manuscript, he covers over this fall from New World paradise, and as readers, we may imagine that by that year Hakluyt sensed a contradiction of an irreversible Eden that had seemingly swallowed his English countrymen.

And what of the anonymous Algonquian woman in John White's drawings who becomes Paul Green's Agona? The woman in the painting stares intently at the artist, and in so doing, she becomes the archival Indian that corresponds to the beginning of English colonialism in the present-day U.S. South. In this way, then, Green's twentieth-century historical imaginings of Agona seem especially apt. Rather than stay beholden to a written archive, Green re-creates Roanoke with an eye toward the archival absences that prefigure a continual narrative of loss. This is not simply a case of modern authors and audiences creating a narrative of loss to understand Roanoke in terms of their contemporary consciousness. Rather, this narrative of absence and loss becomes a settler-colonial epistemology that depends on absence as the archival evidence used to justify and continue a process of colonial invasion—an imperial strategy not too far afield from our recent history in the search for absent items as the justification of war. In the case of Roanoke, Green's play points us toward these gaps in the record and their lasting complications—complications that as we will see in the next section are all too easily taken up by white southerners to understand their own lost causes.

A Recovery of Feelings

In the summer of 2009, Robert Richmond, then director of Paul Green's outdoor drama *The Lost Colony*, made a risky decision. For the first time in the production's seventy-two-year history, the performance would include a curtain call. In the previous seventy-one seasons, the actors playing the ill-fated colonists had either departed downstage right into the wilds of the island, or they had ambiguously dispersed from the stage as Spanish ships approached. In any version, they had never come back onto the stage to assure the audience that they were in fact living actors and that the show was the stuff of fiction. The play had always left audiences in a state of profound uncertainty, and it had left the mystery of the colony intact. As represented in the performance, the colony might have gone to live with the Croatan people farther south, or they might have been wiped out by the Spanish, or they might have simply perished. Only one thing was certain for the viewers before the 2009 performance: these were not actors deserving of applause from the audience of vacationers. They *were* the Lost Colony. During the 2009 season, the town of Manteo, North Carolina, on Roanoke Island was abuzz with the scandal of Richmond's decision. During my conversations with cast members, they noted that the people of the town were indeed upset that summer. Attendance on the first night seemed to be up precisely because of the question: would Richmond really go forward with the curtain call? This controversy, while it might seem to be a trivial bit of small-town politics, speaks to the very core of the performed history of the performances that I examine throughout the book.[22] Richmond's decision and the town's reaction to it render visible how the outdoor drama creates a space in the U.S. South that exceeds and supersedes what an audience might think of as historical reality.

These outdoor dramas constitute an important site of investigation for understanding multiple versions of the red state. The fact that the genre of the outdoor drama depends largely on the history of the region as it relates to Native American history further complicates how local audiences might understand something as simple as a curtain call. They each make claims to the literal ground on which they are staged, and they all deal in recursive time through their design as yearly recurring events that recapitulate historical moments. The plays retell historical events, and additionally, they are retold every year, offering a site to examine how historical retellings change over time and take on the inflections of the present. As subsequent chapters explain, these outdoor dramas have long been written, produced, and performed by non-Native southerners, yet in some instances they have also been rewritten, reproduced, and reperformed by Native individuals and tribal nations.[23] As a genre, it has its beginnings in North Carolina, though during its peak as a mid-century tourist attraction, the outdoor drama was performed in locations from Ohio to Texas, with the heaviest concentrations in the Carolinas and Virginia.

In examining these performances, I often turn the lens of inquiry toward the audiences who view these works. This is not simply an exercise in the affective fallacy, but instead an inquiry into how the audience responds—and is conditioned to respond—to claims of Indigenous history, land claim, and identity. This arena of reception has been as much a shaping force of the red state as the creators of these works. As such, the outdoor drama represents a site of affect in abundance. Although at times I do examine the effects that these performances have on the audience, I do not seek some understanding of the truth of the text in and of itself; rather, I argue that these understandings and this realm of affect have the precise ability to create lived realities for the Native people of the region today. Looking at the outdoor drama performance over the years shows how Indigenous history in the U.S. South has been created and deployed for varying ends as the plays literally restage a "timeless" history in the context of the audience's lived reality. These deployments and receptions of affective history have created what I discuss in the introduction as structures of feeling, which may at once appear as nonconsequential as a simple curtain call but maintain structures of power that have repercussions for Native people of the U.S. South, both at home and in diaspora. These feelings, as Raymond Williams offers, "cannot without loss be reduced to belief-systems, institutions, or explicit general relationships," though they may include all three (133). Rather, in the case of these outdoor dramas, they are those moments that lead us to examine "meanings and values as they are actively lived and felt" (132).

In order to approach these texts, I ask several questions regarding the use and reception of Native history in these pieces of lived and performed southern literature: How have Native and southern identities been mutually negotiated and performed? How do these compulsive tellings of historical events create a performative link between the past and the present that troubles our understanding of linear temporality? What versions of these histories are being restaged, and toward what ends? Who is the intended audience for these performative histories? How does the sanctioned space as part of the regional tourist industry propose a space of the red state that troubles temporal and geographic designations of the region? And finally, what conceptual genealogies of land claim do these plays suggest? These questions foreground the concepts of regional space and historical identities, and they look to the outdoor drama as a site of compulsive history where narratives of the region become shored up year after year as the plays are staged six nights a week for the entire summer. In querying the role of feelings and reception in the creation of alternate visions for a red state, I also consider the ways that Native communities in the region may indeed have differing motivations for the staging of their histories, as I examine in chapter 4 regarding the Lumbee outdoor drama, *Strike at the Wind!* In the early days of the genre, all of the outdoor dramas were written, produced, and staged by non-Native people. Later, however, tribes and individual Native people began to take control of their own participation in the genre through their casting in key roles (as was the case with *Horn in the West*), their consultation in initial script-writing and staging (*Strike at the Wind!*), and their wholesale tribal takeover and revision of the production (*Unto These Hills*). The motivations behind these plays certainly differ from community to community and from individual to individual, but nonetheless, in each case the occurrence of these dramas in the U.S. South necessarily challenges the reception of both tribal and regional histories. Together, these questions lead us to consider the complicated issues of periodization when Native and southern histories are held together in view.

These plays produce histories, and these histories, whether real or imagined, produce realities for the actors and viewers alike. They create historical genealogies where connections to the land are legitimized through story. The production of these dramas asks us to reconsider the production of histories and how our understanding of a dynamic, rather than static, historical narrative opens up possibilities for the future. I examine the precise ways that these plays illuminate the possibilities of a shifting landscape where histories can be understood as products of discourse rather than as litanies of fact. In these plays, it is not simply that they are accurate or inaccurate, true or untrue, but that their very production of stories creates systems of power and, perhaps more importantly, unequal distributions of power in the region. Therefore, the nature of these performances as recurring and continual shores up the type of Foucauldian power that requires constant enforcement in its production of pleasure, knowledge, and discourse. Through an analysis of these texts, both in their performed and written versions, I investigate how Native and southern and Native southern histories map the region, demonstrating how in the red state narratives of indigeneity frequently shore up the construction of whiteness.

These texts foreground the issues of periodization through their linking of historical events, their twentieth-century moments of inception, and their continual staging into the present. Do we say that these plays are of the historical archives they call on? Or are they products of the moment of their initial writing? Or perhaps they are of their staged moment each time they are performed? These questions go alongside the issues of reception in that in each instance of performance, the regional audience has changed both literally and figuratively. It is in this way that these plays engage structures of feeling through the reception archives that they leave behind. In a sense they allow us to glimpse the emerging changes of thought in the region. The received histories called on in these performances return me to my earlier reference to Greg Sarris, when he asserts that each time one hears and tells a story, there is more to the teller and listener and *that* is the story. Tracking the archival, performance, and reception histories of these outdoor dramas allows us to render this interstitial space visible, and it undoes the colonial parameters of period in showing the ways that Native communities have been able to change the histories through the stories in both subtle and overt ways. It demonstrates the ways that the performance of Indigenous identities and histories have continually formed the construction of red states in relation to both time and space.

The outdoor dramas I examine engage in a strategic dehistoricization even while they are obsessed with historical "accuracy." The plays, both Native and non-Native, use this space of the stage to construct legitimate identity and land claims in the Native South. They produce a relationship between the fictive and nonfictive in order to make claims to specific geographic and genealogical claims regarding a particular group's connection to the ground where the action is staged. This relationship emerges in a careful analysis of the performances as well as the archival materials and stated intentions of the genre's founders. In terms of the red state that I examine, the impetus behind these performances becomes central. Claims to land and Native identity in the U.S. South can be fraught, and in the case of these performances, we see both the historical construction of these claims and their contemporary repercussions for lived people, both Native and non-Native, in the region. Examining the genre, content, and historical and factual mobility of the outdoor drama allows us to reconfigure common assumptions about the region, including the effacement of Native people from the earliest colonial landscapes, the assumptions of the U.S. South as an empty post-Removal space, and the continual linking of Nativeness with fetishized versions of "loss."

Furthermore, we might conceive of these performances as precisely engaged in the possibilities for new emotive registers that can correct or challenge the old, faulty politics of the red state. One problem that emerges is that as cultural critics we often cannot successfully answer the power of affect with a bombardment of historical facts and accuracies.[24] These plays, indeed, all engage in historical inaccuracies, but it is not my intention to simply point out how the initial texts and yearly performances get history wrong. Rather, I am interested in examining how these performances, and the revisions of these performances, open up new affective spaces for considering the Indigenous history in the U.S. South. The need to tell and retell the same story every year suggests an affective register where the urge to rehash the region's history exceeds the realm of the conscious and instead speaks to a host of psychological imperatives. This compulsive retelling, then, does not necessarily refer to theories of trauma or repetition but to a sense that the accretion of representation of the region's Indigenous history creates a space where the narratives of significant historical events are displaced in favor of performative histories that have real and material implications for Native people of the U.S. South. These issues have been a part of the outdoor drama since its inception.

In some sense, these performances might be thought of in terms of Philip Deloria's work in *Playing Indian* (1994). Deloria invokes a theoretical backing from Mikhail Bakhtin's ideas of "carnival" and "play," and from that he thinks through "playing Indian" as a dialogic and contradictory process of negotiation. He points toward the Indian in the "American" imagination as a site of ambivalence where white culture has appropriated Native culture and dress in order to shore up its legitimacy as a nation with historical roots, and conversely, white people have deployed Indian identities to express the anxiety over white America's perpetual liminality. Playing Indian for Deloria works as both closure and aperture for white identity in the United States. From new American to New Age, Deloria traces what has changed and what has remained constant in these instances of "disguised" identity. Ultimately, he maintains that "to be American is to be unfinished," and that in this liminal space Native people continue to be imagined and played as answer to the U.S. culture's larger anxieties of colonial conquest and doubt (191). These doubts, however, take on a specific resonance once one adds in equally popular narratives of southern exceptionalism, which depends on its own set of strategic memories. As with this work of memory, Joseph Roach's critique in *Cities of the Dead* (1996) also informs my analysis of these performances, as he sees the act of performance working within issues of remembering but also forgetting. As he states, "circum-Atlantic performance is a monumental study in the pleasures and torments of incomplete forgetting. But more obdurate questions persist: Whose forgetting? Whose memory? Whose history?" (7). Though these plays are not necessarily of a circum-Atlantic tradition, their staging of Indigenous history in the U.S. South brings up the same questions. These query a specificity beyond Deloria's unfinished American identity as they layer regional and national questions that depend on several other competing sovereignties including those of Native, U.S., Confederate, and European nations.

The Lost Colony layers these competing sovereign claims across time and space. Green was commissioned to stage the story of the Lost Colony of Roanoke Island for the 350th anniversary of the colony's disappearance. Loss, it would seem, constitutes an odd anniversary to celebrate. At the moment of this play's inception, the whole country was experiencing a state of loss as the Great Depression continued to affect the lives of many, and as Laurence Avery notes, *The Lost Colony* began as a product of the late 1930s political-social climate: "At no other time could it have been gotten together in just the way it was in 1937. With its grassroots origin, community spirit, and celebratory aim, the production was precisely the sort of effort to attract national attention during the New Deal phase of the Great Depression" (3). The "symphonic drama," as Green called it, was a four-hour spectacle including elaborate staging in the Waterfront Theater on Roanoke Island. As documented by several regional newspapers, audiences loved the play, and even President Roosevelt attended that first summer. It seemed that in the combination of outdoor setting, epic scale, historical material, and extended pathos, Green had hit a mark. From his work at UNC he, along with Samuel Selden, who served as director and/or producer of many of the performances, began to cultivate the talent of other young playwrights. One of these, Kermit Hunter, whose work *Horn in the West* I examine in the next chapter, went on to become the most performed playwright in U.S. history. As I note above, the plays—not all written by Hunter and Green—even branched out to locations across the nation. Many of these plays staged across the North and Midwest eventually lost their popularity, but in the U.S. South, particularly in North Carolina, the outdoor drama created by Green, Selden, and Hunter has held on.[25]

For those from North Carolina, these performances are a part of the collective ether. Many theater students land their first professional acting jobs in these performances, and it is a common occurrence for families to spend a week in the mountains or at the beach, where the itinerary includes a visit to see the show. For some people, these are yearly expeditions. On the surface, this may seem odd. After all, the show rarely changes. There may be minor adjustments here and there, and almost all of the plays have been edited and condensed from their initial three- to four-hour run time, but at the end of the day, we all know that the Lost Colony is lost and how the Revolutionary War ends. The history does not change. However, this is the interesting thing about these performances. Sometimes the history does change—sometimes in slight, almost imperceptible ways and sometimes in large sweeping motions—and this is where these outdoor dramas become especially telling for formulations of a red state that depend on building a geographic space via layering histories across deep time. As Samuel Selden wrote regarding these performances: "The outdoor drama presents the essence of history" (7). Significantly, an essence is not the same as a fact or a truth, and it connotes an inherent and intrinsic spiritual quality that may bend accurate details in the service of emotions. This essence may be akin to the affective realm, where the culmination of these feelings can signal shifts in the region's ideological ethos. Tracing these shifts in the historical essence of the outdoor drama tells us not only about the politics of their moment of inception, but also about the dynamic nature of the audience's understanding of the region's received history. In other words, these plays have significant implications even while they remain relatively understudied. In my experience, audiences, actors, and directors tend to discuss the plays relative to their present realities. The plays make little to no effort to recount which parts of their performance stem from archival knowledge and which parts spring entirely of the writers', producers', or directors' imaginations. In many cases, they appeal to or even depend on the idea that their "essence" of history is indeed fact. They are presented as history with few winks or nods to the audience, allowing them to traffic in lofty notions of historical memory without much grounding in the archive.

Such an analysis is informed by critical inquiries established by Diana Taylor in *The Archive and the Repertoire: Performing Cultural Memory in the Americas* (2003), where she isolates the archive as the written historical records—the places of colonial conquest and narratives of subjugation. Taylor sees the repertoire as a not-quite-opposite of this, where cultural (and often counter-) memory takes hold as a means to resist the absences of the archive. She does not, however, position these two items as participating in a pure binary, and she shows how the two can elide one another in ways beyond both the performers' and archivists' control. Taylor thinks of these moments as situations that call all of us into the realm of knowledge-making where we have to order the events into a manner that allows us to process cognitively their significances. For Taylor, it is not simply that we see our ontology as extant in the evidence of the performance, but that the performance allows us to witness knowledge-making in process. Therefore, how one knows and perpetuates the idea of the Americas is based on the context in which one performs an identity in relation to one's situation. She closes by noting that this is not an action that will simply bind the Americas; it will also fragment them, which will allow us to "remap" the hemisphere—an act that in and of itself implies the performance of constructed and situated knowledges. I extend this construction to my consideration of the U.S. South as a region that has depended on the performances of multiple histories across competing sovereignties. These competing sovereignties inform the regional contours I wish to add to Deloria's analysis, offering a significant new branch to the analytical tree he plants in *Playing Indian*. As Angela Pulley Hudson and others have argued, American colonialism is localized, flexible, and responsive to microconditions, and scholars must pay attention to the ground conditions of the region to understand how ideas of performed Indian-ness and American Indian history cling to the local terrain.[26]

To live in a region that must compulsively retell its histories, even its unpleasant histories, has an effect on its inhabitants, both those who have resided there for thousands of years and the relative newcomers. As actor Brian Clowdus, who played the role of Sir Walter Raleigh/the Narrator Historian in the 2009 season of *The Lost Colony*, observed regarding a regional audience's particularly intense investment in these performances, "When a director or performer makes changes to these plays, audiences react strongly. They seem to feel, 'You aren't just changing the performance; you're changing *my history*'" (Clowdus, personal interview). This well-conceived point from Clowdus about the outdoor drama forces us to reconsider the power that these performances have. If history is dynamic via production, then it opens up great space for possible futures where people become empowered through the production of their own histories. As Clowdus suggests, though, audiences too must be willing to engage with the reimagining of this historical space.

Significantly, in each of the plays I examine, at some point in the action, a character or characters literally hold up handfuls of dirt from the earthen stage or speak almost directly to the ground in an expression of immense attachment to the geographic space of the performance. Because each of these outdoor dramas claims to be staged on the site of the historical event it recounts, the audience is made fully aware that these plays are about who claims the ground on which they stand, which as Eric Anderson reminds us in "On Native Ground" is an act fraught with significance. Through this, each of the plays makes claims about who constitutes the rightful inheritors of the geographic space of the region, and these performances call up this issue through fictive genealogies, both familial and conceptual. The claiming of space and the reverence for southern earth occur precisely for audiences when the play encourages a visceral link between the history of the geographic space and the stage on which the performance takes place. When the performances make these appeals, they engage perceived histories and structures of power that determine who gets to claim the land.

While Selden saw these performances as offering an anecdote to "our cramped way of living in a modern world," Green was more obtusely critical of the southern audience when he wrote in 1959 that the performances emerged from "a guilty sense of intellectual and cultural lack" (Selden 7; P. Green, "Letter"). Green also admitted that the spectacle of the show might find its appeal in the importance of spectacle in southern culture, and he admits, "we in the South love spectacles. We used to like lynchings and public hangings" ("Letter"). This admission, while shocking to a contemporary audience, should not be read as Green's endorsement of such a paradigm, and may be understood as a jab at the history of southern mob feelings. Green, a lifelong activist against the death penalty, was among one of the staunchest opponents to neo-Confederate and white Agrarian activism in the U.S. South, working to write opinion pieces such as his "Farewell to the Civil War" for the collection *We Dissent*, which was to put forth an intellectual southern voice against the calls of southern agrarians and other racists as the authoritative representatives of the white South. In this piece Green writes of southern fiction: "I am tired too of the misshapen fiction characters who moan their wails and woes in the long-winded pages of what is called the Southern literary renaissance. In my present mood at the fallen prestige of American idealism in the world, these characters seem to me as sorry and as untruthful representatives of human life as the old magnolia, honeysuckle, crinoline, roses, and mockingbird folks a hundred years ago. True, they are not as empty-headed, but since they are stuffed with their own excrement they give off a viler odor" (P. Green, "Farewell"). Green keeps us from simply dismissing these plays as products of a racist South and forces us to consider the history of the genre and the genre as history in order to see where they both create and legitimate romantic narratives of the region that push against common assumptions of race and land claim in the U.S. South.

While none of the plays, especially in their original form, could be held up as a shining exception to the racial politics of their original time, they transform as a part of a living and changing landscape where people have created and re-created narratives to register with the changing audiences who see these performances as history. These plays evolve out of a specific place and time, and when we read them today we have to remember the contextual histories—the Great Depression, the Indian Reorganization Act, the Termination period, the Vietnam War—that inform their own inceptions as texts. Within the genre, there exists the possibility for an affective mobility, but given that a large part of the work of affect happens within the audience, we must maintain a touch of skepticism on how shifts in feelings and facts register for the viewers. Despite Green's stated disavowal of southern fiction as invested in the paradigm of magnolias and mockingbirds, the original scripts for these outdoor dramas often do construct Native history in the region as part of a narrative of legitimate white ascendency. In many ways, the contemporary performances have worked to counteract the narratives of white supremacy, but the audience's understanding of these historical shifts is more difficult to control, leaving the history of the Native South as a shaking terrain between fictive performance and material reality. For *The Lost Colony*, I engage the question of colonial critique as the play elicits nostalgia from the viewer while simultaneously undermining romantic attachment to the region's history. Because of Green's combination of attention to historical detail and imaginative license—the "authenticity" and "feelings" he describes in this chapter's epigraph—in his review of the first season of the outdoor drama,

James Gray wrote for *American Motorist* that "'Succeeding where science and history has failed,' art has found the Lost Colony."

With the exception of the much later *Strike at the Wind!*, among the outdoor dramas Green's *Lost Colony* attempts the most fidelity toward the historical records. Even more significantly, the fictional play makes an explicit reference to itself as history through the use of the narrator who is labeled in almost every version of the script since 1937 as "The Historian." This inclusion of the Historian who records and serves as the authoritative voice for the audience suggests that the performance attempts to establish itself as some type of accurate rendition of life on Roanoke Island and in England in the 1580s. What many audience members take away from the play is a sense of some "truth" behind the mystery of the colonists' disappearance and their relationship with the local Algonquian people. These truths have lasting effects as many in the region and state view the Lost Colony as the initial moment of racial mixing in North Carolina. Such a misconception creates a conceptual genealogy for the region where residents can imagine themselves as both English and Indigenous through distant ancestors.

In the 1930s few people in the United States remembered Raleigh's efforts at colonization as the beginnings of English settlement on the American continent, and the narrative genealogy of "America" had moved far north to the stories of Plymouth Rock and William Bradford. The Roanoke Island Historical Association (RIHA) sought to correct what they saw as this false U.S. genealogy through a production of a play about Sir Walter Raleigh's Lost Colony. They wanted to use the 350th anniversary of the colony as a way to reinsert this piece of "southern" history into the popular narrative of the beginnings of English America. However, this task would not prove to be so easy because even though 350 years had passed, Roanoke Island was still geographically isolated, only accessible by a combination of floating roads and ferries. Manteo, the town that was expected to host this epic performance with a projected cast of more than a hundred, was itself home to only 547 people. However, the problems of an isolated location and limited resources did not dissuade the RIHA. In conjunction with extensive support from the Federal Theatre Project, and using resources from the Civilian Conservation Corps, the Rockefeller Foundation, and the University of North Carolina at Chapel Hill, the play opened successfully to an audience of 2,500 on the evening of July 4, 1937, marking the RIHA's attempt to reinsert North Carolina into the narrative birth of the Anglo America.[27]

Such a reinsertion into the historical record speaks to the concerns of emotional histories as well as a new way to conceive of the early American historical periodization. From this expressed anxiety over the regionalization of history, we can understand the RIHA as precisely invested in a type of red state construction that looks to create a new narrative of national beginning in order to reimagine the U.S. South's place in the larger nation's consciousness and create pride in the region at home. Significantly, *The Lost Colony* shares a striking homonymic resonance with the Lost Cause. As Charles Reagan Wilson offers, unlike the national founding narrative and resulting civil religion that focused on issues of democracy and immigrant inclusion, the southern civil religion of the Lost Cause looked toward a history of righteous defeat that "offered confused and suffering Southerners a sense of meaning, an identity in a precarious but distinct culture" (13). This analysis supports Taylor's work, and it offers another point of evidence in the ways that narratives of Native history become confused under the post–Civil War rubric of the Lost Cause. However, as I demonstrate earlier, the very concept of "loss" figures into the discourse surrounding the colony from even the late sixteenth century. So while the later play indeed traffics in the logic of the Lost Cause, the conditions for such a conflation far predate the later emotive attachments. Religious studies scholar Michael Zogry identifies the problems of the religious rituals depicted in the play, and he argues that "Though the drawings, engravings, and play describe late sixteenth-century 'Indians,' they continue to influence constructions of the category 'religion' [...] because such images and the ideological ciphers that they contain resonate with contemporary authors and audiences; more broadly, they remain constituent elements of generalized teleological grand narratives of the United States" (2). I do not disagree with this assertion, but Zogry's analysis does not account for the specifically regional character of these plays.[28] *The Lost Colony* does not simply offer a founding for the United States through a performative understanding of religion. Instead, it offers a distinctly southern founding narrative of loss counter to the teleology of the nation, and as such it requires an analysis that remains attuned to the region as an organizing space for settler-colonial logics.

The conflation of the Lost Colony and the Lost Cause is not simply an act of scholarly synthesis of the two ideas. In fact, a local reverend noted during his opening benediction for both the performance in 1937 and its second run in 1938 that "It is well to consider the glory and significance of lost causes, the splendor of noble defeat, the eternal beauty of those who die for a cause." He was not, however, even speaking of lost causes in the abstract, as he is reported in the local paper as explicitly stating that "the world called the broken dream of the Confederacy 'The Lost Cause'" ("Lost Colony Lives Again"). This narrative interpolation represents a proposed shift in the historical and affective registers, showing how the performance both pushed and pulled away from a historical genealogy of the U.S. South. *The Lost Colony* both reinserts the U.S. South into a larger nation, signaling a shift away from the isolationist and dejected Confederacy, and appeals to an exceptional history still grounded in the profound narrative of loss. Notably, the article appears just below an image of a Confederate soldier and a Union soldier shaking hands, signaling their "forgiveness." In short, the southern civil religion deployed itself via ritual and pathos, and it worked to coalesce a sense of loss into the very fabric of southern identity that imagines itself as at once oppositional and indicative of the nation. But again, it remains important to remember that when it comes to Indigenous history on the American continent, the language of loss had represented a *modus operandi* for the logic of colonialism long before the Confederacy had been imagined, won, or lost. Instead of a later convergence between the two ideas, we might understand the coterminous use of loss as a layer to the palimpsest of the U.S. South where various losses accrue meanings and redactions across the region's history and enact new meanings across a spiral of time.

Indeed, the addition of white southern loss to Indigenous beginnings may lead viewers to invent a shared sense of colonial defeat between the two groups—a convergence rather than a shared background—and it makes the questions of identity and land claim a fraught space where Indigenous history can be remapped to encompass southern feelings of loss. As ethnohistorian Michael Harkin argues, "Paul Green's play is as much about the painful transition from an agrarian to an industrial society as it is about the Lost Colony itself" ("Performing Paradox" 109). Such a restructuring of affect through history enforces and even extends a dangerous structure of discursive power in the region, where the wages of whiteness become enforced through feelings of colonial rule following the Civil War.[29]

This is not to argue that some cases of shifting history are *ipso facto* negative while others are positive, but that each enforces or challenges structures of southern feeling that can have consequences for lived realities. In this case, the narrative of loss as historical fact informs structures of power in the region that remain undergirded by dangerously racist paradigms that inform people's conception of who they are and where they live. As Laurie Langbauer argues of the Lost Colony narrative:

> The obsessive iterations within this originary myth of lost origins—all the endless missed possibilities, all that forgetting and oblivion (first of the colonists themselves and then of the history they represent)—suggest that its meaning lies precisely here: in a gap that cannot be closed, an enigma inhabiting the fringes, an obsessive rememoration of a forgotten trauma, an alternative that persists because it remains open—history circumvented, short-circuited, stuck in a loop. That this story takes place in the Virginia territory, and not in Massachusetts Bay, is probably only coincidence, historical accident. And yet accident shapes identity. (4)

The fact that this shaping of white southern identity works in conjunction with the perceived loss of the English to the Native demonstrates the ways that these outdoor dramas continue to matter for the use of history in the construction of a space-time that we now might collectively shorthand as red state politics. In this gap that cannot be closed, the conservative ideology that depends on white nativism is able to imagine itself as originary. This spirit of nativism depends on a myth of lost Native presence that can be easily replaced by feelings of white nostalgia for a history that never existed.

Signaling the play's trouble with dynamic histories, one of the most frequently reimagined roles has been that of the Historian who narrates the play's backstory and fills in the historical details of the colony. As Avery notes: "A narrator is an efficient vehicle for introducing historical background and for bridging the gap between episodes a few months or years or an ocean apart. The trouble with narrators is that they are not part of the action of the play but outside of it [and they] tend to be a drag on performance" (4). In 1937 the Historian was cordoned off from the stage in his own separate cubicle, physically separated from the play's action. In the 1960s, with Green's approval, the Historian became mobile and was described as a "kindly, elderly man, dressed in a scholar's dark robe and carry[ing] a ledger book" (4–5). In 2000 the Historian was cut as a character, his lines distributed to members of the chorus. Details regarding the various characters' cultural or collective histories were often taken by those characters; for example, as Avery describes, "Lines having to do with the life of Native Americans, for instance, are taken by Wanchese and Manteo" (5). In addition to adding a curtain call, in the summer of 2009 director Richmond controversially combined the role of Sir Walter Raleigh with the Historian, dressing each differently as to create the illusion of two separate characters until a dramatic transformation on stage in the final scenes when the audience definitively realizes that Raleigh and the Historian are one and the same.[30] Through these shifts of this character, we see the slight ways that these plays do in fact change the history of these events as subjective experiences and thus create competing narratives of the implications of English colonization for the Indigenous people of the Atlantic shoreline.

Combining the character Raleigh with the Historian highlights the subjective nature of historical telling, and it opens up a slight critical nuance to the historiography of the Roanoke colony. Such a move shifts the reception of the history and for many viewers likely complicates their ideas of who tells what history for what ends. This continual reconception of the Historian is interesting for what it says about the play's deployment and the audience's understanding of how the performance functions as history. While some of the details the Historian narrates are indeed factual tidbits from the extant sources, the Historian's continual narration of the events in the colony following Governor John White's departure in 1587 must be pure speculation. Likewise, his romantic imaginings of the Algonquian people come more from Green's imagination than they do from any historical details. More than simply a narrator of facts, the Historian focuses mainly on reminding the audience of the noble dream of the colony's hopes at creating a "New World." The Historian delivers these lines:

> Now down the trackless hollow years
> That swallowed them but not their song
> We send response—
> 'O lusty singer, dreamer, pioneer,
> Lord of the wilderness, the unafraid,
> Tamer of darkness, fire and flood,
> Of the soaring spirit winged aloft
> On the plumes of agony and death—
> Hear us, O hear!
> The dream still lives.
> It lives, it lives,
> And shall not die!' (P. Green, *Lost Colony* 32–33)

With his initial physical separation from the action and even with his later scholar's robe, the Historian—in name and essence—serves as an authoritative narrative voice, one that the audience trusts for the "truth" of the Lost Colony. However, when this character moves from historical detail to romantic maxim, the audience receives the effect of the two as joined. The historical details then justify the outcomes as part of a perceived inevitable destiny of colonization in the Americas.

The play, however, is not without its critique of this "dream." As I discuss shortly, Richmond's decision to make the Historian the same as Raleigh showcases a subtle critique of bias in the historical narrative that finds its basis in a written English archive. But even in his original script, Green undermines the romantic narrative of English colonization as a dream. In a scene at the English court, the "drunk" Old Tom, who later becomes one of the colonists, passes out as Queen Elizabeth, Raleigh, and other members of the court debate the colonization of the Americas. Raleigh urges the queen to realize that the strength and perpetual power of England rest with their ability to plant permanent colonies across the Atlantic. And as Raleigh assures Eleanor Dare and the commoner John Borden, "You and hundreds more shall go—someday" (P. Green, *Lost Colony* 58). After this scene, Old Tom awakes to address the audience: "Whee-oo, I had the most frightful dream! The world was most monstrously overrun by lice with two legs," to which Raleigh, overhearing him, replies, "An apt dream, old man" (62). This critique of colonization as likened to invading lice comes and goes quickly in the play's action. Furthermore, it is delivered by the town drunk, Old Tom. While Tom later becomes a hero in Roanoke, at this point in the action he hardly represents a character to whom the audience looks for any reasoned discourse on the implications of

Brian Clowdus in 2009 as the Historian in *The Lost Colony*. Courtesy of the Roanoke Island Historical Association.

English colonialism. Instead, he functions as the fool whom the play permits to speak unpleasant truths. However, when the reliable character Raleigh responds in endorsement, it creates a slight pause in consideration of what the colonial "dream" might really mean for the rest of the globe.

Once in the Roanoke colony, Tom falls in love with Agona, whom I discuss earlier in the chapter. When asked what Agona's name means, Old Tom replies, "which is to say in the Indian tongue, 'Agony'" (117).[31] The significance of Agona renders visible through performance Philip Deloria's assertion that the figure of the Native woman was used by colonists as a way "to evoke female sexuality in picturing the fertile landscape or to show the colonies as available and vulnerable to the desires of English men" (*Playing Indian* 29). The shifting portrayals of Agona both support and undermine this specific function of the Native woman in the colonial imagination.[32] For the first several decades of the performance, Agona was played as a slapstick figure who had more romantic feelings for Tom than Tom had in return, thus rendering her as the colonial "helper" ready to do the male settler's bidding. Despite this, some still saw the relationship as part of Green's subtle attempt to refigure the conceptions of interracial intimacy in the U.S. South. Green was an intense opponent of segregation, and as noted earlier, he worked throughout his life to challenge narratives of southern white supremacy. As Drew Harris notes to Avery: "That was Paul Green's slyest move [...] To make that relationship palatable by treating it on the comic level. How many people in those early audiences realized, do you think, when they felt a warm glow at the success of the relationship of Tom and Agona, that they were responding favorably to an interracial marriage? I'll bet not many" (Avery 7). Here, Harris points toward a possible shift in the affective registers of racial relations that the play might have on an unsuspecting southern audience in the early twentieth century. While Harris has a valid point, two factors limit the progressive lens through which we can see Agona in 1937: one, she serves as comic relief—much like the character Look in John Wayne's *The Searchers* whose hurtful and crass treatment at the hands of the other characters represents the abuse suffered by Native women while onlookers find humor—and two, Agona never existed. The interracial marriage the audience sees represents a created and performed history that some might realize as such, while others may take it as the "proof" of their own possible Indigenous ancestry. The fear of interracial amalgamation can be mitigated by the fact that half of the combination of this progressive interracial relationship remains as a fancy of Green's imagination and that Agona seemingly exists in the play's action insofar as her absurdity makes her worth the colonists' notice. However, one might argue that this representation remains dangerous for the very possibility that it suggests: an interracial relationship. However, even this possibility of representation begetting reality creates a structure of feeling that, rather than signaling danger for a southern audience, enforces a narrative of land attachment. Agona's relationship with Tom creates a founding narrative of legitimate land ownership.[33] The audience afraid of racial mixing can seek comfort in Agona's nonexistence, and the audience looking to identify with the region's Indigenous population can point to the fictional Agona as the beginning of a New World mixedblood identity that draws Indigenous and English ancestry into a narrative of early land attachment. Almost like the lost silver cup of the Roanoke archive, the myth of Agona creates action through imagined absence.

Additionally, Agona might represent what Richard White conceives of as the realm of "middle ground" in the early Americas, where we see the history of colonization as anything but the inevitable destruction of a Native culture under the wheel of the forceful European culture. Instead, this middle ground shows where colonists and Natives were able to meet and coexist on their own terms, creating a space that incorporates new, dual meanings for Natives and non-Natives. However, while Green may be attempting to showcase such a narrative with the character Agona, this is again problematized by the fact that she exists only in his imagination. The fact that Tom and Agona seem to be the colony's best hope for survival establishes a narrative where resulting North Carolinians can imagine identities that encompass English and Algonquian ancestors—and therefore offer them material land claims on Native ground.

So far my evidence of the idea that Agona and Tom allow audiences to imagine themselves as descendants of English and Native people has been limited mostly to my analysis of the performance. However, the very tourist institution of *The Lost Colony* depends on this unlikely narrative.[34] During the week, *The Lost Colony* hosts backstage tours where actors from the show guide patrons around the reconstructed Fort Raleigh and lead them through the backstage areas explaining how the cast and crew stages the show. My tour guide was an affable young man who played a small part in the chorus. While he was friendly and knowledgeable enough regarding the ins and outs of the performance, his relation of any historical factors surrounding the colony seemed to be lacking. I imagine this resulted more from the script he was given rather than from his personal stake in any narrative of the colony. Just after guiding the crowd past the earthen reconstruction of Fort Raleigh, he paused to tell us that while nobody knew for sure what happened to the colonists, a document from the early modern period said that just south of us, on Hatteras Island, there was a "tribe of Indians with grey eyes who spoke perfect Elizabethan English." In response to this revelation, the tour group gave an interested murmur. Indeed, there have been rumors of these "grey-eyed Indians" in present-day North Carolina since Jamestown, but their exact location or tribal affiliation remains the source of much conjecture and little evidence. When *The Lost Colony* performs these narratives as history—both on and off the stage—it disorients the registers of material fact that continue to influence the ways that non-Natives imagine living Native people today. Rather than understand tribes as sovereign nations made up of citizens from multiple racial backgrounds who live contemporary lives, they are encouraged to view Native people as out of time and place, a grey area between the black and white "reality" of the region.

For example, as I was sitting in the audience waiting for the performance to begin one evening, my mother, who had accompanied me to the show, asked, "So what do historians think about the whole Croatoan, Lumbee, Native connection with the colony?" As I began to explain that the issue was complicated by several sources whose origins seemed dubious and that even Paul Green had his own serious doubts about the Lost Colony–Lumbee connection, a woman seated in the row in front of us turned around and began to speak loudly—some might call it yelling—at me. She claimed that she had grown up on the Outer Banks, and that she *knew* those "Indians with grey eyes" and that they must have come from somewhere and that she had no doubt they were the ancestors of the ill-fated colony. She went on to say that she always felt bad for those Indians—the way that they couldn't fit into white or "Indian" society, stuck between two worlds. I nodded politely while resisting the urge to point out to her that while she appeared to be around seventy years old, the initial "mixing" she was alleging happened more than four hundred years ago, leaving little likelihood of some sort of direct visual phenotypic register between those English and Algonquian people who may or may not have initially produced children and any Native people she claims to have known personally. This anecdote serves not to mock her faulty math but to think through how, for this particular viewer, the play not only seems very real but also establishes possibilities for an initial contact that has real implications for her thoughts—which notably fell into a tragic mixedblood narrative—about contemporary Native people.

These combined factors of historical narrative construction and its reception by the audience through performance help illuminate the importance of Richmond's decision to cast Raleigh as the Historian. With the combining of the Historian and Raleigh into one part, Richmond showed how the history of the colony can no longer be removed from an archive based on the early modern performances of men such as Raleigh and his colonial-minded counterparts. The archive becomes just as much popular myth as the show. The very culture industry of the show encourages this association for the present-day viewer as indicated by the banner in the theater from the 2009 season, which promises under the heading "The Lost Colony in History" that "you can be remembered." This linkage between the audience and history carries through every decision of the play's eighty-year history. When the Historian

Banner from the Waterside Theatre in Manteo, North Carolina, for the 2009 production of *The Lost Colony*. Photo by the author.

is cordoned off from the action, he exists in a realm of pure authenticity, and consequently the audience fails to see how all history can result from one's performance for others in a specific situation. When the Historian's authority is doled out to the other characters such as the Native characters of Manteo and Wanchese, as in the 2000 performance, it makes it seem as if they are giving their own truths. Yet this too is an inaccurate representation of events. It suggests that the Native characters accept this history as representative of their reality. These words—this archive—is the stuff of Raleigh and his men's point of view, not the coastal Algonquian people they encountered. English colonization was Raleigh's—not impartial history's—dream, and while it indeed lives, so does the nightmare for many people of living in a world overrun with lice on two legs.

These performances demonstrate how many versions of the red state have long relied on the realm of emotive excess to shore up narratives of white supremacy and Euro-American land claim. They engage questions of truth as a set of perceived discourses that have specific effects on who can claim what identity and history to what contemporary material effects. As such, these histories exceed the space of the stage. When Old Tom critiques English colonialism as a project of overrunning the world with "lice on two legs," he creates an alternative colonial history that refuses to valorize a supposedly inevitable English ascendancy. From this space of possibility perhaps we can more effectively read Richmond's controversial decision about including a curtain call in the 2009 season of *The Lost Colony*. Familiar and local audiences resisted this decision, for as they perhaps intuited, this story means far more than a two-and-a-half-hour performance on Roanoke Island. Through his inclusion of a curtain call, Richmond's implicit critique of this type of performative history—one that allows a fluidity between performance and lived reality—jostles the very core of how these plays create structures of power through affect. Richmond's decision to limit *The Lost Colony* to the stage pushes the audience to understand themselves as a part of the lived history depicted before them. Whether the audience fully appreciates this push is certainly up for debate. However, the curtain call reminds them that to a certain extent all history is performed and that when they leave, they are part of a power dynamic between historical actor and lived inheritor. They are not simply passive receptors of a specious historical inheritance of lived land claim. Rather, they are an audience that must choose to either accept and endorse the history before them or question it for the structure of power that it maintains. This is an uncomfortable position for many who live in a red state, and it seems likely that this small decision in this small town speaks to larger shifts in understanding the history, and material impact of that history, of the Native South.[35]

I argue that understanding the history of Roanoke and the way it recurs and evolves through popular narratives offers a way to understand the obsession with loss and recovery that finds a problematic home in some approaches to Native and southern studies. If scholars do not jostle ourselves loose from these narratives, then we run the danger of producing our own sacrificial bodies to the butcher of settler colonialism, our own "recoveries" that depend on "loss." Ultimately, we keep an American horror story alive because we continue to feed it, perhaps in our own service to the land claims of colonialism. Furthermore, understanding that loss exists as one of the earliest imagined conditions of English settler colonialism should help trouble a continued fixed stare at the Civil War and Lost Cause as "foundational" southern moments. These narratives, as I will demonstrate in the next chapter, do not simply appear from thin air in their later iterations. Instead, they represent some of the earliest tenets of an English presence in what will eventually become the U.S. South. These concerns of how to understand the U.S. South alongside the Native histories of settler colonialism continue to appear in narratives of the American Revolution, taking up the questions of land claim and narrative order as they intersect with the earliest moments of regional identity within a new national framework. Like histories and narratives of the Lost Colony, these red state fantasies reappear across time to buttress regional distinction at the expense of the dispossession of living Native people.

CHAPTER TWO

Revolution

> Things come full circle, back to where they started. That's Revolution.
>
> —Russell Means, 1980

As with most other states—states of exceptionalism, states of emergency, and state fantasies—red states recur and evolve to fit the needs of a contemporaneous moment. Rather than fetishize discrete events as "game changers," the concept of the red state allows us to see how some narratives reappear over time in order to do different work. As a state of being, a geographic space, and a political concept, the red state reappears in our understandings of the U.S. South as more than a single temporal moment. Thus, linear time—with its breaks and interruptions—cannot always account for how the red state operates. Rather, as I outlined previously, the red state might best be understood through concepts of spiralic time that move forward even as they loop back onto themselves. As such, I continue this study with a discussion of literature that centers the American Revolution as a plot point, particularly on the southern front. As with the Lost Colony narratives I examined in the previous chapter, many narratives of the American Revolution depend simultaneously on ideas of national founding, Indigenous dispossession, and land claim. Through a careful examination of how narratives of the Revolution reappear and readjust their aims, we begin to see how these Revolutionary stories stand in for larger anxieties over the continued presence and vitality of Native nations alongside the need to indigenize whiteness to the U.S. South.

Revolution serves as a useful metaphor for understanding how the red state operates. Of course, when one imagines a revolution several distinct meanings might spring to mind: the process of social upheaval; the overthrow of a government; the act of moving in a circular fashion around a central point; a period of time; or the recurrence of a particular event or task.[1] As the red state recurs and evolves, it moves around the spiral of time in order to return to a previous narrative for a new moment. These new moments frequently represent instances of social upheaval as they look back to old stories for contemporaneous justifications.[2] In this way, the base of the word "revolution," "volute," bears significance. A volute is a spiral form, referring to items as divergent as scrolls to snails. At its core, then, discussions of revolutions are discussions of spirals.[3] Indeed, the American Revolution and the subsequent (re)tellings of the event have long served as touchstones for American cultural studies when considering foundational narratives of the United States. These narratives continue to do work for how one imagines the nation's beginning, its subsequent trajectory, and one's place within the nation's future. Frequently, narratives of the American Revolution are used to establish legitimacy for almost any political claim. When incorporated into political movements over time—from South Carolina's Nullification Crisis to the Civil War and from the civil rights movement to the Tea Party—the American Revolution becomes caught in its own genealogical vortex. The event generates new meanings for these new moments, and as such the event itself changes in the minds of those attempting to look back through a cross-section of spiralic time. While we might return to the Revolutionary moment, we must also remember that another revolution has occurred and that we are now one more layer out from the center. The Revolution, then, exists both synchronically and diachronically. The story has evolved as it has revolved. Thus, narratives of the American Revolutionary War might best be understood as the American *revolution*—a returning to the foundational moment to erase what came before: Indigenous land claim and sovereignty on Indigenous soil. When the American Revolution asserted independent settler-colonial nationhood in the Americas, the understandings of landed sovereignty necessarily changed. Despite earlier treaties with the imperial and colonial nations of Europe, Native nations had to reimagine their relationships to their invaders. The return to this moment when settler colonials imagined themselves as new (lowercase) native Americans illuminates how fantasies of state belonging remain dependent on narratives of Indigenous presence, absence, and resistance. In this chapter I read several recurrences of Revolutionary narratives in order to illustrate one instance of the red state, a familiar one that demonstrates the intersection between the use of Native history and conservative political structures. I trace a spiralic pattern of American Revolution narratives in the U.S. South from Thomas Jefferson's writings to William Gilmore Simms's early nineteenth-century romances of the Revolution and from the mid-twentieth-century outdoor drama *Horn in the West* to contemporary political rhetoric emerging from conservative red states.

Over the last few years a rather mediocre film about the American Revolution has become something of an American cultural studies discussion piece as a result of Donald Pease's work in *The New American Exceptionalism* (2009). Ronald Emmerich's *The Patriot* (2000) is not a great film, but I am not concerned with questions of merit here. Rather, *The Patriot* and the subsequent critical discourse surrounding the film offer an introductory illustration of how an American revolution works at the level of narrative use over time. I read the film—and the critical discourse surrounding it—as indicative of how fantasies about southern red states reveal themselves as deeply embedded in concerns over Indigenous land claim and identity even when they do not acknowledge them as such. The film follows Ben Martin (Mel Gibson), a veteran of the French and Indian War who now wishes to live out his days as a chairmaking widower on his farm in South Carolina. He has seven children to whom he frequently refers as "the heathen," and of these children, seemingly all of his sons want nothing more than to serve the American Revolutionary cause. As an important point of note, Martin was a famed killer known as the "Ghost Rider" during his previous wartime, and now he values freedom so much that he only has free people of color work for him rather than use the enslaved labor that pervaded South Carolina plantation agriculture at the time. He has no desire for either himself or his sons to become involved in the Revolutionary cause (even though he eventually relents after the British murder one of his sons and destroy his farm), and he spends much of the film either lamenting his "sins" during his days as the Ghost Rider, or mourning yet another dead son, or hacking to death British troops who have threatened his family. Occasionally, he makes musket shot from silver "Red Coat" army figurines, which—judging by the intense camera work—seems like it is supposed to be heavily symbolic, though admittedly I remain a little unclear what exactly it symbolizes aside from the obvious. Sometimes he proves his folksiness by hanging out with the "poor whites" that he recruits to the militia because they are unscrupulous fighters. And not to spoil the film for anyone who has not seen it, but the Americans win the war. In short, *The Patriot* is not a great film. However, it has seemed to raise some American studies hackles, and that is what I would like to discuss briefly.

As much as I find the film mediocre and irritating, Donald Pease *hates* it. He dislikes it so much that he blames it for the current state of far-right political ideology that permeates what passes for political discourse in the United States, or as he calls it, the "Southernification of the American Revolution" (*New American* 36)—or, as I would call it, the rise of the red state. As Jon Smith notes in *Finding Purple America: The South and the Future of American Cultural Studies* (2013), Pease's strongest ire seems to be directed not at the general whitewashing historical revisionism that *The Patriot* participates in but rather at the fact that the film is set in South Carolina, representing what Pease sees as a "discredited" region that, rather than remain quietly relegated, comes to stand in for the entire nation. Smith also takes on Pease's faulty logic and rightly calls him out for reinscribing American exceptionalism by imagining the U.S. South as an exceptional space because of its history of racial and civic violence. Furthermore, I would add that Pease fails to acknowledge two crucial historical facts in his critique of the film and the supposed ideological fantasy it promotes: one, logistically and politically speaking, South Carolina was an incredibly important front in the American Revolution, and two, while South Carolinians were even then viewed as somewhat of firebrands among their continental state allies, their way of life—rather than being exceptional—buttressed the economy of the aspiring nation precisely through their practices of exploitative labor policies (read: enslavement) and quickness to enact civic and racial violence to enforce the needs of the plantation economy. As Jennifer Rae Greeson notes, "This bipolar Plantation South served U.S. writers working through an ideological bind that had been created in the very language of the American Revolution. [...] By identifying the imperial power extremes of both 'domination' and 'bondage' with the Plantation South, early U.S. writers increasingly were able to produce a triangulated placement of the new nation on their moral-geographical imaginative map of the world" (81, 82). Though here Greeson speaks specifically about earlier American writers, I argue that the continued popular and critical reception of Emmerich's film reveals the same anxieties. *The Patriot* may only be so far off in that it manages to quarantine colonial violence, Indigenous land theft, and slavery to the U.S. South rather than acknowledging their central role in both the ideological and material development of the entire nation.

In addition to historical contextualization, Pease neglects at least two other significant details in his reading of the film. While I agree with his assessment that the film replaces the frontier narrative for one of the Lost Cause, I would also like to account for the significant work the film does to demonstrate class divides among white people in the region. According to the film, those with land and money have good morals. They go to church, and they believe in a cause of justice and liberty. Specifically, Martin's oldest son Gabriel imagines a postrevolutionary "New World," where enslaved African Americans will be equal to their white counterparts. However, these noble-minded, landed gentry are terrible fighters. They are not "the sort" that win wars. That "sort," as the film calls them, are poor white alcoholics, enslavers, Indian killers, thieves, and uneducated rapscallions. They have missing teeth and noticeably stronger southern accents. They are openly racist. However, the morally minded Revolutionaries need these individualistic poor white people to fight for them, to do their dirty work, as it were. The poor white masses in *The Patriot* may be shiftless, but when riled up, they dig in for the cause. This dynamic might indeed seem familiar as political pundits scratch their heads attempting to understand the "reddening" of the Midwest, and it proves Smith's critique—red states are more than a southern problem.

Coupled with neglecting these class dimensions, Pease's analysis also pays little attention to the other important force that powers the film: the specter of Native presence and dispossession that generates the entire narrative. Historically speaking, from the character's description of events, Ben Martin was not fighting in the French and Indian War as the film claims. He was fighting in the Anglo-Cherokee War (1758–61), which indeed was something of an offshoot of the larger conflict but had more significant local implications for how southern states eventually dealt with Native peoples, especially around calls for removal over strategies of diplomacy and productive alliances.[4] The fact that Martin quite literally fights his battles with a Cherokee tomahawk should signal the viewer to the fact that the Native defeat that haunts him is the very thing that buttresses his Revolutionary fervor. He fights with Native weapons on Native land for the right to be a "native" to this American geography; his new world is won at the expense of the very old. Rather than simply ghosting the Native people as Renée Bergland, in *The National Uncanny: Indians Ghosts and American Subjects* (2000), argues is the desire of much American literature, *The Patriot* allows Martin to be the "Ghost" himself, attempting to remove perhaps even the specter of indigeneity that should haunt the film as it haunts the character. Given the significance of the U.S. South's history with both Native peoples and poor white people in establishing and supporting states of exceptionalism and state fantasies, including eventually the South Carolina Nullification Crisis, Indian Removal, and Confederate secession, it proves productive to extend Pease's arguments to consider this historical context.

Perhaps the most telling scene in the film comes in its opening. The viewer sees Martin attempting to fashion a rocking chair—homespun folksy widowerhood at its finest.[5] Martin's "free laborer" and his children, or as he calls them "the heathen," look on as he completes his work. Martin takes the chair down from its rack, and he sits carefully in it before he begins to rock back and forth. He can hardly contain his excitement as it seems he has constructed a perfect chair. In this moment, then, we might witness the Adamic spark for the Agrarian's perfect chair: "a container of a 'whole way of life'" (qtd. in Romine 5).[6] The tight focus of the camera and the slow pace of the scene signal a moment of dramatic irony to the viewer: we know the chair will break. In the next second, Martin is on the floor as his creation splinters apart underneath him. Thus, from the beginning, we know that this film cannot hold the weight of its subject.

However, if we pay attention to the core narrative of the film, one based on the American Revolution, we might be signaled to antecedents that lend support. In other words, the film may be less about the American Revolution and more about American revolutions, or how stories get told again and again in order to understand contemporaneous moments. This is where we might productively extend the arguments from Pease, and even Smith in his brief but strong critique, in order to see the development and continued return to a red state. Few, however, have given extended consideration of the film's significant resonances with prolific nineteenth-century southern writer William Gilmore Simms's romances of the Revolution, *The Partisan* (1835), *Mellichampe* (1836), and *Katherine Walton* (1851), as clear precursors to Emmerich's film. While the screenplay was written by Robert Rodat, it is obvious to anyone who has read Simms's work that *The Patriot* comes straight from his South Carolina novels with an extra bit of historical upstreaming of the Lost Cause, an added flair that would likely make the nineteenth-century author happy. It also bears a striking resemblance to Kermit Hunter's 1952 outdoor drama *Horn in the West* with its interfamily dispute over joining the Revolutionary cause. To be clear, I imagine that the Hunter narrative connections are coincidental, but as for the use of Simms's material in making the film, I remain more than suspicious that Rodat read the author when conceiving the screenplay. Even if not directly related, the compelling reappearance of this Revolutionary narrative over time suggests the spiralic pattern of its success in reception.

However, direct connection is not the point. Rather, narratives of the Revolution do a particular kind of work in creating red states. They accrue meaning over time with each revolutionary turn around the imagined foundational moment. Regions, causes, and people frequently attempt to draw a genealogy from this historical moment in order to support their own ideologies and actions. For instance, the Confederate States of America rhetorically positioned themselves as the true inheritors of the Revolutionary spirit through the secession from a tyrannical North. Segregationists and other white supremacists again appealed to a throwing off of tyranny as federal troops moved south to enforce desegregation. Today, the Tea Party clearly and eponymously signals their affiliation with the Revolution in order to lend credence to their cause. These returns to the scene of the Revolution, particularly in the U.S. South, can tell us something about how narrative works to buttress political discourses that attempt to legitimize paradoxically regional difference from and affiliation with the larger nation.

This chapter examines representative texts from these moments and focuses on the ways that issues of indigeneity bolster these Revolutionary narratives. As I outline below, frequently narratives of the American Revolution in the U.S. South depend on interactions and critical disorientations between Native people and poor white people. In these moments, we see one formation of the red state emerge. As I examine here, this formation remains a particularly conservative one in contemporary terms, but as I will examine in later chapters, it does not have to be. Through the use of narratives of Native presence and absence, the authors and audiences I examine here come to indigenize whiteness to the region via their return to a Revolutionary moment when settler-colonial men imagined their sovereign land claim to what would become the United States of America. This occurred across the colonies from North to South, but as whiteness took on a specific relationship to freedom in the southern plantation states, white people imagined their relationship to the land and their racial ideology developed additional vectors of meaning. The living, sovereign Native person and nation becomes effaced as white people of the U.S. South imagine their own belonging through the birth of a nation in the Revolutionary moment. I trace these Revolution narratives and narrative revolutions from Thomas Jefferson to the mid-twentieth century to demonstrate how the region emerges in the form of a volute that allows us to see the recurrence of red state fantasies of landed belonging.

Beginning with a brief reading of Thomas Jefferson's written material on Indian affairs, I then move into a sustained analysis of William Gilmore Simms's historical novels that reimagine the Revolutionary era, specifically *Mellichampe* (1836). Focusing on the mixedblood Catawba character Blonay, I demonstrate how narratives of the American Revolution in the U.S. South came to stand in for contemporaneous arguments about southern Indian policy—what we might see as one of the first instances of conservative red state politics. As with my earlier analysis of Lost Colony narratives, this reading signals the ways in which reperiodization can illuminate moments when structures of feeling resonant with a Lost Cause may in fact predate the Civil War and legitimate the necessity of other southern counternational moments, including, as I mentioned earlier, South Carolina nullification, Indian Removal, and eventually secession itself. I continue with a reading of Kermit Hunter's outdoor drama, *Horn in the West*, which deals with the onset of the American Revolution alongside Cherokee conflict in the Appalachian Mountains, demonstrating a beleaguered whiteness that finds no recourse in the British government. Given the play's continued yearly staging in Boone, North Carolina, I read the play's moment of inception during increased debates about racial segregation in the mid-twentieth century as well as its contemporary appeals to land claim in the Appalachian South, demonstrating the revolving nature and continued consumption of red state logics. Furthermore, despite the play's decidedly non-Native production history, it manages to call up Cherokee critic Daniel Heath Justice's concepts of the Beloved Path and Chickamauga Consciousness from his seminal work *Our Fires Survive the Storm* (2006). As the play literally stages a conflict between Dragging Canoe and Nancy Ward, it seems useful to read it both within its history as a conservative non-Native text and through a Cherokee studies methodology that might illuminate the higher stakes of its yearly staging. I close the chapter with a quick analysis of our contemporary red states, buttressed by Tea Parties and treasons, R*dsk*ns and revolutions.

Thomas Jefferson and the Fantasy of the Revolutionary Native

Before examining later uses of Revolutionary narratives, it is useful to consider the rhetorical use of the Indian figure alongside actual Indian policies that pervaded the Revolutionary era. Perhaps no other founding figure offers such ambivalence and doublethink around issues of Native people than Thomas Jefferson. At once steeped in romantic respect and immersed in tactical disdain, Jefferson's writings represent almost a full range of the ways for a non-Native person to consider Native people and issues of Native policy during the late eighteenth century. Alongside these sentiments, Jefferson also offered paradoxical assessments of southern character, noting its emotive hotheadedness while also championing its justified if not impractical desire to throw off the "tyranny" of northern states as the colonies had with the monarchical rule of the British. Of course, one should never come to Jefferson for easy answers or cut-and-dried distinctions concerning the social or political issues of his time. His numerous contradictions of character, philosophy, and action have been noted in numerous other venues, particularly as they concern his feelings on enslavement, race, and his own relationship with Sally Hemmings.[7] Greeson in particular demonstrates how in writing about his home state Jefferson creates a "synecdochical Virginia, emerging idiosyncratically from a southern state, worked antithetically to the Plantation South construct, defining the new United States not by providing a foil to it but by expanding to encompass it fully" (51). Her analysis of Jefferson's non-South proves fruitful, and I would like to put it into dialogue with Jefferson's writings about Native people, history, and policy. In these contradictions, specifically as they form around his thoughts on Native peoples, their history, and their future, we see the emergence of a red state. It creates and grounds a revolutionary potential in the figure of the Indian while at the same time dispossessing living Native peoples of their land in order to assert an affective power of rebellion grounded in white land tenure.

Jefferson's sentiments in his private correspondence during and immediately following the Revolution reveal the fomenting of these ideas. In January 1787, Jefferson composed two letters that offered his romantic view of Indians as existing in a pure state, free from all government. He writes to Edward Carrington: "I am convinced that those societies (as the Indians) which live without government enjoy in the general mass an infinitely greater degree of happiness than those who live under the European governments" (880).[8] And to James Madison, he offers: "Societies exist under three forms sufficiently distinguishable. 1. Without government, as among our Indians. 2. Under government wherein the will of every one has a just influence, as is the case in England in slight degree and in our states, in a great one. 3. Under governments of force: as is the case in all other monarchies and in most of the other republics" (882). He wonders, "It is a problem, not clear in my mind, that the 1st condition is not the best," but he speculates that "it [is] inconsistent with any great degree of population" (ibid.). Thus, for Jefferson in 1787, the Indian in the abstract represents a pure state where men may govern themselves without interference from the state. While he wonders about the impracticability of this, he fails to mention, despite his certain awareness of the fact, that Native people had complex and varying tribal governmental systems. Instead of dealing with this reality, he creates a revolutionary Native who exists in an idealized condition: a state without state interference. This particular state fantasy for Jefferson, however, falls apart with the weight of actual human beings, much like Ben Martin's chair in *The Patriot*.

As Robert Berkhofer, Anthony Wallace, and others before me have illustrated, Jefferson's opinions on Native peoples were in large part influenced by his feelings on his selective affiliation with environmental determinism, and he imagined Native people as equal to European Americans in theory yet inferior in practice due to their differing lifestyles and heritage.[9] As Berkhofer explains, this allowed Jefferson to both claim a universal human equality and forward policies for the control and removal of Native populations. As Katy Chiles notes: "Jefferson argued for the nurturing quality of the American environment by refuting Buffon's allegations about Native Americans. As scholars have noted, it is interesting because Jefferson seemed to agree with Buffon's supposition that the environment could affect humans—at least, for Jefferson, Native Americans (and perhaps whites)—but he vehemently disagreed with Buffon's claim about the quality of the New World environment and that, as Jefferson says, animals 'degenerated in America'" (16). This shuttling between racial nature and environmental nurture categorizes much of Jefferson's thinking, but as Chiles reminds us via work from Peter Onuf, it should not be thought of as standing in for the popular thought of the period.[10] Although perhaps unique in their perspective, Jefferson's thoughts demonstrate an attempt to establish convergence and divergence between those who inhabit the American continent. In his ruminations on climatic determinism, Jefferson ponders how individuals of different races might share traits and why those of the same phenotypic classification might differ across geography. When approaching Native southeastern issues today, there remains an imperative not to fall into the pseudoscientific language traps that plagued Jefferson's limited understanding of humanity.

Few have examined Jefferson's opinions on Native people in direct relation to his writings on southern people, with whom he somewhat and occasionally self-identified, depending on the audience. In two separate letters to the Marquis de Chastellux in 1785, Jefferson outlines the character traits of Americans—Native, African, northern, and southern. Jefferson's remarks to Chastellux in 1785 regarding Native Americans as a people with "a masculine, sound understanding" are made to counter the American degeneracy arguments made by Count Buffon's racial taxonomy of the time (801). These remarks appear as revised in Jefferson's later *Notes on the State of Virginia* where he describes Native people as "brave," and obsessed with a "point of honor" that consists in the "destruction of an enemy by stratagem" (184). According to Jefferson, "the Indian" is utmost interested "in the preservation of his own person free from injury," and "that he will defend himself against a host of enemies, always chusing [sic] to be killed, rather than to surrender" (184). Jefferson asserts that Native men are weaker owing to their lack of labor, which Jefferson attributes to the stronger Native women. He offers to Chastellux that "As to their bodily strength, their manners rendering it disgraceful to labor, those muscles employed in labor will be weaker with them" (801). And in *Notes*, he argues that the Native "meets death with more deliberation, and endures tortures with a firmness unknown almost to religious enthusiasm" (185). He again echoes his earlier 1785 letter to Chastellux in his later *Notes*, writing that the Native is "affectionate" and "indulgent in the extreme" toward his children, and his friendships are "strong and faithful to the utmost extremity" (185). In other words, Jefferson's invented Native is independent, emotive, adverse to particular labors, and invested in individual honor. This revolutionary Native for Jefferson is an extremist, bound to protect land and family at all costs, and in these descriptions his Enlightenment discourse belies his romanticism.

Jefferson's southerner is also created via climate, although for the worse. It also bears mentioning that Jefferson's southerner is almost certainly a white man. He wrote to Chastellux in September 1785 of his own Virginian countrymen, "I have thought them, as you found them, aristocratical, pompous, clannish, indolent, hospitable, and I should have added disinterested, but you say attached to their interest." Continuing, he ascribes these traits, particularly disinterest, "to that warmth of their climate which unnerves and unmans both body and mind" (826–27). In this letter, he lists the traits of southerners as "fiery; voluptuary; indolent; unsteady; independant [sic]; zealous for their own liberties, but trampling on those of others; generous; candid; without attachment or pretensions to any religion but that of the heart," reiterating that these qualities are a result of the hot clime (827). Notably, he advocates something of a "civilization" policy for the southerner, asking that Chastellux send a copy of his observations on the southerner to James Madison that he might be induced to advocate for a more thorough introduction of artistic education to the Americas.

Jefferson's Native and southerner are not identical, but in his rendering, they share some important traits. They are incited by key passions and have a natural resistance to work. They each have a generous spirit and follow an enthusiasm attached to personal preservation. Notably, Jefferson seems not to take into account climatic differences that might occur in Native societies, which according to his schema would appear more distinctly as Native peoples would have been in their respective northern or southern climates much longer than the northern or southern Euro-American. Either way, according to Jefferson, both the southerner and the Native need a certain level of reform and cultivation to reach their preferred state as true human beings. Their emotive natures seem to interfere with their potential, and they each seem to deal in extremes. While neither is explicitly a figure of the American Revolution in his schema, the terms by which he constructs their identities remain popular ones for the collective imagination of each.

This conflation of the backward and emotive Native and the southerner will continue for the next several hundred years. For instance, *The Education of Henry Adams* (1918) connects noble southerner and noble savage. Adams writes that his boarding school companions from Virginia are "as little fitted [for school] as Sioux Indians to a treadmill" (52). He continues by stating, "no one knew enough to know how ignorant [the Southerner] was; how childlike; how helpless before the relative complexity of a school. As an animal, the Southerner seemed to have every advantage, but even as an animal he steadily lost ground." He closes by noting, "The Southerner, with his slave-owning limitations, was as little fit to succeed in the struggle of modern life as though he were a maker of stone axes, living in caves" (Adams 53–54). Unfit for modern life like the "Sioux Indian," the southerner—and by extension the region—becomes a site for loss and out-of-place time. While we might be tempted to imagine this backwardness as a result of a Civil War loss, the return to Jefferson allows us to see the ways in which ideas of Natives and southerners fomented in the Revolutionary period. This romantic codetermining moves the red state from the narrative lost colonies I discuss in the first chapter into the new national framework. This key instantiation of the red state forms when white southerners are able to indigenize their whiteness to the region by claiming romantic affiliation to the figure of the Indian while at the same time dispossessing living Native peoples of their lands. This process is helped by those who see each in need of civilization policies. This sentiment allows the southerner to imagine themselves as victims of colonial oppressions (via England and eventually the U.S. North) all the while victimizing Native people.

However, these are Natives and southerners in the abstract. They are neither tribes nor individuals, and this is where Jefferson's revolutionary Native, free from government control and deserving respect for his fierce independence, begins to break down. In a 1776 letter to Edmund Pendleton detailing the promise of a return to Saxon land tenure policies for the new nation, Jefferson also mentioned in closing a particular clash between the Cherokee and white southerners, specifically those of the Watuagan settlement who battled Dragging Canoe and his faction of Cherokee warriors known as the Chickamauga:[11] "I hope the Cherokees will now be driven beyond the Mississippi & that this in future will be declared to the Indians that invariable consequence of their beginning a war. Our contest with Britain is too serious and too great to permit any possibility of avocation from the Indians. This then is the season for driving them off, & our Southern colonies are happily rid of every other enemy & may exert their whole force in that quarter" (754). The removal of Native peoples was never far off from the founding of the nation during the Revolutionary era. In this moment, Jefferson pits the southerner against the Native, recognizing that they are enemies fighting for the same lands. The fact that Jefferson calls on this policy in a letter that specifically deals with the details of how land tenure will be established in the new nation signals that abstract, romantic, and revolutionary Natives are just fine so long as they do not interfere with land occupation.[12] As Wallace reminds us, one can never fully appreciate Jefferson's Indian policy, particularly as it applied to western Appalachian lands, without remembering that Jefferson himself was involved in an intense series of "off-the-books" land speculations. Interestingly, in *Jefferson and the Indians* Wallace also notes that the defeated Chickamauga after moving to the area near present-day Chattanooga came to be known as "secessionists" (57–58).

While real Native people with functioning governments and complex war strategies fighting against the theft of their lands proved a hurdle for Jefferson's idealized revolutionary Native, their fierce resistance might have inspired something in his own thoughts about the proper ways to resist one's own government. By 1798, Jefferson expressed strong feelings regarding his belief in the internal oppression of the southern states, writing to John Taylor of the "reign of witches" (1050). He offers, "We are conpleatly [sic] under the saddle of Massachusetts & Connecticut, and that they ride us very hard, cruelly insulting our feelings as well as exhausting our strength and substance" (1049). He urges patience against scission as it might result in a total dissolve of the union, state by state, asking, "are we not men still to the south of that, & and with all the passions of men?" (1050). He predicts that even the individual states will quarrel, noting that "an association of men who will not quarrel with one another is a thing which never yet existed, from the greatest confederacy of nations down to a town meeting or a vestry" (1050). Despite his statement that "It is true that in the mean time we are suffering deeply in spirit, and incurring the horrors of a war & long oppressions of enormous public debt," Jefferson wonders, "But who can say what would be the evils of a scission, and when & where they would end?" (1050). There are a couple of notable issues in this letter. One, despite his resistance to a breaking off of any individual or set of states from the union, Jefferson clearly forwards a feeling of southern beleaguerment. He considers the "rule" of New England states unnatural and despotic. However, he also forwards the idea of internal quarreling as a natural state and that no idealized association of men without conflict ever existed. On the surface, this contradicts his previously stated beliefs that the Native people of North America existed in an idealized state free from all government, but one also has to remember that Jefferson likely did not conceive of Native people as full men. As noted above, Jefferson himself could not reconcile this belief with his other stated resolve that any organization of too many men would eventually have conflict. And of course this also goes against his certain knowledge of Native governmental and military practices involving wars, treaties, and land claims. Taken together, these contradictions of sovereign governments—federal, proto-Confederate, and Native—reveal significant inner workings of the cogs that begin to mechanize our understanding of the conceptual red state within the national framework. In Jefferson's postrevolutionary writings, he ponders the consequences of another internal scission based on the throwing off of government. He imagines a revolutionary figure in the white southerner that lives up to his previous ideals around the revolutionary Native.

One significant hurdle to the indigenizing of whiteness to the U.S. South remained the physical presence of Native people. As I mentioned earlier, Jefferson had long articulated a plan for what would become Removal. While serving as president in 1803, Jefferson outlined his Indian policy in what he identified as "unofficial" and "private" correspondence with William Henry Harrison. He states that the intended goal is peace; however, this peace is to be achieved through the accumulation of lands by the artificial driving up of debt of individual Native leaders. As governmental policy, he offers that "At our trading houses, too, we mean to sell so low as merely to repay us cost and charges, so as neither to lessen or enlarge our capital" (1118). Tellingly, he adds, "This is what private traders cannot do, for they must gain; they will consequently retire from the competition, and we shall thus get clear of this pest without giving offence or umbrage to the Indians" (ibid.). While forwarding public policy, Jefferson will use the power of the state to undercut private trade. Even though the free market might very well also have deprived Native peoples of their land, Jefferson maintains state power with the illusion of market value in order to take lands for his new nation. Moving tribe by tribe, Jefferson assesses the value of tribal lands and speculates on the future of what will eventually become the policies of Removal, Allotment, and Termination. Most significantly, Jefferson notes the importance of keeping this plan and his future visions for Indian policy a secret, noting, "For their interests and their tranquility it is best they should see only the present age of their history" (1120). This closing is significant as it imaginatively constricts the view of Native people for what will become their political fights for the next two centuries. He wishes them cut off from their past, and Jefferson also desires that they be cut off from a future. They are to be retained in the present while their past idealized state can serve as a revolutionary cipher. With a corrupted, romanticized past and little future, Native people can simultaneously serve as spiritual fodder for future revolutionary moments while leaving "empty" lands for the possession of a land-hungry plantation economy. For Jefferson, Native people represent an imaginary ideal free from government while they can simultaneously be oppressed under a collusion of a monied government working alongside and against private interests to deprive them of their landed sovereign rights. Jefferson proposes a Native figure held in a permanent timeless state. In so doing, he renders visible the connection between temporality and spatial connection as he suggests disrupting Native people's temporal framework in order to remove them from their land. This logic informs the spiralic pattern of one conservative fantasy of the red state.

Jefferson's revolutionary Native—free from government and invested in land identity—allows the non-Native southerner to imagine something worth dying for: soil and freedom. The abstraction of freedom combined with the material benefit of land claim allows the Revolution to make sense. In fact, it does this so successfully that as I examine in this chapter, we see a continued return to this Revolutionary narrative for a shoring up of white southern identity based in oppositional freedom and land tenure, or as I describe earlier, an American revolution. While other critics have placed this equivalence within a framework of the Lost Cause, I continue to trace this argument back through the pre–Civil War period to the region's earliest colonial moments in order to see what these older narratives can tell us about the formation of a conceptual red state beyond the hangover of the Confederacy. In other words, this examination of the red state can illuminate ways in which secession was not the result of a fundamental national break but rather the next predictable event in a long series of revolving practices for a region obsessed with its own loss and beleaguerment. Through the use of the conceptual red state, I examine how these structures form primarily from interactions between Native and non-Native people in the region.

William Gilmore Simms's Unromantic Natives and Romances of the Revolution

During the 1830s, prolific southern writer William Gilmore Simms composed several novels and tracts about the American Revolution. These works, and in some cases the critical responses to them, reveal how narratives of the Revolution that address southeastern Native people and their white counterparts traffic in the joint ideas of individual freedom and land claim. The 1820s and 1830s represent a time when concrete secessionist sentiments began to emerge in the southern states over issues of federal tariffs, Indian Removal, and abolitionists' activities aimed at the region. Even though as early as 1790 George Washington wrote to David Stuart of "jealousies [...] gaining ground, & poisoning the minds of the Southern people," the combination of South Carolina's nullification of tariff laws along with Andrew Jackson's refusal to enforce the Supreme Court 1832 ruling in *Worcester v. Georgia* allowed many white southerners to believe there would be little consequence to challenging federal authority (756).[13] As Chief Justice John Marshall wrote to fellow justice Joseph Story in 1832, the plans for a "southern confederacy" led by South Carolina and Virginia represented to him "insane dogmas which have become axioms in the political creed of Virginia" (826).[14] In 1833 he pondered, "Have you ever seen any thing equal to the exhibition in Charleston and the far south generally? These people pursue a southern league steadily or they are insane" (835). This climate of "insanity" surrounded the emergence of Simms's Revolutionary War narratives, and indeed, narratives of the Revolution were later used by both southerners and northerners to justify their respective positions in the ideological battles leading up to the Civil War.

Much of Simms's work about South Carolina depended on the intersection of Native and southern histories. As W. Matthew Simmons notes, "A significant aim throughout Simms's work is to provide South Carolina, and the South generally, with pride of place in the emergence of the American nation, its people, and their national character" ("Life of Francis Marion"). Perhaps more than any other of his contemporaries, Simms concerned himself with the production of narrative history. As an author whose life and work stretched through the pre– and post–Civil War years, Simms saw his world and politics change drastically. During the South Carolina nullification crisis, Simms remained staunch in his support of the Union, and he faulted those in his state who seemed bent on pushing South Carolina to a dissolution from the general government. However, as the debate over states' rights intensified, during the 1840s Simms became a supporter of the secessionist movement. During the Civil War, his own estate suffered ruin from Sherman's march across the region, and Simms published his account of the destruction of Columbia, South Carolina. Simms frequently linked the production of a southern regional history with the foment of a Confederate nationalism, and he continually referred to the production of history and the ways that contemporaneous memory shaped one's understanding of the past. Many of his novels begin with a treatise on the responsibilities of the writer and the historian. In his practical shaping of historical narratives ranging from the life of Captain John Smith to Francis Marion, Simms explicitly acknowledged how the shaped truth of history and fiction remained dependent on what the audiences know, imagine, remember, and forget.[15] As such, he remained interested in, if not obsessed with, the southern front of the American Revolution. Like many white southerners of his era, he expressed concern that the southern contribution to the cause of American independence had been neglected in favor of that of the Northeast. As with many of his contemporaries, he also alluded to the idea that the U.S. South was the rightful inheritor of the Revolutionary cause in their quest for an escape from the tyranny of the U.S. North. Frequently, he employed Native history in his narratives of the past, including *The Yemassee* (1835), *The Lily and the Totem* (1850), and *The Cassique of Kiawah* (1859). He also appealed to Native histories in his trilogy commonly referred to as his romances of the Revolution: *The Partisan* (1835), *Mellichampe: A Legend of the Santee* (1836), and *Katherine Walton* (1851). In order to engage Simms's work as contributing to the formation of a conservative red state logic, I examine a repeatedly forgotten work and vanished character in Simms's oeuvre. *Mellichampe: A Legend of the Santee* appeared in 1836. By some accounts, *Mellichampe*, as a loosely connected sequel to the popular Revolutionary-era romance *The Partisan*, was not particularly successful.[16] However, some reviewers noted that it was among the best of his works.[17] Both of the novels follow a fictionalized account of the ongoing Revolutionary battle between South Carolina militia leader Francis Marion and British general Banastre Tarleton. *Mellichampe* deals with two fictionalized men, one from each camp: the honest and virtuous rebel Ernest Mellichampe, and his nemesis, the underhanded Tory Captain Barsfield. Shortly before the action of the novel, Barsfield has acquired Mellichampe's father's estate, and he desires winning away Mellichampe's true love, Janet Berkeley. Mellichampe has two loyal companions: his poor white friend, Thumbscrew, and the enslaved black man, Scipio. Instrumental to almost the entire plot is the "half-breed" Native character, Ned Blonay, who is occasionally called "Goggle" because of his large and clouded eyes. Despite what reads as a relatively standard Simms historical romance, somewhat strangely, *Mellichampe* suffers from some neglect even among the world of Simmsonia. For instance, the 1988 collection *"Long Years of Neglect": The Work and Reputation of William Gilmore Simms* does not deal with the novel. More curiously, despite the centrality of the novel's Native character, John Caldwell Guilds and Charles Hudson, editors of the collection *An Early and Strong Sympathy: The Indian Writings of William Gilmore Simms* (2003), do not include the novel in their bibliography of Simms's works with Native American themes and histories. Blonay is not catalogued as a Native character, and the book remains largely underexamined in many critical studies of the author. *Mellichampe*'s Blonay collapses the Native and poor white southerner into one figure. Most interestingly, this collapse comes just as much if not more in the later critical analysis of the character as it does in the novel.

Guilds, Hudson, and others have long maintained that Simms was among the most sympathetic figures of his time in his feelings toward and writings about Native people.[18] In fact, in his recent study of the author's use of history, Sean Busick notes, "It is surely no exaggeration to point out, as John Guilds has done, that Simms produced the most realistic treatment of American Indians in nineteenth-century American literature" (65). Of course, such a pronouncement is certainly an exaggeration as one considers the numerous Native authors writing "realistic" portrayals of their own lives during the 1800s, and here Busick seems to conflate the "sympathy" of Guilds and Hudson with "realism," demonstrating that the measured authenticity of Native history remains for many audiences the representation of an emotive suture to their hardships and loss. In yet another example of the relatedness of sympathy, authenticity, and forgetting, Guilds posits in his introduction to *"Long Years of Neglect"*: "But perhaps the chief deterrent to a sympathetic reappraisal of the man and his work is that, measured by present-day standards, Simms is a racist" (4). This assertion hinges on the critic's duty to be sympathetic toward Simms, which not only foregrounds the question of critical investment and distance but also problematically links Simms's posture toward his Native characters with his reception by present-day critics through the rubric of sympathy. Seemingly, *Mellichampe*'s mixedblood character Blonay is not portrayed sympathetically, and on the surface it seems that his absence within Simms scholarship may have to do with one of the following three issues: one, for some critics a mixedblood character does not "count" as an Indian; two, Catawba history fails to fit a perceived narrative of southeastern Native nations; or three, Simms's portrayal of the character is so unsympathetic that to include Blonay in the category of the author's Indian writings challenges the thesis that Simms was somehow exceptionally progressive or unusually responsible in his stance toward Native people and their political issues.

Much southeastern Native history centers on what have been referred to problematically in the past as the "Five Civilized Tribes": the Cherokee, Chickasaw, Choctaw, Creek, and Seminole. Such a distinction is problematic not because these tribes were not in fact complex societies with significant cultural and political structures, but because the designation emerged largely from nineteenth-century white ideas of civilization based on tribal adoptions of print cultures, plantation agriculture, and hierarchical, male-dominated governments. There were, however, numerous other Native societies that existed across the U.S. Southeast aside from these tribes. One of these groups is the Catawba, first referenced in Spanish documents of the mid-sixteenth century, when Spanish *conquistadores* including Hernando de Soto noted the "Katapa" peoples. As historians have outlined, the Catawba were likely a group that coalesced from loosely connected tribes that maintained confederated relations through shared language, trade, and kinship networks.[19] By the beginning of the eighteenth century, they were largely recognized as a singular group, specifically identified as such by the writings of John Lawson. They were key players in the Yemassee War of 1715, which was fought largely over the Indian slave trade as described by historians including Alan Gallay and Christina Snyder.[20]

In 1763 the Catawba had negotiated for a reservation in order to protect themselves from land-greedy settlers. However, over the years, they became involved in private lease agreements, rendering a fair number of European settlers as tenants of a Native nation in South Carolina. Increasingly, these settlers pressured the state that they should not have to pay rent to a Native landlord. By 1830, the settlers had agitated the South Carolina government enough that it began to negotiate lease terms with the Catawba Nation that would dispossess the tribe of any remaining land. However, during this era of forced Removal to Indian Territory across the region, the Catawba people managed to hold on. In essence, despite some significant losses, they waited out their opponents. In 1840 they signed the Treaty of Nation Ford, which promised that in return for ceded lands in South Carolina, the state would find and purchase land, possibly in North Carolina, where the tribe could move. Then the state would pay them $2,500 to relocate and, for the next nine years, $1,500 annually. If they could not find a suitable new home, the state would pay the Catawba Nation $5,000 outright. Given the larger climate of Indian policy, this was a fantastic win for the Catawba people. However, the execution of this plan proved much more difficult. For one, North Carolina failed to cooperate. The Catawba people themselves were understandably divided about where to move—how does one plan to choose the space to relocate an entire nation? With the cession of leased lands, there were no more rent checks coming in, and as with almost every other Indian treaty in the United States, the state never paid the promised monies. This unfortunate turn of events led many outsiders to see the Catawba Nation as effectually destroyed. However, this proved not to be the case. The Catawba persisted in the region and in South Carolina, managing to maintain their sovereignty even during the disastrous Termination period of the 1950s. However, despite being a federally recognized tribe in the U.S. South today, with continued strong traditions of local policy leadership, language education, tribal advocacy, and pottery making, rarely do we see their experiences catalogued in the histories or studies of a Native South.[21]

The absence of Catawba people in many considerations of the Native South might result from several factors having to do with their persistence and survival as a sovereign tribe. For one, by many accounts, they were understandably skeptical of outsiders, acting judiciously in the sharing of their tribal happenings. Two, because of their long history of interaction with Europeans and

Africans in the Americas, many people believed them no longer to be "Indian." And three, because so much of the history of the Native South rests on Removal narratives as the defining experiences of the region, many people fail to see how some Native nations struggled to remain. We might draw from these factors the idea that non-Native people of the U.S. South fetishize narratives of Indian history and identity that confirm purity and authenticity from histories of loss and disappearance rather than careful survival and persistence in place—stories that tell of convergence rather than divergence. All of these factors—nullification, Removal, the fomenting of secessionist ideology, and Catawba persistence—surrounded the publication of Simms's first two romances of the Revolution. Simms's work is one of the few places where we see an acknowledgment of the significant ways that Catawba people shaped the present-day U.S. South. However, even he has a difficult time imagining how Catawba people survive.

For instance, *Mellichampe* begins with a rare narrative attachment to the Catawba character Blonay. The novel, while in third person, opens as Blonay buries his mother and proceeds to follow his enemy from *The Partisan*, Humphries, in order to avenge his mother's death. Given that the main plot of *Mellichampe* revolves around the conflict between the titular Mellichampe and Barsfield, the extended third-person omniscient beginning with Blonay leads the reader to develop a potential, even if tentative, attachment to the character over and above simply a side plot. The opening of the novel clearly centers the Catawba man's losses as present even if seemingly absent. Simms describes Blonay in these opening scenes: "his countenance as immovable and impassive as if he had sustained no loss, and was altogether unconscious of privation" (21). Here and throughout the early chapters of *Mellichampe*, Simms characterizes Blonay as odd, lacking emotive expression, and encumbered by the natural desire for vengeance that comes with his "Indian blood." Additionally, his facial expression belies his numerous "privations." He has lost, and he has lost dearly. Other characters find Blonay's actions and motives difficult to read, but despite his later absence in catalogues of Simms's Native characters, there exists little doubt that Blonay is indeed Native and that the audience should remain attentive to his actions despite their imperceptibility.

Blonay has an interesting history in the critical reception of the novel. Although in many cases critics disregard him entirely, some have noted his side plot as compelling. In 1936 Arthur Hobson Quinn wrote of Blonay: "The way in which this disfigured, ignorant being, ignorant and half-savage, tracks Lieutenant Humphries, whose troop has trampled Blonay's mother to death, and the mixture of greed and of a queer sense of gratitude towards Janet Berkeley, the heroine of *Mellichampe*, makes Blonay unforgettable" (117). Ironically, for many years Blonay has indeed been forgotten as a Native character, even though a handful of critics have concentrated on his mixture of "good" and "bad" "blood" or his grotesque nature resulting from the mixture. Mary Ann Wimsatt notes that "Goggle, the product of his mother's liaison with an Indian, is a pop-eyed, double-dealing rascal who likes to pick at a large, ugly sore on his arm," and that "Simms uses Goggle's physical ugliness to suggest his essential depravity, claiming that he is 'as warped in morals as he [is] blear in vision'" (79). She reads him into a rubric of the southern Gothic as does later critic Masahiro Nakamura, who argues that "Blonay's atrocities are attributed [in *The Partisan*] to dissatisfaction with his lot resulting from his mother's immorality and passion, which in turn incites his demonic hatred towards society," but in *Mellichampe*, "the capacity of good latent in Blonay comes to the surface through the catalytic medium of the virtue of beautiful Janet" (80–81). All of these assessments rest on the same thing: Blonay's confused state as mixedblood. However, it remains unclear both in the novels and in the resulting criticism whether Blonay's poor white or Native heritage results in his good or bad qualities, posing a conundrum similar to Jefferson's uncertainty on racial and climatic determinism. This lack of clarity signals an initial and continued confusion over the relationship between racial and class-based inheritance in the plantation South, and this confusion continues into the contemporary assessments of both the region's literature and its history. It represents a moment by which we catch a glimpse of the red state as it positions readers to consider, albeit erroneously, whether or not poor white southerners and Natives do in fact share a temporal backwardness and a sense of their own spatial privation. It continues the spiralic logic from Jefferson into a retelling of the period that ponders the causes and consequences of seeing wronged Native people as having anything in common with their white counterparts.

As an example of how the function of race and class intersects with concerns over land claim, the narrative development of Blonay coexists with the undercurrent of place naming within the text. After "leaving [Blonay] upon the road for a while," the novel "change[s] the scene to that beautiful tract of county lying close along the borders of the Santee" (27). This scene takes place on what Simms tells the reader is known as "the river Kaddipah—a stream which, according to modern usage, has shared the fate of most of our Indian waters, and, exchanging the more euphonious title conferred upon it by the red man, is now generally known to us as Lynch's creek" (27). The use of the Indigenous name Kaddipah, reminiscent of de Soto's Katapa, for the creek throughout the narrative exemplifies one of the central ways that Simms begins to link the question of Blonay's racial determinism to his actions and the physical geography of the novel. Thus, it is not simply that Blonay exists at the margins of the text, weaving his way in and out of the reader's view. Rather, the reader's knowledge weaves in and out of the Indigenous land claim, ultimately confusing what might be Blonay's concerns as the lone

Native character with the use of a Native landscape for the glorification of an emerging southern nationalism during the nullification and Removal periods. This shifting landscape serves as the novel's construction of a historical genealogy from the Revolutionary rebel Marion to the fomenting secessionist sympathies of the author. For example, Simms notes of his usage of the name Kaddipah in the text: "With a patriotic hardihood, that will be admitted to have its excuse if not its necessity, we choose to preserve in our narrative the original Indian cognomen whenever we may find it necessary to refer to it; and the reader, whose geographical knowledge might otherwise become confused, will henceforward be pleased to hold the two names as identical, if not synonymous" (27). Simms's linkage of patriotism, Indigenous naming, and geographical knowledge suggests that an understanding of the Indigenous geographical landscape will affect the love of nation, but in these increasingly confused national times, he does not specify whose nation.

The power of the name Kaddipah even seems to overtake the novel's Tory villain, Barsfield, as he argues with his lieutenant over renaming the estate he has acquired from defeating Mellichampe's father. Lieutenant Clayton states that the Indian names "have no meaning—none that we know anything about," while Barsfield counters that the Indian name is "musical," and "seems to me a history" that would be lost if he were to change it (50). The fact that the loss of the Native name would foreclose a history, even for the novel's clearly evil loyalist, suggests a desire for an unrecoverable history even if it exists in loss (much like the narratives of Roanoke that I examined in chapter 1), and that for the European, the Indigenous name legitimizes the ownership of the dispossessed Mellichampe's estate. This connection between place name and right of possession via the harmonious sound and historical legacy again supports the white southern desire of indigenizing an Anglo presence to the region while the Native character wanders throughout the story seemingly disconnected from his land, history, and family. At the metadiscursive level, however, Simms has informed his reader that the name Kaddipah is indeed changed to the possessive Lynch's Creek, suggesting an incomplete national identity for the pre–Civil War South. We know from Simms's own *The Geography of South Carolina: Being a Companion to the History of That State* (1843) that he considered the real-life Kaddipah as part of the landscape of Lancaster, which was located squarely within traditional Catawba lands. The dual naming as an indication of Simms's feelings of patriotism seems to indicate that the novel, and perhaps its author, felt the impulse to connect national feeling to an appeal to indigeneity, and it calls on a "split-earth" methodology for understanding the landscape of the novel.

This connection is complicated by the seemingly nationless and offensively termed "half-breed" character Blonay, whom some audiences may know from *The Partisan* is the son of a "poor white" woman, regarded by many as a witch, and "an Indian of the Catawba nation," who may or may not have been a "mulatto" or a "horse-thief" (*The Partisan* 198, 97). More complicated still remains the fact that Blonay eventually double-crosses the Tory Barsfield to assist the Revolutionary rebel Mellichampe even though his political sympathies have previously been with the Loyalists. Together, these shifting loyalties within a changing Revolutionary landscape expose the slippage around which the novel, written on the heels of the Removal debates in Georgia, desires an indigenizing of whiteness to the region where even the dispossessed Native people find cause to join the rebels against the corrupt British. However, historically speaking, the Catawba had long been allies of the Revolutionary cause. As Merrell notes, this allegiance occasionally came at the logic of "or else," but nonetheless, the Catawba, even if not a determining presence in any one battle, remained instrumental to the Revolutionary cause in South Carolina even fighting against their sometimes enemies, the Cherokee. This historical detail makes Blonay's shifting loyalties and localities all the harder to read. There is little doubt that Simms knew of the Catawba's role in the Revolution, but like the rest of the state that began to forget their service as it became convenient to forget Native land claims during the Removal period, Simms undoes Blonay's national connection to the Revolutionary cause.

Furthermore, it seems little coincidence that the white hero Mellichampe's anger results from a complaint that sounds strikingly similar to that of Native people during the Removal period as he laments: "my father cruelly murdered—my mother driven away from the home of her ancestors—that home confiscated; and given to the murderer" (*Mellichampe* 36). Over and above an implied indigenized whiteness to the U.S. South, in the character Mellichampe the audience sees the pain of Native land loss mapped onto the white consciousness. If the Native people of South Carolina can be forgotten or rendered non-Indian through the logic of mixedblood calculus, and white southerners such as Mellichampe can experience land loss and beleaguerment, then the formation of the red state is complete, where white southerners can fight for freedom and soil unentangled from the particularities of Indigenous land claim.

The specter of the genealogy between a Native South Carolina and the novel's so-called Revolutionary "rebels" also occurs a little over midway through the text when Janet assists Mellichampe and the rebels with a plan to overtake the Tories. Just as hope seems lost when the rebels have been relegated to the overseer's house as the Tories have taken possession of the Berkeley estate, Janet comes up with a rather violent strategy. She eavesdrops on the rebels as they ponder their ill-conceived plan to use fire to remove the Tories from the Berkeley house, and she then emerges to proclaim: "'I have a plan for you. [...] [L]ook at this bow and these arrows,' pointing to a noble shaft, which leaned in the corner of the room; 'they were the gift of a Catawba warrior to my father when I was but a child. They are as good as new. They will convey combustibles to the roof—they will do what you desire'" (196). The sudden appearance of the saving Catawba weapons passed down from the nameless warrior reveals the novel's understanding of an inheritance of ascendency in this land. These weapons that will ultimately fulfill the "desire" of the rebels represent the burgeoning desire of the white South to trace its own national genealogy through the American Revolution back to Native nations. As the white southern heroine Janet offers on the burning of her own home with the Catawba arrows, "in its ruin the people and the cause I love must triumph" (196). This use of the Native weapon prefigures Ben Martin's use of the Cherokee tomahawk to exact his revolutionary revenge in *The Patriot*. This named inheritance from Native weapon to the triumph of the American Revolutionary cause both predicts and echoes southern causes to come.

In contrast to this isolated recognition of one seemingly past-tense Catawba Nation, Blonay continues to figure into the narrative both in his own side plot and in his relationship to the main set of intrigues between Mellichampe and Barsfield over the war, their mutually claimed estate, and Janet's hand in marriage. Barsfield hires Blonay to kill Mellichampe in a convoluted scheme that requires facilitating Mellichampe's escape from Tory capture so that he may be executed under a rubric of justice rather than murdered over one individual's jealousy. Barsfield knows that if Mellichampe stays in the judicial system, he will likely be acquitted as he predicts that everyone knows of his own bias against Mellichampe. Therefore, he wants to facilitate the escape so that Mellichampe may be killed under the quick justice of the anticipated ensuing scuffle in his recapture. Barsfield keeps this complex thought process to himself and simply asks Blonay to arrange Mellichampe's escape so that the two of them can meet equally on the battlefield without the specter of the system's perceived biases. Blonay challenges Barsfield's scheme and points out that "it's easier to shoot a man than take a journey" to which Barsfield informs him: "men who rank high in society must be relegated by its notions" and that "to gratify a feeling is not so important as to gratify it after a particular fashion" (294–95). The fact that Blonay suddenly feels sympathy for the individualistic ethos of the Revolutionary rebels and rejects Barsfield's plans suggests that the mixedblood Catawba man comes to feel enjoined to the Revolutionary cause over the structure of society's colonial notions. In the logic of the novel, Blonay becomes good when he rebels.

This conflation of Blonay as rebel and Blonay as Native has been perpetuated through some troubling critical readings of the novel over the years. Although Simms repeatedly—almost continually—refers to Blonay as Indian or "half-breed," even some contemporary critics have read onto the character his stand-in quality as "poor white." This shift represents a troubling move as it not only removes the Native character from the novel but also renders him landless and confuses the relationship between race, class, and land claim for the region. It creates a scholarly turn of the red state where critical discourse enforces an idea of indigenized, backward whiteness to the U.S. South. We may very well expect Simms to get this distinction wrong. However, when contemporary critics read their own racial and class-based structures into the pre–Civil War southern novel, we must consider how critics continually approach the Native South not on its own terms but on the terms of a biracial, class-based society in a post–Civil War framework. This critical lens maintains the myth of a southern system's loss that erases Native presence. For example, Susan Tracy reads *Mellichampe* for the way it establishes clear racial and class-based hierarchies. Even though she initially states that Blonay is a "mixed-blood poor white" (a designation not entirely clear in and of itself), she immediately dismisses any implications of his Native identity and begins referring to him solely as "poor white," arguing that "The Humphries-Blonay contrast lets the reader draw the distinction between a sturdy yeoman/villager type and a degenerate poor white" (206). She continues to remove all mention of Blonay's Native identity and asserts that "Simms draws a clear distinction between Humphries and his cowardly and thus unmanly poor white adversary. [...] Simms makes his point: in the moral world of the yeoman and the poor white, disputes are not settled by either formalized dueling rituals or expensive lawsuits" (207). This complete morphing of the Native character into a "degenerate poor white" becomes even more problematic in Tracy's argument when she finally argues of Simms's work that "While honorable men like planter Singleton take human life only in self-defense or in defense of their family, land, or nation, dishonorable men like Hell-Fire Dick, Ned Blonay, and Samuel Bostwick wage civil war against their countrymen to *obtain illegally*, in a time of turmoil, what they cannot earn through their own efforts because they are naturally inferior" (211–12; my emphasis). Finally, according to Tracy, "Although poor whites are degraded, they still possess their own women and children, and some even have *squatters' rights* to land" (212; my emphasis). To completely erase Blonay's Native identity and render him a "squatter" on Catawba lands, which he "obtains illegally," is at best absurd and at worst dangerous. It completely misses the point of Simms's character as a Native man whose wrongs might very well be akin to the titular hero Mellichampe as someone who had his "father cruelly murdered" and "mother driven away from the home of her ancestors," and then suffers "that home confiscated; and given to the murderer." In this echo, we see the only difference between Blonay and Mellichampe is in the parental designations of mother and father in their respective injuries. Blonay has to be removed as Indian character in the subsequent critical literature so that an easier understanding of the plantation economy can emerge. The noble planter class, as represented by Mellichampe, can be the wronged and mourned, and their indigenization to the region through structures of loss and land dispossession can be made complete.

In *Mellichampe* Simms enacts a logic of the red state when he trades on the discussion of Blonay's racial identity to establish the saving Catawba arrows and to shift the landscape between Kaddipah and Lynch's Creek. Simms, however, does not quite finish the job. He maintains Blonay's identity as Native, and he maintains the region's Indigenous connection. He shifts the desire and loss in the novel to Mellichampe, sewing a neat narrative suture between the Native man and the white hero, rendering an almost—but not complete—removal. When critics such as Tracy jettison Blonay's Indian identity and render him a white squatter, then removal *is* complete. Therefore, perhaps Blonay disappears from Simms's perceived Native characters because he makes the narrative a little too difficult to fit into the preconceived arguments around the plantation South and the received knowledge of how a Native character should look and act. In some critics' work, he remains, but rarely as his Native self. And the novel—despite the fact that it might actually lay bare more than any other of Simms's work the dynamics of the Native South—fails to hold up to the idea of what many expect this history to look like. It is neither Simms's romantic *Cassique of Kiawah* nor the ferocious and tragic *Yemassee*. Rather, *Mellichampe* demonstrates the complexity of race, loyalty, land claim, and history writ small onto the details of one mixedblood character.

In the novel's penultimate climactic scene, Blonay finally locates Humphries, whom he holds responsible for his mother's death. On finding the Marion rebel, Blonay is then pursued in turn by Humphries. Eventually, however, Blonay crawls inside a cypress tree to hide and secure a continual vantage point from which to track Humphries. Once Humphries realizes that Blonay is inside the tree, he attempts to pull him out of his location. When this fails, Humphries then decides to encase Blonay alive within the cypress. When Blonay exposes a hand to facilitate his release, Humphries crushes it with a mallet. After this grisly act, Humphries feels secure in his defeat of his enemy. However, as he ponders the nature of the slow, encased death he begins to experience a haunted sensation. In the extended description of Humphries's horror, Simms writes:

> He had triumphed yet he could not keep down the fancy, which continually, as he went, imbodied the supposed cries of the half-breed in little gusts of wind, that seemed to pursue him; and, when he emerged from the wood, a strange chill went through his bones, and he looked back momently, even when the gigantic cypress, which was the sepulchre of his enemy, no longer reared up in solemn spire in his sight. It was no longer behind him. It seemed to move before him faster than his horse; and he spurred the animal furiously forward,

seeking to pass the fast-traveling tree and to escape the moaning sound which ever came after him upon the breeze. (381)

As Bergland has demonstrated in *The National Uncanny*, this embodied and continual haunting guilt regarding Native death is a common trope in literature from the early nineteenth century. However, given the immediate historical context of the novel when southern states were concluding their devastating decisions that they hoped would result in the national and physical death of the many Native people in the region, this sudden guilt of the rebel reveals an anxiety over these policies. The novel suggests that the land remembers over and above psychological repression and that in the attempt to vanish the Native past, the rebel will only see the guilt from this decision in his future. As I discuss in the next chapter, this guilt emerges in equally troubling ways when non-Native southerners attempt to retell Removal stories to buttress their own versions of red states.

Quite remarkably, this scene has been lauded for its initial and continued originality since the novel's publication. Keen Butterworth and James Kibler's extensive bibliography of Simms notes that one of the novel's initial 1836 reviews by Caroline Gilman of the *Southern Rose* proclaims that "The use of the prison cypress tree is Simms' most excellent invention and marks him as a genius" (36). Likewise, a century later Quinn also praises the scene and Blonay's "stoical conduct" despite what he sees as the plot-based flaw of Humphries's repentance and guilt (117). In his biography of Simms, Guilds calls the scene a "gripping episode [where] Simms combines well-motivated characterization with his penchant for sensual, visual depiction of the lush Carolina low country" (*Simms* 79). Wimsatt even goes so far as crediting the characterization of Blonay and the scene as presaging the southern grotesque and psychological gothic of twentieth-century writers such as William Faulkner, Erskine Caldwell, and Flannery O'Connor and even "anticipat[ing] Poe in 'The Cask of Amontillado'" (79).

However, as any critic of colonial or postcolonial literature should know, putting Indians in trees is no new trick. This plot device goes all the way back to Shakespeare's *The Tempest* when Prospero frees the "good" Indigenous spiritual being Ariel from his prison tree of the witch Sycorax. It even continues through Grandmother Willow of Disney's *Pocahontas* all the way up to the Na'vi of *Avatar*. Simms is not inventing a new structure of imagery around Native characters but merely rehearsing what seems to be a tried and true plot device for understanding indigeneity. And quite tellingly for Simms's novel, it seems little coincidence that while Blonay acts as the "bad" and deformed Indian, he reminds the reader of that other disfigured Shakespeare colonial character with an evil mother: Caliban. When Blonay converts to the "good" Indian who needs to be free in order to save Ernest Mellichampe for his bride Janet, suddenly Blonay is released from his tree prison just as Ariel is freed to facilitate Prospero's many plans, one of which includes the marriage plot of his daughter Miranda. In this shuttling between the Caliban and Ariel archetypes, we see the move of Blonay from the position of the "bad" Indian, who demands material retribution for the wrongs he sustains from a settler-colonial plantation economy, into the "good" Indian, who forgoes these complaints to unite the white colonial family and then willingly remove himself from the action.[22]

Of course, this plot turn likely occurs because the reader is supposed to believe that the novel's rebels are in fact the good guys. Humphries changes his mind and decides after much psychological self-torture to free Blonay. However, his exhortation on freeing the Catawba man sounds much like the logic for how Native people should remove themselves from the landscape for their own protection. He commands Blonay as he frees him: "Go, Blonay—you are free this time. [...] Go now, but better not let me meet you. My blood is hotter at other times than now. I'm sad and sorry now, and there's something to-night in the woods that softens me, and I can't be angry, I can't spill your blood. But 'twont always be so; and, if you're wise, you'll take the back tracks and go down quietly to Dorchester" (407). Here, Humphries's "hot" blood echoes Jefferson's southerner. This revolutionary command presages the eventual and many Indian Removals across the U.S. South, and it reminds the reader that though this one Native man's blood has been spared and sympathy has prevailed, 'twont always be so. In this red state fantasy, Native people buttress the American Revolution, legitimize its procreation, and then are made to quietly and willingly disappear.

"My people!": Confused Land Claim in the Appalachian South

One of the most productive places to witness the revolutions of narrative over time remains in the genre of the outdoor drama. As I explained in the first chapter, the long staging histories of these plays allow us to see how narratives change as they (r)evolve into new moments. In Kermit Hunter's Revolutionary history play *Horn in the West* we see American Revolutionary histories staged and rewritten that create a narrative of white southerners' attachment to the land and a lineage of identity that incorporates Native people through their eventual disappearance and absorption into a generalized American identity. For example, the souvenir program for the 1952 opening of *Horn in the West* states of the performance, "During the early part of 1950, a small group [...] began to discuss frequently the possibility of an outdoor drama to show the Anglo-Saxon heritage of the mountain people." This same article notes that the Southern Appalachian Historical Association is "primarily interested in collecting, preserving, and transmitting the historical heritage of the people of the Southern Appalachian Mountains," and that "The heritage of the Southern Appalachians is, in a very true sense, the heritage of America. Here, perhaps, was preserved longer the purest Anglo-Saxon culture." Among this culture, land attachment registers the most highly, as the writer states that "The love for private ownership of land, the love for freedom and the hatred of oppression—these are part of the traditional heritage of the mountain country" (Greer 17). This rhetoric of "pure Anglo-Saxon culture" registers as indicative of a mid-twentieth-century invocation of white superiority and fears over interracial contact. It also centers a particular form of capitalistic ascendency where the private ownership of land links an economic feeling with a racialized identity of belonging. In sum, the original discourse surrounding *Horn in the West* continues the invented historical genealogy of Anglo-Saxon land ownership in the Native South. This lineage marks one of the central concerns of the red state, as an idea of lineage creates a specific structure of periodization where legitimacy through time signifies a fomenting of inherited land attachment. However, if examined closely, the play also critiques these paradigms. Within the performance there stands the imbedded colonial contradiction of how to create a foundational history from counterhistorical narratives of legitimation. This concern informs many narratives of Native history in the construction of a red state looking to legitimize its presence and land claim in a region simultaneously seeking to disregard Native landed sovereignty while creating its own counternational identity.

The imagined histories of Anglo-American origins as attached to the American landscape serve as sites of desire for an original land claim in these performances, but these foundational histories must continually dance around (literally and figuratively) the Native presences that far predate their moments of inception. These contradictions can be seen differently in the performance—sometimes explicitly and sometimes implicitly through extradiegetic gestures that push audiences' perceptions past the immediate action and staging. In what follows, I examine the legitimizing genealogy of *Horn in the West*, where the play performs a history based entirely on a fictional foundation of Anglo-Saxon land claim. I argue that this outdoor drama, through both its original script and its continual production in Boone, North Carolina, reinscribes a continual red state through the use of a Revolutionary narrative. It indigenizes whiteness to the Appalachian South through an imagined genealogy from Native rebellion to American independence.

Horn in the West might be best explained by Scott Romine's work in *The Real South*, which he offers as "a study of the fake South, which I argue becomes the real South through the intervention of narrative" (9). Hunter's narrative, then, creates real fake space via the work of narrative. However, as Romine articulates: "the difficulty lies in untangling how, as narratives go about performing cultural work—mobilizing desirable pasts and futures, reconciling the arrangements they describe with the arrangements that ought to be, weaving space into time with both subtlety and violence, all in an effort to provide an account of the relation between subjects and environments—they do so *now*" (3). Indeed, this is the difficulty of understanding how *Horn in the West* works to build narrative connection between real, material land claim for invented white characters while using relatively historical Cherokee characters to enact some version of "authentic" connection to the region. It is this weaving of space into time that replicates and revolves as this narrative of the southern front of the American Revolution is reperformed every year.

Horn in the West tells the story of a band of Revolutionary Regulators, who participated in the local rebellion against colonial officials in North Carolina from 1764 to 1771 and fled the central part of the colony after the Battle of Alamance in 1771. In the battle, the young protagonist Jack Stuart fights with the Regulators against the local government controlled by Britain. The young Jack is the son of Geoffrey Stuart, a respected doctor who remains loyal to the Crown and the colonial governor, William Tryon. Geoffrey's wife, Martha, is the governor's sister, making the battle a complicated family affair. Governor Tryon employs a sinister general, William MacKenzie, to quash the rebellion by executing all of those captured, including Jack. When Geoffrey learns of the execution plans, he goes against his ethical obligation to the Crown and frees his son along with the other ragtag band of fighters. As a result, MacKenzie vows revenge. After the escape, the Regulators, their families, a Baptist preacher named Isaiah Sims, and the Widow Howard flee into the Blue Ridge Mountains to escape colonial rule. The Stuarts depart on their own, but they soon catch up to the other outlaws who have lost their way and are wandering around the Yadkin Valley. In some way, then, this play also begins with a lost colony, and the registers of geographic disorientation figure in my analysis of the play's action and parerga. In understanding this performance, I also draw from the play's opening-season souvenir program as well as interviews with contemporary cast members to highlight the performance's evolving registers.

After reaching their destination with the help of the legendary Daniel Boone, the Alamance Regulators build a thriving town. Geoffrey keeps his Tory loyalties while his son reads the writings of Benjamin Franklin and dreams of an independent and free government. Soon after establishing a home, the villagers encounter the local Cherokee people who come to Dr. Stuart's house to request his help in curbing a smallpox outbreak. Led by Cherokee Beloved Woman Nancy Ward, the delegation takes Geoffrey to their village, which remains unnamed in the play, where he meets Atakulla and Dragging Canoe.[23] While Atakulla and Ward seem sympathetic and cooperative with the settlers, Dragging Canoe explains his continued resentment against "the white man." Shortly after this speech, the malicious MacKenzie appears, and Stuart recognizes that the Cherokee are divided between two groups: one supporting their British alliances, led by Dragging Canoe, and another expressing their sympathies toward the illegal and Revolutionary-minded settlers in the area, led by Ward and Atakulla.

In the second act, Jack marries the young Mary Greene, an orphan whose parents were killed in the Battle of Alamance and who is now being raised by the Widow Howard. Immediately after saying their "I do's," a man appears with a newspaper. As Jack reads the newspaper aloud, the play's audience recognizes Thomas Jefferson's Declaration of Independence. This serves as a call to arms for the village, and Jack decides to leave his bride to go fight in the Revolution. His father, however, remains recalcitrant, but Jack offers a moving speech. Reluctantly, Geoffrey agrees to join his son in the march toward King's Mountain to join John Sevier's army. The night before they depart, Nancy Ward appears, warning the town that Dragging Canoe, encouraged by the British colonel MacKenzie, has planned an attack on the settlement. Despite this threat, the men leave the village and go to fight the British army. When the group reaches the battle, Jack engages MacKenzie in hand-to-hand combat. Jack successfully kills MacKenzie, but MacKenzie fatally stabs him in the process. The play ends as Jack dies in his father's arms. Just before the stage goes black, Reverend Sims prays aloud, "Oh Lord, we've been chasing phantoms of a dead past, so freedom can go on. Lord, teach us to be still and listen!"[24]

Although the play works with several historical events and includes many historical figures, it is almost purely ahistorical. Geoffrey Stuart never existed, nor did his wife, Martha, nor his son, Jack. The Regulators in the mountains seem like the people of the historical Wautauga Settlement, but they are not. Daniel Boone is real, as are John Sevier and Governor Tryon, but aside from that, none of the play's main characters have any archival or historical antecedents—all except for the Cherokee characters. Hunter goes to great lengths to create a fictional white family in a fictional white town full of fictional white people, but he pulls all of his Cherokee characters—down to their clothes—from archival sources. However, the play does not offer this distinction. It flattens the reality of the stage to suggest that all of these characters are historical figures who lived on the land where the audience now watches their personal and collective drama play out. This historical razing of fact is a significant feature of the revolutionary red state formation, and because of its ubiquity, viewers seem primed to accept it as "real." Audiences are encouraged to see this play as history, and the fact that they are attending the play in Boone, North Carolina, certainly enforces this reading. Furthermore, as one walks into the amphitheater, s/he walks past a "historical village" complete with replica log cabins from the Revolutionary period of the play's performance. They encounter the stage amid the forests and rhododendrons, evoking an affective experience where they have happened on real reception just as much as it does through the author's creation. This suture between the audience and the character Stuart sustains a structure of power where white psychology imbues the landscape and creates a naturalized link between performative history and contemporary land claim. When Native characters are rendered timeless through strict archival "accuracy" it effectively keeps them in the past, away from the non-Native audience of the present, which in turn essentially empties the landscape for present-day material claims of geographical heritage. It constitutes a type of removal that clears the way for the appropriation of land that the Revolution requires.

This friction between representational truths plays out at the level of concerns over historical accuracy. Unlike *The Lost Colony*'s Agona, *Horn in the West*'s Nancy Ward, Atakulla, and Dragging Canoe all existed, and the performers I spoke to seemed conscientious, aware of a responsibility to play these characters respectfully and "accurately." Some even apologized to me for what they saw as the occasionally inaccurate representations. The young man who performed the "Indian" fire-hoop dance in 2009 said to me after one show, "Yeah . . . we sometimes play pretty fast and loose with the Native history," and admittedly, the popular "fire" scene in the Cherokee village illustrates one of the more difficult parts of the show in terms of its representations of an "exotic" Native culture. Perhaps not coincidentally, it is also an audience favorite. Jeff Hatley, an eighteen-year veteran of the performance and a history professor, talked about the difficulties in taking a script written during the mid-1950s and making it respectful to Native people today—especially when the show is still made up primarily of non-Native actors in red body paint. In the 2009 season, Hatley played the part of Atakulla. He noted that Hunter himself even changed the script over the years to reflect more historical fidelity to the Cherokee characters, and he said that numerous cast members over the years worked to learn Cherokee words and phrases rather than communicating in the stereotypical grunts and broken English. For example, Hunter researched the lives and political positions of the historical Attakullakulla and Dragging Canoe and by all accounts wanted to produce a portrayal of his Native characters that respected the historical archive.[27]

The performance has changed over the years in attempts to increase its historical fidelity while maintaining the spirit of the initial script. For many years, the character Atakulla offered a speech in the Cherokee language to thank Dr. Stuart for his help with the smallpox epidemic. This speech has now been cut. Hatley said this happened when a cast member who was Cherokee took the speech to an elder to translate. Although the speech contained actual Cherokee words, it amounted to a string of random nouns. Because of this, the actors and director at the time decided to remove it from the performance. I noticed during the show that Hatley simply responds with a "Wado" when Stuart helps the town. When I asked him about this addition, he said that it was a personal ad-lib he used the opening night of the 2009 season because to him it seemed right that Atakulla would express his thanks for the doctor's assistance. Through these subtle changes, Hatley sees the show as doing the best it can with the given script. The performance, then, finds itself in two—perhaps irreconcilable—histories: the colonial archival history and the history of the performance. Because the outdoor dramas are performed every year, often to returning audience members, the viewers have expectations of these plays, and from the plays, they have expectations of the history.[28] Such expectations of representation and history have material implications for how a regional audience in the U.S. South views Native history and living Native people today, including debates about land use, tribal sovereignty, and self-determination.

Unlike many of the purely romantic and ahistorical elements of Cherokee culture represented in the play, Nancy Ward appears as a slightly more complex character whose actions mirror her representations in much of the historical archive. In the play, Ward comes across as a strong cultural interpreter and diplomat. She does not fall into gender stereotypes, a mixedblood/fullblood dichotomy, or a caricature of Native people. She speaks English and Cherokee, and even though she sympathizes with the white settlers, she ultimately defends her nation. When Stuart first refuses to go with her to treat the smallpox outbreak, she challenges him: "You'll save white children but let Indian children die?" She also argues that white people brought "the disease of red spots," and therefore it is their responsibility to fix it. Ward does not agree with Dragging Canoe's tactics or positions, but she staunchly defends him as Cherokee, illustrating a solidarity despite strategic differences. When Stuart asks why she risks so much to negotiate between the settlers and the Cherokee people, she proclaims to him, "These are my people!" Ultimately, her desire for peace and her seeming sympathy with the white mothers and children in the settler town lead her to warn them of the imminent attack. In this way, the character Ward works as a relatively historically accurate figure as drawn from her archival representations. As Theda Perdue argues, historically speaking, Ward, as the Beloved Woman of Chota, exercised considerable influence as a diplomat. She often used the rhetoric of kinship, mothers, and children when speaking to U.S. representatives, and Perdue notes that this had less to do with blood and more to do with an understanding of the kin networks based on clan identification. Perdue writes that "The political power of Ward and other Cherokee women rested on their position as mothers in a matrilineal society that equated kinship and citizenship" (*Cherokee Women* 101).[29] Thus, Ward's rhetoric and autonomy in the play have their foundations in her historical position as a respected woman in Cherokee society. However, in some ways this representational power becomes negated because some audience members—and by extension historians of this period—may view her as yet another colonial helpmate to the colonists who simply betrays a political faction of her tribe. Without the background of this character's functioning within Cherokee society, some audience members may impose their own well-trod assumptions of the function of a Native woman in the protonational narrative.

Daniel Heath Justice also works from an understanding of Ward as a Beloved Woman in developing his readings of Cherokee literature. In his productive Cherokee-centric methodology, he refers to Ward by her Cherokee name, Nanye'hi. As he articulates, "Nanye'hi was a strong advocate for peace allegiance with the fledgling United States" as she "lived in times of extraordinary cultural change and conflict." She represents the Beloved Path of peace despite its "difficult nature." For as Justice explains, "When the focus centers on the survival and endurance of the People, peace itself can be as much an assertion of defiance as the Chickamauga consciousness of war" (38). In this way, we might attempt to reread the representation of Ward in the play. Justice reads the historical actions of Ward through the previous historical work of Virginia Carney: "Her behavior during the U.S. Revolutionary War has been read outside a Beloved Path context as a betrayal of her people to an enemy state, but Carney asserts that '[i]t was, in fact, a legal requirement among the Cherokees, as among many other Indian nations, that warning be given of an impending attack'" (qtd. in Justice 39). Even though *Horn in the West* is thoroughly a fantasy of the non-Native southern imagination, Justice's methodology for reading the Beloved Path serves as an important node in understanding the history represented in the play. Whereas some might dispense with Justice's model of Nanye'hi as an instance of a Native-produced "compensatory fiction," Justice explains, "Cherokees today understand Nanye'hi's often contradictory approach toward preserving her cultural identity while adapting to the demands of the present. [...] [M]ost of the Cherokee people have long fought to survive on the Beloved Path by shaping Eurowestern cultural, religious, and political structures to serve the interests of Cherokee nationhood" (41). Justice's view here is important for understanding how we cannot lump all historical fictions into one category. While we have to be clear about how, as Romine explains, labels of "reality" do work for the region, it is crucial to realize that in the case of *Horn in the West* the Stuart family is a pure fiction that justifies an illegal land claim whereas Ward was a living Cherokee person who represents a powerful genealogy within a contemporary Cherokee worldview. While both narratives do work, the causes behind these figures have vastly different resonances. However, even with Justice's thoughtful analysis of Ward's epistemological legacy for Cherokee people, it remains important to remember that this reading of the character remains dependent on viewers' reception of the history before them. Do audiences understand the potential behind her representation, or does she remain as psychological backdrop for the non-Native characters? How does the reperformance of her character over time change the way that she is understood? As the play restages the Revolution, what are the logical revolutions of the red state embedded within the reception of her character?

Indeed, Hatley noted that the biggest hurdle in playing a Cherokee person on stage was the audience's overt lack of awareness about Native people. While he said that the audience understood that professional actors played the roles of Daniel Boone and the Stuart family, they would often be completely unaware that the Native characters were also played by actors. At the end of every show, the cast invites the audience on stage for autographs and pictures with the performers. Hatley and his wife, Shannon (a twelve-year veteran of the show), told me about times when audience members would approach the Cherokee actress who played Nancy Ward for many years. One concerned woman attempted to convert the actress to Christianity after the show, explaining that while she might be tied to her "tribal" beliefs, she should know that those were frowned on by God as pagan sins. Another man once approached Hatley and asked him if the actress playing Ward spoke English (this despite the fact that he had presumably heard her speaking English throughout the entire performance). On another occasion, a man asked Hatley and his fellow actors "where they kept the Indians," seemingly unaware that the same chorus members played the Wataugan settlers, the British soldiers, and the townspeople in the Cherokee village.

On the first night I attended *Horn in the West* I saw the reaction that the show can elicit from the viewers. As the mosquitos bit me and the persistent drizzle kept me writing notes underneath a cheap poncho, I tried hard to ignore the woman sitting directly in front of me. She jumped out of her seat every time an "Indian" came on stage, and she yelled in a way that might be best described as "war whoops." As the actors in red body paint danced, she kept exclaiming loudly, "Yeah! My people!" Just before intermission, the stage went black as the actors entered the set for the Cherokee village. The villagers appeared from upstage dressed in buckskin and holding torches. Then, one man came to center stage and completed what is a quite impressive dance with a hoop that had been set on fire. During the fire dance, the woman in front of me continued to scream like something out of *Stagecoach*, and yelled "My people!" with such enthusiasm that I began to wonder if her people were in fact half-naked, white, college-aged summer theater actors in red body paint. Maybe they were, but I doubt it. I suspect that the spectacle of the "Native" performance combined with the generalized pathos of the play allowed this woman to identify with her desire for indigeneity in the Appalachian South. She had entered something of a red state. Indeed, this one viewer's reaction may represent an outlier of enthusiasm, but combined with some of the Hatleys' anecdotes, I think we have to pause to consider why such a response is possible at all. Via the intervention of place-based narrative, the fake Indians of the show elicited a real response from a viewer, one that evokes a romantic attachment to disappearance, where revolutionary Natives buttress American sovereignty against their own interests.

Despite the cast's best attempt at creating a staged show that respected Cherokee people, in these cases some audience members remained relatively dismissive of the historical—and interpretive—nature of the representations. I offer these anecdotes not to make fun of the audience or criticize the show but to offer examples of the complicated ways that Native history remains staged and understood in the U.S. South regardless of the good intentions of the performers. As my sister, Jessica, hypothesized one night after a performance, "I think those reactions from people come because they have no understanding of Native people or realities today. They understand white history and white lives, but they have nothing but 'cowboys and Indians' in their head when they think of any real Native people." In other words, Native history and people remain in the eighteenth and nineteenth centuries while "American" history and people have completed a full revolution and can now occupy both the past and the present. Like Jefferson's plan to hold Native people in a perpetual present, Hunter's play creates a static, historically present Indian figure through referents to a legitimate positivistic archive. This production of history speaks back to the play's confinement of Native characters to the archive while allowing white characters to transcend history. And ironically, the invocation of a psychological depth represented by purely ahistorical characters creates a greater feeling of historicity in the play's reception.

This divide between archival history and historical representation speaks to the difference in psychological depth noted by Selden. He argues that Nancy Ward must have *influenced* the imaginary Geoffrey Stuart. In Native American literary studies we often think and talk about the imaginary, or invented, Indian influencing the "real," Euro-American author.[30] Instead, Hunter has created an imaginary British American who is influenced by the real Native. This reversal creates an odd paradox in the play. On the one hand, this structure suggests that Nancy Ward underwent no psychological change of her own despite the extremely trying times in which she lived. It makes her exist only to influence a burgeoning Revolutionary American identity and reduces her autonomy to the space of psychological incorporation. It denies any psychological depth to her character, and because audiences often refuse to see her as a *character* and instead as a real person straight out of the eighteenth century, it renders all past/present Cherokee people as mere influences on the formation of revolutionary whiteness. On the other hand, it questions what audiences view as Native history. As a character, Ward speaks a powerful amount of truth about the negative influences of illegal white settlement on Cherokee land, and she stages an alternative of diplomacy and respect between Cherokee and British Americans in the eighteenth century. Unfortunately, half of this alliance happens to be Geoffrey Stuart, a man who never existed, pointing audiences toward an ultimately unfulfilled possibility where the Cherokee and British Americans engaged one another on the terms of mutual respect.

This slippage between the reimagining of history and the misunderstanding of history remains one of the core material problems of the red state for living Native people and their land claims in the U.S. South. When the audience refuses to understand the Native history of the play, or they fail to see the interpretative nature of the show, they unwittingly participate in a colonial logic of the region. On some level, these types of misunderstandings reveal the deeply threatening idea that contemporary Indigenous existence poses for the non-Native population of the U.S. South. These audiences fail to understand the reality of living Native people because to see Native characters or actors as contemporaries opens up a dangerous realization that Native people are twenty-first-century humans with a legitimate moral and legal claim to the land. When audience members engage in their own colonial acts—attempting to convert the actress playing Nancy Ward, assuming a language barrier with the "Cherokee" actors—they reassert their position in a continued settler-colonial dynamic that the play encourages through the appeal to history and place. Despite its best effort, the performance remains in a red state revolution. From the original script to the accrued meaning of the performance over the years, the play moves in a spiralic time around the region's Indigenous connections, drawing on ideas of Native history while positing a legitimate Anglo-Saxon claim to the "emptied" tribal lands.

Once again, though, this consideration of Native history in the region exists in such a way as to support what I have been calling a red state revolution where whiteness becomes indigenized through an appeal to Native history as rebellious and counternational. This continual narrative works to place the U.S. South within the foundational framework of the nation while at the same time attempting to maintain its beleaguered and exceptional status. It is true that some historians look to the Battle of Alamance in central North Carolina as an early precursor to conflicts with the British Crown. However, this would be just one early historical flashpoint among many in the lead-up to the American Revolutionary War. Yet the play produces a history where this one event becomes precisely emblematic of the contradictory feelings of European settlers regarding their position as colonial subjects. Just as we must understand Paul Green's *Lost Colony* as invested in the placement of the U.S. South within the foundational colonial narrative, we should also query how *Horn in the West* engages the same emotive registers that place the U.S. South as exemplary in the nation's Revolutionary history.

On some level, *Horn in the West* subtly links British rule with Reconstruction "Northern rule" in the U.S. South. The concerns of isolation and freedom from the state figure heavily in both instances, and although the audience knows that the Revolutionary War is not a lost cause like the Confederacy, the play ends with young Jack's death, leaving the viewer with a heavy sense of loss. This sense of a southern nostalgia in suffering and loss represents one of the major components within the strategic misrecognition of truth as it engages questions of Native history in the region. Like *The Lost Colony*, it sutures feelings of white southern loss with the experience of Native colonization, which dangerously conflates lived histories and material legacies of settler colonialism within the region. Such a conflation supports Huhndorf's argument that "going Native comprises a cherished national ritual," and it supports Melanie Benson Taylor's assertion that in the U.S. South this ritual takes on specific regional undertones that at once enforce racial power and collective loss (*Going Native* 18). Therefore, as noted earlier, this is a context for the machinations of power that construct truths for the region, which both enforce and subvert narratives of national belonging for white southerners, ultimately legitimizing a conservative version of the red state.

Although so far I have critiqued the play for allowing the white characters to exist ahistorically, this lack of historical grounding offers a significant commentary on Anglo-Americans' paradoxically imaginary and real sense of land attachment in the U.S. South. Toward the end of the play, Jack argues with his father about the imperative for them to fight on the American side in the Revolutionary War. He implores his father, saying, "This is my home, my land, and these are my people!" Geoffrey reacts by responding, "Nine years ago, Nancy Ward said the same thing—my people—said as if it was first and all else was secondary." Jack replies that it is. This echoes Daniel Boone's earlier call to arms when he asks Geoffrey to imagine "If his whole family lived right here." These statements pose a crucial historical problem. Given that all of these settlers have just moved to the area, the Cherokee people such as Nancy Ward are the only people whose "whole families" live "right here," as even the play makes clear. Most of the colonial characters' families would presumably still live in Europe, or at the very least farther east in the Piedmont of North Carolina. With these statements, Jack's invocation of the land draws a parallel between home, land, and kinship. Jack and Boone's argument suggests to the audience that kinship is what determines one's claim to a geographical space and that identifying "one's people" makes fighting for the land a worthy cause. Because Jack and Geoffrey are purely fictional, they have no people, and likewise, these fictional people have no claim to the real land. The play, however, creates a space of ahistorical reality for the audience, and a regional audience is compelled to romanticize a southern sense of home while erasing legitimate Indigenous land claims.

Although the play makes a serious claim to history, it also subtly foregrounds this specious story through its convoluted geographical placement. While the original souvenir programs of the other major outdoor dramas in the state, *The Lost Colony* and *Unto These Hills*, both include detailed maps, *Horn in the West* does not. This disorients the audience as to the geography of the performance. Furthermore, when the Regulators flee the community of Alamance in the center of the state, they become lost. While Reverend Sims and the Widow Howard debate their next turn, Daniel Boone appears silently upstage. The crowd often emits an excited murmur at this point, knowing that the celebrity of the performance—and the town of Boone, North Carolina—has appeared. As Sims and Howard argue over directions, Boone climbs a tree and continues to observe the other characters unnoticed. Sims points "west" toward their desired destination, but Boone points the opposite direction, creating a moment of dramatic irony where the audience knows that the reverend's sense of geographical direction is all wrong. Again, Sims asserts confidently, "this is west; this is the direction we want to go!" For a second time, Boone points in the opposite direction, offstage. While this moment of dramatic irony seems on the surface only a humorous exchange, it may also signal another meaning. Boone literally points away from the stage, suggesting that the space and people portrayed on stage are not the "real" story. Boone's actions might be understood in the tradition of Brechtian gestus, where the physical action reveals an aspect of the character's political and social place within the larger political landscape of the epic drama.[31] The drama is the stuff of fiction, and Boone points away from this action, gesturing to another history that an audience might find if they look in another direction, thus rupturing the bond of empathy with the errand of the Regulators and alienating the audience from the action on stage. When Boone finally reveals himself to the settlers, he goes over to Reverend Sims and turns his map 90 degrees, noting that it is hard to know where one is going if he is holding the map wrong. These are indeed Jack's people, but they are lost. From the beginning, then, this outdoor drama of the southern Appalachians queries the audience's understanding of geographies and historical genealogies. When we take *Horn in the West* as establishing a legitimate claim between the land and the Anglo-Saxon people, we are looking at the map all wrong.

As the original souvenir program claims, *Horn in the West* was originally conceived by the Southern Appalachian Historical Association as a way to indigenize Anglo-Saxon culture to the Appalachian Mountains and to the foundation of the early American Revolution, much like the Roanoke Island Historical Association desired to create a space for North Carolina history in the larger national narrative of English colonialism. When Hunter wrote *Horn in the West*, he started his genealogy from purely imaginary people, and he mapped a territory that even his own characters cannot navigate, thus exposing that a pure Anglo-Saxon identity as one with the land is nothing more than a fiction drawn from a specious historical inheritance. Whether such moves were intentional on Hunter's part remains to a certain extent irrelevant. What remains clear is that when Hunter tried to write the history of a legitimate and genealogical Anglo-Saxon claim to the Appalachian Mountains, he had to begin from a family-tree branch that never existed. While Nancy Ward has a historically "real" people who have a Native claim to the land, Jack's people—and by extension his land claim—have to be invented.

Indeed, constructions of historical fiction must rely on both history and fiction. Furthermore, we might even dismiss the specious history as a simple dramatic trope in that in creating Geoffrey Stuart the play is simply appealing to a logic of the "common man" to whom audiences can relate. However, these plays do not poise themselves as solely historical fiction. They make claims to legitimate history, and furthermore, I argue that the "common man" protagonist in such a drama ultimately buttresses the red state revolution through an ahistorical land attachment for non-Native people in the U.S. South. The use of the common man in Geoffrey Stuart allows the white southern audience to project their personal histories onto the character. They fill in the historical blanks with their own ancestors, making *Horn in the West* not simply a history but *their* history. The gestures toward the historical in the fictive performance mobilize the audience toward an affective connection to the land. In so doing, the play creates a whiteness in the U.S. South that is mobile and emotive. It claims reverence for southern earth despite the material history of Indigenous land claim.

"Dress Like an Indian So You Can Commit Treason": Tea Parties and R*dsk*ns

During the 2013 Modern Language Association Convention, two of my friends and colleagues, Hupa/Karuk/Yurok scholar Cutcha Risling Baldy and Cherokee/Wasco/Warm Springs scholar and filmmaker Brook Colley, decided to spend the day touring Boston instead of going to panels. Quite regrettably, I decided to attend sessions. Throughout the day, they sent me picture texts under the theme of "Indians Around Boston." Their most interesting stop of the day was at the site of the Boston Tea Party, where they, along with the other tourists, were told to "Dress up like Indians so you can commit treason," to which Cutcha responded, "What if we're already dressed like Indians? Do we still have to dress up?" She says this caused the tour guide to backtrack awkwardly from her previous statement. I do not mean to tell this story as yet another non-Native account of a Native experience in this country in order to make a point. But after discussing the story with Cutcha in order to make sure I had my account correct, she and I decided the point stands: Native people in the abstract stand in for all sorts of revolutionary ideas.

Indeed, many years ago Philip Deloria made a similar point about the original Boston Tea Party's use of Indian disguise. In *Playing Indian* Deloria discusses New England as the site for the misrule tradition and the historical societies who initially deployed Indian identity as a fraternal exercise. Explicating the revolutionary impulse to play Indian, Deloria writes, "Through Indianness, colonists articulated a revolutionary identity" and they "invoked a range of identities [...] all of which emerged from the categories Indian and Briton" (20, 36). He articulates this American identity as contested between these spheres, but he never turns toward a consideration that at this time, American colonials were also deeply invested in their regional and state-based differences. Furthermore, interaction with Native people also occurred in deeply localized contexts. Before the consolidation of trade with Native nations under the general government, states largely conducted their own treaties and policies with Native nations. Though in several instances colonial Americans engaged in playing Indian as a universal stereotype, they were also informed through their regional experiences. As Deloria offers, "Beyond the Tea Party and the Revolution lay a land characterized by uncertain identity and a progressive hope for future clarity, a place that Americans would continue to explore and refigure as they consolidated the new nation" (37). However, as we know from Greeson among others, this identity formation had deep regional vectors and implications that even playing Indian could not resolve. This complicates Deloria's hypothesis regarding the consolidation of national identity. The recognition of the regional shows how settler colonialism acted on and was acted upon by specific interactions with specific tribal nations. Just as colonialism is localized and flexible, the ways that settlers understood their land claims as emerging from interactions with living Native people in their midst surely affected how they understood generalized "Native" performance. These differences have generated specifically regional histories that, while not being exceptional, are indeed particular and deserve to be parsed. As such, the consideration of the regional pushes against Deloria's argument regarding the category of the national when people choose to play Indian.

The Indian figure frequently stands in for the idea of committing treason, which is why it has remained such a potent image for those who want to express counternational sentiments. These sentiments have a certain type of half-life as they expand, replicate, and mutate across regional divides. However, these rebellious Indian figures work only insofar as Jefferson's revolutionary Native figure does—they stand in for a state fantasy that imagines no state control. As Jefferson failed to conceptualize how this ideal state could exist, he also promoted aggressive policies against real Native people who articulated their own national sovereign sentiments in the protection and defense of their land claims. They were, to echo Thomas King's work in *The In-*

convenient Indian: A Curious Account of Native People in North America (2012), incredibly inconvenient. When white southerners have taken up Indian identity it has not just been, as Deloria argues, to foment national identity. Rather, it has been to disrupt a homogeneous national identity through a counter-national framework that imagines a throwing off of the federal government—it has been to imagine a state with no state control, a red state where southerners remain, to echo Jefferson, "zealous for their own liberties" but willing to trample "on those of others."

In other words, it looks a lot like the contemporary Tea Party. According to one of the organization's websites, they are "born from obscurity, without funding, without planning," noting that they welcome "all red-blooded U.S. Citizens."[32] Fittingly enough, they are rather upset about possibly losing the right to dress up like "Indians," and instead of dump tea, cheer for football. Under the headline of "TYRANNY UPDATE: Obama Strips Washington Redskins of their Trademark," a teaparty.org exclusive criticizes the U.S. Patent Office for canceling the trademark for the Washington R*dsk*ns because they concluded it was disparaging. It remains unclear from the Tea Party's coverage how not being able to have a desired football mascot constitutes tyranny, but there you go. Teaparty.org cites the oft-quoted study from the football team's owners that improbably concludes that most Native people have no problem with the name. As a response, the Constitutional Rights PAC has started a petition to change the team's name to the Washington Tea Party. Their petition appeal reads: "The Tea Party movement aims to put power in the hands of the people, not in the hands of the government. The movement is made up of Patriots who stand up to government intrusiveness, and fight for the principles set forth in the U.S. Constitution. Given the recent events regarding the fight to change the 'offensive' Redskins team name, the Tea Party is the perfect representation of the fight of the American people against political correctness and government intrusion" ("Change the Redskins Name"). This suggestion implies that if fans cannot pull for fake Indians, then they can cheer for a mascot that faked Indianness in order to stage a revolution. Furthermore, this appeal exposes the desire to merge a largely beleaguered whiteness suffering under perceived governmental oppression with an abstract Native. And thus, this American narrative completes another revolution, one that most recently has moved from the Tea Party to the Trump Party.

However, by way of concluding, I would like to suggest that we might have another, more subtle revolution on our hands. When the Washington R*dsk*ns took to Twitter to ask their fans to tweet to Senator Harry Reid about their "#RedskinsPride," they got substantially more than they were asking for. A flood of tweets poured in with responses ranging from, "What a clown show. I hate my team," and "Ignorant commercialization of race" to "The fruits of genocide?" and "The Redskins only integrated because the government forced them to. And now they'll change their name for the same reason."[33] Such are the problems with freedom of speech and public forums—as people may very well not take the intended bait and instead turn the forum on those who ask leading questions. As Cutcha Risling Baldy relates, the battle to change the R*dsk*ns mascot and against Native mascots in general has a long history, dating back to at least the Red Power era.[34] However, this may be the first time that a large portion of the non-Native public has taken notice of the issue in a concerted and effectual way. The Twitter user who reminds us that the R*dsk*ns have been through this before as they battled integration demonstrates the power of these revolutionary turns. The name of the team and the cliché appropriated Indian figure it represents takes on different valences over the turns in political power. These previous battles show the team's owners working against the specter of an interfering government that refuses to grant the individual liberty to be racist. However, as the overall Twitter case shows, it is not "Obama-esque tyranny" forcing the team's owners to get rid of one more vestige of a genocidal history, and I hope that by the time you, the reader, encounter these lines, the name *will* have changed.[35]

Of course, in 2018 such a hope might be far-fetched, as the contemporary political moment suggests that America has entered a more regressive phase. As I demonstrate in this chapter, these "conservative" claims often link narratives of land claim to a desire for an indigenized whiteness to the continent. The American revolution, then, is not just about the turning of abstract cogs as history repeats itself. Rather, it is nourished by fantasies of Indigenous history that buttress whiteness while attempting to efface Native sovereignty through new national and regional identities. As these stories move through the spiral of time, they gather added valences as settler colonialism refreshes its own roots through the binding of a white landed class to its "home." This work, as I demonstrate, occurs through the intervention of the regional within and against the larger construct of the national. As white southerners began to imagine themselves as distinct from their northern counterparts, they began to foment their own sense of regional, state-based sovereignty. In order to do so, they looked to the actual sovereign nations in the midst: the Native nations who controlled land and resources that the white South coveted. The non-Native narrative of the American Revolution slowly became one about the removal of these competing sovereign claims in the southern states. As I demonstrate in the next chapter, Removal stands as a site that might better organize considerations of the U.S. South under rubrics of settler colonialism. The historical and narrative legacy of Removal might be considered the ultimate crescendo of the red state: a location in time where the battles of land claim play out in the starkest relief.

CHAPTER THREE

Removal

> It is hard to be poor, and unlettered, and friendless, and to live neighbors to people who care so little to exercise brotherly kindness; but we hope that we have friends even in Georgia; and it is wished that we may be treated like human beings, at least.
>
> —John Ridge and David Vann, March 3, 1826

> The government and people of the United States will always find the Muscogees anxious to preserve peace and do justice; and all they ask in return is to be treated in like manner, and spared the afflictions in which the people of Georgia appear determined to involve them. *Justice is Justice.* There is not one kind for the White man and another for the Red man.
>
> —Opothle Yoholo, John Stidham, Mad Wolf, Menawee, Yoholo Micco, Tuskeekee Tustenuggee, Charles Cornnels, Apauli Tustenuggee, Selocta, Timpoochy Bamnett, Coosa Tustenuggee, Nahetlue Hopie, Ledagee, March 3, 1826

The 1863 *Geographical Reader, for the Dixie Children* offers brief lessons for schoolchildren in the Confederate States of America, and as one might suspect, it has a distinct political and regional bias as the only reader of its type during its period. After the main body of the *Reader*, which offers many lessons imbued with climatic determinism and anti-Union propaganda, the author, Marinda Branson Moore, poses a series of catechismal questions for the children's review. One series of questions asks the following to the presumed white southern child audience:

Q: How do the Indians live?
A: By hunting and fishing.
Q: Where did they once live?
A: In all of America.

Q: What has become of them?
A: The white people drove them away and took their lands.
Q: Are they all gone?
A: A few of them live in some places but do not seem much happy.
Q: Was it not wrong to drive them away and take their lands?
A: It was, and God will judge the white man for it.
Q: May not some of the wars we have had have been such judgements?
A: Very likely. (Moore 38)

This series of questions is curious for a number of reasons. Before this moment, the *Reader* is not particularly inclined toward the Indigenous peoples of the Americas, aside from noting that before Removal, the Cherokee had "advanced" to enslaving people and creating a newspaper and that the Inca of Peru were the most similar to white people due to their gentle and benevolent ruling class (Moore 16). Moore draws several conclusions regarding the economic and military turmoil of countries such as Mexico and Peru precisely due to the violent colonization of the Spanish, who she says "have never prospered in any country, as much as some nations," because "judgments will always follow wickedness" (16). According to Moore, "The curse of heaven seems to rest upon them, for treating the poor Indians so cruelly" (15). Not surprisingly, these sentiments follow the logic of the Black Legend where English colonizers can be conceived in relative piety because of their imagined better treatment of Indigenous peoples.[1] What is surprising, however, is that Moore connects the recent treatment of southeastern U.S. Native peoples to the same heavenly judgment as the previous actions of the Spanish. Not only does this link the Confederate States of America in a nexus of a global South of Latin America, but it also provides a small glimpse into the complex ways that white southerners were attempting to articulate their antebellum and wartime identities in relation to the two major events of the nineteenth-century U.S. South: Indian Removal and the Civil War.

This chapter interrogates the structures of feeling that informed the act of Removal alongside the fomenting of an oppositional southern identity. How did examples of regional sentiment such as these move in thirty years—virtually the space of Marinda Moore's lifetime (she was born in 1829 and died in 1864)—from the virulent disdain for Native people to the romantic bond in anguish or, as Moore speculates, to the profound religious guilt and retribution that would lead her to suggest to "Dixie children" that the Civil War itself was punishment for the sin of Native dispossession? This chapter engages this question through an examination of the print cultures and later narrative accounts of Removal. From newspapers to religious tracts and popular novels, the period from the 1820s to the Civil War saw a proliferation of printed materials throughout the region. These materials allow us to catch a glimpse of the myriad of popular sentiments that surrounded the Removal debates. Whereas the previous chapter focused on the lineages drawn from recurring narratives of the Revolution in order to justify feelings of land attachment, this section focuses on the caesuras within this process. Two events, Indian Removal and the Civil War, mark crisis moments for the region, and these traumas have a tendency to recur as foundational myths of a white southern national identity. Looking at these two ruptures within formations of Native and non-Native conceptions of the U.S. South allows us to reperiodize later southern phenomena such as a "sense of place." This disjoining of a sense of place from a material land claim is important for then considering the geographic and temporal fantasies that undergird much of white southern exceptionalism. In a way, this attempt at detangling echoes Martyn Bone's excellent work in *The Postsouthern Sense of Place in Contemporary Fiction* (2005), yet because the Native South is also not "postsouthern" just as it is not in Anderson's words "presouthern," the work needs attention from a specifically Native studies perspective. The Native South exists alongside these "pre" and "post" markers without adhering to their temporal determinations. While for Bone the Agrarian invention and reliance on place represents a ground zero of sorts in his analysis, my forwarding of land claim attempts to recognize the material theft of Indigenous lands from sovereign Native nations that exist in practice and policy while "the South" covers over this history with affective and sensory myths. One place to examine the affective registers of this crisis is in the print culture that circulated throughout the region during this time, which I examine in the first two sections of this chapter. As with the previous chapters, I follow the recurrent narrative accounts of an event. After examining the popular discourse of the Removal moment, I look at one of its earliest retrospective narrative accounts in William Gilmore Simms's 1844 "The Broken Arrow, an Authentic Passage from an Unwritten History," which tells the story of the prominent Creek citizen William McIntosh. From there, I turn toward more contemporary imaginings of the period as I analyze in the following order texts including Charles Frazier's *Thirteen Moons* (2006) and *Cold Mountain* (1997), Blake Hausman's *Riding the Trail of Tears* (2011), and Alex Timber and Michael Friedman's *Bloody Bloody Andrew Jackson* (2006). Together, an examination of the primary materials from the Removal era alongside the later popular imaginings of this time period help us understand how the red state engages narratives of Removal in order to solidify a sense of loss that will eventually coalesce into narratives of the Lost Cause.

Beginning with the Removal era itself allows us to think through the ways in which conservative versions of the red state attempt to consolidate land claim alongside narratives of Native cultures. Two figures in particular emerged as significant in the long history of the print culture of the Native

South: Cherokee author and editor Elias Boudinot and, as I examined in the previous chapter, South Carolina's William Gilmore Simms. Boudinot served as the editor of the *Cherokee Phoenix*, which began printing in 1828 and was forced to stop in 1834 due to the increasing pressure over Removal.[2] The paper included printed material in English and in the newly developed Cherokee syllabary. Simms also worked as an editor and writer in several southern print venues including newspapers such as Charleston's *City Gazette* and the literary venture *Magnolia*. While there exists little direct evidence to suggest that Simms and Boudinot were actively aware of each other's work, it seems unlikely that they did not know of one another. As the editor of the *Cherokee Phoenix*, Boudinot's name was ubiquitous with the Cherokee case against Removal, and as a rising figure in antebellum print cultures, Simms's name and works circulated throughout the southern cultural landscape. Given the culture of newspaper exchange and reprinting during this period, it seems entirely probable that Simms knew of the *Phoenix* given that he wrote columns during the same time for Charleston's *City Gazette*, some of which address Cherokee affairs directly.[3] Simms's popularity, of course, began a bit later than Boudinot's, but we do know from Simms's 1844 literary essay "The Broken Arrow" that by that time he was aware of the *Cherokee Phoenix*, accusing it of doing "an infinite deal of mischief in the hands of small politicians" (86). Regardless of their possible implicit or explicit connections, both men understood the print cultures of their periods, and both found promise and peril in the use of the medium.

Today, both Boudinot and Simms suffer from somewhat tarnished reputations that result from political decisions each man made during his lifetime. Boudinot became part of the Treaty Party, a group of thirty-two Cherokee men who signed the spurious Treaty of New Echota with the United States in 1835. Against the wishes of the vast majority of the Cherokee Nation whose official and elected leader was John Ross, the Treaty Party traded the Cherokee land east of the Mississippi for land in Indian Territory. According to Cherokee constitutional law, selling any Cherokee Nation land without the permission of the Nation constituted a capital offense. After many years of active campaigning against Removal, Boudinot ultimately signed the fraudulent Treaty of New Echota that gave the United States the ultimate paper backing to effect what became known as the Trail of Tears. Put simply, Boudinot and the other members of the Treaty Party signed a treaty that they knew they did not have the national authority to sign.[4] Of course, questions of intention remain difficult to answer. It is impossible to know what each member of the Treaty Party, including Boudinot, hoped to achieve either personally or nationally in this decision.[5] Boudinot and the other members of the Treaty Party, including Major Ridge and his son John, removed to Indian Territory ahead of the majority of the Nation. After Removal, Boudinot, along with the other members of the Treaty Party, was eventually killed for his violation of the Cherokee law that made it a capital offense to sell Cherokee lands without the permission of the Nation.

Many today read Boudinot through the lens of his eventual treason. As Theresa Strouth Gaul notes of Boudinot:

> Despite the availability of many of his writings in Perdue's *Cherokee Editor*, he has not shared in the critical attention accorded other American Indians who produced texts during this period. Possibly the neglect stems from a generic cause, since most of his writings were journalistic, a form of writing often ignored by literary critics. Perhaps the perception of him as an entirely assimilated and Christianized Cherokee does not attract critics interested in "authentic" Indian voices, or maybe the historical infamy attached to his subsequent role in the Cherokee removal proves problematic to modern scholars. (50)

Frequently, Boudinot is labeled as simply "pro-Removal," a designation that flattens the reality of his long work against the state and national forces that relentlessly assaulted southeastern Native nations.[6] As Daniel Heath Justice offers, the Treaty Party members are also read continually as "tragic martyrs," yet as he argues these readings of romantic sympathy do little for understanding the complex moral and ethical negotiations between those who eventually signed the treaty and Chief John Ross who persisted with the Cherokee people's resistance. In his analysis, Justice offers a reading of the Treaty of New Echota itself and Ross's writings. Although examining a different set of materials, I take his intellectual lead in contextualizing the archive I offer in order to contribute to a "critical conversation between the individual and collective histories, writings, and struggles that emerged from a troubled time" in order to "better [understand the] more vexing issues of Georgia's campaign of ethnic cleansing and the Cherokee response" (Justice 58, 57). In my contextualization of Boudinot and his work in the *Phoenix* within the southern print landscape, I also seek to foreground the region-wide dynamics from the Carolinas to Alabama that precipitated the large-scale human rights abuse of Removal.

Like Boudinot, Simms's reception has also suffered. According to many critics, this results from a long critical neglect that emerges from a largely New England focus on pre–Civil War literature.[7] Simms's work embodies almost all of the elements of his antebellum southern cultural mores, including intense racism and an excessive belief in the superiority of a well-bred white southern ascendancy. Simms represents for many readers and critics a southern Confederate, a designation that he himself would not have shirked. As John Caldwell Guilds offers, Simms was "always a Southern nationalist," and based on a reading of his correspondence, "there can be no doubt that the novelist strongly advocated secession" (*Simms* 272–73). He even went so far as to draw up strategic plans complete with diagrams for the defense of

Charleston, which he submitted to South Carolina's secretary of war, General David Flavel Jamison. Interestingly, however, despite his staunch defense of the region in letters to his northern contemporaries where he "vigorously defended South Carolina's every action and painted favorable pictures of the quality of plantation life," when writing to fellow southerners, "he lamented [...] the state's inefficient leadership and its people's financial hardships" (Guilds, *Simms* 278–79). Thus, Simms shifted his information for his audience, and in so doing he gives us a glimpse into the contradictions of a white southern point of view that defends the Confederacy while acknowledging the problems of the region's morally, legally, and logistically precarious economy. Nonetheless, Simms's public and private writings reflect his Confederate nationalism, and this stance renders him as an author who might (rightfully so) be difficult to appreciate in our own time. Furthermore, to attempt a "recovery" of Simms by claiming he was not really as racist or as "Confederate" as we might initially think is a fruitless task. Rather, Simms's critics need to accept that his thoughts were likely as reprehensible as he himself represents them. It is not presentism to acknowledge his flaws, and his deeply troubling ideology does not mean we should not study his works. I argue that by giving Simms our full consideration we might better understand the mechanisms by which racist ideology finds root in our own time. In short, we must read more authors than the ones that simply confirm our own political values or our imaginations of who or what we might have been or the decisions we might have made in the same situation.

The first half of this chapter reads the cultural artifacts of print that surrounded Boudinot and Simms as largely staged and dependent on what the audience may or may not see given their vantage point. In other words, just because two events occur on stage at the same time does not mean the audience notices both simultaneously. Likewise, two articles' proximity to one another in a newspaper does not guarantee that any given reader would see or even notice both works. However, like the stage, examining the print cultures that circulate throughout a period gives us a sense of the possibilities of understanding that permeated the cultural milieu. The correlation of Boudinot and Simms in the period does not suggest a causation between their works and the cultural attitudes pervasive across the region; however, placing the two authors in the context of one another and the surrounding print culture allows us to imagine what the multifaceted and diverse nineteenth-century southern audience might see. This in turn can help us understand the eventual ability of the white southern audience to consume readily a linked history of Native dispossession and white southern defeat. As Elisa Tamarkin has argued, newspaper editors and printers during the mid- to later nineteenth century formed their papers in ways akin to how we might discuss painters, arranging the news in terms of perspective. However, as she points out, perspective depends on one's vantage point, and "The problem with perspective in a painting or a newspaper is that it takes a great deal of control to ensure that we 'get the picture' when we see it" (199). Within this framework, questions of audience become paramount.

Therefore, I examine the southern print cultures from just before the Civil War in order to understand how varied southern audiences engaged in debates over Removal alongside fomenting secessionist ideologies. By tracking this narrative as it played out in the print cultures of the period, we can illuminate the crucial tenets of white southern identity that allowed for the shift into a narrative of the Lost Cause that incorporates Native history and identity into the eventual red state. In this shift, we can see the ways that the complexities of the plantation economy allowed white southern audiences to displace their own concerns over the unsustainability of their own system onto the cipher of Native nations. As John Boles outlines, social and economic historians have long debated the worth of the plantation economy in the region. Numerous critics have attempted to articulate the economic structure of the region in terms of its profitability on either an individualized micro or collective macro scale.[8] Like Boles, I contend that this focus on profit only reifies the plantation economy at the expense of ignoring the very unsustainable nature of the system. No doubt, many in the U.S. South profited from the system. However, this profit was at the expense of a land depleted in pursuit of a one-crop commodity market, a people forced to perform brutal labor without wages or human rights, and yet another people who, although free, had their earning power negated by the presence of the enslaved labor system. In addition to this, the corrupt market system in turn corrupted those of racial and economic privilege who were conditioned in inhumane and anti-ecological practices. This conditioning led to widespread abuses of power and likely resulted in the internal corruption that Simms complains privately about in his letters to fellow southerners. While we cannot definitively know how people in the U.S. South understood these conditions in the contexts of their own lives, it takes little to imagine that like Simms, many in the region were recognizing the effects of an economy based on land and human abuse. Within these moments of recognition, I isolate how the region's Native presence—as a group who suffered the material effects from both the land and human abuses of the plantation economy—came to stand in as a convenient cipher for white regional concerns over the system the U.S. South had created. This allows us to see how neither Removal nor the Civil War were entirely states of exceptionalism but rather predictable events in the creation of a conceptual red state that depends on narratives of indigeneity to make claims to an exceptional status.

In the case of both Simms's and Boudinot's work, we can see a continued critical reception that seems to recapitulate the contemporaneous discourse of their careers. This continued critical reception of these authors flattens the registers of reception across varied audiences and across centuries, and it reinscribes the same logic of Removal onto the Native South. While Boudinot has been read largely as an assimilated sellout, Simms receives an increasing reputation as a "sympathetic" author of the region's Native history. This continued trend is troubling. It neglects the historical pressures on Native communities, and at times it runs counter to Simms's printed sentiments from the period.

In the recapitulation of this logic through present-day critical discourse, this structure seemingly goes unchallenged in ways that continue to fetishize the loss of the ascendent white South at the expense of everyone else. Furthermore, as I examine later, we can see Native communities pushing back against their incorporations into white southern feelings, demonstrating their distinct national and cultural identities. Ultimately, in contextualizing the period's print cultures, we may be able to see how for authors such as Marinda Branson Moore, American Indian identity and land claim went from an intolerable fact for the U.S. South to a cause for divine retribution in the onset of the Civil War. From there, we can see how these narratives have been reimagined in the contemporary red state. Taken together, these issues signal the ways in which reperiodization can illuminate moments when structures of feeling resonant with a later Lost Cause predated the Civil War and worked to legitimate the "necessity" of Indian Removal. These supposed crisis moments in the U.S. South seem to coalesce around anxieties about a plantation economy that must continually subsume land and people and render itself "necessary" to the larger U.S. national economy through myths of indigeneity. I close with an examination of how these debates have been reread and re-presented through the spiralic time since Removal and leading up to our current political moment when Donald Trump has decided to hang Andrew Jackson's portrait in the Oval Office as a guiding spirit of his own political legacy.

Reading Removal in the South: The Devil, the Details, and Georgia

Like most historical narratives and their popular afterlives in the cultural imagination, Indian Removal in the U.S. Southeast was a far more complicated and drawn-out process than the most frequently considered moment of the Cherokee Trail of Tears. This is not to downplay the significance of this singular event for the Cherokee but to foreground the ways that many accounts of Removal do not fully consider the constellation of events ranging from the Choctaw Treaty of Dancing Rabbit Creek in Mississippi to the Creek Indian controversy with the McIntosh Party in Georgia. Such a larger view also necessitates that we consider the longer temporal range of Indian

Removal as a process that dates back to at least Thomas Jefferson and entered the public consciousness well before the 1830s. Additionally, while much of the history of Removal focuses on Andrew Jackson and the U.S. Supreme Court decisions in the Cherokee cases, particularly *Cherokee Nation v. Georgia* (1831) and *Worcester v. Georgia* (1832), recent scholarship such as Tim Alan Garrison's *The Legal Ideology of Removal: The Southern Judiciary and the Sovereignty of Native American Nations* (1997) demonstrates how questions of American Indian sovereignty played out largely in the state courts. Garrison's analysis is important because a narrow focus on the individual actors in the Removal debates obscures the systemic mechanisms of the pre–Civil War juridical and economic structures that made the large-scale human rights abuse of Indian Removal—and to a certain extent, the enslavement of African people—possible.

Because of the frequent flattening of the history of Indian Removal into a single exceptional narrative of the Cherokee Trail of Tears, I would first like to offer a general (and admittedly broad-stroked) overview of the multifaceted events occurring in the U.S. Southeast at this time with respect to Indian policy and Native resistance. Throughout the chapter, I will refer back to these moments in more detail, but for now, I outline the larger constellation of events that serve as a historical background to the Removal accounts I examine. Pressure for southeastern Indian Removal began in earnest during the early decades of the nineteenth century. Encouraged by Georgia's insistence on the enforcement of the 1802 compact with the federal government to remove any Indians within the state's borders, other southern states began pressuring the federal government to make good on its troubling promise. The Creek Red Stick War, where the United States was led by General Andrew Jackson, exacerbated the regional feelings of white people against Native people and resulted in the Treaty of Fort Jackson in 1814, which ceded 33 million acres (approximately half of all Creek lands). In the mid-1820s pressure from Georgia continued to mount for Creek Removal. Now aided by Alabama, the state created largely by the Treaty of Fort Jackson, Georgia put pressure on then-president John Quincy Adams to gain further cessions from the Creek and the Cherokee to support a growing plantation economy. In the first Treaty of Indian Springs, Creek leaders, including the notoriously problematic William McIntosh, whom I discuss later in the chapter, ceded even more territory to the United States and to the state of Georgia in particular. McIntosh had supported the United States against the traditionalist faction of the Creeks in the Red Stick War, and he was first cousins with Governor George Troup of Georgia. While this first treaty was controversial, it was nothing compared to the second Treaty of Indian Springs. Called by historian Angela Pulley Hudson "by far the most transparently fraudulent, self-interested, and deceitful of all the treaties conducted between the United States and the

Creeks to that date," this treaty represented a policy shift into wholesale land acquisition and explicit language extinguishing title in exchange for Indian Removal beyond the Mississippi (*Creek Paths* 141). Notably, many Creeks vociferously opposed the treaty and recognized McIntosh as a traitor to his nation who involved himself in backroom politics. As part of the protest of this treaty, Creek leaders solicited the assistance of two prominent young Cherokee citizens: John Ridge and David Vann. These men quickly became targets of pro-Removal southerners, and in this case, we can glimpse the intertribal discourse of the period where tribal nations assisted one another against the threats of Removal.[9]

Following the Treaty of Indian Springs, Andrew Jackson defeated John Quincy Adams for the presidency. Jackson openly supported southeastern Indian Removal during his campaign, and it came as little surprise when he signed the Indian Removal Act in May 1830. This federal law, however, only buttressed the work and sentiments of many in the southern states. The first Removal treaty signed after the passage of the federal legislation was with the Choctaw in September 1830. The Treaty of Dancing Rabbit Creek called for the cession of 11 million acres of Choctaw lands and the removal of the Choctaw Nation to Indian Territory. Those Choctaw who chose to remain in present-day Mississippi would have the laws of the state extended over them. The Choctaw suffered numerous deaths during their removal to Indian Territory, and although in what we might see today as tragically romantic terms, Alexis de Tocqueville recorded their passage through Memphis as a somber and despairing sight.[10] After Choctaw Removal, the state governments put even more pressure on the remaining tribal nations. Having lost their Georgia lands in the second Treaty of Indian Springs, the Creek eventually were forced into signing away their remaining territory in Alabama in the Treaty of Cusseta in 1832. The Chickasaw relied heavily on monetary compensation for their ceded lands and eventually used the acquired money to purchase lands from the Choctaw in Indian Territory. The Seminole fought a military campaign against their removal from the Florida territory, and while some removed in 1832, the Seminole Nation largely held out until the late 1830s and 1840s through a series of events known as the Seminole Wars.[11]

In contrast to the Seminole, who waged military battles against the federal and state governments, the Cherokee relied primarily on legal strategies in their fight against Removal. This history is largely well known as it is the most frequently cited in a general understanding of the period. Despite the continual pressure from Georgia to extinguish Cherokee title, the Cherokee Nation held on, forming a constitutional government, founding a national newspaper, and launching a nationwide public relations campaign for their cause. Eventually, they filed suit in two famous cases now known as the Cherokee cases. In the first, *Cherokee Nation v. Georgia* (1831), the U.S. Supreme action in its location. Through these elements, it becomes easy to see how audiences might view *Horn in the West* as offering a mostly accurate historical narrative given that the performance space draws on a concrete sense of history as physical presence. Ultimately, this immersion in constructed place overrides any suspicion that the audience might have regarding the play's fictionalized characters and history. Audiences are invited into the "action" on their entrance to the theater, encouraged to participate in the drama's sense of place, and subsequently presented with a selectively ahistorical narrative that evokes feelings of land attachment.[25]

Outdoor drama director, historian, and UNC theater program affiliate Samuel Selden argues that this modified history, particularly through the use of the protagonist Geoffrey Stuart, marks the true genius of Hunter's work. He writes of *Horn in the West*: "By using such a person as the pivotal character of his drama the author has given himself a liberty not possible in his other heroes. Not having to bind himself by historical fact he has had the opportunity to do some exploring of the psychological factors in Geof Stuart's career" (Selden 8). Selden also notes that "the times and circumstances in which he finds himself are all in the records. Proud Governor Tryon, handsome John Sevier, brave and humorous Daniel Boone are all real. Even Geof's brother, John, is in the books," suggesting that Dr. Geoffrey Stuart is the brother of the British superintendent of Indian affairs for the Southern District, John Stuart, who was wrongly accused of inflaming the Cherokee against the colonial communities and Revolutionaries during the war (ibid.). By extension, then, Geoffrey is also a brother to the historical Henry Stuart, who continually wrote letters to the Wataugans on behalf of the British, urging them to vacate their settlements in acknowledged Cherokee territory. Hunter then throws the fictional Dr. Stuart in a convoluted family situation with numerous loyalties, allowing him to explore what Selden calls the "psychology" of early British American settlement.[26] Selden states that Hunter "shows how his protagonist, still true to his fundamental loyalties, is driven to the mountains to escape the blind intolerance of the sterile Colonial government and he is there changed through personal struggle and closer understanding of his fellow pioneers' search for political, economic and religious independence, into a vigorous revolutionist" (Selden 8). The play, then, according to Selden, represents a psychological experiment about the formation of a Revolutionary American identity. Over and above this, the use of the descriptive adjective "sterile" connotes that the British colonial government will not reproduce in this space, allowing for the genealogical possibilities for the future history to reside solely with the new nation. This narrative of the Revolution again uses Native history in order to legitimize a new American whiteness in the region.

This identity comes from historical circumstances, but according to Selden this psychological depth can be explored only if the characters have no historical antecedents. Selden asserts that all of the "real" personages in the play, including Nancy Ward, "have a part in influencing the mind of Geof Stuart" (Selden 8). Thus, while the audience expects history with a big "H," what they really receive is an exercise in ahistorical identity formation. When the play allows white characters to float free from history (even insists that they do so) in order to explore their complex psyches while it simultaneously pulls the Native characters from carefully documented archives and insists on their historical antecedents, it suggests that Native people serve as either periphery or exotic markers of authenticity within a British American family drama. Such a construction confirms and complicates the analysis offered by Berkhofer when he asserts that white people conceived of Indians as "ahistorical and static" (29). Interestingly, however, this static identity comes precisely from a perceived archival accuracy. While one could argue that Hunter's play must focus on the psychological depth of the colonial characters because they are in fact the protagonists of the play, it seems curious that Hunter could not have imagined a white psychology from the archives. The colonial characters become bigger than history while the Native characters in Hunter's play are confined to what was recorded about them in the archive. Nancy Ward and Dragging Canoe serve as backdrop to a larger Anglo-Saxon identity drama of fictionalized settler colonials. Grounding their representations in the archive demonstrates how "historical accuracy" does not preclude the use of Native figures to justify ahistorical land claims.

This difference in psychological history and archival antecedents speaks to the power of "truth" in these performative histories as they build and buttress the red state. As Foucault reminds us, this form of truth consists of "the ensemble of rules according to which the true and false are separated and specific effects of power attached to the true." These differences in psychological depth resonate to "a battle about the status of truth and the economic and political role it plays" (*Power/Knowledge* 132). This battle around truth allows a recognition of how certain affective attachments create narrative ties between the audience and the viewer that enable a lived continuation of ahistorical frameworks of indigeneity and original land claim. In a Foucauldian sense, the question of Geof Stuart's existence exceeds the level of correct and incorrect histories and instead speaks to how audiences understand their role as the space for the incorporation of received history into daily struggles over political and ideological presence. When the mid-century Southern Appalachian Historical Association invokes the "purest Anglo-Saxon culture" alongside "the love for private ownership of land, the love for freedom and the hatred of oppression," it creates a discursive tie linking these ideals to the psychological invention of the ahistorical Anglo-Saxon protagonist and his investment in capital through land attachment. As such, the characterization of the play, then, relies upon an affective psychology of the audience's

Court did not hear the case on its merits, as they ruled that they did not have original jurisdiction in a matter arising between tribes and states. In the second, *Worcester v. Georgia* (1832), the court did hear the case as the pursuant party was a U.S. citizen and white missionary, Samuel Worcester, who had been arrested by Georgia within the bounds of the Cherokee Nation. In summary, the court upheld the territorial and legal boundaries of the Cherokee Nation, recognizing their sovereign right to exist in their southern homelands. The executive branch, led by President Jackson, refused to honor this ruling, essentially giving Georgia the go-ahead to effect Removal on its own terms. After this ruling, the Ridges along with Elias Boudinot and others signed the Treaty of New Echota, which, as I mention above, was not only unconstitutional in a Cherokee legal sense but also represented a considerable act of personal treason on behalf of the members of the now-designated Treaty Party. While the members of the Treaty Party removed ahead of the rest of the Nation, those remaining in their homes were eventually rounded up into stockades and removed to Indian Territory in 1838, which resulted in thousands of deaths. Many of the Cherokee people in North Carolina had already taken individual 640-acre reserves, accepted state citizenship, and were under the impression that Removal would not apply to them. However, in several cases the authorities did not respect these individualized land claims, and many Cherokee people in North Carolina either hid out in order to avoid Removal or offered refuge to their Georgia counterparts.[12]

Although members of all southeastern tribes remained in the U.S. South after Removal, including what became the Eastern Band of Cherokee Indians, the vast majority were relocated to Indian Territory at great personal and national costs. Many Native people died, and the social, cultural, and legal landscape of the region was forever changed. This complex nexus of intertribal and international alliances and conflicts must be foregrounded as without it conversations about Removal run the risk of contributing to what Justice calls a "well-traveled history" that foregrounds tragedy or what Julia Coates terms a "litany of loss." As Coates argues, histories of Cherokee society often fall into two camps. She calls "progressive histories" those that center the experience of "mixed blood elites" who are considered responsible for the progress and survival of the Cherokee Nation through the venues of what might be thought of as "white" enterprises in government, religion, and business. The other camp includes the "revisionist histories" that center the experience of "full bloods" who are considered responsible for the Cherokee Nation's survival through their staunch attachment to traditional practices. Coates argues that this mixedblood/fullblood binary fails to account for the complex history of the Nation and that it ultimately serves to take responsibility away from the federal and state governments who were the real antagonists of the Cherokee Nation.[13] As Justice writes about Cherokee Removal:

"the story of the Trail isn't one just of tragedy, although it's unmistakably that, too. It's also a story about defiance, about enduring the unimaginable and still continuing on, living to rebuild and emerge from the ashes sadder but stronger than ever" (58). This fact is best represented when the chaotic machinations of Removal history are kept in view even when examining seemingly overanalyzed Cherokee figures such as Boudinot or non-Natives writing in this period such as Simms. Without this backdrop, the print cultures of the period make little sense because the original audiences of these print documents—Native and non-Native alike—were living within this very chaos.

Just as with the often underconsidered complicated nexus of events in considerations of Removal, a similar phenomenon happens when scholars discuss the *Cherokee Phoenix* or Elias Boudinot in the context of antebellum print culture. While several critics have thought about the newspaper in terms of its exceptional place as the first Native-published paper or in terms of its circulation among an antebellum New England audience invested in social issues such as abolition, there has been little work that examines the *Phoenix* as a part of the antebellum print culture in the U.S. South.[14] Indeed, the *Phoenix* had a non-Native readership in New England, but it has remained unclear to what extent non-Native southerners engaged with material from the Cherokee Nation's newspaper. Additionally, while Boudinot was without a doubt the driving force behind the content and production of much of the *Phoenix*, he was not the lone Cherokee or Native person of the U.S. South who appeared in print during the period. A survey of numerous newspapers from across the antebellum U.S. South, particularly from the early 1820s through the Cherokee Removal in the late 1830s, reveals that readers were exposed continually to Removal coverage from a variety of sources including reprints from the *Phoenix* as well as statements from Cherokee and Creek leaders such as John Ridge, George Lowery, Chilly McIntosh, Little Prince, and Yoholo Micco. An examination of figures in print culture beyond those such as Boudinot and Simms allows us to reconstruct a picture of the macrodiscourse surrounding their individual authorial acts, and it illuminates what average reading audiences in the U.S. South might understand in regard to their personal investments in and relationships to the policy of Indian Removal.

Even before publication of the *Phoenix* began, evidence from southern newspapers suggests that non-Natives in the U.S. South already viewed Cherokees as audiences and participants in the debates that circulated through the print of the period. When covering the controversy surrounding the second Treaty of Indian Springs in Alabama, the *Alabama Journal* noted in the summer of 1827: "The finger of the Cherokees may be seen in this business. That crafty people, convinced from the tone of the Georgia papers, that as soon as the difficulties with the Creeks is settled, their own nation will be the next object, are anxious to keep the excitement alive among the Creeks until the latest hour" ("Cis-Atlantic"). This reference to the Cherokee influence in Creek affairs likely has to do with John Ridge and David Vann's work with Creek delegations who protested the suspect Treaty of Indian Springs that the McIntosh Party made with the government. More interestingly, it shows the perception of the Cherokee as precisely engaged in the print cultures in its appeal to their interference and their acquired information from the Georgia papers. This reflexive logic demonstrates the danger of a critical flattening audience in the antebellum period. Not only is it entirely logical that Cherokee people were in fact consumers of the period's print cultures, but it was an acknowledged fact among other consumers of newspapers, indicating that the imagined communities of the antebellum period were both varied and aware of their differences in perspective.

As might be suspected, excerpts from the *Phoenix* indeed appear in numerous non-Native southern newspapers. However, these inclusions are frequently undermined by their textual proximity to other events. Continually, when non-Native southern newspapers printed excerpts from the *Phoenix*, they included material from other current events that sent an almost cross-purpose message to the audience. The tacit implication of many of these inclusions remains that Native people, despite their coalescence around a new print culture, will lose the bureaucratic and legal battles that have been rigged against them from the start. For example, from 1824 until 1830, the *Augusta Chronicle and Georgia Advertiser* offered linked coverage of the Creek controversy over the Treaty of Indian Springs and battles over Cherokee Nation activity within what they argued were Georgia's territorial borders. It is apparent from a close survey of the paper from this period that these two events were not perceived as separate in the paper's editorial decision-making. If anything, they were linked by rhetoric, notable players, and legal questions over nullification and states' rights. As with the previously quoted *Alabama Journal*, the Georgia papers draw a clear line between the work of John Ridge and David Vann and the Creek Nation's dissatisfaction with the Treaty of Indian Springs. In one instance, the *Augusta Chronicle* refers to the two Cherokee men as "intermeddlers" and "mischief makers" who manipulated the Creeks with their "cunning and interested talk" ("Creek Treaty"). The prevalence of these linked issues in the pre–Civil War southern papers indicates not only that non-Natives in the region were exposed to debates about Native policy and sovereignty, but also that the print coverage of these issues was foundational in many pre–Civil War conceptions of a fomenting idea of states' rights. I argue that in these moments, we witness a consolidation of the conceptual red state that depends on the idea of Native loss combined with land dispossession.

For example, the *Augusta Chronicle* printed numerous articles indicating that the overarching questions of Native sovereignty, print culture, and state "internal improvement" projects were bound together in one tangle of systemic questions over the nature of Native nations existing within the plantation-based economy of the U.S. South. On Tuesday, November 6, 1827, the *Augusta Chronicle* included a quick piece headed "Cherokees" that notes the new Cherokee government seems to be in "full swing" as evidenced by "the first exhibition of its power," which "was the public execution of an Indian for murder." It follows this with the mention that the Cherokee government's printing materials have arrived, and then the short piece closes with the following, seemingly decontextualized fact: "They are universally opposed to the opening [of] the Canal through their country, between the Tennessee and Coosa Rivers" ("Cherokees"). This quick linkage of power, print, and infrastructure demonstrates a process by which the paper's audience becomes conditioned to questions of what Foucault deems "governmentality," where the exercise of power on the juridical body is bound up with other subtle mechanisms of social order.[15] Interestingly here, the Cherokee Nation's own development of a hierarchically enforced power on their own subject's bodies leads the reporter to the question of which government will determine the power of infrastructure for the region—a concept that has lasting implications for the debates over Removal and land use in the region.[16] The categorization of the Cherokee people as dependent on the spectacle of their internal power is subtly opposed to the more blatant exercise of a power based on infrastructure to promote the movement of materials and goods from the South to the North. In this debate, we see the concern over the development of internal national sovereignties and the ways these relations might render challenges to, or even usurpations of, the region's plantation economy.

Meanwhile, the language of race subtends the arguments. When white southerners perceive that Native governments are beginning to exercise internal structures of power, they express nervousness. When this exercise of power then extends to the ways that infrastructure will control the flow of goods and capital from the North to the South, this seems to add to the cause for alarm. Furthermore, the fact that this discussion bookends a quick mention of the development of the Cherokee Nation's print culture brings us back to considerations of reading publics and audience. Therefore, ultimately, what this quick article implies for its non-Native audience is the inherent danger of a reading audience of Cherokee people with the power of their own structure of enforced governance. As Hudson argues of the Creek, the development and use of roads through Native lands constituted a significant node in the articulation of a Native sovereignty. As evidenced by coverage in the *Augusta Chronicle*, this argument extended to Cherokee sovereignty. Additionally, the exercise of Cherokee governance and the means by which to announce these explicit and implicit exercises of sovereignty clearly put the non-Native U.S.

South on notice that the Cherokee meant very clearly to remain and control their territory. One way to undermine this increasing power of the Cherokee Nation in the non-Native southern print cultures is, as I mention earlier, to manipulate the coverage of these matters through the coplacement of selected news items with countering coverage of other related issues. As the Creek controversy abated for Georgia, the debates over Cherokee Removal increased. On March 14, 1828, the *Augusta Chronicle* printed its first excerpt from the *Phoenix*: Boudinot's editorial mission statement for the paper addressed "To the Public." There is little remarkable about this inclusion except that on the back page of the same issue, the paper included an advertisement for the "Indian Spring Reserve" land sales. This advertisement began its weekly run in the paper just the week before on March 7. It reads, "In conformity to an act of the Legislature of the 22nd day of December last, 'to dispose of the McIntosh Reserve in the county of Butts'" ("Indian Spring Reserve"). This advertisement for the sale of the Creek leader McIntosh's estate potentially reminds at least some members of the reading public that there will be material land benefits for non-Natives as manipulations of the law can result in the dispossession of Native leaders.

McIntosh was one of several Native people who had established numerous internal improvements on Native land. He ran a successful inn at Indian Springs, and he established a profitable ferry service on the Chattahoochee. As Hudson notes, McIntosh "was willing to facilitate American movement through Creek lands if it meant that travelers would pass his plantations, taverns, stores, buy his goods, and keep him connected to the southern market" (*Creek Paths* 138). In other words, he facilitated and capitalized on the very internal improvements that the southern newspapers said Native people prevented. As he was well positioned in both Creek and white society because of his parentage, he used every mechanism at his disposal to succeed financially in the early U.S. South. He was eventually executed by other Creek citizens for signing the second Treaty of Indian Springs, and this fact was covered extensively in the region's newspapers during this period.[17] Many newspapers expressed ambivalence over his death as the Treaty was widely acknowledged to be fraudulent even if it did produce the desired outcome for many in the region. Furthermore, there emerges some undercurrent within the papers that many white Georgians saw McIntosh as a corrupt ally with their own Governor Troup. The inclusion of the sale of this estate represents a site where the region reveals its own ambivalences around the desire to support the participation of Native people within the region's plantation economy.

The proximity of this advertisement for the auction of former Creek lands to Boudinot's editorial mission statement for the *Phoenix* signals to the reading public that, with the "excitement" ended with the Creeks, the Cherokee Nation is indeed the next object of the battles over sovereignty and land claim in the U.S. South. It also renders public the concept of the divided Native nation, which through publicized internal disagreements, may be brought to the brink of Removal. Like the eventual Cherokee Treaty Party, it is impossible to know McIntosh's intentions in signing the Treaty of Indian Springs. However, unlike Boudinot, from many accounts, McIntosh never seemed particularly against Creek Removal so much as he was against his own personal removal from land and property that he had invested a lot of time and money into "improving."[18] With the fraudulent treaty, he ultimately secured the right for himself to remain in his estate as granted private property. However, it seems unclear to what extent the Georgia government knew that by signing the treaty McIntosh was in fact rendering himself a capital criminal by the Creek Nation.

All of this complicated intrigue aside, what remains is the fact that for nineteenth-century southern audiences there was not necessarily a clearly demarcated line between Native people and those invested in the plantation economy; these were not mutually exclusive categories. In other words, McIntosh represented a person clearly invested in the economic system of his place and time, and just as his land now appeared for public auction, so might the Cherokee Nation's if there was a steadfast course of divide, systemize, and conquer. Through projection and fantasies of beleaguerment that support the Native state, white southerners were eventually able to read their own defeat within the framework they had previously established. From the revolutionary Native imagined in the previous chapter, the tragically defeated Native emerges in narratives of Removal, and because across both of the narrative formations white southerners identified themselves as suffering oppression from northern states and the federal government, the psychological leap from disdain of to bond in anguish with Native people is not as wide as one might imagine. This is all the more true given that each is but a projected fantasy of the "Native" rather than living Native individuals engaged in self-determination.

The instances of complicated textual proximity that support the conflation of Native and southern loss continue throughout the Removal debates, and excerpts from the *Phoenix* appear throughout the 1820s and 1830s in non-Native newspapers. These editorial decisions were not limited to the *Augusta Chronicle* or to Creek matters. Under this subject heading of "Indian News," editors often printed excerpts from the *Phoenix* alongside coverage of the Seminole affairs in Florida, suggesting that the violence farther south stood in direct correlation to the dangers of Native national sovereignty. Most disturbingly, reprints from the *Phoenix* also appear alongside news of gold finds in the northern part of the state, and like the *Geographical Reader, for the Dixie Children*, at least one of these instances from the *Augusta Chronicle* links the U.S. South in a nexus of Mexico and Peru where the newfound abundance of gold will endanger stability in the region as people turn from agricultural enterprises to "gold fever." On April 21, 1830, the *Augusta Chronicle* noted that such a shift in the economy will only benefit individuals at the detriment of the country's larger prosperity as the "injurious" economy will supplant the "sugar region" with the "gold region." While the article names no Native tribes, it highlights the significant concern in the region for the necessity of animating a plantation, agricultural-based system over and above any newfound wealth. Tellingly, the article is placed immediately below correspondence from one Abraham A. Heard through a transcribed Q&A for the senatorial record where Heard accuses the Cherokee Nation of being based on a corrupt economy where a wealthy and powerful 10 percent control the land and money of the entire Nation. He claims that the "suffering majority" would prefer removal if they were educated beyond their "miserable, ignorant, and debased" condition. Such a concern for the maintenance of the imagined egalitarian agricultural sugar economy (read: enslaved labor–based plantation economy) alongside a condemnation of the wealthy 10 percent of the Cherokee Nation is surely an exercise in strategic consciousness where the white audience is led to believe almost oppositional arguments about their very same economic structure.[19]

In at least one case, on November 13, 1830, the *Georgia Journal* completely undermined the content of the original publication by printing a rare pro-Removal appeal to the Cherokee from the *Phoenix*. This excerpt takes up almost the entirety of the newspaper's front page, and alongside it sits an advertisement for "Georgia Gold." The letter from Secretary of War and prominent Jackson advisor John Eaton enumerates the arguments for Removal and attempts to convince the original Cherokee audience that their corrupt leadership desires to prevent Removal in order to maintain their own land-hungry power and that Removal would constitute an opportunity for more Cherokee people to have more land. The reprinting of this letter from the *Phoenix* in the *Georgia Journal* complicates the registers of reception as it appeals to the non-Native audience's desire for Removal by demonstrating the awareness of the pro-Removal argument among the presumed *Phoenix* audience. This combination of faulty contextualization with the other instances of cross-purposed placement renders the inclusion of the *Phoenix* in these southern newspapers evidence of more than simply an "exceptional" Native paper, but rather a paper fully a part of its pre–Civil War southern print culture. This culture of reprinting and reception serves as a type of intelligence gathering between the Georgia and Cherokee print cultures that demonstrates the continual question of audience in the U.S. South. This leads to the perpetual and necessary question of the field: whose South do we imagine in the region's print cultures? How does the conflation of these audiences lend itself to a later critical flattening of the Native and non-Native experiences of the region?

Front page of the *Georgia Journal*, November 13, 1830, showing reprinted material from the *Cherokee Phoenix* and advertisements for "Georgia Gold." Courtesy of the American Antiquarian Society.

> Milledgeville, Oct. 30—wtd   JOHN MILLER, Secretary.
>
> ## INDIAN AFFAIRS.
>
> *From the Cherokee Phœnix, of Oct. 16.*
>
> FRANKLIN, TEN. 29th July, 1830.
>
> DEAR SIR—On the subject of removal it is matter of regret to find, that with all the

Reprint from the *Cherokee Phoenix* in the *Georgia Journal*, November 13, 1830. Courtesy of the American Antiquarian Society.

> Milledgeville, Oct 30
>
> # GEORGIA GOLD!!
> ## L. PERKINS
>
> HAS just returned from New York, with a rich assortment of
>
> ### FINE JEWELRY,
>
> manufactured of GEORGIA GOLD, and under his immediate inspection—consisting of Gentlemen's and Ladies' Patent Lever Watches, Seals and Keys; Cable, Loop, & Basket Neck Chains; Breast-pins, Ear-rings, and Finger-rings; Minature Lockets; Medalions, gold and silver leaf—Also, Silver Patent Lever and Plain Watches; Silver and Plated Table, Tea, Desert and Soup Spoons; ever pointed Pencil Cases, Plated Castors, Candlesticks, Cake Baskets, Snuffers and Trays, Silver Spectacles and Thimbles, Britania Coffee and Tea Pots, do. Spoons and Ladles, Shell Combs, Pocket Books and Purses, Dirks and Knives, Rodgers' Pocket and Pen Knives, Razors and Scissors, Walking Canes.
>
> ### MILITARY GOODS,
>
> Consisting of Gilt and Plated Epaulets, Belts, Spurs, Hats, Lace, Buttons, Cord, Cockades, & Eagles, Travelling & Pocket Pistols.
>
> The above added to the former stock will make a very complete assortment, which are offered at wholesale and retail, as low as at any other establishment in the Southern country.
>
> OLD and NEW GOLD or SILVER received for any of the above articles. WATCHES and CLOCKS repaired as usual.
>
> Milledgeville, Oct 16—0t

Advertisement for "Georgia Gold" on the front page of the *Georgia Journal*, November 13, 1830. Courtesy of the American Antiquarian Society.

More problematic than the coplacement of print and displacement of economic structure is the rhetoric of the beleaguered U.S. South that appears in the debates over Removal. Several decades before the Civil War, the issue of Indian Removal represents one of the hotbeds of the question of states' rights. Alongside the South Carolina Nullification Crisis, Indian Removal constitutes a place around which white southern identity expresses its sense of abjection. This rhetoric is akin to what we now think of as Lost Cause–style appeal for the region. However, this is before the Confederate Lost Cause existed, and as such we must nuance our periodization of the concept of loss as informing white southern ideology. During the Removal period, Georgia and Alabama papers in particular expressed the language of total repression in the states' inability to persuade northern states or the federal government to support the removal of Indian people within their borders. They use this language in relationship to both the Creek and the Cherokee as far back as the 1820s, demonstrating that the imagined period of Native loss around the Trail of Tears in the late 1830s constitutes but one moment in what was a protracted debate around the question of land use and the psychological construction of an oppositional white southern identity beleaguered by a backwardness attributed to the Native people in "their" borders. For example, a letter from Andrew Dexter printed in the *Alabama Journal* in August 1828 speaks of the "Indians that remain within Alabama's borders"—a statement likely directed toward the Creek Nation—and notes that their removal is necessary as "They may also oppose as heretofore, the improvements of our roads and navigable waters, within their limits; prevent new roads and canals, which may be necessary for the convenience of travelers, and for the transportation of the products of agriculture and merchandize; and may thus diminish the intercourse and trade between different parts of the State, and of our sister States, which may be of the greatest importance to their mutual interests" (Dexter). Furthermore, he accuses the very population of Native people as "exclud[ing] a much greater population of white settlers, which would increase our agricultural products, and add greatly to the strength and political importance of our State, as a member of the federal confederacy." Dexter argues that "Indians [...] can add nothing to the value of our products, and constitute what Adam Smith calls an unprofitable class."[20] Here, Dexter creates an imagined burden of the Native population for the white southerner.

Similar rhetoric appears time and again throughout the pre–Civil War southern newspapers. In several instances it seems that the Georgia papers attempt to make the case that the Native people are, in fact, the very thing holding the state back from progress in that they stand in the way of internal improvements. On July 12, 1826, the *Augusta Chronicle* noted that the state is "disgraced" by their neglect from the general government over the Creek controversy and the Creek Nation's denial to allow a surveyor to enter their territory and exhorts, "shall Georgia wait till she is completely crushed to cry *revenge* and to demand and require satisfaction for the manifold injuries she has received!!" ("News from the Cherokees"). Later, *The Southron*, published in Washington, Georgia, argues that if the larger country imagines the state as backward, and if Native nations prohibit internal improvements, then "the privation of the lands yet in the occupation of the Indians, must be ascribed the backwardness of Georgia in internal improvements, [thus] measures ought to be adopted by which those lands could be immediately obtained" ("Cherokee Indians—Proceedings in Congress"). And in a clear example of the tone of the Georgia papers as imagining themselves persecuted by the general government while their northern neighbors are encouraged, two years later, on January 23, 1830, the *Georgia Journal* alerted their readers that "The state of New York more fortunate, and better favoured than Georgia, is left free to manage her local concerns as she pleases," as "She can hold treaties with the few Indians still remaining within her chartered limits, for land in their occupation without the intervention of the federal government." It continues: "Meetings have not been held to prevent New York from *inducing* the Indians to emigrate to Green Bay; and no memorials have been presented to Congress, praying the federal legislature to interpose its authority, in order to protect the unfortunate Indians from the *rapacity* and *inhumanity* of the people of New York" ("New York Indians"). While there may be an element of truth to the argument that Removal was not simply a southern phenomenon, the constellation of this rhetoric from the numerous papers indicates that the issue of Removal was one by which southern audiences imagined themselves as both backward and neglected by the federal government while their northern counterparts reaped material rewards from being encouraged and indulged in their autonomous decisions regarding Indian policy.[21]

Another problem that appears across some of the Georgia papers is not only the belief that Cherokee people stand in the way of "internal improvements" but that they are inherently corrupt because they have an economy that is divided into two classes: one that controls the money and resources through their privilege, and one that labors. In several places the Cherokee people are critiqued for their supposedly hierarchical system. The pro-Removal lobbyers attempt to use the rhetoric of sympathy with those "unfortunate Cherokee people" who can only be saved from this system if they are moved to Indian Territory to have their own lands so that they can compete with those of privilege within their own tribe. As I quote above, the *Augusta Chronicle* notes in their reprinted senatorial Q&A that certain "informants" charge that the Cherokee have a hierarchical society and that Removal would allow for the larger populace to have a greater share in the potential for success via land acquisition. In December 1830 the *Augusta Chronicle* informs their readers that "it is known that there are two classes among the Cherokees very widely separated from each other. One consists of white men with Indian families, and the half-breeds. This class has both wealth and intelligence, and by its influence now controls the tribe" ("Executive Department"). This corrupt economy with a wealthy 10 percent who exploit the land and control the tribe sounds not so much like a Cherokee economy but an economy of the plantation-based U.S. South.[22]

This turn in logic, which faults the Native people and nations for the problems of Georgia and places Georgia in an imagined oppressed state because they cannot simply kick all of the Native people off the land as their northern counterparts had done, represents a tacit acknowledgment of some of the inherent problems of the plantation economy that controls the state. In other words, Georgia places its own systemic problems onto the Cherokee, which allows them later to easily render their own Civil War trauma onto the same loss of the Native nation. In essence, Georgia was already mourning its unsustainable enslaved labor–based system before that system was jeopardized by the Civil War. Perhaps, then, it is little surprise that during the height of the war, the Dixie schoolchildren were told that their own misfortunes represented retribution for their dispossession of Native people—people who they are told had become "civilized" through their adoption of plantation society and use of print culture.

The Cherokee recognized the irony in the comparison between themselves and their non-Native Georgian counterparts. Under Boudinot's editorial leadership, in August 1831 the *Phoenix* directly satirizes the sympathy of many of their "supporters," particularly the ones who call for Removal because of their supposed "degraded condition" in Georgia. The short article reads:

> Some of our good neighbors have lately shed abundance of tears on our account, and have mourned over our wretched and degraded condition. We cannot blame them for their tender sympathies, when they are sincere, and when not prompted by selfish considerations. But is there not something nearer home which may command a portion of their commiseration? Is there not a degree of savageness among some of the citizens of Georgia greatly superior to that existing among the Cherokees? But we see no tears shed for *them*—we hear no editors mourning over them—no exertions are used to better *their* condition, and to teach them better manners by inducing them to remove beyond the limits of the state. We rather suspect, therefore, that our *humane* friends are not as sincere as they pretend to be, and that their tears are but "crocodell teres." ("Civilized Correspondence")

Aside from the clear satire of the power of sympathy in its inability to feel anything for the "poor Georgians," the editorial comment also does a remarkable job of critiquing the virulent sentiments of at least one non-Native Georgian reader of the *Phoenix*. Additionally, it again points to the interchanges between the Cherokee and larger pre–Civil War print cultures in its appeal to "editors mourning." Not only does the article mock those who pretend to sympathize with Native people in favor of Removal, but it also makes fun of a letter to the paper from a man named Ralph Scruggs. His original letter to the *Phoenix* represents some of the worst of Georgian sentiments against the Cherokee, but the *Phoenix* prints his remarks nonetheless. Scruggs writes: "In looking over the last Cherokee Phoenix I noticed the remarks you made in that paper concerning the Georgia Guard &c and about the President &c Now you d—d little frog eater and worsp destroyer if you dont mind I will sell you as a negro, for you favor a negro more than a d—d Indian." He continues, "I intend to tie you and [David Vann] up and give you five hundred lashes if any more complaints are made about Georgia. There is that d—d broken leged Andy Ross I have sold him to a free negro in Georgia. Now where is all the Indian simpathisers and the crocodell teres that has been shed about the Georgia law you d—d * * rascals" (Scruggs). Closing by calling David Vann and presumably Boudinot "d—d scunks of hell" and warning if they do not remove to "the Arkansas" that he will scalp them, Scruggs then signs his letter, "Yours with indifference." The letter is filled with hatred, and so completely far from "indifferent" that one wonders if Scruggs even knows what the word means. It also exposes the lack of reason and degree of hatred coursing through the pro-Removal Georgian populace. Alongside this indictment from Scruggs, the *Phoenix* prints a drawing they received of a man being hanged, clearly suggesting the level of violence their white neighbors were threatening ahead of Removal. Boudinot's editorial choice to print this material shows his full engagement and awareness of the climate that surrounded the Cherokee Nation, and it helps later readers fully appreciate the paper's existence within the U.S. South.

As for the later marriage of southern loss and Removal within the southern consciousness, we have to look toward the continued duties of the paper after Boudinot's ousting as editor. Boudinot is eventually relieved from his editorial duties at the *Phoenix* because of his desire to express the pro-Removal argument as a means of national survival. Importantly, without him the Cherokee remain resolute. They do not represent a litany of loss, nor do they accept defeat. In the last issue of the pre-Removal *Phoenix*, before the press was seized by the state of Georgia in 1835, Elijah Hicks, the editor who replaced Boudinot, closes with this moving exhortation, printed in both English and the Cherokee syllabary: "To our Cherokee readers we would say, DON'T GIVE UP THE SHIP; although our enemies are numerous, we are yet in the land of the living and of our clearly recognized rights. Improve your children, in morality and religion, and say to intemperance now growing at our doors, depart ye cursed, and the JUDGE of all earth will impart means for the salvation of our suffering nation" (*Cherokee Phoenix* May 31, 1834). This plea to the Cherokee readers is more than a last gasp of survival, and it certainly marks a refusal to be caught up in a lost cause narrative. Rather, it reminds the reader that justice, though slow, and perhaps operating on a differing temporal scale, may prevail, and that the Cherokee then—as *today*—are yet in the land of the living. It is not enough to imagine the *Phoenix* as only a rhetorical tool aimed at non-Native readers to garner sympathy. It also stands as a profound tool of resistance against the Removal South, refusing "crocodell teres" in favor of sovereignty.

After Cherokee Removal in the late 1830s, Simms published "The Broken Arrow, an Authentic Passage from an Unwritten History" (1844), which detailed the assassination of the Creek leader William McIntosh. Guilds and Hudson note that Simms was "fascinated" by the story of McIntosh as a young man, and the short narrative historical tract demonstrates that deep interest as it foregrounds Simms's sympathy for the executed Creek leader. Like many other Native people, McIntosh was indeed bound up with the plantation and speculative economies of his time. However, his ties may have been even more complicated as his explicit family connection to the governor's office certainly enhanced his ability to capitalize on shifts in policy. As Benjamin Griffith notes, "Thus the question becomes complex whether McIntosh was the manipulator or the manipulated, the money-hungry entrepreneur or the realist who wished the best for his people in a situation that was inevitably to worsen" (230–31). I cannot say if the situation would have "inevitably worsened" without the signing of fraudulent treaties such as McIntosh chose to do, so rather than spend time faulting McIntosh for these decisions, I wish to interrogate one red state fantasy through Simms's sympathy for McIntosh.

McIntosh was a Creek man. This may seem like an unnecessary statement, but repeatedly, historians have suggested that McIntosh was largely or even totally assimilated, thus negating his Creek identity.[23] This was likely not the case. Rather, he used his powerful position in both societies in order to achieve as much material gain as he could. As Andrew Frank has argued, he was Native *and* southern. He exploited the mechanisms of the plantation economy to their limits, but this did not mean he was any less Native. He used his standing as a member of the Wind Clan of the Creek Nation to the fullest extent. He was also certainly a member of a landed class as he adopted many of the strategies of his surrounding political economy. This decision eventually cost him his life as the majority of his people recognized him as a lawbreaker, who at the expense of the many tried to secure material gain for himself. This decision, however, does not render him a "white man"; it makes him a member of the plantation economic system.

The plantation system was largely unsustainable. Southerners' willingness to identify this unsustainability in their Native counterparts signals a tacit awareness of this fact even before the Civil War. We might say that McIntosh represents a casualty of the system. While there might be many similarities in the original motives of McIntosh and the members of the Treaty Party of the Cherokee, one has to remember that the Ridges and Boudinot fought for many years against Removal. Although they too were members of the surrounding plantation economy, their specific actions differ from those of McIntosh. However, these men may have, as Griffith argues of McIntosh: "being offered continued wealth and prestige as headmen of the most powerful tribe in the West—as opposed to a position of dwindling rank and increasing white encroachment of the East—[not found] it difficult to rationalize a decision to remove, no matter what his logic or his instinct for survival dictated" (231). Therefore, we may illuminate some of our understanding of Removal under the rubric of the plantation system, but one does not simply trump the other. The surrounding economies caused numerous individuals—Native, black, and white—to make complicated decisions within their own time that do not signal the mitigation of any of these identities. When contemporary critics confuse these detailed mechanisms, they run the risk of seeing the same hierarchical faults that contemporaneous white southerners used as the justification for Removal. They make the mistake of seeing convergence as evidence of sameness. Rather, these moments, though appearing at times similar, must be held in view for their divergent genealogies.

Simms's "early and strong sympathy" for Native people, particularly those such as McIntosh, must then be reread. Echoing the papers of the 1820s, Simms writes: "the people of Georgia [. . .] felt all the inconvenience, annoyance and insecurity, which ensued from the proximity of a people so capricious and treacherous" ("Broken Arrow" 82). He then argues that in terms of national perception, "The desire of Georgia was assumed to be one growing rather out of her cupidity, than because of any real annoyance or danger from the Indians" and that as a result, in other parts of the Union, "False ideas of philanthropy prevailed" (83). Once again appealing to the logic that the southern newspapers had used a decade earlier, he argued that any sympathy for Native people "was assumed by Fancy—who sometimes puts on the habit, and looks grave, like Philosophy,—as a monstrous evil, that a people should be expelled from homes in which they had made no permanent habitation—which they had neither enriched by culture, nor made attractive by art or ingenuity" (83–84). This "injudiciously and unreasonably expressed" sympathy, he argues, *resulted* in the Native people taking the irresolute position not to be removed from their homes. He then uses the same logic that the Native "headmen" were white or "descended from white men" and that they constituted a landed class that kept the masses of their nations in a state of poverty and ignorance. These masses were not, he asserts, capable of understanding the debates, and in any case: "their nomadic life made them really indifferent to place" (84). As one can see, there is very little language of sympathy here for the majority of Native people and in no way does Simms seem to advocate against the recent past of Removal.

Simms uses the language of good and evil throughout the tract, demonstrating a red state fantasy of morals. He demonizes the Cherokee leaders for their "cupidity" and their obtaining of "money and arguments" from northern sympathizers (85–86). He argues that they only wished to retain the land after they had learned from white squatters that it possessed gold, and he noted that their mixedblood status rendered them "one of that class, which, for good or evil, will always have the most influence among the Indian tribes of our country" (86). However, when describing McIntosh, he notes that he was "an artful politician, an able orator" and that his innate gifts resulted in the jealousy of his "associate Chiefs" (87). Even though he praises McIntosh's immense natural skills, he calls the Treaty of Indian Springs a "consummated" evil (95). However, he states that McIntosh, in an effort to assure the safety and independence of his people, favored Removal. Simms renders the treaty a selfless act that results in McIntosh's death, and he fails to mention the enormous sums of money or earmarks that McIntosh guaranteed for himself alongside the retention of his own estate at Indian Springs. He romanticizes McIntosh by neglecting some details and elevating others, all of which aggrandize the paternalism of the plantation economy in his portrait of the Creek man.

When Simms mourns McIntosh, he does not mourn the man, he mourns the system. When he waxes poetic about McIntosh's death, Simms prefigures the eventual uprising throughout the region when people made decisions on both large and small scales to challenge the logic of the plantation economy. As noted at the beginning of this chapter, Simms privately acknowledged that the region, and South Carolina in particular, suffered from internal corruption and financial difficulties. The fact that he juxtaposed this acknowledgment to his fellow white southerners alongside his defense of the plantation system to his friends in the U.S. North suggests that he saw these problems as inversely related, and he sought to hide the truth from his correspondents and perhaps even himself. In so doing, he transferred his sympathies for a devilish system onto the Native man McIntosh. Simms marks McIntosh as a man of a lost cause—a true citizen of a red state. In closing the piece, Simms writes of McIntosh's execution: "Alone,—hopeless, but fearless, the beleaguered chief, like the wolf driven to his den, and rendered furious by the fire, rushed boldly to the entrance" (98). And Simms speculates of the Creek Law-Menders, "Could they but be brought to look and listen—hear his voice, feel his arguments, understand his reasoning" that they would ignore their national duty to exercise the law (98). The language of beleaguerment and feelings suggests that Simms does indeed have sympathy for the Creek McIntosh. However,

McIntosh is a Native man who acted out of accord with the laws of his own nation, who in his full participation of the plantation economy made unsustainable decisions at the expense of his fellow Creek citizens. As such, the people rose up and brought justice to what they saw as his misplaced priorities. In this act, Simms ultimately sees tragedy.

One cannot help but wonder, in this narrative of Removal and retribution, does Simms see in McIntosh the future demise of his own plantation system loyalties? Does he draw together the loss of McIntosh with his own forthcoming losses? These are questions of intention and psychology that cannot be answered fully. However, when critics today label Simms as "sympathetic," perhaps we should examine the object of this perceived sympathy. When we, as twenty-first-century audiences, read the nineteenth-century Native South, we have to ask what we choose to see. Can we see Boudinot, Simms, and others in all of their complex details as individuals caught in a nexus of choices largely overdetermined by the surrounding plantation economy? Or do we see them merely as archetypes of their respective lost causes? Readers of Guilds and Hudson's anthology *An Early and Strong Sympathy: The Indian Writings of William Gilmore Simms* will open the book to see as the frontispiece a portrait not of Simms but of McIntosh. While this decision might seem odd, it almost inadvertently hits the mark. That ultimately *is* the object of Simms's sympathy: a man who believed in the promise of a southern plantation economy and still lost it all.

"Anyone Seeking Historical or Geographical Fact Should Look Elsewhere": Narrative and Loss in Charles Frazier's *Thirteen Moons*

After the nineteenth century, southeastern Indian Removal continued to remain a narrative touchstone for many who wanted to establish a shorthand for tragedy and loss. However, from a Native perspective, the story of Removal is much more complex. Indeed, there is loss, but there is also survival. As Coates offers, "In the end, the lesson of the Trail of Tears is not one of division, betrayal, or tragedy, but one of triumph" (*Trail of Tears* xiv). From the tribes who reasserted their inherent sovereignty in Indian Territory to those who remained in the U.S. Southeast, there are numerous stories that recount how southeastern Native people refused to bend to their attempted annihilation. Likewise, there are numerous stories that, like the *Geographical Reader, for the Dixie Children* or Asa/Forrest Carter's *The Education of Little Tree*, attempt to read Removal in terms of a white consciousness of a Confederate Lost Cause.[24] Rather than acknowledge living Native people, the post–Civil War U.S. South has repeatedly returned to the narrative expectation that transforms its crimes against Native people into its own sense of defeat. Since the late nineteenth century this moment of transference has happened for authors and audiences alike. Such a conflation must be examined for the ways it denies the subjectivity of both the living Native people who have survived despite Removal and those Native people in the U.S. Southeast who remained. The white U.S. South is largely built on the narrative of Indian Removal as complete and the resulting loss as total—and this narrative is not confined to an easy periodization of the southern novel. When narratives emerge that challenge this structure, audiences have a difficult time of incorporating them into a revised worldview. Melanie Benson Taylor does a sound job of explaining this trend, but I want to push this argument a bit further into how non-Native audiences latch on to these stories and with almost a gratingly exact precision refuse to attribute anything more than loss to stories of Removal. As such, I take on some of the more problematic recent texts that attempt to retell Removal for contemporary audiences. In each case, the retelling seems to emerge from what could be considered a place of progressivism, and this is what makes these texts so difficult for audiences, both critical and commercial. Despite what might be read as attempts to pull apart white beleaguerment from Native survival, texts such as Charles Frazier's *Thirteen Moons* (2006) and the recent off-Broadway sensation *Bloody Bloody Andrew Jackson* (2006, off-Broadway season 2010) manage to snap white landed privilege back into place via the vector of audience reception that cannot account for their traffic in ahistorical epistemology and satire. In contrast, Blake Hausman's recent novel *Riding the Trail of Tears* (2011) takes this approach to task, using a speculative near future to undermine non-Natives' claim to the narrative of Removal. Together these texts demonstrate the ways in which Removal is never complete but represents an ongoing red state battle where conflicts over land claim continue to emerge as non-Native southerners buttress their own conservative fantasies with abstract ideas of Native history all the while investing in concrete policies that erode landed tribal sovereignty.

In the "Author's Note" to *Thirteen Moons*, Charles Frazier issues a somewhat stern warning to the novel's readers. He claims that not only has he altered the history of the events surrounding Cherokee Removal and the resistance to Removal with regard to the Eastern Band of Cherokee Indians, but he has also altered the very landscape on which these events take place. While a large portion of the novel narrates the actions of the protagonist, Will Cooper, in his quest to help the remaining Cherokee buy up land in the North Carolina mountains, Frazier reminds us that this is the space of fiction. Of course, such a proclamation is complicated by the historical fact that the real-life William Holland Thomas, who Frazier insists is *not* Will Cooper, did help negotiate land deals for the future Eastern Band of Cherokee Indians and by the fact that the 640-acre reserves taken by some tribal citizens did eventually become part of the present-day Eastern Band's territory.[25] These overlapping historical and geographical worlds ask us to reimagine the landscape of the southern novel as it creates a red state, where the historical narratives of land claim and attachment create structures of power that continue to affect how non-Native southern audiences perceive the continued Native presence in the region. Frazier's constant narrative refrain to the mapped space of the North Carolina mountains elicits feelings of geographical certainty for the reader, yet his direct appeal to the nonfactual nature of his geography leaves the reader disoriented as to how to understand the land's continued attachment to the sovereignty of the Cherokee people, both remaining and removed.

Thirteen Moons presents an uneasy map of the U.S. South and its corresponding southern identities. Frazier's fictional remapping of this space allows audiences to reimagine the construction and significances of the Appalachian region. Rather than a natural space associated with "hillbilly" abjection or a merely romanticized narrative such as Asa/Forrest Carter's *The Education of Little Tree*, the novel's landscape exudes sacred significances. Here I read the novel for the geography of the U.S. South that it proposes and the genealogies of the red state that result from its remapped territory. When Frazier tells audiences that locations in the novel "will not be found on a map," he precisely points to the power of colonial cartography as the overarching system by which we imagine the region's physical geography. His novel builds a new, but simultaneously very old, landscape in the U.S. South. Incorporating the complicated history of the Eastern Band of Cherokee Indians' land claims, *Thirteen Moons* attempts to propose a way to think about the region as a Native space with deep ties to its Indigenous inhabitants whether remaining or removed. Furthermore, this new construction of landscape has material implications for contemporary debates in the region regarding the use and protection of sacred sites such as Kituwah Mound, and it ultimately asks audiences to question their notions of historical and geographical knowledge when considering the U.S. South. As with Ronald Emmerich's *The Patriot*, I am not concerned with the merit of Frazier's sophomore novel, and the reader may notice that I depend heavily on the verb "attempt" when discussing what the novel does and does not do. There are many reasons, which I examine later, why the novel should be considered an incredibly unsound depiction of the Native South, not least of which is its romantic portrayal of the nineteenth-century Appalachian region. Rather, what concerns me more is how audiences—critical and popular—have responded to the novel. In these responses we see desires for the red state in a merging of the white narrator's consciousness and Cherokee characters' "losses" via Removal and the Civil War.

The desire for a detailed History (capital H intentional) in *Thirteen Moons* reverberates throughout the novel's reviews. Indeed, the novel makes a claim toward the genre of historical fiction, yet given Frazier's somewhat cryptic warning at the end of the novel, it seems that readers might remain wary of the spaces between the histories of a novel, the actual events, and their own desires. As *New York Times* book reviewer Adam Goodheart (also author of the popular and critically acclaimed *1861: The Civil War Awakening*) argues in the opening of his 2006 review of the book: "There's a certain kind of history that's made in out-of-the-way places: the swamps, the borderlands, the barren mountain ranges that no one claims. No grand political gestures, or even any memorable battles, unfold here. It's the terrain, rather, of squalid little deals, nasty skirmishes and forgotten massacres—where the reverberations of great events wreak distant havoc on singular, unchronicled lives. This is territory where novelists, not historians, sometimes make the truest guides." Goodheart's pronouncement rings true for much of Frazier's novel or almost any attempt at the genre of historical fiction. However, Frazier's novel seems intent on challenging this fetishization of local space and small-scale event as an insatiable longing of readers who desire more than fiction or history can reasonably give. The results of Frazier's subtle provocation can be found in Goodheart's later critique of the book when he expresses his irritation at Frazier's refusal to pin down the exact events of the fictional Charley's death (based on the historical Eastern Band hero, Tsali): "There's one particularly revealing moment, a climactic scene of a duel between two of the main characters. Instead of telling us how it played out, Frazier gives three alternative versions. It's as though he's saying that he doesn't know or care what his characters would really have done—or perhaps, couldn't decide which of his rough drafts he preferred. Moreover, he has his narrator announce, 'Readers may feel free to choose the story of their liking and consider it true history . . . Something happened. Beyond that, nothing is knowable.'" Goodheart concludes of this passage, "If that isn't the worst possible epigram for an author of historical fiction, I don't know what is."

Goodheart has a point about the irritation an audience might experience with Frazier's refusal to lay the imagined historical details before them, but his critique remains more interesting for the way it completely fetishizes what Kathleen Stewart calls "ordinary affects," where large-scale political and historical events may be explained by the "squalid little deals" of what Goodheart clearly considers minuscule players in the larger history of the Native South. Furthermore, Goodheart's desire to have the novel reveal to him "forgotten massacres" necessitates the question of whose memory he is inferring. Massacres are rarely forgotten by the few survivors of the victimized side, and in this comment Goodheart demonstrates the slippery nature of measuring narrative history by its affective power. Likewise, his fantasy of "barren mountain ranges that no one claims" clearly circumscribes the reality that much of the Americas *is claimed* by Indigenous people. This desire for affective history—forgotten and occurring on unclaimed land—is not so much suggestive of the world that Frazier gives the readers as the specious one they seemingly desire. Notably, this review represents the criticism of almost all other reviews of the novel on its release.

There has been relatively little, if virtually no critical reception of the novel aside from the popular reviews. Melanie Benson Taylor takes up the book in a brief mention. She calls the book deeply problematic and argues that by the end, "the merging of anticapitalist values, the Old South, and [Will Cooper's] Indian romance are complete" (*Reconstructing* 46). I agree that the novel has numerous problems regarding romantic narratives, but I would also argue that such a merging remains overwhelmingly incomplete unless the critic does the merging. Indeed, Will Cooper, the first-person narrator, desires this associative bond, but as I argue below, the narratological distancing of the first-person narration from the constructed history he attempts to tell creates a potential awareness of how the "Old South" can never merge with Native resistance even when it desires nothing more. If, as Taylor argues, readers "celebrated the romance at the novel's core and the humanistic fervor of the white chief" (a popular reader reception I have been unable to locate in my research), then this is an act of audience desire, not the narrative structure of the text (*Reconstructing* 47). She notes that it reads much like "a defense of the antebellum South," which is true given that this is *exactly* what the fictional Confederate narrator aims to do. I agree that the novel is problematic but in ways slightly different from those that Taylor suggests, and in this attempted narrative complexity it solicits the ire of popular critics, such as Goodheart, who want their historical fiction to pin down concrete details.

As evidenced by the reception trends of the novel, I argue that Frazier's work precisely points to the desire of audiences for a neatly bound narrative of affective history, and his novel implicitly critiques this desire for the narratives of southern history that result. For instance, it is hard not to read the novel as challenging the longing for the epic narrative when the narrator Cooper tells of the way that he and Bear, who seems to be modeled on the historical Yonaguska (Drowning Bear), compiled the events of Charley's death: "As a narrator, I had an overconcern with the *why* of people's actions, when really the *what* is largely all that matters. So of course it was Bear who came up with the idea of leaving everything exactly as it was, telling the story straight through just the way it happened, but flipping it with the underside up. It would be Charley who sacrificed himself for the good of his people, not the other way around." This narrative construction, as Cooper explains, "made a better story and was certainly better for Charley" (Frazier, *Thirteen Moons* 291). After Bear and Will render the events the way they see fit, "Bear told his version of Charley complete from start to finish in great detail, touching up the dignity and the tragedy, giving it a high degree of shine. And it was so good that about all I could think to add was a little *Et tu, Brutus?* touch at the moment before execution. It was not much of a creative contribution, but I'm proud of it nevertheless. And later, the journalists ate it up" (291). These later journalists from the novel who "ate up" the constructed story may be akin to the very real-world reviewers who find themselves irritated by Frazier's insistence at the unknowable. Given the long historical debate about the details of Tsali's death, Frazier's ending is not only the most likely summary of the actual events, but it also renders visible the narrative construction of all history. Perhaps even more importantly, it distances the actual history from the teller—an aging Confederate general who many real-life historians speculate died after experiencing the effects of late-stage syphilitic dementia. In this way, *Thirteen Moons* frustrates the desires of readers who long for the narrative history of ordinary affects.

The first chapter of *Thirteen Moons* signals that mapping, fictional genealogies, and loss will represent the novel's central concerns. The chapter begins with Will describing death as "the last unmapped country"; he writes in the Cherokee syllabary while reading *The Knight of the Cart* and contemplating that "The gist of the story is that even when all else is lost and gone forever, there is yearning" (3, 5). He asserts that in his reflective old age, "Memory is about the only intoxicant left," and that "if you don't watch out you can spend all your time tallying your losses and gains in an endless narrative" (5, 6). Together these three elements inform the construction of a history of the Native South. Rather than offer a totalizing narrative of how this or that event occurred, the novel pushes against these concerns, asking the audience to consider what productivity lies in attempting to know the unknowable, remember the unrecoverable. It forces audiences to consider what narratives they expect or desire when considering Native history. The novel attempts to dislodge the narrative of the white Confederate narrator from the loss of the Cherokee people. It creates a distance between the narrator's subjective memory as a totalizing story that recounts a litany of loss based on his own Lost Cause posture and the emplotment of small victories that the Cherokee characters seem to be winning.

As a narrator, Will Cooper obsesses over narrative structures that render tragedy onto the physical space. As such, the specter of mapping hangs over the text, cordoning off what remains unknowable from the ordered rendition of space onto the page. As the orphaned Will travels west into Cherokee land to make his start as a storekeeper after having been indentured to this profession by his aunt and uncle, he notes that his "map was a real map, from a printer's shop, the result of a survey commissioned by some variety of government that claimed sovereignty hereabouts," and that the "land I had already traversed was displayed in fine detail regarding state and boundary lines, towns, and turnpikes and traces, mountains and rivers" (28–29). However, as Cooper continues on the map he observes, "But westward, at a point where I guessed I was, the map turned abruptly white and all the geographic opinion it ventured further was the words INDIAN TERRITORY, lettered rather big. No fading or tapering off. Everything halted all at once" (29). This construction of space is not lost on Will, and he tells the reader, "So the lesson the map taught was that knowledge has strict limits, and beyond that verge the world itself might become equally unspecified and provisional" (29). This unknowability relates to the abdication of facts on which Frazier insists in his author's note. *Thirteen Moons* refuses to make the connection between narrative history and mutable land claim. Will's map does not claim the blank space; rather, it recognizes that such a space exists in another possible realm. It is not the renamed "Lynch's Creek" from my discussion of Simms in chapter 2, and it is not the "lost" space of Roanoke begging for recovery. It halts at what it does not know. Such a refusal echoes Franco Moretti's assessment of the internal border present in the European novel: "Internal borders define modern states as composite structures, then, made of many temporal layers: as *historical* states—that need historical novels." He continues, "Historical novels are not just stories 'of' the border, but of its erasure, and of the incorporation of the internal periphery into the large unit of the state" (40). Unlike several of the texts I examined earlier, Frazier's novel unsettles the link between the reception of history and the setting of its events through its use of the internal border between the Native and U.S. South. It is not simply a failed historical novel, but rather a novel that attempts, successfully or not, to name and to challenge the desire for an internal subsuming of Native land into southern space.

While the scene with the map notes the construction of knowledge as strictly limited, the novel reminds the reader that the land does indeed keep going. What cannot be rendered on the map is known, but only to certain cultures and individuals willing to see the world in particular ways. Presumably, the Cherokee people know the territory that Will is about to enter very well. Their connection to the earth precedes that of the "real map," offering a verbally ironic turn to how the novel positions Western and Indigenous knowledges as positing various claims to the real. As Will closes this section by noting of this unmapped land, "Or just give it your own name, Will River. Put your impress on the land and see if you could force it to stay how you had decided to call it," echoing the same concerns over place naming that Simms explores in *Mellichampe* (29). Such a pronouncement asks the reader to reconsider how and why places retain names, undoing a structure of power that always assumes that the mapmaker has naming rights over a land. It suggests, instead, that the land exerts its own agency in questions of naming. Later in the novel, when Will and Bear work to figure out a way to begin buying back land, Will shows Bear the government map of the territory. Bear disregards this map that "bore no resemblance to the ragged and often vertical terrain" and proceeds to "draw his own in the dirt of the floor" (279). Will asserts that Bear's "dirt map was a claim of ownership on a space of earth. Not his claim alone, but his people's" (380). Bear's knowledge of the "real places and speculative places" determines how they will go about the acquisitions for a homeland, something that Bear sees as essential for the people's identity. Therefore, in a moment of prolepsis at the novel's beginning, Will notes of the white space on his "real map" that he "knew that the white only stood proxy for a real world, an indication merely that mappists had not reached that far in their thinking" (33). In this way, the novel renders land claim and attachment as epistemological concerns rather than simply economic considerations. The novel shows the Cherokee characters as valuing their geography in wholly separate ways from their non-Indigenous neighbors in their active purchase of land precisely to avoid and/or delineate the limits of economic and commercial development at the expense of sacred earth. Furthermore, it also calls on "white" and "white space" as a fiction or "proxy" invented by those "mappists" who attempt to carve space. This invention of white map space also invites a consideration of the consolidation of whiteness in the U.S. South. In addition to this epistemological attachment to the land, the novel goes on to render this attachment as one of identity. However, in the white U.S. South's desire to create structures of attachment via the land, this construction ignores Indigenous land claim. Conversely, Bear argues that land and identity must work together, suggesting that the danger of Removal lies not simply in the economic dispossession of the territory, but in the attempt to undermine Native identity through the separation of Indigenous peoples from their sovereign lands.

The battle over land and identity emerged in political public discourse not long after the novel's publication in 2006 when Duke Energy began building the power station on the Kituwah Mound located just west of the Qualla Boundary in western North Carolina. This case played out largely in the court of public opinion, and the Cherokee success in this instance marks an interesting moment in the region where the larger audience saw a Native presence in the U.S. South and seemingly understood the impulse toward a sacred earth on Indigenous terms that should be under Indigenous control.[26] While I would not go so far as to say that this is a first, it certainly represents a different outcome than many previous battles over Native presence and land claim in the U.S. South. In what follows, I offer a brief analysis of the discourse surrounding this case in order to imagine what future might lie ahead for the region as people from all backgrounds in the U.S. South reexamine the histories of their traditional, adopted, and occupied homes.

The Cherokee people consider Kituwah as the Mother Town, a sacred space that connects them as a people. The Eastern Band of Cherokee Indians purchased the 309-acre site in 1996 after local activism spurred the initiative to reacquire the land from non-Natives. For many years after the purchase, tribal members debated the potential uses for the regained land: leave it for sacred significance or use it to generate a tourist economy. In order to have a sense of the site's former use as sacred location for ceremony and burial, the tribe enlisted the services of archaeologists to conduct a relatively noninvasive survey of the site. This survey demonstrated that the site did indeed have human burials and, as Cherokee oral history claimed, served as a location for sacred ceremonies. This confirmation quieted some of the debate within the community, and the general sense seemed to be that the site should remain as it was—a sacred space for the Cherokee people. However, in January 2010 local residents noticed that construction vehicles and material seemed to be moving up the side of the mountains in clear view of the Kituwah Mound. According to several news reports and public blogs, many community members were puzzled because there had been no announcement of or pending bids on construction in the area. Furthermore, because the mountains were in the Nantahala National Forest, many were confused about how there could be what appeared to be commercial-scale building within the federally protected space. Soon, local residents found out that Duke Energy had filed an "express" erosion permit to install a new power substation within view of the mound—a location that would obscure the Kituwah Mound from view and damage the sacred landscape.[27]

The legal wrangling continued for months as the Eastern Band of Cherokee Indians along with the Cherokee Nation and the United Keetoowah Band of Cherokee Indians together called for an immediate cessation of Duke Energy's construction project. The Eastern Band of Cherokee Indians passed a formal resolution stating it was their "solemn responsibility and moral duty to care for and protect all of Kituwah from further desecration and degradation by human agency in order to preserve the integrity of the most important site for the origination and continuation of Cherokee culture, heritage, history and identity" (McKie). Incidentally, officials of Swain County were also irritated by Duke Energy's move as they had not informed the local county officials of their construction plans. In a battle that involved several legal entities—the feds, the state, the tribal nations, the county, the utilities commission—working against and in alliance with one another, the rhetoric and popular discourse seemed especially telling around issues of cultural persistence and economic advancement of tribal peoples in the twenty-first century. Richard Thornton, amateur archaeologist and contributor for the now-defunct freelance-content site *Examiner.com*, noted that "The precedents set by this legal case could have effects elsewhere in the United States. The relative legal rights of states, Indian Tribes, counties and interstate utility companies have never really been defined by the Supreme Court," suggesting that the case may force the courts to determine the relationship of imminent domain, utilities, states, and tribal nations, an outcome that may have made many nervous given the long history of Supreme Court cases addressing other instances of tribal sovereignty in the U.S. South. The *Raleigh News and Observer* called the conflict a "modern variant of a treaty negotiation" (Murawski). However, Thornton went on to speculate in July 2010, "Duke Energy apparently gambled that it could quickly build its project before any significant legal opposition could form ... and if it was taken to court, the opponents would not have the financial strength to match Duke's legal department. However, it is a whole different Indian Stickball game when Duke goes against a Native American tribe with lots of casino money rolling in. This writer's bets are on the Cherokees." This questionably phrased linking of a new "Stickball game" and the casino economy precisely points to the tension around twenty-first-century tribes with the financial clout to buy back their sacred sites and fight in court to have those sites protected. This juxtaposition renders visible many of the historical debates around Indian Removal, and it calls on the shift in material power in the region alongside a shift in tribal economies based on casino revenue, all the while remaining tied to traditional conceptions of space and place.

Duke Energy attempted to capitalize on the idea of the "casino tribe" in their response to the public outcry. They claimed in their motion to hold the complaint in abeyance that the only reason such an upgrade was needed in the first place was to support the Eastern Band's $600 million expansion of the Harrah's Cherokee Casino and Hotel. They went on to warn that not building the power station could result in blackouts for numerous customers in the area. In this rhetorical move, the power company hoped to pit twenty-first-century gaming politics against traditional values, likely hoping to stir up resentment against a false presumption of "rich casino Indians."[28] However, this plan seemed to backfire, and many within the state and surrounding area supported the Cherokee people's call for Duke Energy to find another location. Writer John Murawski of the *News and Observer* even said that Kituwah Mound "may well be the most sacred spot in North Carolina." Even after Duke Energy relented and decided they would be a "good neighbor" and work with the tribe and county to find an alternative site, a writer for the Charlotte edition of the lifestyle magazine *Creative Loafing* noted, "Good neighbors would have been all, 'my bad, I'll find another site,' instead of duking things out bureaucratically and in the media," and she speculated that what many realized was "The rest of us have to read between the spin, yo. This story is about David v. Goliath, not about being a good neighbor or penny pinching" (Fionn-Bowman). Despite their attempts to rally an age-old resentment toward "Indians with benefits," Duke Energy failed to convince most North Carolinians that the need for a power station trumped a reverence for sacred earth.

Furthermore, as Lisa Brooks notes, this debate brings the ancient and contemporary sacred space into an immediate and visceral contact. She speculates that the Cherokee coalescence into a concentrated web presence ultimately offered part of the material victory against the energy company. The protection of Kituwah may have had more to do with the power of the people rather than their casino money. She links Kituwah as "simultaneously the place where the nation and its 'laws' emerged, where its oral traditions were inscribed, and from which its national fire was renewed and redistributed every year" along with this contemporary legal battle waged in the public web space where "the image of Kituwah makes us hold the land and its stories, ancient and contemporary, in our mind, our wired present spiraling us back to the primacy of place" (Brooks 313). This spiraling points toward another way to conceive of the way that Native sovereignty may emerge in the volute of temporalities that do not depend on linear time.

Within these new ways of imagining place, one wonders about this moral and material victory for the protection of a sacred site over industrial development. It cannot simply be that such a recognition of sacred land comes out of the larger U.S. South's own obsession with the religiosity of southern dirt. Currently, over the objections of local tribes and concerned non-Native allies, throughout Alabama sacred mounds are being destroyed for development projects such as Sam's Clubs and sporting complexes.[29] Of course, many of these tribes in Alabama either do not have federal recognition or the federally recognized tribes connected to these sites were removed in the nineteenth century by the settler-colonial governments that surrounded them, making the practical approaches to maintaining the sites more difficult. And some of these tribes do not have the backing of a tourist economy. While sacred sites farther south have been caught up in what seems to be a perpetual fight against development, the Cherokee in North Carolina pushed past a narrative of loss into a notable victory. They got Duke Energy to the table without significant government intervention, largely supported by the will of a regional non-Native public that expected the energy company to do the right thing. These contemporary power struggles between Native people and the drive for economic development in the U.S. South have long antecedents in the cultural and literary productions of the region. Repeatedly, the anxiety over land use coalesces around real or imagined concerns about the region's (cultural and material) infrastructure and perceived backwardness relative to the rest of the country.

The Eastern Band's victory in the Kituwah matter stands in an odd relationship to Frazier's novel. Released four years before Duke Energy showed up on the hillside within two hundred yards of the Kituwah Mound, the novel prefigures an expectation of sacred earth beyond the material concerns of development and maps. When Will argues for reparations from the U.S. government on "ceded" Cherokee lands he demands, "And if America doesn't stand for property rights, what does it stand for? The land of the Nation was our heritage, ancestral homeland. Sacred places, et cetera, et cetera. Lost for all time. And—by the way—what land is not sacred? It all is. It's all sacred or it's all just fit to be shit upon" (302). Will argues after his assertion of sacred land, "It is impossible to construct an argument to prevail against that last assertion, and also hard to live up to its strict requirements" (302). More interestingly, Frazier's novel calls this work of saving the land a "lost cause" despite Bear's numerous victories in preserving enough of the space to eventually coalesce and "[become] fairly autonomous, at least as much as the modern world allows" (303). Thus, the novel with its non-Native, Confederate general narrator deals in lost causes even when the Cherokee people of the same novel seem to be winning hard-fought battles. Such an attitude is underscored in Will's own life where he—not his Cherokee counterparts—links space and sadness. Even though toward the beginning of the book, Will speculates that he and Bear both feel "There would be no regaining what was lost," and "A world once gone was gone for good," toward the end of the novel it seems that Will's losses become personal while the Cherokee people will be able to regain at least a partial victory through the strategic land buys (178). Will begins to relate his life to a Lancelot theme where he, unlike his ultimately doomed hero, fails to get in the cart: "Hesitate," he says, "and you are lost" (218). The novel begins to separate these two losses, showing Will's inability to see the Cherokee victory within his own scheme of post–Civil War loss.

However, not all audiences are content with this dissociation of white narrator and historical narrative. As Bob Hoover of the *Pittsburgh Post-Gazette* critiques: "Unlike Inman [the protagonist of *Cold Mountain*], who was driven by love to return home in a kind of American 'Odyssey,' Will, the orphan, decides he has no home to return to. His love has vanished, his Cherokee 'family' has died out, and his North Carolina property has been lost. 'Everyone and everything you love goes away,' Will says in old age. 'You're left with nothing but your moods and memory. Pitiful and powerful tools.' And that is that." Here, the reviewer fails to see that the first-person narration offered by Will creates the ironic distancing between Will's view of his personal tragedy (coupled with his desire to live an epically shaped narrative of loss) and the preservation of Bear's Cherokee people whom he has helped persevere. The novel, then, points to a rupture in the red state between the southern white narrative of pathos and the Cherokee narrative of persistence. This narrative attempts to unbind an overdetermined Native tragedy into a metanarrative of the U.S. South, showing a rift between the perception of history and a continuation of a people. Such a gap in individual white southern loss and Native tragedy makes the novel stand out among many of its textual predecessors. The novel refuses to render a knowable history dependent on loss. Will Cooper's history is indeed forlorn, but this narrative of one fictional southerner does not and cannot map onto Cherokee national survival. Frazier reiterates this point throughout the novel in demonstrating the construction of narrative history. Regarding the Charley incident, Will narrates, "Bear and I spent a long night figuring out how best to tell Charley to the future. Not his history, his story. For that is what it would become, a narrative, with our help or without it" (290). The story, embellished by Will with the final *Et tu Brutus?*, meets Bear's desire to shape the history just as much as what he says others do "who get to make up the stories and furthermore that they have a great deal of leeway in regard to adherence to facts and especially interpretations and opinions, not to mention outright lies" (290). In other words, two can play the game of strategic dehistoricization. Or, as Will says, "Neither history nor journalism nor sausage-making is a pretty business" (120).

This unknowable history marks precisely what many reviewers found so distasteful about Frazier's sophomore novel. Like Jon Smith points out regarding Pease's outrage over *The Patriot*, it seems curious to me that critics are drawn only to what they want from the narrative in terms of knowable history rather than the general and frequently offensive white-washing this ahistorical story proposes for the region. Only Stephen Metcalf of *Slate.com* measures the novel's flaws by its jettisoning of the hard life of subsistence and enslavement in the pre–Civil War Appalachian Mountains. His assessment rests on Frazier's romantic rendering of all mountain life, and he argues quite rightfully that "The ahistorical conscience gets quite the workout in *Thirteen Moons*" (Metcalf). I would argue that there exists at least some attempt (and again possibly a failed attempt on Frazier's part) to render CSA general Cooper's own unreliability as a narrator as the very thing that creates this troubling ahistorical U.S. South. Nonetheless, Metcalf's criticisms of the book remain the most sound given his serious engagement with the (a)historical factors of the audience's desires. While Metcalf seems well aware of the problems of history in the book, his insight stands in direct opposition to the other critics such as Goodheart at the *New York Times* who want *more* knowledge—even if it has to be wrenched into ahistorical knowability. Frazier's attempt to pry apart the specious convergence narratives of Confederate and Native loss via the first-person narrator remain provocative, but ultimately this attempt bumps up against an ideological ceiling of what the narrator or the critical audience can imagine.

Most reviews compare the book to Frazier's runaway success in his first novel, *Cold Mountain*. Considering this, one might expect that this first novel does something quite in opposition to the problems of unknowability catalogued by the reviews of *Thirteen Moons*. In fact, the review excerpts for *Cold Mountain* almost all note one particular strength of Frazier's first novel: its use of detail. Frank Conroy says it is "richly detailed," while the *Christian Science Monitor* calls it "finely detailed"; *People* says it is "loaded with vivid historical detail," and John Brendt says it is "elegantly told and convincing down to the last haunting detail." All these details might seem overwhelming, but I suppose they are mitigated by what the *New York Review of Books* called "Charles Frazier's *feeling* for the Southern landscape" (my emphasis).[30] This appeal to detail, and by extension authenticity, through the author's deep feeling for the southern landscape begins to seem awfully familiar, and thus, it seems little surprise that like *The Education of Little Tree* before it, *Cold Mountain* won the ABBY award.

Certainly, it is possible that Frazier took a detour from his use of rich historical detail when he wrote of the unknowability of the geographical and historical fact in *Thirteen Moons*. However, this seems not to be the case. In many editions of *Cold Mountain*, just past the title page and dedication and before the beginning of the narrative, readers find a "Map of the Southern Blue Ridge Mountains." Perhaps this map offers some confidence to readers as a sort of geographical positioning system to the narrative they are about to encounter. However, this appears to be *the exact same map* as the one described by Will Cooper when he is sent west to open his store in Cherokee Territory. The map is richly detailed until it hits that same "white space" of Cherokee land where everything halts at once, marking what *Thirteen Moons* calls the limits of "mappists' knowing." Perhaps, then, the reader just knows that because this narrative occurs in the mapped territory of the state, the narrative remains knowable, loaded with the same vivid detail of rivers and streams. Yet this too seems unlikely.

Throughout *Cold Mountain*, we see the movement of Cherokee land from a "white space" to a red state. The novel's protagonist, Inman, speculates on his making sense of his visual memories, and the third-person omniscient narrator tells us, "Those pieces together seemed to offer some meaning, though he did not know what and suspected he never would" (8). This same lack of knowledge continues as Inman later "has no idea where he was," as he proceeds on his journey, and at one point, "He passed a rock cairn that the Cherokee in times long past were in the habit of building along the way to signify something, though whether way marker or memorial or holy place was now unknowable" (351). The novel's other protagonist, Ada, also thinks about a vanishing Cherokee landscape, wondering, "Whatever word they had called it would soon be numbered among the names of things which have not been passed down to us and are exiled from our memories. She doubted that its people, even in the last days, had ever looked ahead and imagined loss so total and so soon" (388–89). Unlike *Thirteen Moons*, *Cold Mountain* marks a total loss for the Cherokee people in both language and land, two things rendered unknowable but two unknowables readily accepted by the novel's reviewers. All non-Native people need or want to know of the Cherokee, the evidence suggests, is their loss.

Even this rather cynical reading of the novel's reviews is complicated by the specter of unknowing throughout *Cold Mountain*. At the end of the novel, Inman and Ada tell stories of their lives. However, "When Inman reached the war years, though, he accounted for them in only the weak detail of a newspaper account. [...] What he wanted Ada to know was that you could tell such things on and on and yet no more get to the full truth of the war than you could get to the full truth of an old sow bear's life by following her sign through the woods" (431). This inability to tell and know the truth of an event is further described when the narrator concludes, "Inman figured he himself might only know something as fleeting as the smell of her breath. No one could know the entirety any more than we can know the life of any animal, for they each inhabit a world that is their own and not ours" (431). This unknowing seems analogous to the gaps in knowledge addressed by *Thirteen Moons*. In both books Frazier calls out the inability of certain claims to epistemology. What, then, makes some moments of uncertainty palatable for the readers while others seem like an affront to the very genre of historical fiction?

The discrepancy in response seems likely tied to ideas over epistemological rights in the red state. Non-Native readers seem inclined to expect a certain knowability of Native cultures. This power of the gaze and historical construction is deeply embedded in a contemporary culture that continually renders Native bodies and history as the object for study or tourist consumption. Once inside this structure, histories that conform to the litany of loss meet many non-Natives' readerly expectations of what can be seen and known: Indians died and lost their land, and this is how it happened. This settler-colonial structure appears comfortable for the reviewers of *Cold Mountain*. The bias in these reviews suggests that, as in Hunter's *Horn in the West*, white audiences expect psychological depth to white people and their history, and this history is complex and therefore, obviously, must be shaped into a narrative. However, when *Thirteen Moons* shows Bear and his ally Will constructing a Cherokee narrative history, covering over and manipulating the known and unknown through their respective agencies, reviewers express feeling cheated. "How *did* the Indians lose?" they seem to ask. "Show us," they demand. This impulse and denial becomes further exacerbated when the use of the white narrator separates a Confederate Lost Cause from a set of Indigenous losses. Ada of *Cold Mountain* draws the two together in her own subject position, but Will in *Thirteen Moons* shows us that this drawing together of tragedy constitutes an affect of white emotive narratives of the U.S. South. It is not indicative of the region's Native cultures. This unstitching, this lack of knowing, becomes unbearable for those seeking historical and geographical fact.

Thirteen Moons demonstrates the stakes of narrative cartography in the Removal narrative. With its abdication of historical and geographical fact, it elicits and possibly subverts the material claims inherent in a red state project. Multiple maps exist for any space, and they can be put to use in order to generate new cultural narratives about issues such as Indigenous land claim. In his call to "look elsewhere," Frazier may not simply be encouraging readers to go to "factual histories," but rather this call might be thought of in a more revolutionary way, akin to Daniel Boone's gesture of *Horn in the West*. Look elsewhere—to other possibilities of space, to other narratives of land claim, to other maps, to other languages—and see what settler-colonial cartography and history attempt to cover over: that no space exists in static fact but is continually created by the people who call it home and know it as sacred.

This might all easily seem to be a problem confined to fiction. However, two extratextual events demonstrate how these narratives and the desires for them have real-world antecedents. One, the Kituwah Mound case represents a significant win for the Cherokee people. It demonstrates a vitality that would likely make the fictional Bear, and his likely real-world counterpart Yonaguska, happy. Two, the "Removal" section of *Thirteen Moons* was translated into the Cherokee language by Myrtle Driver Johnson in 2006 for the Eastern Band of Cherokee Indians' Yonaguska Literature Initiative. This represents the first major work of literature translated from English into a Native language of North America in well over a century and a half, maybe longer. Indeed, it may seem to be a strange decision that of all the texts available for translation, the Eastern Band chose a portion of this particular novel, and some critics might scoff at the tribe's choice. However, sovereignty means that a tribal nation gets to make their own choices whether any outsider likes it or not. In the choice to translate a non-Native text, the tribe incorporates a story and makes it their own, reminding audiences that Native peoples, just like their white counterparts, are allowed to decide what work any given story might do for them, what long-overdue compensation it might hold.

Spiraling Down: Timing Removal in *Riding the Trail of Tears*

Blake Hausman's novel *Riding the Trail of Tears* offers a compelling corrective to the red state logic that has long used Indian Removal as a cipher for a Confederate hangover of loss. Set in a speculative near future, it follows Tallulah Wilson, a Cherokee woman who works as a tour guide on a virtual reality attraction where tourists "ride" the Trail of Tears as simulated nineteenth-century Cherokee people. Tallulah ponders her role as a Cherokee guide, ruminating on whether her participation in the ride constitutes a selling out that lends "authenticity" to the troubling tourist attraction. Significantly, the entire novel is framed through a Cherokee "Little, Little Person," who has hung onto Tallulah's scalp, causing trouble in her life and wreaking havoc on her work environment. These "real" Little People, we are told by the Littler Person narrator, were "cut from the stories, spliced out like a track on an old reel-to-reel recording that no one wanted to hear anymore" (5–6). The novel begins just a few days before we are told of Tallulah's impending vacation to Nags Head on the Outer Banks in North Carolina (which is, incidentally, the closest Atlantic beach to Roanoke Island, site of the Lost Colony). On the day before her vacation, the ride "malfunctions" and a number of events ensue as Tallulah's tour group endures a much darker and more painful experience than they bargained for. Hausman's novel complicates an affective attachment to the Cherokee history of Removal, and it encompasses everyone—Tallulah included—in its critique. Plagued by self-doubt over her participation in a genocide-based tourist attraction, Tallulah considers her own complicity in the retelling of Removal stories for profit. However, the novel does not deconstruct the primacy of Cherokee stories of Removal. Rather, it calls out those who use these stories as some sort of catharsis over those who remember these stories as a means of survival and sovereignty. Tallulah's self-reflection and personal investment in these narratives is different than that of her paying passengers, and despite her participation in the stories, the audience has no choice but to reflect on the non-Native consumption of Removal narratives that buttress their own sense of settler-colonial guilt and "sympathy."

In its very structure, the narrative links the history of Removal with a speculative near future. Past, present, and future loop together in one virtual compression. The Little Little Person who has troubled Tallulah (though unbeknownst to her) underscores both the perils and possibilities in acknowledging the synchronic and diachronic joining of events. In essence, the novel takes place over just one day, ending with the Little Little Person losing its grasp over Tallulah and being washed down her shower drain in northern Georgia. In closing, it asks the reader to imagine a cycle, "Endless water, underground, moving somewhere. Maybe it all flows back to where it began. Do you know where it comes from? Do you know where it goes?" (370). This question links the readers back to the beginning of the novel that they may have not previously understood when the narrator complains, "These sewer pipes are endless, and I don't want to think about the shit I'm swimming in. It would be easy to just forget and drown" (1). In this way, the novel links beginning and endings rather than points of finality or national Cherokee rupture. The water spirals down the drain, counterclockwise as Choctaw author LeAnne Howe would remind us, moving in the direction of hurricanes and calling up the counterclockwise directional movement of southeastern Native stomp dances.[31]

The novel jostles the temporal order, compressing time as it sends riders back into a linear history. As a tourist version of Removal, the ride attempts to control time. The novel explains, "The Trail of Tears ride, like the actual Removal, exists because of causality. Cause and effect—actions and reactions, the universal continuum of motion toward and away" (70). Within this causality, the ride operates by spinning groups off in simultaneous universes from the same starting point: "Each time a tour group jacks into the Trail of Tears, they enter through the same point of origin, moving away from the real and into the virtual through the same place—the First Cabin. The First Cabin is an authentically ransacked 1838 Cherokee summer home. It is the gateway to virtual time" (70). The ride, then, begins with a point of loss rather than ending with the beginning of the Trail like many accounts of Georgia Native history. In contrast, as with Removal histories that depend on reception, the ride accounts for tourists' reactions: "However, the Trail of Tears always changes after this origin point. No two rides are exactly the same. Each tour group experiences the same historical cycle, but the details change based upon the tourists' reactions" (71). In the ride's normal functioning, the time compression resolves itself neatly, leaving the tourist with an "authentic" experience. However, on the day in question, this compression of linear time breaks down, spinning Tallulah and the other tourists through recursive spirals. Like the water that flows down the drain moving from the ending to the beginning, taking the Little Little Person with it, the ride spirals off into a temporality that the engineers and Tallulah cannot control.

One character in particular, Irma Rosenberg, a Jewish grandmother from New York, finds herself in an alternate universe of ride "extras" known as the Misfits. She tries to leave this area and exhorts the Indians that she meets there (distinguished by their sports team baseball hats) to join her. They attempt to explain their temporal conundrum as it relates to their spatial occupation. As "Giants hat" explains, "'We're not supposed to be here, [...] but here is where we always come back'" (119). Irma protests that Tallulah can help them out of their problem, but they insist, "'Every time the loop starts over, so do we.' [...] With each new loop [...] we all begin again'" (119). They attempt to explain that within the game, they exist only to be killed. Irma encourages them to "Do your march to Oklahoma or whatever, and get it over with. You're supposed to be characters on the Trail of Tears, right? Well, if you're supposed to walk to Oklahoma, why not just do it and see what happens? Maybe you won't come back here" (120). In cacophony they respond, "'We do not belong on the Trail of Tears.' [...] 'We belong *here*,'" ultimately explaining again, "'We *do* belong here, but we are *not supposed* to be here'" (120). This dialogue echoes Cherokee historian Julia Coates's work "'None of Us Is Supposed to Be Here': Ethnicity, Nationality, and the Production of Cherokee Histories" (2002) when she quotes a Cherokee Nation citizen in diaspora, explaining the problems of being a Cherokee person "out of place" *and* a Cherokee person who has survived what Removal was meant to destroy: Cherokee people. In this way, the novel links land claim and narrative order. For the United States and for the

U.S. South, the narrative of Cherokee existence was supposed to end in the nineteenth century. Their survival has looped them through numerous other attempts to annihilate their sovereign existence. Hausman's novel theorizes these recursive routes and through Tallulah offers an embodied Cherokee existence that privileges continued survival and sovereignty over loss and beleaguerment.

Tallulah's name—ironically positioned against the waterfall in northern Georgia—also calls up the linkage between temporality and land claim. When informing inquisitive passengers that she was not named after the actress Tallulah Bankhead: "[S]he'll tell them how Tallulah Falls was once the second-largest waterfall in all of North America. How Tallulah Bankhead's grandmother was given that name because her parents honeymooned at the Falls back in the nineteenth century, some time not too long after the Removal. How Miss Bankhead inherited the name from her grandmother, and ultimately how it all comes back to Cherokee words and ancient rivers and things that lived here long before the Old South began to imagine itself as Old" (23). In her very name, then, Tallulah pushes her non-Native passengers to evaluate the temporality of the region, split into Old and New Souths that do little to explain the region's Indigenous connections. It also points not so subtly to the recognition of a tourist space opened up in the post-Removal dispossession of Cherokee lands. In this "coming back" to Cherokee lands and rivers, the passengers of the ride are asked to see that the region's familiar and linear divisions conceal more than they reveal.

Significantly, before Tallulah takes her tour group on their ill-fated ride, they quiz her about her own name and the names of many places in Georgia while they wait in the Meeting Grounds for the ride to begin. She goes through many sites, rehearsing a well-worn conversation about Tallulah Gorge, Amicalola, Atlanta, Allatoona, Chattanooga, and Dahlonega. Amid this geography and history lesson, "She checks the time and calculates her dwindling meeting minutes in the Meeting Grounds. Soon it will be time for Tour Group 5709 to enter the Chamber" (65). This movement from the discussion of "real" geography to the calculation of dwindling clock-minutes again creates a link between how the passengers understand their physical space and how time appears to be working inside and outside of the ride. When they step into the specific calendar date of 1838, they are still timed and placed within a universe that is imbued with Western temporalities. Tallulah herself seems beholden to this time-space construction despite the fact that she appears to know better. When the ride spirals out of control, the readers are left to wonder which temporality is real: the minute-clocked one of Tallulah's watch or the temporality born of an apocalyptic Removal.

The Little Little Person narrates its own apocalypse as it removes itself from the ride despite being made to believe that as a "digital" creation, it could not survive in the "organic" world. It opens the novel by attempting to place its time: "It's true. I dreamed with her last summer, for four months. At least I think it was four months. I watched her watching the calendars. I saw the reflections of her eyes in the plastic of her digital clocks" (1). Of course, its truth claim at the beginning of this narration should give the audience some pause as a moment of unsolicited protest. Yet it itself waffles on the time lapse of its existence, going back between the four and five months it was surely living via Tallulah. And just a few paragraphs later it confesses, "I lack the means to keep track of time" (2). From this point on, the audience should remain aware of the way that its narration cannot account for any stable temporality: linear, spiral, or otherwise.

However, the Little Little Person, unreliable as it may be offers some temporal positioning to the narrative that makes suspect all other claims to ordered time. It claims:

> Anyways. Long ago—well not that long ago in a geological sense, but long ago in a human sense—things were quite different. It was back before the big colonization, before Cristóbal Colón, before Hernando De Soto, before all the mess you Americans breathe every day in this twenty-first century. And I don't mean that in a nostalgic sense, because yes it was already a mess before invasion happened. Capitalism just made it a lot more obvious. But before that, before invasion, something happened. A revolution. A revolution that is, as far as I'm concerned, the first American revolution. (3)

This "first" American revolution returns me to my argument from chapter 2 where the volute of time exists as a spiral that can have many valences from both a non-Native and Native perspective. In the universe of Hausman's novel, this revolution means something for the narrator quite different from the non-Native tellings of any discrete event. Despite the Little Little Person's attempts to date its revolution, "In Christian time it was around 1400," what matters for the novel is that time revolves. It moves through the spiralic form from the unreliable narrator's proclamations to his own counterclockwise journey down the drain (3).

Removal not only jostled spatial conceptions of the U.S. South with its land grabs in defiance of Supreme Court order, it also fundamentally shifted the region's temporality. Old and New Souths make little sense in an Indigenous temporal framework of the region, and scholars would do well to remember that the apocalypse of the Civil War is a *white apocalypse* in the region. Removal leaves its own mark—one that has been considered in only spatial terms for far too long. As such, it requires methods from Native studies to think through the productive understanding of alternate temporalities that do not begin or end with colonialism and have their own punctuating moments not easily categorized in traditional understandings of the region's literary periodization. In this way, Hausman pushes his audience to consider the relationship between claims to land and claims to time. Indeed, Tallulah too is linked to a Western temporal order, but as she is cleansed of her Little troublemaking companion, the audience is left to wonder what new time she will find as she spirals forward. The speculative future that ends Hausman's speculative novel thrusts us forward into our own political moment—whatever the present may be—and I close this chapter with a consideration of the return of Removal logics in the twenty-first century.

The Reprise of Andrew Jackson

In 2009 and 2010, something curious began to happen in my courses on Native American literatures. On more than one occasion, during our readings of the Native-produced literatures debating and depicting Removal, a student referred to the "fact" that Andrew Jackson's parents were killed by Indians. I corrected this inaccuracy and moved on. However, I remained perplexed at the general traction this bit of apocrypha had seemed to acquire. Notably, in September 2010 *Bloody Bloody Andrew Jackson* opened on Broadway after spending most of 2009 enjoying a successful off-Broadway run. In quick summary, *Bloody Bloody Andrew Jackson* is a horrible musical and failed satire of the seventh president of the United States and Indian Removal. Perhaps I should maintain more critical distance, but I would like to be clear: I think the musical is atrocious, and I find nothing so dangerous as satire that fails to hit the mark. But, alas, it has had some success, and this success has generated a few interesting repercussions—not least of which is that one of its main plot points showed up in my Native American literature classes as a presumed "fact."

Indeed, the musical outlines in hipster-emo overtones numerous "facts" of the nineteenth century in its attempt to satirize the early populist movement and, speaking generously, draw the disturbing parallels between the past and the present-day rhetoric of the Tea Party. Scott Manning Stevens, former director of D'Arcy McNickle Center and current director of the Native American and Indigenous Studies program at Syracuse University, first turned my attention to the play. When I spoke with him about my project, he said, "Well, you have to talk about *Bloody Bloody Andrew Jackson*." Stevens had managed to see the show while it was still off-Broadway and subsequently wrote an op-ed to the *New York Times*, which they elected not to publish. In his piece, Stevens writes:

> The tone of the musical is somewhere between an extended SNL skit and the requisite irreverence of a South Park episode. That the musical strives mightily to be over-the-top is an understatement but therein lies much of what smacks

of bad faith. Who knew Indian removal could be such fun? The camp hilarity of its characters and parodically serious emo tunes are genuinely entertaining. Nor does it hurt that Jackson is portrayed by a twenty-something hottie. [...] And, to be sure, the piece does not endorse Jacksonian Indian policy, which is registered by some oddly heavy-handed gestures in the midst of all the ribaldry. But why present the audience, even a likely well-educated audience, with such reckless historical fictions?

Elsewhere in the op-ed, Stevens expresses his concern as a Native person that this particular moment of overt hipster racism serves to do real damage for how non-Native people in the United States imagine the era. The musical allows people to be "edgy" and "in-the-know," but at the same time, the narrator figure, who positions herself as somewhat the only reliable figure in the musical, narrates completely bogus historical "facts." Her untimely death at the hands of Andrew Jackson leads to the refrain throughout the play, "You can't shoot history in the neck." However, I remain skeptical that the average audience member knows his or her ins and outs of nineteenth-century Indian policy enough to get the "joke." In other words, I have more problems with *Bloody Bloody Andrew Jackson* than Donald Pease has with *The Patriot*.

I was finally able to see a version of the performance in the spring of 2013 in Atlanta, Georgia. Already, I was dubious. To stage a counterhistorical romp through a national genocide is one thing, but to do so at the very site where that genocide occurred seemed to be a whole other. The play was staged in the round, giving me an excellent vantage point from which to watch the audience's reaction to the events staged before them. At least one of the audience members was wearing a T-shirt emblazoned with "I ♥ AJ." From the way he cheered at key scenes, I did not get the sense that his love was ironic. To its credit, the performance was well staged. As a performance, it has merit.

However, this is even all the more dangerous for the message. Snippy dialogue about Susan Sontag and Michel Foucault fails to stand up against the numerous times that Jackson and other characters offer lines such as "And even the land that isn't our land is the land that shall be our land, so pick up a GOD-damn rifle and make those land-grabbin' Injuns bleed! All of 'em! BLEED!" or "I also gotta kill the entire Native population!" Or even: "Well can I tell you something? I think the only remaining menace comes from within this country. Uh-huh, from Congress, the White House. You guys don't give a shit about the frontiersmen. There's no equal representation in your one-party system. The Era of Good Feelings? Huh! More like the Era of Bad Feelings! You guys are so dead. The Republican Party is so dead. The American people deserve an alternative to you croquet-playing cock-gobblers. I'm gonna fucking ... shit all over you guys with my brand of maverick, egalitarian democracy." Just in case I have not yet expressed the flavor of the performance, consider these additional lines: "That means it's our time. Time for the real people of this nation—you and me—time for us to take this fucker back!" And "Beginning tonight, we're gonna change things in Washington. We're gonna take this country back for the common man: for you, and for me. Together we will see our greatest hopes fulfilled because, people of America, people of the World—this is our moment!" Given the general proximity of these statements (minus the Indian killing) to actual, contemporary Tea Party and Donald Trump discourse (although his executive order on several pipeline projects as well as the reduction of Bears Ears National Monument leads to fear that violence toward Native people is quickly forthcoming), I reiterate my point that I do not think the man in the T-shirt ♥s Andrew Jackson ironically.

Rather, I argue that the play induces the audience toward these counter-national desires. As Scott Stevens speculates: "In a time of Tea-Partiers and demonstrations by the descendants of immigrants against immigration or calls by the heirs of settler colonialism to 'take back America,' it is hard as a Native American to look on in silence. Perhaps then the popularity of *Bloody Bloody Andrew Jackson* is a symptom of our current condition and not a sly corrective. Americans demonstrate a notable contempt for the study of history even as they are fond of invoking it for partisan reasons. Ideally the two impulses should not co-exist." As I have demonstrated so far in this study, these impulses almost always coexist in the red state. In fact, the conservative, familiar red state *depends* on this coexistence. It cannot think itself without it. While I suspect that the play attempts to invoke satire in order to show the flaws of present-day politically coded red states, it may actually encourage the ahistorical narratives on which it depends. In almost any performance situation, it is difficult not to cheer for the protagonist, and the play asks us to see Jackson as a sympathetic, flawed man who just happened to let populism—and popularity—get away from him a bit. Even though the musical may very well attempt to create an ironic distancing, I argue that perhaps like *Thirteen Moons* it facilitates an even more intense suture.

This narrative connection likely reads as stronger given the play's staging in the U.S. South. At several points, characters specifically point toward New England as an oppressive force on the rest of the country. I remain fairly certain that this is also an attempt to make fun of southerners (I will leave it alone that this satirical jab is in and of itself offensive in its flattening of the population of the region). However, when staged in the U.S. South, these moments take on a different tone, and not surprisingly, the audience cheered at some of these key moments, including: "We're just as good as those Northeastern cities and their aristocrats!" and "Those wealthy New England congress-fucks would rather tax us and play polo all day than defend our frontier. No one's gonna do anything about it. Everyone 'round here's pissed off but no one's takin' a stand." I do not think the ironic distancing that the writers may have imagined stands. The play then becomes nothing but an apology for the worst kind of red state. Indeed, this analysis of the play is made all the more eerie as Donald Trump has decided to hang a portrait of Andrew Jackson in the Oval Office, signaling that the seventh president's proposed removal from the twenty-dollar bill was little more than a promotion.[32]

While Marinda Branson Moore imagined Indian Removal as a sin precipitating the Civil War, *Bloody Bloody Andrew Jackson* only imagines Removal as a cipher for our contemporary wayward political discourse. This is a problem. Indian Removal is not a cipher. It is not simply a narrative where the non-Native audience can project their own desires, anxieties, and guilt. As the excerpts from the region's print cultures have shown, this projection even worked to legitimate Removal itself. This is a problem of the red state. Rather, this is a problem of the non-Native, conservative red state. As I have outlined in the first half of this book, white southerners have repeatedly attempted to link their desires for southern identities grounded in land claim to the region's Indigenous history. Frequently, this linkage has buttressed counternationalist arguments that serve to reify southern identity as tragically white and beleaguered by northern interests. However, it does not have to be this way. The red state can be more than its worst impulses. As I examine in the remainder of this book, when Native people have built anticolonial and resistance movements based on land attachment, narrative continuity, and appeals to complex regional identities, they have demonstrated new possibilities for the red state. We have seen glimpses of these possibilities in my quick analyses of the anti-R*dsk*ns and Kituwah Mound campaigns. In the final two chapters I look more closely at how Native people have used narratives of persistence in place in order to shift our understanding of the red state as a given white space.

CHAPTER FOUR

Resistance

> Well, [*Strike at the Wind!*] was very controversial because of the nature of what it was saying. It raised awareness about things that people in Lumberton didn't even want to talk about. Our culture. Our existence. Our presence and our being there, period, was a fight and a struggle. That's where Henry Berry came in.
>
> —Willie French Lowery, 2008

Through their literature and other cultural productions, Native people connected to the U.S. South have used key articulations of land claim and regional belonging in order to resist popular red state logics. In the second half of the book, I examine ways that Native people have formulated their own red states: sovereign spaces of indigeneity that can both center material land claim and engage in a mobility that neither undermines nor diminishes claims to Native independence on this continent, and more specifically within the U.S. South. Like the recurrent narratives that I outline in the previous chapters, these resistance movements also reappear and evolve, taking on new meanings over time. Like almost all communities, Native people draw on past events to shape and understand the present. The productive retelling of these events might appear to have a similar structure to those used by non-Natives to justify settler-colonial occupation and land claim, but audiences should remain attuned to the significant differences between the use of the past to commit colonial violence and the retelling of stories to survive. As I demonstrate in the next two chapters, these differences matter when considering how and why Native people use stories to make countercolonial claims that forward their landed sovereignty on the American continent. While many of the non-Native texts I examine use specious narratives of Native history to undergird myths of white southern exceptionalism, Native people make use of their own history, building and constructing it to their own political ends.

To a certain extent, all of these narratives may be constructed, but without falling into relativism, it must be possible to acknowledge that Native people have the right to self-determine the uses of their own historical accounts, stories, and myths for their continued sovereignty. Rather than critique and dismiss the Native use of recurring narratives in the region as simply wrong or misguided, audiences should pay attention to how these stories are retold in order to stage resistance to colonialism, white supremacy, and land theft, examining the ways that the retellings of key moments link temporality and land claim to call for a more complex, robust, and just U.S. South. In this chapter, I consider the way that narratives of the Lumbee hero Henry Berry Lowry demonstrate the stakes of this resistance in the Native South.

As an opening example, I want to consider a particularly localized vector of the Red Power movement from the late 1960s and early 1970s. The *Raleigh News and Observer* from July 11, 1971, includes within their "Perspectives" section several articles that examine Lumbee history and identity in North Carolina. At the beginning of this section, the newspaper features a pull quote from Herbert Locklear who asserts that "It's not that we love North Carolina so much ... It's difficult to explain, but what we are attached to is one particular place in North Carolina where our people live. It's the center of our nationalism." Within the article, Locklear goes on to explain, picking up where the pull quote leaves off, "our nationalism, our social milieu ... but those words don't get it either. They are too abstract, too sociological, really, too Anglo-Saxon. What I'm talking about actually is tied up with the while [sic] concept of what it means to be American Indian." Next to the article is a photograph of a middle-school–aged Lumbee boy holding a homemade cardboard sign that reads, "Better *Red* Than Dead." This insistence on "Red" as an identity flips the popular anticommunist slogan of twenty years prior, and it centers the Lumbee's identity as Indigenous, linking together questions of race, nation, and economic structure. The corresponding pull quote, placing the Lumbee Tribe of North Carolina geographically within the colonial state of North Carolina but also apart from it, foregrounds questions of tribal sovereignty and geography while the image of the boy and his slogan critiques the capitalist nationalism of the United States, asserting a resistant stance to Euro-American hegemony. Locklear's explanation of the ill fit of Western terms such as "nationalism" to account for Native continuance asks us to consider Native presences in the region that do more than follow the teleology of the U.S. South as counternational space. When taken side by side, these words and this image succinctly demonstrate a Lumbee resistance to being brought under U.S. national or southern regional founding myths.[1]

In attempting to shift inquiry away from the United States as a discrete cultural and political system that maintains the U.S. South as an exceptional space, this chapter examines Lumbee history in the region, demonstrating how the Tribe has refused to be co-opted into either a U.S. nationalist framework or a southern oppositional antinational rhetoric. Instead, through cultural productions such as the outdoor drama *Strike at the Wind!* (1971) and Willie French Lowery's albums *Plant and See* (1969) and *Proud to Be a Lumbee* (1971), the Lumbee, whose federal recognition status remains complicated, have challenged both the U.S. nation-state and its founding European narratives as well as narratives of southern exceptionalism that are based on white supremacy and biracial classifications. Rather, they create their own *Red* state, one that exceeds any popularly held images of what such a space entails.[2] In pursuing this Red reading of the red state, I turn frequently to the work of Lumbee scholar Malinda Maynor Lowery. In her seminal study *Lumbee Indians in the Jim Crow South: Race, Identity, and the Making of a Nation* (2010), she explains, "While the history of Native Americans in the segregated South may seem exceptional at first glance, a closer look reveals many commonalities with Indians all over the nation and sheds new light on 'Americanness' itself" (220). Following this logic, I wish to hold on to the particularity of Lumbee resistance without rendering it exceptional for the region or the nation. To do so, I examine the literary and popular productions of Lumbee resistance, attempting to sketch their varied significance as materials produced by the community and/or in collaboration with their allies. As I track these resistance narratives—many of which focus on the figure of Henry Berry Lowry—through their own spiralic time, I attempt to demonstrate how the contemporaneous political moments matter for the reception and legacy of the stories themselves.

Henry Berry Lowry Will Never Die

The most popular resistance figure in Lumbee history is Henry Berry Lowry. His spirit permeates the Lumbee community and its attendant narratives of resistance. The story of Henry Berry Lowry has long been a subject for writers of fiction and nonfiction, ranging from George Alfred Townsend's 1872 quasi-news tract *The Swamp Outlaws or, The North Carolina Bandits, Being a Complete History of the Modern Rob Roys and Robin Hoods* to Josephine Humphrey's popular novel *Nowhere Else on Earth* (2001).[3] Without a doubt, Henry Berry Lowry serves as one of the most significant figures in all of the Native South. During the Civil War, Lumbee men had to hide out to avoid being abducted by the North Carolina Home Guard and conscripted into service in Wilmington, where they were forced to construct the Confederate Fort Fisher. At this time, the Lumbee were most frequently classified as "free persons of color." Because of this, they could not own weapons or officially serve in the Confederate army. Many Lumbee opposed the Confederacy and sympathized with both escaped and later emancipated African Americans. As the community legend goes, with this backdrop of civil war and intense racism, Henry Berry Lowry and his family were harassed and arrested by authorities for refusing conscription. Two of his relatives had been murdered when they attempted to evade the Home Guard. These events escalated into a series of reprisals that echoed across Robeson County. One of the men responsible for murdering Lowry's family members, James Brantly Harris, was sent to the Lowry home to investigate a spurious charge of stealing. Later, the authorities found the bodies of Harris and the white planter who had charged the Lowrys with theft. They immediately suspected Henry and his relatives. As a result, they executed Henry's father, Allen, and brother, William, after a hasty trial—essentially in the family's backyard. After this, Henry gathered several men who eventually became known as the Lowry Gang. They retaliated against the Home Guard and evaded capture by living in the surrounding swamps. On two separate occasions, the local authorities captured Lowry, but both times he managed to escape from custody before his trial. Even after the Civil War, the "Lowry Wars" continued as the state authorities put a bounty of $12,000 on Henry, dead or alive. Despite this, many in the community actively supported his evasion. Lowry became known as the "Indian Robin Hood," and his entire operation quickly became one that robbed monied white families and redistributed the wealth to the entire community, marking him as a figure resistant to both racial and economic oppression. After robbing a store with a safe containing $20,000, Henry Berry Lowry was never heard from again. As Adolph Dial recounts, some say he used this money to escape from North Carolina to Mexico or South America and only to return home in disguise many years later. Others claim that he went west and participated in the Modoc resistance. Still others speculate that he accidentally shot himself while cleaning his gun, and the community surreptitiously buried him in the swamp to protect his body from desecration at the hands of his enemies.[4] The rest of the Lowry fighters were either captured or they surrendered, but because of the mysterious circumstances surrounding his seemingly complete disappearance, the saying in the Lumbee community remains: "Henry Berry Lowry will never die."

I am not as interested in the verified and unverified historical events of the "Lowry Wars" as I am in the later tellings and retellings of them. Nor do I spend too much time dwelling on the relative accuracy or authenticity of these retellings. Rather, I am interested in the *ways* that the story gets told over time and the work such retellings do for the cultural imagination of what constitutes a red state. While in the previous chapters I examine the use of narratives about the Lost Colony, American Revolution, and Indian Removal to demonstrate how southern feelings of whiteness and land claim have depended on the figure of the southeastern Native person, here I would like to examine how narratives of Henry Berry Lowry illuminate a tradition of resistance to the ideas of a homogeneous white South built on the oppression of Indigenous sovereignty as well as racial minorities. As Lumbee scholar David Wilkins argues regarding Lowry, "[B]ecause of the interracial nature of this band, it has been argued that Henry Berry was able to forge a pluralistic alliance that served to bond, at least temporarily, the dispossessed and disenfranchised of other races as well in a way that had never occurred before" (110). Wilkins continues by placing this resistance within its context as an event occurring in North Carolina: "[T]his single individual has risen to legendary status among the Lumbees and even local whites because he dared to defy the white political and economic power structure of a staunchly conservative state and challenged the injustices being perpetrated against not only Indians but others as well" (ibid.). Put another way, stories of Henry Berry Lowry allow for the formulation of a resistance to the Confederate, neo-Confederate, and eventually conservative red state. In its ability to stage an essentially secessionist movement from the secessionist Confederate States of America, the figure of Lowry challenges the narrative of what southern resistance means in broader terms. As Maynor Lowery explains, "the Lowry War seems to contradict the standard narrative of the racial and political dynamic of the post–Civil War South. But what seems like a contradiction can also reveal the underlying systemic nature of white supremacy in rural areas and help explain why Indians would later embrace segregation" (*Lumbee Indians* 16–17). The fact that this resistance carries over into the Reconstruction period when Native people along with other disenfranchised minorities were realizing that the end of the Civil War did not usher in a new era of opportunity but instead served to calcify racial prejudice under an emerging Jim Crow system further positions Lowry as a figure of resistance to both regional and national ideologies of discrimination. However, as Maynor Lowery explains, the Lumbee—like almost all people in the United States—were themselves not immune to the pressures of Jim Crow logics that forwarded discrimination along color lines. This fact drives my investigation not so much into the "what" of the Henry Berry Lowry narratives as into "how" different versions have been told over time.

Frequently, these resistance narratives coalesce around issues of land claim. Henry Berry Lowry's father, Allen, owned a relatively large amount of land, and although reportedly respected by both his white and Native neighbors, during this period any nonwhite person who seemed to be achieving success on "white terms" likely drew the enmity of racist white people. This question of land use and attachment remains central to narratives about Lumbee history and resistance. For Maynor Lowery, this concern over land permeated her youth: "Adults seemed inordinately focused on finding a way to keep land in families or at least to avoid it passing out of Indian hands. Keeping the land for Indians ensured a cycle of give and take that would keep future generations together" (11). This desire for the land is both material and epistemological. For example, the title of Lumbee historian Adolph Dial's history of the Tribe, *The Only Land I Know*, comes from a quote attributed to Henry Berry Lowry. When asked by North Carolina adjutant general John C. Gorman why he would not simply leave Robeson County rather than stage a guerrilla war against local authorities, Lowry reportedly responded, "Robeson County is the only land I know" (qtd. in Wilkins 109, Dial and Eliades 54). While on its face this might be read as a simple assertion, I argue that we must pause and take into full consideration the epistemological claim in this statement. Whereas I demonstrate earlier how non-Native southerners came to a sense of feeling southern via an affected attachment to the land through story, Lowry here asserts a claim to the land through Indigenous knowledge. It is the *only* land he *knows*. He, along with his entire Lumbee community, has a creation story from this space of earth that grounds his knowledge. And this knowledge is fundamentally different from the knowledge of a space as determined by settler colonialism. Lowry asserts an Indigenous land attachment. He is not a lost colonist. He does not simply *feel* attached to Robeson County as a southerner or North Carolinian with a "sense of place" or an "essence" of history. Instead, his knowledge of the land grounds his unwillingness to leave, and it foments his resistance against the affected pathos of both the Confederate secession and the later Lost Cause ideology that emerges after the Confederate defeat.

Whereas this Confederate defeat traffics in the language of death and reemerges time and again in the literary genre of the southern gothic, I would like to return to the important and often-repeated assertion that "Henry Berry Lowry will never die." As Eric Anderson, Daniel Cross Turner, and Taylor Hagood argue in their collection *Undead Souths: The Gothic and Beyond in Southern Literature and Culture* (2015), the Lost Cause rhetoric following the Civil War "suspiciously bears the marks of undeadness in its symbolic resurrection of fallen C.S.A. hero-saints. Indeed, the post-Appomattox, postemancipation, postplantation South was the site of numerous reburials of Confederate dead, physical resurrections that kept undead the searing memory of that nationalist insurrection against the U.S.A." (2). They position this "undeadness" as an important component in the southern imaginary, and their work examines how this concept works as "a metaphor, a receptacle, a mode" that turns our focus away from the horror of the gothic toward a more nuanced understanding of how "'undeadness' is rooted in and routed through a surprisingly dynamic physicality" (5). I follow this important work, but as is the case with Henry Berry Lowry, what I find significant is that future simple adverb, "never." Whereas the U.S. South might traditionally be considered under a rubric of that which will not stay dead, Henry Berry Lowry never enters this state in the first place. He secedes from a stereotypical southern pathos of defeat. He is, to return to the opening of this chapter, "Better *Red* than Dead." In a close look at the Lumbee cultural productions that follow his legacy, I argue for Henry Berry Lowry's red state: one where Indigenous resistance to settler colonialism lives.

In contrast, some such as Fox News's John Stossel would claim that the Lumbee represent ideal American capitalists and that they exist in a perfect "Tea Party" red state. For Stossel, the Lumbee are the Native people that other Native people should strive to be because, according to him, they have fully embraced capitalism and are "thriving" in Robeson County, North Carolina—despite the fact that this assessment flies directly in the face of available economic data about the area.[5] In 2011 Stossel used the Lumbee in a political attack on the Obama administration and the federal government, claiming with little sense of irony that "no group has been helped by the U.S. government more than the Indians."[6] In contrast, he asserts that the Lumbee have done incredibly well as individual capitalists due to the continued nonrecognition of their sovereignty (and by extension the full rights that other federally recognized tribes have) by the federal government. In this 2011 segment, Stossel interviews Lumbee tribal member Ben Chavis, who, using personal anecdotes, gives him ample ammunition to carry these claims.[7] As a point of contrast, Stossel interviews individuals on the Oglala Lakota Pine Ridge reservation in South Dakota, and he blames their struggles with poverty and alcoholism on their status as a federally recognized tribe. Despite being difficult to watch, the Stossel-Chavis interview is interesting for the way it completely muddles the concept of tribal sovereignty under the rubric of capitalism and instead equates federal recognition of tribal sovereignty with *acceptance* of the U.S. government and, simultaneously, socialism.[8] The convoluted logic of the Stossel-Chavis interview is almost too difficult to parse, but at its base it represents the Tea Party rhetoric that I examined earlier, and it attempts to use the experiences of four individuals as stand-in for a Lumbee population of 56,000. As Rob Schmidt of *Blue Corn Comics* summarized in his 2011 response to Stossel: "Most of the nation's 565 recognized tribes could list businesses similar to the three Lumbee successes Stossel lists. Yet not one of them is demanding to be terminated and 'set free.' Not one of them wants to disband the BIA, sell its reservation, or eliminate its sovereignty. Not one of them is ready to abandon its treaty rights, which is the source of the government programs Stossel mislabels 'freeloading.'" He goes on to explain the conservative agenda attached to this rhetoric, noting that "These Tea Party Republicans are launching hateful, racist attacks on Indians and other minorities to see what they can get away with. It's like launching a trial balloon for white supremacy" (Schmidt). Given the political events of 2017, it seems Schmidt hit the mark.

While we might at first dismiss Stossel's attempt to co-opt the Lumbee story as just another way for right-wing rhetoricians to demonize all things having to do with an Obama-led federal government, I argue that this tactic derives from a long tradition of how politicians have used Lumbee issues in order to make larger political points. The Lumbee Tribe of North Carolina's quest for federal recognition offers several significant antecedents to the political struggles of other Native American groups over the past century and a half. In 1885, 1913, 1924, 1933, and 1956, the Lumbee sought federal recognition. In each case they were ultimately denied (with the 1956 quasi recognition and denial proving the most vexing), yet on all five occasions the Lumbee history grew more complex as the Tribe (with significant nudges from the state and white "experts") repeatedly supplanted tribal names and origin theories to justify their case for recognition. Anyone familiar with the trajectory of American Indian law and politics will realize that at least four of these dates also signal significant shifts in the federal government's policies toward Native groups: in 1887 the United States enacted the disastrous Allotment Act; in 1924, the Citizenship Act; in 1934, the Indian Reorganization Act; and 1956 signals the center of the Termination period around Public Law 280 and House Concurrent Resolution 108. Historians and legal scholars have noted these correlations between Lumbee recognition requests and shifts in federal Indian policy but rarely do they go beyond the correlative to assess the deep entanglement of logic pervading each of these moments. I argue these correlations signal a long history of how the Lumbee have repeatedly been made to serve as justifications for federal policies that force Native nations to take up Euro-American values and narratives of capitalistic nationalism—values that, as a community, they have frequently repudiated.[9] Maynor Lowery also summarizes these shifts in policy, noting in the case of the 1913 and 1924 legislation that "neither branch of government wanted to interject itself into white southerners' control of race relations" and that particular "rationales reflect the federal government's use of Indians to establish white political, social, and economic dominance" (94). So while the Lumbee have frequently been asked, cajoled, and forced to exist in a traditional red state—one where political ideologies of white supremacy use Native nations, histories, and identities to justify their own desires—they have just as traditionally worked to flip this logic on its head.[10]

As these shifts have occurred in policy, we have also seen shifts in the narratives of Lumbee history. Frequently these narrative shifts have come from outside the community. Even more frequently, however, when they have emerged from within the community, they have focused at least in part on the story of Henry Berry Lowry. Both R. W. Reising and Christopher Arris Oakley have previously chronicled this process and its relation to narratives of the Lumbee hero Lowry. While Reising focuses more directly on narratives that circulate outside the community, Oakley looks specifically at the stories that emerge from within the community, specifically as they deal with the soil, and use enslaved labor. Having already been absorbed into the "mass of citizens" via the logic of plantation-style farming, the Lumbee could become the "poster Indians" for the success of assimilation via land title and European-style agriculture. McMillan continues: "Some of these Huguenots penetrated the interior as far as the Lumber River in the early part of the last century, and found the country north and east of them thickly populated by Indians who had farms and roads and other evidences of civilized life, and had evidently resided there for a considerable time before the approach of white men" (20). And again, he belabors the point of Lumbee "civilization" via the methods of the English assimilation: "In building they exhibit no little architectural skill. In road making they excel. Some of the best roads in North Carolina can be found within their territory. They are universally hospitable and polite to strangers. They are proud of their race and boast of their English ancestry. Like their ancestors, they are friendly to white men" (26). The settler-colonial logic in these extended examples is quite clear: adherence to white civilization via farming, infrastructure, and language will result in a fully functioning, independent, and proud American Indian tribe. In this way, the Lumbee become the success story of assimilation, able to have functioning tribal schools because they quickly and eagerly adapted English ways on first contact. In further evidence of this, McMillan also discusses the first land grants made to the Tribe and uses this evidence as a way to prove the familial lineage of the Tribe as both Indigenous and English. He writes: "They held their lands in common and land titles only became known on the approach of white men. The first grant of land to any of this tribe, of which there is written evidence in existence, was made by King George the Second in 1732, to Henry Berry and James Lowrie, two leading men of the tribe" (14). Here McMillan asserts the way that individual land grants can make Indigenous people legible to the state and ensure their recognition through land title, surname, and archival presence. This serves to further appeal to the benefits of land allotment, as it will create documents by which to solidify Native identity along the parameters important to government officials. These remarks combined with the above statements all work to legitimate allotment policy as the best way to ensure the "success" of a tribe via assimilation and individual land title. Despite the public popularity of the Lumbee–Lost Colony theory, in the late nineteenth century the Lumbee's application for federal recognition under the name the Croatan Indians of North Carolina was denied. However, the Tribe accepted the state of North Carolina's recognition of them under the name "Croatan."[12]

I do not mean to claim a one-to-one relationship here between McMillan's theory and the Dawes Allotment Act, but the discourse surrounding both Lumbee recognition and Allotment policy appears as more than coincidental. It reveals the discursive parameters of the period, and it once again returns us to the English Lost Colony as a ground zero for much of the ideological framework for what becomes the U.S. South. It works to place the Lumbee within the southern Lost Colony creation story, and it figures their success not as a result of their own will to survive a colonial invasion but rather because of their willingness to assimilate to the newly created region around them. Their "rediscovery" in the early eighteenth century by Scots and Huguenots finds them in the perfect stateless existence imagined in the figure of Thomas Jefferson's revolutionary Native that I outline in chapter 2. A thorough examination of Lumbee narratives of existence and resistance reveals a lot about how white southerners imagined the Native people in their midst following Removal and how Lumbee people refused to be brought under the rubric of a southern identity on anyone's terms but their own even when internal disagreements about how to assert their Native identity divided the Tribe.[13] In what follows I offer an admittedly broad-stroked explanation of the numerous additional attempts that the Indigenous people of Robeson County have made to be recognized by the federal government and the ways that these moments have aligned with the larger shifts in American Indian policy over time. This general overview helps those unfamiliar with the complexities of Lumbee history understand the larger stakes that any narrative of Lumbee identity holds for their material claims to land, labor, and identity.

In 1913 the Lumbee Tribe initiated a new attempt at federal recognition in order to gain federal funds for their Indian Normal School. At the same time, the Tribe had become increasingly dissatisfied with the name Croatan Indians of Robeson County. Additionally, the Tribe was moving away from a relationship with Hamilton McMillan and entering into a relationship with A. W. McLean, a Democratic senator, who would eventually become governor of North Carolina. Because the name "Croatan" had become colloquially shortened to the word "Cro," and because this term had become a racial pejorative that signified "Jim Crow," many tribal members wanted to be disassociated from the word.[14] To this effect, in 1911 the state agreed to recognize the Tribe as simply Indians of Robeson County. This vague name, though, certainly left little room for federal recognition, as it served to make the Lumbee even more ambiguously Indian than McMillan's Lost Colony theory. For reasons that are somewhat convoluted, A. W. McLean was committed to the idea that the Indians of Robeson County were actually Cherokee that had moved east in order to fight white settlers and perhaps other Eastern Seaboard tribes. While some tribal members such as D. F. Lowery agreed with McLean regarding the Tribe's Cherokee relation, many tribal members were unhappy with the classification and viewed it as erroneous. Nevertheless, in 1913, against the wishes of the Eastern Band of Cherokee Indians, the state of North Carolina recognized the Tribe as the Cherokee Indians of Robeson County.[15]

That same year, the Tribe once again sought federal recognition and support for their Indian Normal School, which was severely underfunded by the state of North Carolina. However, this attempt was unsuccessful, and in the statement from Superintendent of Indian Education C. F. Pierce, one sees the protologic of the Termination legislation that was to come into play just a few decades later:

> It is the avowed policy of the Government to require the states having an Indian population to assume the burden & responsibility for their education as soon as possible. North Carolina, like the State of New York, has a well organized plan for the education of Indians within her borders, and I can see no justification for any interference or aid, on the part of the Government in either case. Should an appropriation be made for the Croatans, it would establish a precedent for the Catawbas of S.C., the Alabamas of Texas, the Tuscaroras of N.Y., as well as for other scattering tribes that are now cared for by the various states. (Lumbee Tribe, "Federal Recognition" 3)

Pierce's statement reveals the concern of states as absorbing responsibility for tribes, and thus negating any sovereign-to-sovereign relationship between the United States and Native nations. Furthermore, the Catawbas and Alabamas later become "terminated" tribes (although reinstated), which suggests the long institutional technique of targeting tribes who might be successfully legislated out of existence.[16] Additionally, these hearings in 1913 focused quite exclusively on how the Indigenous population of Robeson County acquired its land. In a piece of testimony quoted at length by historian Gerald Sider, Senator Simmons and McLean discuss the use and distribution of land owned by tribal members. McLean testifies: "I should say there are several thousand acres. Most of them settled on it time out of mind. They have divided those tracts up into small tracts, probably 25 or 50 or 75 acres" (qtd. in Sider 84–85). This discussion of tracts, inheritance, and land use works to demonstrate the federal government's clear interest in the relationship between land claim and indigeneity. Furthermore, this appeal to "time out of mind" demonstrates the ways that what might at first appear as abstract notions of periodization find their resonances in the realm of policy.

Having been denied federal recognition as Cherokee, the Tribe attempted to find a more comprehensive theory of historic origins. Based on the work of John R. Swanton, a Smithsonian anthropologist, the Tribe concluded in the 1930s that the most likely connection to any BIA "historic" tribe would be the Siouan group, the Cheraw. Working from several migration theories and the presence of other Siouan groups in the region, Swanton proposed that the Tribe descended from an intermixing of Siouan-, Iroquoian-, and Algonquian-speaking people who moved west into the swamps in order to escape aggressive European invasion. However, he concluded that the most dominant influence of the group would likely be the Siouan Cheraw. With this new theory of historical identity, the Indians of Robeson County again approached the federal government in 1933, asking to be recognized as the Cheraw Indians of Robeson County and to receive funding for education. This request was denied.

Shortly after, the Lumbee decided to resubmit the request for recognition to the U.S. Congress, but this time the secretary of the interior chose (against Swanton's recommendation) the more general name, Siouan Indians of the Lumber River. The less specific designation of Siouan was selected because since there were now both "professional" anthropological evidence and a continued oral history that suggested that the Lumbee were connected to at least three various groups—the Pee Dee, Waccamaw, and Cheraw—it would be more respectful to choose a name that would not alienate any tribal members. Of course, several Lumbee tribal members maintained that they were descended from eastern Algonquian people, and yet others were committed to the relationship between the Tribe and the Eastern Band of Cherokee Indians. Even other tribal members asserted that their ancestors were Tuscarora, a theory that has gained significant purchase among many tribal members today. However, the request for recognition under the name Siouan "gained the support of only a handful of the Lumbee people, and the opposition of most, because it threatened, by offering an imprecise name, to introduce a new element of confusion into their history" (Dial and Eliades 18). The question of a name once again complicated the Lumbee's appeal for federal recognition, while it seemingly solidified white society's idea of the Indian as a single, racialized, and "historically accurate" entity rather than an identity informed by complex formations bounded by commonalities across Native nationalisms.

In 1934 Felix Cohen, who had been hired by John Collier to think through the significant legal issues of the IRA, contacted the Tribe in Robeson County and told them that they might be eligible for federal recognition under the new policy. He told the Tribe that if they could prove that any members were one-half or more "Indian blood," then these individuals could write a constitution and submit it for approval, which would lead to federal recognition and the possibility of establishing a reservation. Of the community of roughly 18,000 people, 209 submitted to a physical examination in order to determine their status as Native people. Of these 209, 22 were confirmed to be one-half or more "Indian blood." This physical examination, and the results from it, were obviously problematic and racist. Using pseudoscientific techniques such as cranial measurement and an evaluation of facial structure, these individuals were selected when even some of their full siblings were denied.[17]

During the 1950s, the Lumbee worked to reconsolidate their community and power. At the same time, the federal government was working through

Public Law 280 and House Concurrent Resolution 108 to terminate Indian tribes' trust relationship with the federal government and move their land onto the tax rolls for individual states. At the same time, the Lumbee's strategy for recognition began by petitioning the state to do away with their continued classification as Cherokee, a name that many in the community had come to see as inaccurate and imposed on them by outsiders. In 1953 they succeeded, and the state of North Carolina recognized them as the Lumbee Tribe of North Carolina. Taking the name of the river that runs through Robeson County, the Tribe decided to adopt a name that would accommodate all of their members and their respective thoughts regarding tribal origin. This decision, while understandable in the way that it insists the people belong to a specific place and emphasizes their connection to the land, also has created a significant hurdle for the Lumbee Tribe in its present-day quest for full federal recognition because it supposedly obscured the Tribe's relationship to a "historic" tribal community.[18] Ultimately, the 1956 Lumbee Act, in one fell swoop, both federally recognized *and terminated* the Tribe.[19] While it finally recognized the Lumbee as a tribe, the legal language of Termination was added to the act at the eleventh hour, which prohibited the Lumbee from receiving services provided by the BIA, one of which is the current administrative federal recognition process, resulting in a near-perfect catch-22. This issue has continued to plague the Lumbee Tribe's applications for federal recognition. In December 2016 the Department of the Interior reversed the decision that the 1956 Lumbee Act effectively terminated the Tribe, writing "that the Lumbee Act does not terminate or forbid the Federal relationship and, therefore, does not bar the Department from recognizing the Lumbee Indians by application of the Part 83 acknowledgment process." Solicitor Hilary Tompkins also notes that she cannot say "whether any petition for federal acknowledgment by the Lumbee Indians, if filed, would succeed; I merely conclude that the Lumbee Act does not preclude evaluating such a petition."[20] After the passage of the Lumbee Act in 1956 and today, the Tribe continues to campaign for the federal recognition of their inherent sovereignty, and the Lumbee continue to assert their Indigenous identity in North Carolina, resisting any outsider's definition. This campaign continues in 2018, and this continual political backdrop informs the subsequent Lumbee cultural productions I examine.

"Don't call me boy": The Resistant History of *Strike at the Wind!*

As the opening epigraph from Willie French Lowery indicates, the impetus for the outdoor drama *Strike at the Wind!* might be understood as just one step among a larger campaign for Lumbee cultural recognition in their quest for federal recognition. From the archival records, it seems that the three main reasons for the creation of the outdoor drama included a concern over school integration policy that the Lumbee felt would rob them of their separate identity by forcing them into a southern black/white paradigm; a desire to capitalize on the renewed interest in American Indian cultures as a result of the Red Power movements across the United States; and a sense that like the other communities with an outdoor drama in the state, they too had a story worth telling.[21] The questions of identity and place constitute central tenets of *Strike at the Wind!* both in terms of the drama's plot and the struggle around successfully staging the show. These intertwined issues affect how people see or do not see the Lumbee people of North Carolina, and the history of *Strike at the Wind!* could be considered as much about the history of the Lumbee battle for federal recognition as it is about the outdoor drama itself. The textual material that surrounds the play—newspaper clippings, reports, internal letters between Green, Umberger, and others disputing plot points—all reveal an anxiety over how to represent the Lumbee Tribe to an audience. Interestingly, the audience discussed in this archive extended far past the immediate audience for the performance but spoke to larger audiences across the region. So while *Strike at the Wind!* would be performed in an amphitheater, the Lumbee drama over recognition was being staged in the theater of public opinion.

Despite several successful seasons, *Strike at the Wind!* eventually ceased yearly performances, but it was recently performed for two nights during June 2017. As Lumbee scholar Malinda Maynor Lowery notes in an interview with the North Carolina Folklife Institute, the play has been a "hand-to-mouth" production in terms of funding for the yearly performances. Although the Robeson County area sits just off I-95, which serves as the travel route for many to coastal destinations from South Carolina to Florida, the play has had a difficult time raising the needed money for each year's production. The Institute of Outdoor Drama predicts that the Lumbee drama could attract as many as 65,000 visitors a year, but this has not happened in recent seasons. The performance constitutes a vital part of the region's summer economy, and as Maynor Lowery stresses, audiences should note that when they come see this play they are doing more than simply supporting the arts; they are creating jobs in a rural section of the country with a shaky economy. The play, then, is caught in an economic double bind where it needs capital to stage the play, and the community needs the play to generate capital. Between 2005 and 2007 Maynor Lowery and others worked hard to raise the money to produce the performance.[22] Part of the problem is that despite the traffic of I-95, Robeson County represents an economically depressed section of North Carolina—even before the 2008 fiscal crisis.[23]

In addition to the economics behind the performance's status up until 2017, at least three other issues point to why the Lumbee drama might have experienced difficulty in sustaining an audience. These include the play's provocative and important choice to portray a local story that rings true for the community rather than the more superficially imposed "Lost Colony sequel" that was initially suggested; the play's clear critique of southern paradigms of racism and pathos; and the play's foregrounding of racial complexity in an Indigenous nationalism that refuses to mirror easy classifications of ethnicity in the region. These elements make the script one of the most interesting of all the outdoor dramas, but as the difficulties in its initial staging suggest, these complexities are perhaps not as well received by audiences from across the region and beyond. Thus, like the Lumbee's own constant quest for federal recognition, *Strike at the Wind!* too longs to be recognized by audiences for the important statement it makes about the complicated nature of Indigenous identity in the region. As it turns out, this story does not seem to have the same resonance to attract viewers and sustain a yearly audience. This further demonstrates the problems of inertia in these histories and how concepts of "truth" in the region remain bound up with cultural and political registers of Native existence in the U.S. South.

In 1970 the Lumbee community experienced significant external pressure from non-Native members of the local community to make their outdoor drama about the Lost Colony theory—in other words, recapitulate the story of their "success" as a tribe as owing to their early acceptance of English people, the English language, and the English values of private land ownership and single-family homes. Additionally, in the 1970s many non-Native people hoped that Paul Green would agree to write the Lumbee play as a sequel to the immensely popular *Lost Colony* on Roanoke Island. In fact, this idea was so popular that the *Raleigh News and Observer* reported on August 2, 1970, that:

> Plans are going ahead in Pembroke for a sequel to Manteo's "Lost Colony" outdoor drama. The play, now being written, would depict the legend that Manteo's unsuccessful settlers survived and moved inland to Robeson County and intermarried with Indians. [. . .] Tradition says the settlers died. But Lumbee Indians—some with Caucasian features—and English-sounding names—contend that some of them intermarried with the Indians. The Robeson Historical Drama, Inc. has commissioned Paul Green of Chapel Hill, author of the Lost Colony outdoor drama, and his associate, Randolph Umberger, to write a drama telling of the migration. ("Lost Colony Sequel")

After this article appeared, Green sent an angry letter to Gene Warren, the public relations director at Pembroke State University responsible for the press release, informing him of his error. In correspondence dated September 8, 1970, Green writes:

> As Nixon says—or did before newspaper men made him conscious of his cliché—let me make this perfectly clear to you, I have not been commissioned,

and I have not been hired by your drama association to write the Lumbee Indian drama. I have offered to help out in seeing that a script is provided and have offered to collaborate on this free of charge. And this drama, when and if it comes to pass, is not and won't be a sequel to the Lost Colony. There is not the least shred of evidence that the Lumbee are descended from the Roanoke people. [...] The story so far as I have anything to do with it will be the drama of the Lumbee Indians' struggle for social recognition and a place equal and right among their fellows. So please, Gene, get your news straight. As I say, I want to help but not on the sort of proposed play I've been reading about. ("Paul Green to Gene Warren")

From this correspondence, we can see the controversy and stakes regarding the content of this play. This is not the only evidence from the archive that several non-Native people from the community were convinced that the only possible story that could carry the performance would be a sequel to Green's *Lost Colony*. Such a performance could prove potentially destructive to the Lumbee case for recognition. To have the Lumbee outdoor drama continue this narrative of Euro-American legitimacy could further entrench both the idea that Lumbee people were "too assimilated" to qualify as Native and simultaneously assert a shared Indigenous and European land claim to the continent. In other words, audience members could feasibly leave the play with a sense of the "Native Lost Colonist" as the foundational figure of North Carolina, rendering both material Indigenous land claim and tribal nationalism moot points for the twentieth century. This narrative would also incorporate the Tribe into a U.S. national and southern regional founding myth that would flatten internal Indigenous transnational complexity and instead render tribal nationalisms as mere sequel to the arrival of European forms of nationalism. Green's own fervent denial of the Lost Colony sequel hinged on both its historical inaccuracy and his feeling that the larger goal of asserting the Lumbee's struggle for "social recognition" should remain at the forefront of the play. Although Green uses the adjective "social" before the term "recognition," one could imagine that the attendant issue of Lumbee federal recognition was not far from his mind. The proposed sequel story would only serve to undermine that claim and further force the Lumbee into an obligatory birth of a nation rather than help with the recognition of their Indigenous identity and their long resistance to the racist paradigm that surrounded them in North Carolina.

In a letter dated May 31, 1970, Nell Skinner, a non-Lumbee woman and influential member of the Robeson County Historical Drama corporation, expresses her frustration with Green protégé and eventual *Strike at the Wind!* playwright Randy Umberger. She advocates for a Green-authored *Lost Colony* sequel, writing to Green that "In fact, you might be the only man who could write a drama that the Indians would be open to because, it is my belief, most of them identify with The Lost Colony" ("To Paul Green"). Skinner does not name her sources, and the archive itself proves murky territory when it comes to assessing who thought or knew what any given Lumbee person believed or was willing to share about their tribal origins or history with outsiders. The non-Native opinions circulate heavily, and frequently they appeal to anecdotal evidence about Lumbee history gleaned from unnamed Lumbee friends and acquaintances. The archive of the performance history and backstory can come across as primarily a debate between non-Lumbee outsiders as they each vied for their own interpretation of local history rendered through a Lumbee story. And such a moment is where the archives of these outdoor dramas can fail us. Without a doubt, the story of *Strike at the Wind!* is a Lumbee story despite the ways that non-Lumbee community members seemingly invested their identities into how that story would be told. These archival moments again show the background machinations of a red state that attempts to use Native history to buttress its own claims of belonging in the U.S. South. Despite the archive's foregrounding of a debate between non-Natives, it remains paramount to realize that there is another Lumbee story at work.

For his part, Green seems to have taken more cues from Adolph Dial and other Lumbee scholars and educators associated with Pembroke State University. It seems that Nell Skinner encouraged at least one Lumbee person to write to Green as a potential plea for him to author a Lost Colony–type sequel. However, it is in this correspondence from Reba M. Lowry that we see the forwarding not of the Lost Colony story but of the material from Dakota ethnologist and scholar Ella Deloria's pageant *The Life-Story of a People* (1940), which included the story of Henry Berry Lowry and featured a cast and crew almost entirely made up of Lumbee community members.[24] Lowry had been asked by Skinner to write to Green about Deloria's pageant, which briefly alludes to the potential of the Lost Colony theory. However, Reba Lowry goes on to focus the Henry Berry Lowry story almost exclusively as the central portion of Deloria's earlier production. Despite the rifts in the community that had emerged through the previous articulations of tribal identity to gain recognition—"Siouan" and "Cherokee," "rural" and "town"—Deloria's play served as a site of coalescence "around a common narrative of Robeson County Indian history that did not depend on a particular tribal name but instead on agreement about the identity markers that defined the Indian community" (Maynor Lowery, *Lumbee Indians* 224). Nonetheless, Deloria's play, even with its use of more stereotypical pan-Indian markers, seemingly appealed to the community as theirs, as a space to "express themselves and to control that expression" (ibid.). Even in the play's use of "inauthentic" markers of playing Indianness, Maynor Lowery asserts, and I agree, that "it amounted to an avenue for Indians to control, to some degree, the portrayal of their own identities," and the significance of this should not be diminished by later scholars seeking the "authentic" Indian behind the constructed performance (ibid.).

Taking its cues perhaps from Deloria's earlier text and Paul Green's 1926 *Last of the Lowries*, *Strike at the Wind!* follows the historical events of the so-called Lowry Wars closely, as even without much editing they already make for a rather compelling story. And despite being a non-Native outsider, Umberger seemed to remain conscientious of the legacy to allow the Lumbee community to control the performance of its own narrative. The unclear ending, the "outlaw style" violence, and the love story between Henry and his wife Rhoda, who facilitated one of his escapes by bringing food (and tools) to the jail house, all serve as central plot elements for the work. Most notably, the play critiques the paradigms of the Old and New Souths, and it takes a sharp look at the region's racist history. It does not rejoice or wallow in the civil religion of the southern Lost Cause, and it foregrounds the continued survival of the people. The script opts for the understandably more intriguing possibility that Lowry did indeed escape North Carolina (ironically to Georgia, ground zero for Removal, perhaps suggesting a provocative counterhistory to *that* narrative). The play clearly sutures the reader to the point of view of the Lowrys, and it creates a structure of sympathy between the audience and the protagonist in the fight against a racist and corrupt economic system designed to keep racial minorities oppressed. The play's main framing device is structured around a "Leader" figure that serves as a narrator of the backstory and offstage events. The "Leader," however, does not speak directly to the audience. Instead, he shares dialogue with a staged viewer, whom the casting notes only call "Boy." This figure becomes more important as the play progresses. While narrator figures have served as important dramatic devices in the earlier plays I examine, this "Boy" is unique. In essence, he seems to mirror the audience, offering them a double of themselves on the stage in the form of a young Lumbee child. This doubling, though, is complicated by what audience one imagines for this outdoor drama and who one imagines is represented by this point of view.

Even though Green supported Umberger and the mission to stage a local, counternational, and critical regional history, he was skeptical of the amount of violence in Umberger's first script. Meanwhile, the organization, Robeson County Historical Drama, Inc. (RCHD), remained wary of any play not solely authored by Green. Additionally, the Institute of Outdoor Drama expressed concern that the white characters in the play lacked any real motivation. In a letter to Green, Umberger explains his concerns and thoughts on the violent script: "There seems no way to avoid violence in the story, since the story is the product of violence and any attempt at 'prettying up' the facts would weaken the fabric of the whole. [. . .] I have not removed, as I indicated, the violence from the story, but I have placed a good deal of it off-stage" ("To Paul Green").

Here, Umberger defends his portrayal of the violent history of the Lowry Wars, and he notes that his solution involves removing the action from the stage. Additionally, as Umberger also notes, he found it difficult to provide much insight into the motivation of the white characters involved in the Lowry Wars. He writes in the same letter to Green: "As I say, I think that although the shape of this rewrite is essentially the same as the first, it is clearer, stronger, and hopefully has more motivation for the whites. The fact remains, however, that some actions of the whites were almost beyond explanation—even to the other whites of the period, and certainly to the Lumbees. Some of those guys were just plain MEAN! Nonetheless, I've tried for more rounded characters in this draft." It seems that Umberger felt caught in a battle between accuracy, violence, and performative history. As he writes to Hector MacLean, who was also chairman of the RCHD, regarding the second draft, "My first draft was extremely accurate historically, and therefore, extremely violent" ("To Hector MacLean"). In several places in Umberger's correspondence he refers to the "audience's sympathies" and "giving the audience what they want," yet despite mentioning the audience as a "known quantity," he remains vague about what audience he means: the Lumbee audience of Robeson County, the non-Lumbee audience of the surrounding area, or audiences from outside the immediate community. The expected motivations of and responses to these characters necessarily changes depending on who views the show. As Green expressed to Umberger, he thought the violence remained excessive. Throughout all of the correspondence between Umberger, Green, and the RCHD, there remains an anxiety over what effect restaging this moment will have on local and national viewers.

Despite the fact that Umberger was non-Native, his allied stance with the Lumbee community's version of the Lowry story for the play, alongside his awareness of the fact that these characters would likely be played by Lumbee actors, allows us to think of the play as a Lumbee cultural text. It is from and of the community, and to this day, it remains the community who champions its staging. Therefore, it is important to analyze key moments from the script and imagine how these words sounded echoing across Robeson County during the 1970s. The play offers several core ideas that help us reconsider the red state. Like many of the narratives of white southern pathos I examined earlier, *Strike at the Wind!* offers key articulations of land claim. However, as with Henry Berry Lowry's "only land I know" statement, these articulations are not drawn from a wistful attachment to a sense of place. Rather, they are argued for in terms of a deep time of Indigenous presence in the region. This regional belonging remains one point of contention within the play as white southerners forward a sense of region that differs from their Native and African American counterparts. The resistance figures of Lowry's gang deny neither their southernness nor their attachment to their home. Instead, they promote their landed belonging through their indigeneity and attachment to the land via labor. Together, these elements of the play forward sovereign spaces of indigeneity that argue for Robeson County's identity as *Red*.

The play offers several considerations of the material claim to land. In the opening scene of the 1971 script, a soldier appears and recites a marriage vow from Queen Elizabeth to the land of "Virginia." One Lumbee chorus member speaks up and, in an often-echoed sentiment, questions, "To have and to hold from this day forth? You cannot hold the land!" (Umberger, *Strike* 2).[25] While this statement may strike many as a cliché pronouncement of the nameless "Indian character," it takes on more significance as the play continues. A few lines later, another chorus member asserts that the Americans have returned the favors of Lumbee allies in various wars by "thank[ing] us with one hand, and with the other [taking] our land" (4).[26] A few moments later, Henry Berry Lowry responds to his soon-to-be wife Rhoda's remark that "the Rebs are losing" by asserting, "They're more determined than ever. It wasn't enough to take our land—now they want our lives" (10). In traditionally labeled conservative dramas of the red state, such a sentiment would indicate that the Confederate Rebels' loss signals that it is the federal government out to take southern land and lives. However, Henry is clear: he chronicles the *Confederate* abuse of Native people at Fort Fisher and boldly calls out the Rebels for taking the lives and land of Indigenous people. This flips an old southern strategy on its head. The Rebels are the land thieves, robbing Indigenous people of the land and many people of color of their labor and lives in the quest to make that land turn a profit. The play is clever in the articulation of this sentiment. It maintains a form of pathos that some in the white southern audience are likely to respond to via their own sense of Confederate defeat, and then it turns the feeling against the Confederate structure itself. This shift is made all the more clear when one of the white Home Guard soldiers, MacGreggor, offers that Henry's father Allen is "'bout the only Indian around with much land left" (15). Allen's land ownership is the very thing that drives the racist, white Home Guard to frame and execute Allen Lowry for theft. Over the course of the play, then, the audience must watch the slow loss of Indigenous land at the hands of what many white viewers might have previously regarded as the "glorious Confederate dead."

The script, however, does not foreground the pathos of a slowly vanishing Indian and wistful whittling away of tribal lands. Instead, Henry fights. He fights hard. And as we know, he does not die. The first act closes as Henry seems to be in imminent danger. He has, after all, declared war against the local officials, and by extension the state of North Carolina and by further extension, the Confederate States of America. Rhoda and his mother step forward to exhort his supporters, asking what they will do to help Henry and themselves. The "Leader" narrator picks up on this exhortation, turning to the listening "Boy," asking, "What will you do boy, strike at the wind? Well, answer me. What's next?" The Boy closes act I by rising to his feet, looking at the action surrounding him and asserting, "Don't call me boy" (42). This moment punctuates the 1971 script. Here we have a character called "Boy" denying the very identity that has been placed onto him by several forces, including the "authoritative" narrator; the even more seemingly authoritative script; and the most authoritative of all, the author of the play. In refusing this put-upon, infantilized identity, then, we see echoes of a Lumbee people who will not be put upon by outside definitions of who they are or what their history stands for. Notably, it seems that these lines were eventually removed as the narrator from the 1990s and 2000s productions speaks to the Boy more as an elder and less as a "Leader," signaling perhaps a shift in the resistance narrative that looks outside of the community to one that foregrounds internal dialogue and leadership as the continuation of the Lumbee Tribe.

In the 1971 decision to tell a story of Indigenous resistance in Confederate and Reconstruction North Carolina—essentially a secessionist narrative from both the United States and the Confederate States of America—there stands an inherent claim to landed sovereignty. Furthermore, with the valorization of a man who advocated the redistribution of a white landed class's wealth to the disenfranchised, the play demonstrates an alternative nationalism grounded in Indigenous land claim and independent from Euro-American narratives of manifest settler colonialism. This counternational narrative, however, is a risky one. As I suggest in earlier chapters, it may be hard for many audiences of outdoor drama in the U.S. South to cheer for an Indigenous critique of U.S. capitalist nationalism and Confederate glory. And in this significant move from the Lost Colony sequel to the story of Henry Berry Lowry, *Strike at the Wind!* shifts the meaning of the red state from one routed through narratives of Confederate Lost Causes to one rooted in continued Indigenous resistance.

Rather than belonging to the region or belonging to the audience, the play makes clear that the Lumbee people belong to one another, and they alone will determine who they are. Their identity comes from within their sovereign community. To return, then, to the brief analysis that opens this chapter, it is much like what Herbert Locklear quoted in the 1971 *News and Observer*: "It's not that we love North Carolina so much ... It's difficult to explain, but what we are attached to is one particular place in North Carolina where our people live. It's the center of our nationalism." The Lumbee's land attachment and their identity attachment inform who they are as North Carolinians, as southerners, as Native people with a sovereign claim to their homelands. The play forwards this, offering a sharp division between being of the place and being a "Reb." It manages to unstitch a Native southern identity from a Confederate southern one, demonstrating that a lost cause is not what drives the story of Henry Berry Lowry, and I would argue by extension the Native South.

As we consider the many nonstagings of *Strike at the Wind!*, it seems that this complicated history does not sustain an audience as easily as the more frequently mythologized narratives of national belonging that undergird the narratives of other performances I examine such as *The Lost Colony*, which is quickly approaching its eightieth season. These complicating factors return me to the troubles of a reformulated red state. When a play such as *Strike at the Wind!* works to shift the narrative of how we understand a resistant, localized Indigenous South, how are we to understand the fact that it continues at the brink of precarity?

Willie French Lowery points to this problem of reception as he recounts the ways in which the surrounding community did not want to see the story of Lumbee existence and resistance to a racist paradigm. Lowery, a significant figure in the Lumbee community and a nationally successful musician, wrote the score for the original play. His music for the outdoor drama speaks to the principles of a Lumbee cultural identity that conformed neither to the expectations of the immediately surrounding non-Native community nor to the pan-Indian or Hollywood stereotype that the public expected to see of American Indians. As he notes of the problems of expectation surrounding the play in a 2008 interview with Michael Taylor: "[A]t that time we didn't have a whole lot of people pushing the idea that we do have a culture. We always looked at it like we don't have a culture. I guess in some people's eyes we didn't. We got questioned a lot from our funders about doing more Indian stuff. So we're sitting there going, 'Do more *Indian*?'" (Taylor 100). As Lowery articulates, this is not only a problem confined to what outsiders see as "Native culture" in the region. He notes that even within the culture, the persistence of general stereotypes about American Indians limited the ways that people within the Lumbee community imagined themselves as being Native: "My own people looked at it wrong because they had feathers in their hair and powwows and stuff" (ibid.). Thus, how non-Native people expect to see Native culture can influence the way Native people conceive of their own being in the region.[27] Such a conflation could lead to the rather simplistic conclusion that Native people allow popular myths to drive their expression of identity, and that in this respect they are engaged in romantic fictions. However, Lowery counters these assumptions of American Indian identity, stating, "It's the culture, but our culture exceeds that, I think. It gets more into how we talk, how we lived our lifestyle, and the beauty of how we were raised" (ibid.). This identity coming from within the values of the community speaks to the initial stakes of *Strike at the Wind!* but also to the problems of rendering these values legible to a larger audience. In essence, it returns to the problem of the "Boy."

When a character in a staged drama throws off his assigned identity, how does the audience conceive of him? Do they continue to call him "boy"? Who is this character, and how will he be recognized?

In his initial writings on the possibility of this performance, Green saw the importance of how this play might work for political ends for the Lumbee people. In his personal notes, he writes: "In the play, there is a little boy who loves books, stories. We feel that he represents the future. He starts a school. Maybe the play ends with the Indians finding themselves established as a nation in their own right" (Green, "Notes"). Here, Green alludes to the future of the Indian Normal School, later to become Pembroke State and eventually the University of North Carolina at Pembroke. As Green knew, this school began the long process of Lumbee appeals and denials for federal recognition. Green hoped that the play would end with the Lumbee as a recognized nation. Green looked to stage this possibility for the future rather than a tired history that kept the Lumbee as wayward lost colonists.

The problem with staging possibilities, though, is that for audiences to imagine them, they must be staged. And for these outdoor dramas to be staged, they need an audience. This is the challenge that *Strike at the Wind!* perpetually battles. The play does not take an ameliorated tone, and as such, perhaps the drama does not appeal to audiences in the same way as the other popular shows of the state. This is not to suggest that the Lumbee should change the tone or content of *Strike at the Wind!* A shift of southern feelings is necessarily dependent on reception, but in order for these plays to shift the emotive registers of the region, they must first present a history that can sustain the economic framework to be staged.[28] Indeed, outdoor drama is no group's "traditional culture," and one might say that the story of Henry Berry Lowry is just another lost cause compensatory fiction, designed and filtered through this non-Native genre in order to consolidate Lumbee difference into Lumbee nationalism. I would argue, however, that every once in a while a little compensatory fiction might just be the trick, especially if one has yet to receive any compensation. Furthermore, *Strike at the Wind!* does not stage a lost cause. Instead, Henry Berry Lowry offers a tradition of resistance, and the Lumbee remain attached to their geographic place in the region despite the toughest historical pressures. The Lumbee have proven time and again that they do not believe in lost causes, or they would have given up on their own battle for federal recognition years ago. Rather, they, like Henry Berry Lowry, still *live* in Robeson County, North Carolina.

Plant the Past and See the Future

In 1976 Willie French Lowery released the album *Proud to Be a Lumbee*, which followed the successful self-titled *Plant and See* (1969) from Lowery's multicultural assemblage of musicians from the U.S. South. Lowery's work demonstrates the elements of a complex Lumbee identity that challenged the pan-Indian cultural markers that the larger public anticipated from Native people, particularly in the new age–infused late 1960s and early 1970s. As I mention above, he points to this anxiety as he recounts the ways in which the surrounding community did not immediately recognize the dynamic Lumbee identity staged in *Strike at the Wind!* Lowery's musical output serves as a productive site to examine these complications as he merges elements from African American blues, southern rock, southern gospel harmonies, and folk music into what some have considered a national "Lumbee" sound.[29] The production of this Lumbee sound is in and of itself resistant to the paradigms of race that obscure Native nationalisms. In a superficially imposed concept of "racial" purity onto sovereign national claims, non-Native institutions demand a standard of Native nations to which the United States does not itself adhere in policy (though practice is indeed another matter). As Maynor Lowery explains, "The ways in which Indians in Robeson County have manipulated race, and the ways in which race has been used against them, demonstrate that the concept is a social fiction that has exclusion and inequality at its core" (*Lumbee Indians* 257). Lowery's musical affirms Lumbee national identity and rejects the physical removal from Lumbee homelands or racially exclusionary politics, emphasizing instead the productive dynamism of Native diversity within a sovereign space.

Lowery's first album, *Plant and See*, from a band of the same name, opens with the guitar-driven, raw, and ever-so-slightly psychedelic "Put Out My Fire." This song with its pedal hi-hat opening serves as a relatively straightforward example of Lowery's early musical output. The group recorded the album between New York and California before returning to North Carolina, where they switched out a few members and re-formed as a band called Lumbee (notably, the label wanted Lowery to name the band "Cherokee," which he resolutely refused to do). After that, they released another album, *Overdose*. During the tours for both albums, Lowery shared the stage with the Allman Brothers. In particular, the first two songs from *Plant and See*, "Put Out My Fire" and "Flat on My Face," represent the southern rock sound of the period. I agree with other critics of Lowery's work that this southern rock is not only the blending of European and African influences. As Michael Taylor has written of Lowery, "while thoroughly informed by a variety of southern musical genres, [his music] was highly Indian in intention and representation. [. . .] [T]hese dual musical identities are as entwined as the kudzu and the oak; the only place we might begin to pry them apart is on paper" (80). I agree with Taylor that Lowery's music remained Indigenous in its intention and representation, but I wonder if these other items, namely, his Indigenous grounding in a southern rock tradition, can be pried apart at all—on paper or otherwise.

Just as others have established the Indigenous origins of traditional African American folk tales such as those featuring Brer Rabbit, I argue that we might at least pause to consider the Indigenous influences, origins, and contributions of the southern rock sound.[30] Furthermore, given that musicians such as Lowery, who resolutely identified as Native, traveled and appeared with such major touchstones of the genre as the Allman Brothers, I argue that we do the genre and Native artists a disservice if we do not engage the discussion of what southern rock might owe to Indigenous artists. The 2017 documentary film *Rumble: The Indians Who Rocked the World* foregrounds this legacy, suggesting that numerous elements of the period's music emerged from Indigenous artists considering their sonic worldviews. Furthermore, as Erich Nunn has articulated in his *Sounding the Color Line: Music and Race in the Southern Imagination* (2015), "Sounds constantly leak through the racial barriers such institutions place around and between them" (5). When we combine Maynor Lowery's analysis of the ways that Native people in Robeson County have pushed through the racial barriers that attempted to construct their national identity alongside Nunn's argument that musical sound operates in a similar way, we can begin to understand the significance of Lowery's work. It contributes to a sounded identity for Lumbee people that confounds racial assumptions of both "southern" and "Native."[31]

The second track on *Plant and See*, "Henrietta," exemplifies this Lumbee sound in form and content. This song offers what might be called a southern rock sound, something vaguely reminiscent of the Allman Brothers' "Melissa," and indeed the two songs were written and recorded during roughly the same period. Unlike the single vocal of "Melissa," "Henrietta" features four-part harmonies, sung by Plant and See's racially diverse members: African American drummer Forris Fulford, Lumbee guitarist Willie Lowery, white vocalist Carol Fitzgerald, and Latino bassist Ronald Seiger, offering a compelling aurally integrated example of the U.S. South's diverse population in the late 1960s. But unlike other groups, whose racial diversity during the period may have been part marketing ploy, Plant and See's membership represented the world around them; significantly, it mirrored in some ways the interracial makeup of Henry Berry Lowry's nineteenth-century resistance group (though this was also unintentional). Brendan Greaves, owner of the label Paradise of Bachelors, which recently rereleased *Plant and See*, notes: "I think that there were bands who were kind of assembled with that in mind, that kind of social boundary pushing, but for Willie, I don't think it was an agenda." However, he continues, "I think it wasn't as big a deal for them as it was for everybody else, but I'm sure it had something to do with their inability to really break through" (Melzer). The four-part harmony of a multiracial band may have worked to the ear, but the visibility of racial harmony remained a hurdle for the band. As Greaves notes of the group, "First of all, an interracial band, in

Publicity photo for the self-titled album *Plant and See*. The band later changed its name to Lumbee.

the South, in Southeastern North Carolina, in 1969. They were ahead of their time, and I know they had a lot of struggles in terms of playing venues during segregation" (McCray).

This "ahead of time"-ness of the band is significant. Despite being a common phrase to describe most anything progressive, it also signals the ways in which the Lumbee community of southeastern North Carolina creates their own temporal landscape. In addition to being "Better *Red* than Dead," recognizing that "Henry Berry Lowry will never die," and waiting to see what grows after planting, Lumbee cultural productions often suggest a sustained temporality—a long view. Thus, it isn't that the band Lumbee was *ahead* of its time, but rather it was of *its* time and on its own terms. The difference is that its time is not the Western calendar time of a Euro-American U.S. South but rather an Indigenous time of the region. In fact, the very fact that Lowery's musical works were rereleased in the last few years signals their continued importance and the cycle of their influence. This music remains relevant; whereas it may not have garnered its due praise in the late 1960s and 1970s (with the exception of "Streets of Gold" from the album *Overdose*, which spent some time at the top of the East Coast market of the Billboard charts), its rerelease and critical reception demonstrate its power to exist in a recurrent temporal landscape. It did work then, and it returns to do work now.

Interestingly, in addition to being "ahead of its time," Greaves notes the album's aggression toward its larger cultural milieu. He continues, "There's an aggression in the music that I think speaks to his frustrations as a young man, working as a musician with an interracial band in the South" (McCray). So ironically, despite southern rock's history as a genre that drew from numerous cultural and racial influences, an actual representation of this diversity on stage challenged a "white-washed" version of the sound. Rather than abstract aggression, I argue that we might also term this as a resistant sound. Instead of attributing the aggressive guitar riffs of the first two songs of *Plant and See* to clichéd masculine anger, Greaves hits a more productive note. This aggression emerges from the same anger that Sue Kim delineates in *On Anger: Race, Cognition, and Narrative* (2013), where she lays out the tradition of aggression in communities where histories of disenfranchisement and dismissal result in emotions that dominant groups might consider "unreasonable." This anger is reminiscent of Henry Berry Lowry's aggressive actions and is in many ways necessary for the heteroglossia of resistance literature, which I argue in this case includes the aural musical forms as well as the lyrical poetics of Lowery's work. As Barbara Harlow reminds us regarding resistance narratives, "They challenge the very effort to isolate literature and literary works from other 'spheres of influence,' which has characterized much of western literary criticism and practice. The resistance narrative is not only a document, it is also an indictment" (98). In this way, Lowery forwards a doubly resistant text: an aggressive instrumental musicality alongside lyrical compositions that call for healing, which together indict the southern racist paradigms surrounding the band in the 1970s and, I would argue, surrounding us today.

In addition to its literal representation of interracial harmony, the song "Henrietta," also deserves consideration for its lyrical content, which links the Lumbee homelands to the theme of homecoming. Given the very real presence of Henry Berry Lowry in Lumbee cultural traditions and the song's title as the feminine form of the name "Henry," it is hard not to hear a tale of homecoming to Robeson County in the song's lyrics, particularly from a songwriter who also penned titles such as "Henry Berry Lowry Is My Hero." "Henrietta" opens:

> I heard from Henrietta.
> She wants me back.
> I'm going in my room now,
> And I'm going to pack.
> And daylight tomorrow,
> She'll be standing by my side.
> Henrietta,

> You're on my mind.
> I'm going back where I met her.
> She needs me there.

By this time, Lowery had spent many years as a traveling musician, but he always returned to Robeson County. The singer's desire to return to the place "where he met" Henrietta, and his knowledge that she wants him back potentially reads as a metaphor for the songwriter's attachment to the land of his people. As his widow and Lumbee historian Maynor Lowery explains, "After being on the road, seeing the violence, the drug use, the corruption of the industry, just the craziness of it, that wasn't as appealing to him as having a family and settling down some—again, although not entirely" (Melzer, "Unexpected Revival").[32] His indigeneity has not been reduced by his travel but rather solidifies his love of home and his attention to those who ask him to return. Even if "Henrietta" is not a feminized stand-in for the Lumbee hero "Henry," and I realize that it most certainly was not Lowery's intention, the call home still rings true. The song is about homecoming and return, and it remains a powerful statement. It suggests a connection that refuses to be mitigated by time and distance. When this song engages in four-part harmonies from a racially diverse set of musicians, it asks us literally to hear a sound of Robeson County and imagine a desire to return home for love.

This harmony stands as central to many of the album's songs. A careful listen reveals that the four-part harmony is not an afterthought or window dressing to the instruments but rather the heart of the album. Significantly, *Plant and See*'s vocal harmonies are more than simply representative of racial diversity. They also carry forward the long tradition of Lumbee gospel singing that evolved somewhat uniquely in eastern North Carolina due precisely to the types of intercultural contact represented later by the members of *Plant and See*. As Maynor Lowery notes in her documentary *Sounds of Faith* (1997) as well as her other critical work, Lumbee vocal harmonies result directly from the cross-cultural contacts of Native, black, and white people in eastern North Carolina.[33] While Lumbee people likely used long-meter singing for many years, Maynor Lowery notes the increased influence of shape notes and vocal harmonies that emerged in the community in the late nineteenth and early twentieth centuries. While we might say that this mixing of cultural influences represents a loss of Native cultural forms, Maynor Lowery cautions against this view, writing for the accompanying *Sounds of Faith* online site:

> Many of those that have written about the role of music in religious and political histories have ignored the experience of Native peoples and cultural evolution. They have chosen to interpret our experience and use of Christian hymns as "assimilation," assuming that Native and Christian beliefs are antithetical and that conversion was in all cases a forced and usually violent pro-

cess. This assumption has created several erroneous conclusions, [including] that Native peoples are not capable of determining their own belief systems. This is not to trivialize the often coercive measures used by missionaries, government agents, and others in determining the course of Native cultures' development, but simply to include another voice to the discussion concerning the origins and experience of cultural interchange among Indian communities. Lumbee hymn singing is evidence of a complex process of musical and cultural interchange, and represents a community's agency in determining its own forms of religious and musical practice.[34]

Thus, from traditional religious, cultural, and regional forms, we see the song grow together, and this is where the very name of the band, Plant and See, offers a way to think about Native communities as future-looking agents in their own cultural productions, as creators of their own productive *Red* states.

This future-looking ethos follows the song "Henrietta" in the track "Rockin' Chair." The song begins by placing us on a front porch with a woman sitting in a rocking chair who "don't care about what's goin' on," even though the "world is in chaos." Asking the listener if anyone remembers "love thy neighbor" and *"noblesse oblige,"* the song foregrounds an image of an old woman who sees a remedy to the world's problems in a return to the values of her front porch. The song, though, is not all despair in its positioning of a rural isolation from worldly problems and the core values that might work to answer these vexing questions of the late 1960s. In this way, we see the album contemplating the role of place and politics. Notably, however, in the appeal to *"noblesse oblige,"* it calls on those with wealth to help those less fortunate. The song, then, is not simply seeking a romantic agrarian retreat as much as it is calling out those with wealth and power to remember the rural spaces that long made possible their status. When the song queries the truth of "love thy neighbor," it does not claim that the woman on her porch loves her neighbor; rather, it asks how much each person is implicated in the world's chaos.

This concern continues in the song "Poor Rich Man," which after an opening guitar solo follows with the white female vocalist Fitzgerald (also Lowery's fiancée at the time) setting a city scene and asking, "If I walked down the street with the blackest man, would you blame me?" After asking numerous questions about how people should react to scenes of racial integration and social justice, Lowery and Fitzgerald sing in harmony that they need "to find a place where they belong." This desire for belonging and justice located in place leads the song to pose hard questions regarding "who holds races back" while the "rich man collects the money." Likewise, it constructs images of a racially diverse urban setting within the form of a southern rock song. Synthesizing the album, then, the listener receives a potentially radical vision of a southern rock future. Such formulations challenge what we might think of as typical conservative, lost cause, romantically rural, Dixie-fied anthems of the genre included but not limited to "Sweet Home Alabama" and "Long-Haired Country Boy," or even Mohawk-descended songwriter Robbie Robertson's "The Night They Drove Ole Dixie Down," which he wrote channeling the life stories from his bandmate Levon Helm. In his case, though, by foregrounding place and politics, Lowery offers an alternative genealogy and future possibility for southern rock—one focused on economic and racial justice in both rural and urban spaces.

The considerations of place and politics influenced Willie French Lowery's later career move when he returned home and began working with Lumbee youth in developing arts programs that helped encourage cultural pride for the Lumbee Tribe's children. His 1976 *Proud to Be a Lumbee* is part traditional (in the gospel or folk sense) and part children's record. The album features several tracks about Henry Berry Lowry, including "Henry Berry Lowry Is My Hero" and "Henry and Rhoda's Love Song." In "Henry Berry Lowry Is My Hero," Lowery constructs a folk hero, telling tall tales about Henry scaring off a bear and staring down a snake. This shift from the historical event to the construction of the folk image demonstrates the power that the story has over and above its appeal to accuracy. Henry Berry Lowry *did* face down bears and snakes, albeit in human form. This song renders him a John Henry figure that achieves a larger-than-life status. It adjusts the temporal order of Henry Berry Lowry as one historical person to the timeless resistance figure that continues to exist past linear temporality or finality of event. Notably, though, Lowery asserts that "Henry Berry Lowry [...] is a great Indian man / Whenever there was trouble, he would make a stand." This shift to folk telling in song, though seemingly small, does important work for Indigenous sovereign claims. Of course, there is apocrypha about Henry Berry Lowry and about Lumbee origins. Nobody claims that Native stories are inherently more factual than their non-Native counterparts; each can operate in folk tradition. However, the uses of these stories matter, and as I explained earlier in this book, it is the causes, not the losses, that deserve our attention. The song foregrounds Lumbee Indigenous land claim in its positioning of a Robeson County home, and at the same time its form as folk song calls up the fact that the genre itself depends on the largely unverifiable (and often wildly exaggerated) tale that manifests a larger truth. In other words, the genre acknowledges the problem of (in)authenticity, but it renders that a moot point beside the use of the story for the sovereign survival of Lumbee people. If imagining Henry Berry Lowry staring down the bears and snakes of the Confederacy helps Lumbee people continue their sovereignty, then, why not tell this story? Why not follow this stand? Regions are made of stories, and people get to choose which ones to tell and which ones have productive use value for a better future. Why not deconstruct the ones that continue to promote hatred, play *Strike at the Wind!* I follow these analyses, which each speak more to the way that Lumbee people "assert their Indian cultural and racial identity to outsiders" (Oakley, "The Legend" 59). Rather than focus solely on racial and cultural identity, I would like to focus on the question of Lumbee *national* identity, and the way that their attendant land claims in southeastern North Carolina buttress the assertion of Lumbee national sovereignty. Furthermore, in this chapter I focus on a wider range of Lumbee cultural productions and the community's direct impact on non-Native authored texts such as *Strike at the Wind!* For example, I am interested in Lumbee musician Willie French Lowery's impact on the Umberger script of *Strike at the Wind!* Using this as a jumping-off point, I turn toward an examination of Lowery as a significant figure in a Lumbee cultural and literary tradition through his musical oeuvre. From this I delineate a tradition of Lumbee resistance to the conservative, often white supremacist red state. In doing this, I hope to demonstrate how through their cultural productions the Lumbee people have long created their own Indigenous red state within and apart from the state of North Carolina.

The Return of the Native Lost Colonists

It remains a common story in North Carolina that the Lumbee are descended from the Lost Colonists. This theory, one of the first and now most frequently questioned stories of Lumbee existence, came into being in 1885, when Hamilton McMillan, a white politician from Robeson County, North Carolina, proposed that the Indians in his home county were the descendants from Sir Walter Raleigh's 1587 Lost Colony. His resulting book with its characteristically long nineteenth-century title, *Sir Walter Raleigh's Lost Colony: An Historical Sketch of the Attempts of Sir Walter Raleigh to Establish a Colony in Virginia, with the Traditions of an Indian Tribe in North Carolina, Indicating the Fate of the Colony of Englishman Left on Roanoke Island in 1587*, argued that the current Native population of Robeson County were actually the "Croatoan" or "Croatan" Indians whose name had been supposedly carved into a tree where the colonists had disappeared, some 250 miles away in present-day Manteo, North Carolina. For as Maynor Lowery explains, McMillan probably operated on a faulty deduction that because the Native people he interviewed told him about their Roanoke and Hatteras ancestors and because they were "civilized" farmers, they must have been descended from Englishmen. Additionally, in McMillan's logic, because the Tribe had not been "discovered" in the inland swamps of Robeson by other white men (Scottish immigrants and French Huguenots) until the early 1700s, and because on their "discovery," the Native people already spoke English and engaged in farming, the theory stated that they must be the descendants not only of the English but specifically of the ill-fated colonists. While this theory is certainly provocative for its historical intrigue, it is probably more apocryphal than accurate. However, it has not kept many throughout the state, even today, from asserting this story as historical fact. Even if the theory is true, when analyzed closely, it implicitly justifies the contemporaneous nineteenth-century policy of Allotment. In other words, in 1885 it seems that via McMillan's theory, the Lumbee Tribe was put into an unknowing service of the federal government in order to legitimate the U.S. policies toward other tribes.

While proponents of the Dawes Allotment Act were busy articulating the benefits of individual land title, western agricultural practices, and registered patrilineal surname descent, McMillan's theory emerged regarding the Lumbee as ideal Indians who have benefited from centuries of just this type of existence. Maynor Lowery explains the appeal of this theory: "Identifying a historic lineage was necessary in the minds of white North Carolinians, who desired assurance that these Indians were a distinct racial group and not in fact African Americans" (26). At this critical juncture, the Tribe approached the federal government in their first attempt at federal recognition. Specifically, they hoped to secure congressional funding for their Indian Normal School, which was established to train Native teachers for their Indian primary school. McMillan enacted this legislation and supported the Tribe's efforts for recognition. Such efforts carried with them a type of weight against the heavily racist policies of the U.S. South, for as Maynor Lowery asserts, "Hidden behind the name 'Croatan' was a legend of white ancestry, white sacrifice, and white heroism. For a society obsessed with race and the traits that blood supposedly transmitted, emphasizing the tribe's white ancestry gained much-needed support for separate schools" (26). The combination of white ancestry and land ownership not only appealed to white southerners' sense of "blood" superiority, but it also implicitly attached the Tribe's success at landed sovereignty to their whiteness, thus equating land with the benefits of settler colonialism.

However, despite McMillan's personal motives or best intentions, it seems that his 1885 narrative of Lost Colony origins, combined with his championship of the Lumbee as a fully successful tribe with sustained schools and farms, actually served to help the federal government deny Lumbee recognition, and it echoed in eerily similar terms the great benefits of Allotment policy.[11] In between the initial attempt at Allotment policy in 1883 with the failed Coke Act, and the successful passing of the Dawes Allotment Act of 1887, McMillan's book regarding the Lumbee and the Lost Colony appeared in 1885. In it he writes of the Lumbee: "At the coming of white settlers [in 1709] there was found located on the waters of Lumber River, a large tribe of Indians, speaking English, tilling the soil, owning slaves and practicing many of the arts of civilized life" (14). Here, the Indigenous people of Robeson County are described as "civilized" because they speak English, till the violence, and racial exclusion, and why not build up the ones that promote resistance to these problems? Why not tell stories about Henry Berry Lowry as a hero? It's possible that one might argue that promoting such fictions only shifts the content rather than the form of the U.S. South. If apocrypha is part of the problem, then one might say that it is the form of the story—not the whimsy of content—that needs to change. But such an argument goes to my larger point. Native stories do indeed have different forms—from the basis in traditional storytelling practices and worldviews to the construction of temporalities and realisms. To only see and dismiss them based on any similarities to damaging fictions of the Confederate Lost Cause ignores not only that the content is significantly different but also that their form as Indigenous stories with historical grounding in this land is also distinct. These are not stories about settler colonialism. These are stories about resistance to that paradigm. Even when they use forms that may not be readily recognized as Native, critics should pay attention to the ways that Native artists indigenize these forms for their own purposes, creating moments of resistance through creative innovations.

In addition to promoting Henry Berry Lowry as this resistance figure, the album also forwards a collective sovereignty for the Lumbee people. The title track has gone on to be considered by many as the Lumbee Tribe's national anthem. The song opens:

> I'm proud to be a Lumbee Indian.
> Yes I am.
> When I grow up into this world,
> I'm going to be just what I am.

At this point, a chorus of Lumbee children respond to the call:

> My skin is brown
> My hair is black/blonde/red/brown
> I walk along without looking back
> I can be anything I want to be.

Just as Henry Berry Lowry calls on an alternate epistemological category of land claim in naming the "only land I know," Willie French Lowery creates ontological possibility in reminding the listener that the Lumbee Tribe is made up of people who are allowed to determine their own sovereign identity. Following Lowery's death in 2012, Maynor Lowery noted of the album: "Willie thought, especially with *Proud To Be a Lumbee*, that the need for that record was enormous [...] just watching the kids in our community and how they felt about themselves and understanding that people needed something to look to. We almost haven't had a counterargument [to the wrong stereotypes] to make to the outside world. *Proud To Be a Lumbee* was that kind of counterargument" (Melzer "Unexpected Revival"). Again, in this song we hear elements of gospel—the lead line, the call and response, the harmony of voices—alongside the southern folk–driven guitar sound. In addition to the musical form, however, one might also note the compelling lyrics, where children in their own voices innumerate the possibilities for Lumbee children as they grow up, not disaggregating careers, success, travel, and Lumbee identity as who they are in total. Significantly, they also note their phenotypic difference when they all sing their own hair color, allowing for the space where phenotypic markers of "race" exist but do not override one's national and cultural identity as Lumbee. This might be one of Lowery's most significant musical points both in content and form. The children sing together and individually: as the Lumbee Tribe and as individual people, they look forward. In this way, Lowery's performances that reference Lumbee identity offer a compelling place to think through the attendant issues of Native and southern identities and communities as living and evolving entities. For American Indian communities, frequently the act of existing, changing, and growing on one's own terms is the most resistant act. The song's imperative toward a self-determined "I am" and "I will be" offers a call for sovereignty for tribes based on the history they have created over the long picture rather than the one determined for them by outsiders through measures of perceived "authenticity." Thus, we might ask "what will American Indian identity in the South be today and in the future?" and Willie French Lowery leads the children in a chorus answering, "anything Indian people want it to be."

While this chapter has focused exclusively on the Lumbee, I do not mean to universalize their histories as indicative of all Native peoples and nations of the Southeast. Rather, I hope to have demonstrated how their battles with land claim, race-based hierarchies, and recognition remain important touchstones for understanding how the Indigenous *Red* state can emerge and take shape in one particularly localized space through tribally specific cultural productions. Because the Lumbee Tribe shares an apocryphal connection to the origin narratives of settler colonialism with the Roanoke colony, their stories demonstrate how the spiral of time carries Native resistance to settler colonialism forward. While non-Natives have long imagined that the impressive community organization and the success of Lumbee people have resulted from their English ancestors, it is more productive to imagine that their ancestors include those earliest Algonquian people who, after realizing that hospitality would not satiate the land-greedy desires of settlers, mounted one of the earliest concerted resistance movements against English colonialism. Through the continued assertions of individualized and community-based land claims, Lumbee cultural productions upset the narrative order of settler colonialism. The resistance narratives I outline in this chapter, while neither universal nor paradigmatic, resonate with numerous other Native acts of resistance to both U.S. national policies and local/state-based actions that attempt to abrogate the sovereignty of Indigenous people. As I continue to examine in the next chapter, embedded within these resistance narratives are calls not simply for survival but for resilience, where Native people imagine futures by building off of spiralic Indigenous temporalities that can enliven possibilities beyond the present. In this way, like the authors of the Lumbee resistance narratives I outline here, other Native writers of the U.S. South push audiences to recognize more complex, and perhaps older, red states.

CHAPTER FIVE

Resilience

> And the people, the people, the People. pushed into cataclysm,
> a few generations from alphabet book imposed catechism,
> soon were calamity tragedy storm splinters, fragmented
> particles of a real past, in a world gone away from oratory, song,
> oraliteratures, orations into gyrations reeling.
> —Allison Adelle Hedge Coke, "We Were in a World," 2016

Storms appear in early colonial American accounts as frequently as any other event. From the Caribbean to the Northeast, violent weather comes in as everything from ominous warning to trial by God. Storms, and in particular, hurricanes, however, are not European inventions. The word "hurricane" appears in European lexicons precisely as a result of Spanish invasion in the Caribbean. The Carib word *huracán* was adopted by the Spanish and Portuguese to describe the violent storms in the region.[1] Huracán, however, is not simply a storm. Rather, Huracán is a K'iche Mayan God responsible for acts including, but not limited to, a partial role in the creation of humans; a great flood; and the ultimate destruction of the Gods' second attempt at creating humanity, also known as "the wood people."[2] These beings abused all they encountered, forgot their Gods in prayer, and were generally mean, exploitative creatures. Huracán seals the ultimate fate of the wood people, and during the ensuing chaos, their animals, tools, and even own houses rise up against their cruel treatment. The hurricane, the Caribs might have been warning the colonial invaders, is a vengeful God who punishes bad behavior. Hurricanes are no respecters of wealth or persons, destroying everything in their path. Although related, natural disasters differ from man-made failures of infrastructure and health care. People in the U.S. South have learned these hard lessons time and again as they watch counterclockwise spiraling orbs of color barrel down on them while eager meteorologists anticipate the next apocalypse. Through an examination of these cataclysmic moments, I argue for the necessity of considering Native resilience as another iteration of a resistant *Red* state logic I examined in the previous chapter. It is these apocalyptic moments—and the postapocalyptic survivals that follow—that I focus on in this chapter.

It should be no exaggeration to state that Native American communities have survived their own apocalypses. From disease to Removal, and from boarding schools to diabetes, the onslaught of destructive forces has blown across Indian Country. Such a realization should easily shake up any easy notions of periodization when it comes to Native American literature. While mainstream accounts of literary postmodernism might encourage us to focus on the hand-wringing anxiety of a world without a center, on the apocalyptic future that skulks around the corner, Native American people have already faced down that demon. They have survived—and are surviving—the flood.[3] I do not mean to understand these apocalyptic moments as Revelation-style biblical referents of a beginning and ending linearity as established by European traditions. Rather, from an Indigenous methodology, each ending is in and of itself a potential beginning. This chapter examines those narratives of life through and after the potentially destructive event, offering two complementary arguments: one, that Native authors of the U.S. South write through the apocalypse, using the "natural" disaster as a tribalography to make sense of the past five hundred years of destruction, and two, that such a reading can offer profound narratives of resilience, signaling that the best hope for the future might be the lessons of an ancient God, ready to create the world anew.

Within this argument, I remain aware that hurricanes are typically viewed as "natural" disasters while the forces of settler colonialism represent man-made violence, theft, and destruction. I do not wish to naturalize settler colonialism, nor do I want to suggest that natural events are necessarily created by humans or that we should understand real hurricanes and earthquakes as the vengeance of an angry Christian God as some preacher-pundits like to claim. This chapter's grounding in a textual tradition of the *Popol Vuh*'s Huracán, however, leads me to consider the way that from an American Indigenous tradition, the appearance of the word "hurricane" in the European lexicon does originate alongside a lesson for human behavior. Therefore, I want to hold both of these things in view: the disaster as nature and the disaster as (un)nurture. The link between action and event appears frequently as unseparated in the Indigenous origin stories I use to read the more contemporary works in this chapter: Linda Hogan's ecological Everglades novel *Power* (1999), Janet McAdams's Creek (re)creation novel *Red Weather* (2012), and Monique Verdin's Katrina and BP oil spill documentary *My Louisiana Love* (2012). In keeping the lessons of Huracán central, I attempt to read the Indigenous disaster narrative through the spiralic time of the resilient after.

My readings of these texts make use of LeAnne Howe's thoughts about tribalography, which "show[s] not only how one thing leads to another, but that movement across space and time, i.e. travel, transforms us into something more than we were" (*Choctalking* 173). These stories move across and through flat-mapped space, and they zoom crossways through linear time, showing slices of experience pulled together through deep connections into the land (e.g., sacred mounds) and up through cosmic constellations (e.g., the solar transit of Venus) that organize our understanding of the wider universe.[4] In this movement humans are changed by their orientation to land and space, and land and space are in turn changed by humans. In reflecting on her own work in the novel *Mico Kings* (2007), Howe articulates how the southeastern Native characters in the novel "not only embodied the world and land of the story but that their physical movements emplotted the land with triumph, tragedy, renewal, and return. All attributes of survival" (ibid., 174). Significantly, she links the novel's plot about baseball to the motion of Native ceremonies, noting that she "reflected on the motion of water and wind in the Northern Hemisphere," speculating that these connections "may explain why Natives in the Southeast dance counter-clockwise [. . .] mimicking or expressing water flow, tornado, and hurricane winds" (174). These speculative connections yield a space to explore the storm as tribalography, charting how contemporary southeastern Native writers link time and place into (re)-creation stories for their people that allow us to imagine a different type of red state.

From speculative tribes to speculative places and speculative futures, the texts I examine in this chapter feature disasters and the resilience that follows, points of regeneration from the colonial-imbued chaos. These texts, like the resistance narratives of the Lumbee I examined in chapter 4, map a very different South. Through speculative histories and alternate cinematic pacing, they each challenge our concepts of temporal periodization, and in so doing they demonstrate a future red state—one that focuses on land claim and the possibilities that exist after the storm. They embrace a particular kind of loss that allows survivors to push through their own apocalypses. These works also depict protagonists who choose to live in resilience. This resilience is not purely romantic, and in fact, all of these texts romanticize very little about their subjects or characters. They propose the hard work of survival and sovereignty. In this model, Indigenous sovereignty does not exist as some linear origin to the eventual creation of the U.S. South, nor is it the aftereffect of federal recognition. Instead, it is the thing that allows one to live through. It is inherent, time-bound, and timeless: spiralic. This way of seeing permeates Native studies. From Paul Chaat Smith and Robert Warrior's *Like a Hurricane* to Daniel Heath Justice's *Our Fires Survive the Storm*, the narrative of not only surviving but also creating metaphorical tempests permeates the best Native American studies scholarship. And as I outlined in the introduction, this focus allows for the recognition of Lisa Brook's argument regarding the use of Indigenous temporalities to understand region and literary periodization anew where we might question, in her words, if "'period' and 'region' are deeply linked narratives" and "What different shape might literary history take if we account for distinct conceptions of time that arise simultaneously from particular places?" (309).

Whereas in earlier chapters I traced the recurrent use of narratives to illustrate the linkages across time and space, in what follows I demonstrate how these texts help us theorize ways to read beyond familiar literary critical narratives of periodization. Previously, I examined historical narratives that recur over time in the appearance of different texts, but the texts in this chapter position the recurrent narrative within themselves. These Native-authored texts create worlds where linear temporality fails to account for an Indigenous understanding of the region. I argue that a reconsideration of temporality works on the inside and outside of the text, on how it builds narrative within its southeastern world and what it offers to the Southeast beyond its pages or screens. In other words, these states were red long before our contemporary colloquial understanding, and seeing the larger (and beyond U.S.) South as indigenously red yields not so much an alternate but a profoundly central way of understanding the region. As Keith Cartwright queried in his 2016 *PMLA* manifesto for the future of southern studies, "What to do with or in southern studies?" to which he proposes, "We need a reconfigured disciplinarity open to undisciplined knowledge from beyond accredited timespace" (178). This from-beyond project might very well find a home in a southern studies that begins to take Native studies seriously as a methodological discipline. There is a way forward—in practice and in policy—without romanticizing the Native object and without adhering to the hard time set down in "the chronological organization of anthologies and coursework [that] keeps the peculiar institutions of planters and founders at the center of the master narrative" (178). As Cartwright proposes, "Cross-cultural authority draws from a different temporality (seasonal, musical, ritual, and deep time) in counterclockwise dialogue with eternity. We can move to the time signatures of our own spaces, which turn at their own angles to the sun" (178).

For instance, Allison Adelle Hedge Coke's account of Hurricane Katrina in her poem "In the Year 513 PC" signals the reader to the competing periodization that marks catastrophe for the Americas. Rather than C(ommon) E(ra), Hedge Coke offers the reader a "post-contact, post-Columbus, post-cultural invasion" (57). She links the destruction of Katrina to the five hundred years after European invasion and posits, "We're all a jazz funeral display, singing, dancing, masking ourselves to crypt enclave" (57). This "crypt enclave" calls forth a distinct region linked by the struggle of a death foretold. Like the wood people who ignored warnings from their creators, Hedge Coke recounts later unconsidered omens: "Looking back, signs gave taste to trepidation, foretold all ten years to known. If we'd only seen the writing, bird tracks left etched on earthen wall" (57). This is not, however, straight-ahead prophecy as much as it is an acknowledgment of the potential end of a destructive era. The etchings on the earthen wall call forth images of glyphs telling the story of Huracán, warning of destruction for those who ignore their responsibilities. Hedge Coke puts forth a new era where an anonymous voice calls, "'Saving the Earth is not a competition, but an essential collaboration'" (57). By reanimating time via an Indigenous worldview, she foregrounds another temporality for the Americas, but this is not simply postcolonial time. Notably, Hedge Coke leaves out the term "postcolonial" from her "PC" list. The colonial continues up until the moment of the storm when she notes, "513 you'd scarcely remember until it had all been drowned" (57). Indeed, what was memorable about that year? What does one remember until New Orleans—the U.S. city with what some would argue is the thickest colonial residue—rendered visible on every American's television screen those five hundred years of colonization, slavery, and land exploitation? As Hedge Coke points out, those images only make sense in 513 PC; 2005 CE does nothing to explain them. It is in this spirit that this chapter proceeds.

Downed Trees and Dissolved Salt: Linda Hogan's Collaborative Creation Story

Linda Hogan's *Power* features a powerful hurricane and a speculative tribal world in seeming chaos as it moves from a destructive past into a potentially uncertain future. The world born anew in *Power* may seem to emerge from the central conflict over the killing of an endangered Florida panther at the hands of Ama Eaton, a member of the novel's fictional tribe, the Taiga. Numerous critics have discussed this central plot point and the ensuing conflict.[5] Less attention, however, has been paid to the chaos that precedes the panther's death: the hurricane. The narrator, Omishto, recounts the story of the panther's death and the ensuing trials—state and tribal—that her Aunt Ama must endure as a result of her actions. While as readers we are privy to the fact that the panther was badly malnourished, Ama's actions take on varying significance for the multiple authorities who attempt to get at the truth of her behavior. As members of the Taiga Tribe, Ama and Omishto find themselves caught between a secular bureaucracy, which wants Ama prosecuted for killing an endangered animal, and a sacred tribunal, which would see Ama punished for killing a valued symbol of the Taiga people. Despite this focus on the animal's death, there are numerous reasons to pay more attention to the storm at the center of the story. For one, the novel's setting in Florida and Ama's last name, Eaton, point readers back to another significant fictional storm in Zora Neale Hurston's 1937 *Their Eyes Were Watching God*. Furthermore, Ama's name is the Cherokee word for both "water" and "salt." Although the novel does not point to this fact directly, nor does it make explicit reference to Hurston's work, attention to these details allows a way to see the narrative working within a genealogy that centers the storm not as mere setting or backdrop but rather as a central agent in the merging of earth and sea, salt and water, into the swamp-based land claims of the Taiga people. These land claims orient the chronotope of the novel, and through the use of Indigenous temporalities, Hogan's work asks the reader to consider beginnings over endings, spiralic curves rather than points of finality.

Hogan's novel offers a key to understanding the possibilities inherent in a Native South. It undoes colonial borders through its merging of tribal creation stories and languages as well as colonial power models. In the space of speculation, it weaves a tribal story that can incorporate rich Indigenous traditions across the hemisphere. *Power* looks both north to a Cherokee worldview in the character of Ama and south to sacred understanding of Huracán in Mayan and Caribbean traditions. This linkage becomes the center of survival. This survival, however, depends on the ending of an unquestioned colonial dominance. It asks that audiences reject readings of Native works that continue to foreground Western epistemologies and instead look to regional continuities and knowledges that are based on this continent. While there is certainly a risk in creating specious tribal traditions and peoples, such a move allows Hogan to echo the larger point that Hedge Coke makes in her poem "In the Year 513 PC": "'Saving the Earth is not a competition, but an essential collaboration" (57). Hogan's novel places the center of power within a collaborative Native Southeast, and it reorients readers' understanding of red state models through its emphasis on Indigenous knowledges. It takes the chaos of a colonial tempest and renders it an Indigenous Huracán, who destroys in order to create.

To belabor the point, the Indigenous Southeast of Hogan's novel is fiction. The Taiga Tribe is a fictional one. Hogan's work frequently builds tribes from composite traditions based in each novel's respective region. For example, *People of the Whale* (2008) is set in the Pacific Northwest and features another fictional tribe with ceremonies and knowledges that are loosely connected to tribes in that geographic area, while *Solar Storms* (1997) explores Indigenous issues in the Upper Midwest. While some might term this a pan-Indian approach, I argue that Hogan's work is slightly more nuanced than that term allows. Pan-Indianism would suggest that she uses traditions from wildly dissimilar tribes and geographies or that she merely pulls from a Plains-imbued powwow culture. This is not to dismiss the strategic uses of pan-Indian cultural forms by Native people, but to point out that Hogan's work has geographic specificity even when it does not address tribal specificity. This lack of specific tribal connection allows Hogan to explore the themes of her work without disrespecting the ceremonies, knowledges, and traditions of living Native nations. While one could debate the merits and ethics of her creations, it is important to remember that they are *regional* creations.

Keeping in view the "creative" aspect of her novel, I posit that in this book, she builds a speculative southeastern tribal universe, a collaborative geography of region—one that pulls from Cherokee, Muscogee, Mississippian, and Caribbean Indigenous worldviews. By examining her collaborative regional geography we can think of her as participating in a small-P pan-Indianism, one that respects and draws from regional tribal universes without infringing on real-life tribally specific space. The novel's setting in Florida certainly places it within Seminole land, and the history of the Seminole Tribe looms the largest across the novel. However, hints toward other southeastern tribal languages, knowledges, and traditions also pervade the story. As Hogan explains in an interview with Barbara J. Cook, the main plot of the novel comes from the case of a Seminole man killing a Florida panther. However, as I outlined above, the invocation of the hurricane itself in the space of Florida (just as much a northern Caribbean as a southern United States) should point us to the traditions embedded in that word's etymology. Furthermore, at least two Cherokee words appear in the novel: one in the main character's aunt, Ama, and the other in the name of the wind/breath/life described in the beginning of the book, Oni. While I concede that these divergent lines of inquiry are speculative connections, I assert with little hesitation that reading the novel in terms of its potential connections to Indigenous southeastern and Caribbean languages, histories, and worldviews yields provocative and productive insights not always achieved by analyses derived from searching for the Western symbolism in the work.

Michael Hardin reads the novel through a Western Christian biblical perspective, arguing that the novel undoes apocalyptic narratives as forwarded by Christopher Columbus during his *Voyages* accounts. Stating that these narratives place Native people in the position of "victim," Hardin claims that Hogan's novel argues for a movement past apocalyptic stories. However, he reads the flood as solely of a Judeo-Christian biblical tradition, arguing that "these myths have been appropriated by indigenous peoples" (140). I would like to complicate such a reading and posit that rather than only read the novel within a Western Christian tradition, we stay much closer to home. Perhaps apocalyptic narratives and Noah-like floods are a part of Christian tradition, but the very word "hurricane" signals us to a religious tradition of the greater Caribbean region in which the story takes place. This setting comes with its own narratives of destruction and survival. While within a Western context these narratives may set up what Hardin calls a "binary" or a linear understanding of time, Hogan's novel demonstrates that the hurricane not only destroys those who have behaved badly but also facilitates a new birth for those Indigenous people that have learned how to survive.[6]

When focusing on the conflict over the panther, it is tempting to read the book as one about both loss and a necessary return to tradition. Eric Gary Anderson argues that it is "less a novel about recovering the old ways and returning to the old routes than it is a novel about how these old ways are one teenaged Indian girl away from being not only relinquished but also extinguished" ("Native American Literature" 167). I agree and disagree. The novel is not about recovery, nostalgia, or looking back, but I am not necessarily sure that it is about a future demise of Indigenous traditions. Rather, when focusing on the storm as agent, as Huracán, I argue that the novel puts forth the end of a colonial wood people and instead points us toward an emerging world where new traditions are born from innovations that succeed. Without a doubt, the panther narrative points toward Anderson's argument. My reading, however, stays closer to the storm narrative in order to think through the multivalent ways that it might signal a future past the supposed point of extinguishment.

Hogan signals us toward the (re)generative power of the storm from early on in the novel. Omishto narrates: "This is how the world was created, Ama told me once, out of wind and lashing rain. 'We were blown together by a storm in the first place.' It was all created out of storms" (42–43). This creation, however, is not simply a past time. The novel makes clear that the temporality of the action moves in complex, spiralic patterns that even the characters do not understand although they acknowledge them. As Carrie Bowen-Mercer argues of the novel, "Instead of a world in which circular clocks measure linear time and straight rulers measure three-dimensional spatial structures, Hogan exposes her readers to a Native American epistemology of time and space that involves their inseparable interaction through a circularity of experience" (164). The beginning may not be the only beginning, and the end may only signal another revolution of wind, bringing new life into being, or as Omishto puts it: "The storm was not just wind and rain, not just a house with a shutter thrown open, a door torn off the hinges. It was not just a dying house with a broken window and branches and leaves blown inside it. It was a beginning and an ending of something" (73). This acknowledgment returns us to the origin stories that tempests tell, to the place where Huracán hurls the world into chaos in order to cleanse the wood people and their destructive practices from the earth.

Significantly, one of the largest casualties of the storm is the tree called Methuselah. While Omishto struggles during the storm to get back to the roots of the five-hundred-year-old tree, she starts to realize that it is losing ground: "[T]hrough the dark air of storm, Methuselah falls and I hear nothing but only see that what has lasted this long is being taken down now as if it were nothing, as if it had never been anything that counted. This tree planted by the Spanish, conceived on another continent" (37–38). Although at first we might view the upending of the old tree as another definitive point of loss, I argue that this downed tree is a sign of regeneration, of an end to the five hundred years of European conquest. Whereas Hardin sees this loss only in terms of the overturning of a Judeo-Christian biblical tradition, I argue that it might be more fully understood as a direct link to Huracán's destruction of the wood people. Such a loss is not without its own difficulty as we see Omishto first struggle to get back to the roots of this tree, and then afterward, she mourns its loss. I read this moment, however, as the pain of potential rebirth. The hurricane has claimed the wooden people of Spanish colonialism and along with it other emblems of planetary degradation. As she scans her new earth, Omishto notes, "The oil rig equipment in the distance is tossed down, too, and all the tallest oldest trees are downed by water and wind. Methuselah, gone after these five centuries. It is the young trees that have survived" (52). This survival is both personal and collective for Omishto, as she ruminates on "History [as] the place where the Spaniards cut off the hands of my ancestors," and she laments, "I wish it didn't but that history still terrifies and haunts me so that I dream it in dreams with skies the color of green bottle-glass," but despite this haunting, she adds, "And somehow, against their will, I stole through" (73). In Methuselah's death, she looks and "It seems there is light in between the young trees" (49). Thus, in the loss of the old Spanish tree, light shines through those who have stolen through, those who like the young trees are birthed on this continent, grasping the swampy earth in their roots as Indigenous land claim.

Later, when Omishto recounts the events of the storm and Ama's subsequent killing of the panther, she tells the elders, "'The old tree, Methuselah, fell'" (163). Then, in a curious moment, it seems as if Omishto misreads the elders' response. She narrates, "They consider this deeply, the oldest tree and how it fell as all the centuries have fallen before us like it was the end of all that time. This is important to them" (163). The elders' deep consideration of this loss could indicate at least two important ideas. Does it suggest the tearing up of five-hundred-year-old colonial roots? Does it represent their own destruction? Certainly, in no way does the story of Huracán offer an easy re-creation. Without a doubt, the story is violent and gory. It depicts a total destruction and an inability for the Heart of Heaven itself to create humans successfully. It is not as if the Mayan Gods wanted or imagined their own failure in building the wood people. Just the same, the wood people likely did not foresee or desire their total annihilation. Likewise, within the universe of the novel, the elders must pause at what the destruction of the old tree means. While Omishto seems to continue to see the loss of the tree as her own and possibly her people's loss, the novel seems more ambivalent. The tree is the symbol not of an enduring Taiga people but of a rooted European settler colonialism on this continent. Its death at the hands of the hurricane, then, could signal not the extinguishing of the Taiga but the coming end of European colonial dominance. In this version of the story, rather than Indigenous stories serving as a prior event to European invasion and occupation, colonialism becomes just a phase before the emergence of real human beings. The storm, then, has made the beginning. In either reading, the elders must pause to consider where they fall in this destruction and potential rebirth.

In addition to offering Seminole-based histories and circum-Caribbean-inflected stories, the novel also seems to offer at least two instances of Cherokee language. The book's central word "Oni," which the audience is told means "life itself, for wind and breath," bears a striking similarity to the Cherokee word for "after": *ohni* (73).[7] Though the Latinate alphabet renders it with an H, the Cherokee syllabary form of the word appears as ᎤᎯ or "oni." And despite this spelling difference, it seems likely that the two words would share a pronunciation. Such a double meaning opens up the possibility to consider the relationship of the novel's life and its temporality. The fact that *ohni* can mean "after" in Cherokee, a southeastern Native language (albeit one removed from the setting of the novel by a significant number of miles), suggests that the book depicts a life after the significant event. It speculates a future in the postevent space of the storm. As Omishto narrates, "Back in the days of the first people, the beginning of wind was the first breathing of one of the turbulent Gods, they say. This God's name was Oni. It is said that this word was the owner of wind, and the panther was the one who first spoke it" (178). The provocative connection between the novel's Oni as a first word, a breath of an original God, and the Cherokee *ohni* as meaning "after" suggests that the book tells a story of an afterlife. This afterlife is not the one of death but perhaps better understood as a life-after.

This reading of the novel demonstrates a methodology that recognizes the Indigenous meanings not only possible but inherent in Hogan's collaborative regional geography of the Southeast. The fact that the novel's turbulent God breathed a storm, a wind, further links back to the Mayan creation story of Huracán. Like the Mayan God, the God Oni creates life, but it also represents destruction. Hogan writes, "Oni, first and foremost, is the word for wind and air. It is a power every bit as strong as gravity, as strong as a sun you can't look at but know is there. It tells a story. Through air, words and voices are carried. [...] Sometimes Oni has a woman's voice, they say, full of tender whispers and urgings, and sometimes it is the deep and bellowing rage of a storm" (178–79). This description joins Oni and Huracán in their respective deeds and descriptions. They each create a beginning via destruction. However, they are neither entirely vengeful nor nurturing Gods. Their creative and destructive powers are linked, and in this way the novel ruminates on the power of beginnings and endings. This linkage of beginning and ending resonates with my reading of the word in Cherokee, *ohni*. The "after" of the novel's storm points toward a futurity. It represents a possible new beginning in the breath of destruction from the storm's wind. As Hogan closes the novel, "as the wind stirs in the trees, someone sings the song that says the world will go on living" (235). The novel's wind Oni carries the voices that point to an afterworld of the novel's close. Like Huracán, Oni makes a life-after possible. This depends not on the temporality of death but on a continuation of the Taiga people.

In addition to the use of the Cherokee word *oni* or "after," Hogan also makes use of another Cherokee word for one of the novel's central figures. As I mentioned earlier, Omishto's Aunt Ama's name means both "water" and "salt" in the Cherokee language.[8] Again, though, this is not a Cherokee or even a Seminole story, and Hogan is Chickasaw rather than Cherokee or Seminole. However, Ama's name, like Oni, still stands as significant in the context of a southeastern Native novel, particularly when so many southeastern Native people ended up in closer proximity to one another in Indian Territory following Removal. In some ways, then, Hogan builds a collaborative regional geography between southeastern tribes that "walks" back their interactions and connections from present-day Oklahoma to southeastern Native homelands. The Cherokee words "ama" and "ama," "salt" and "water," (or DᏬ) vary by spoken inflection. (And it is important to note that "ama" was used for water primarily in the Overhill and Middle Towns, while the word "awa" (DᎦ) seems to have been used in the Underhill towns.)[9] The written form in the Overhill and Middle Town dialects, then, would require context for meaning. While some might ponder at the similarity in these words, to my speculation, it seems like a logical instance for seeing Indigenous knowledge about the relationship between the world's water sources.[10] For the purposes of the novel, it creates a profound encounter when we consider the storm itself. Like many ocean storms, hurricanes churn in over the salt water, pulling up the water molecules and leaving the salt behind through the process of evaporation. The accompanying storm surge pushes that salt water on shore, creating damage through both compounds. Furthermore, at least 97 percent of the water on the planet is salt water. In short, salt and water are linked on this planet. Perhaps even more significant is the fact that the very setting of the novel is the place where water meets salt in the brackish water of the fictional Kili swamp.

Given this, we should understand the character Ama as having a double, but related, set of purposes for the novel's action. She is linked to the storm, and she attempts to pull together the past and the present. Through her killing of the panther, Ama seeks to bring the damaged and the renewed into one moment. These doublings, though, are not necessarily sustainable in the world of the story. Omishto reflects on the swamp and the elders who live among the mangroves: "Walking to Kili, I think that at Kili, in their memories, are a thousand storms. The people there remember how to heal themselves and each other. They remember what they were born knowing. Nothing replaced or erased like it has done with me. Me, I am a dissolved person, like salt in water" (231). Here, Omishto imagines herself not as a whole thing: the necessary brackish water that produces life in the estuary, but *only* the dissolved salt. She recognizes a longer temporal scope of memory that precedes birth, pushing the reader to consider histories before moments of creation. After ruminating on the condition of the world around her, Omishto resolves, "But I will no longer be dissolved salt" (232). This is not, however, a rejection of the properties of salt and water combined; this is only a rejection of her focus on what is lost when the salt as a whole thing is dissolved. Notably, her first spoken word after this newfound resolution is a question, a call to the person who is no longer there: "Ama?" (232).

In this moment we see Omishto give up the narrative of loss and begin to embrace the rebirth that the storm provides. Indeed, much is lost in the novel, but this is not a lost cause. It is a reorientation of values to promote continued survival. The reminders of the loss of the hurricane, of the wood people, of the old world, remain, but they are reminders rather than tokens of nostalgia for a world gone. After Ama's "walking death" sentence from the Taiga elders, Omishto feels a great sense of loss. Notably, as she falls asleep in the boat following the tribunal she hears something climbing in the trees, and she thinks, "The monkey, perhaps," and then she notes, "A dog comes to the edge of the water but doesn't bark" (176). Although this silent dog and rustling monkey might seem like small details, they strike a resonance with core scenes from the destruction of the wood people by Huracán. As the *Popol Vuh* recounts, while the wood people were being destroyed by the storm's fury, their abused dogs spoke to them: "Why did you give us nothing to eat? You scarcely looked at us, but you chased us and threw us out. You always had a stick ready to strike us while you were eating. Thus it was that you treated us. You did not speak to us. Perhaps we shall not kill you now; but why did you not think about yourselves? Now we shall destroy you, now you shall feel the teeth of our mouths; we shall devour you" (Goetz and Morley 91). These silent dogs of *Power* look on the scene of destruction, serving as a reminder of the destruction of the second attempt of creating humans. However, in this moment these dogs do not bark like they do in the *Popol Vuh*, indicating to the reader that Omishto is not the target of the hurricane's destruction. From the *Popol Vuh* we know these cruel stick people's "descendants are the monkeys which now live in the forest," and they look "like man, and [are] an example of a generation of men which were created and made but were only wooden figures" (ibid., 92–93). We can then read this scene from the novel as a signal to the destruction of a past world at the hand of Huracán—a destruction that was necessary for the real human beings to emerge. The subtle details here—

the dog and the monkey—serve as assurances that the earth has moved into a new phase of creation.

This creative power of the storm appears throughout the book. Omishto thinks of this almost halfway through the novel: "Now I think of the storm that made chaos, that the storm opened a door. It tried to make over the world the way it wanted it to be. At school I learn that storms create life, that lightning, with its nitrogen, is a beginning; bacteria and enzymes grow new life from decay out of darkness and water" (95). As Goetz and Morley explain of the three Heart of Heaven Gods, while collectively known as Huracán, each of them has a name that signifies lightning and the flashes of light from storms (82n7). In her merging of Indigenous and Western knowledges, Omishto comes to an understanding of how this storm functioned as creator much like the Mayan Huracán and her own world's Oni, and later she realizes her place in this process, differentiating herself from her school peers, who represent children born of settler colonialism. She notes, "I am not a tree, broken by wind. I am not a building fallen with the storm. I am not a brick, collapsed. I glance around knowing I am not one of these people, either, not these people who are like vines grown over this land, smothering it" (106). In her realization she sees that she is not who the storm has been meant to destroy. She is not a tree—a wooden person—and notably she is not the clay brick, a reference perhaps to the first attempt at creation by the Heart of Heaven. She will not melt into the land, and she will not be torn apart. She is also not the shallow creep of settler colonials represented by vines that, though they may evoke a sense of place like kudzu, have shallow roots in their land claim. Her awakening depends on this realization of the power of storms. She thinks of "a storm that brings thunder and lightning and rain, renewal [. . .] rain that is nourishing but has to fall. And when it does, the world rises up once again and grows" (186). In this way, the hurricane becomes more than a fulcrum in the novel; instead, Huracán and Oni show themselves as protagonists, leading the world to a new time: not a time of loss, but a time of creation, a time of the after.

South to a Speculative Place: Janet McAdams's *Red Weather*

Just as Linda Hogan's *Power* deals in Indigenous world renewal narratives, speculative tribes, and new creation stories, Janet McAdams's novel *Red Weather* (2012) calls on shifting terrains, worldly (re)creations, and speculative places, as the main character, Neva, shuttles temporally between past and present. Neva also moves geographically from the "South" in Atlanta even farther south to the fictional country of Coatepeque, a no-country "that barely made the news" somewhere between southern Mexico and Guatemala (5). Likewise, the novel's title hurls the reader through multiple referents of meaning from Wallace Stevens to Hurricane Katrina and from Muscogee

Creek creation stories of earthquakes to socialist "red" revolutions. I follow these lines of spatiotemporal transit in order to argue for the novel's creation of a profound possibility for new conceptions of Indigenous identity through its engagement with fictional settings alongside its grounding in a Muscogee Creek worldview. Unlike *Power*'s attempt to create an amalgamated southeastern sacred ceremonial narrative through Seminole, Mayan, Carib, and Cherokee referents, McAdams takes the reader to the center of a Creek universe via her creation of a speculative setting in Central America. The novel features its own tempest in the form of an earthquake, mirroring the Creek creation story where, as Craig Womack explains, "the earth opened up in the West near the Continental Divide and spit the people up from below its surface out into the broader landscape. The people journeyed eastward on a quest to discover the origin of the sun until they reached the Atlantic and could travel no more. Turning back, they decided to settle in the area of the Chattahoochee River in Alabama" (*Red on Red* 26). In this way, *Power* and *Red Weather* speak to one another as literary works that simultaneously ground the audience in southeastern Indigenous worldviews while opening up new possibilities for Native resilience in the region. Importantly, each novel calls into question the very spatial and temporal borders of the South, demonstrating how the idea of the red state hinges on questions of land claim and narrative order. Like Hogan's collaborative regional geography, pulling together traditions and worldviews into a fictional Taiga Tribe, McAdams also links multiple Indigenous peoples and belief structures. This collaborative space generates possibilities for a red state of futurity rather than one of backward-looking nostalgia and loss.

Red Weather follows a young Creek woman from her Alabama childhood, which was disrupted by the disappearance of her parents, to her young adult life married to Will—a troubled and troubling non-Native academic who is alternately fascinated with his wife's American Indian identity and abusive of her body and identity—to her eventual relocation to Coatepeque to search for her lost parents. Notable to the plot is the fact that Neva's parents disappeared because of their Red Power activism as they worked to expose the government's systematic sterilization of American Indian women during the middle of the twentieth century.[11] These vectors of movement throughout the text shuttle the reader along what Jodi Byrd constellates under her concept of the "transit of empire"—where "As a transit, Indianness becomes a site through which U.S. empire orients and replicates itself by transforming those to be colonized into 'Indians' through continual reiterations of pioneer logics" (*Transit* xiii). The locations of McAdams's novel call on deep historical affiliations: from Dauphin Island (a rich space of shell-mound peoples) to Butler City in Choctaw County, Alabama (named for Pierce Butler who died in the Mexican-American War) and from Ponce de Leon Avenue in Atlanta (calling up the history of Spanish colonialism) to a further south of Central America. This movement signals the ways in which McAdams's novel challenges colonial borders and histories as falling along present-day demarcated national and state borders. In so doing, she creates a layered South that is as presently dynamic as it is referential to the histories of the Indigenous people who inhabit the region.[12]

The novel's primary setting in the fictional Coatepeque, which at once seems reminiscent of Nicaragua, El Salvador, Guatemala, and Chiapas, Mexico, but not quite, leads the reader back through time to the Los Altos state of The United Provinces of Central America (UPCA), which existed between 1821 and 1841.[13] Described by historian Hector Perez-Brignoli as "ephemeral," the Los Altos state included parts of present-day Chiapas, Mexico, and Guatemala, and as such had a significant Mayan population.[14] This shift in space through the fictional setting also moves the reader backward in time to the era of Creek Indian Removal in the southeastern United States. Taken together, we might then better understand the novel's movement from Alabama and Georgia to Coatepeque, or South to South. In fact, nineteenth-century southern newspapers including the *Augusta Chronicle* covered the formation of the UPCA, publishing the U.S. recognition treaty with the country in the same issues where debates over Creek Indian Removal and Native versus U.S. state sovereignty were debated. The movement then from the U.S. South to the fictional country of Coatepeque creates an alternate historical trajectory bound up with different sovereign powers where Indigenous revolutions may work to counteract past and present removals. Furthermore, the earthquake toward the end of the novel then moves the reader back even further in time as it calls on a Muscogee creation story where the people emerge from a split earth that opens to give them life. This ending signals an emergence of Neva's character as a re-created Indigenous person, born of composite, alternate, and speculative histories. *Red Weather* moves the reader from the literal "red states" of the U.S. South to a "red state" of Native American resilience, demonstrating the importance of thinking hemispherically when we engage both southern and Native American literatures.

In this way, my argument builds from Byrd's recent interventions into the idea of Native Souths when she thinks through the "challenges that indigeneity, as both a mode of being and as a reading practice, poses to the past, to regionalism, to the nation-state, and to the bio- and geopolitical governance structures that have forced peoples, lands, and histories into the cacophonous entanglements that forged the Americas out of the new world event" ("Return" 614). To this end, Byrd asks what imaginative possibilities might emerge if we are to jostle our affective historical understandings. I propose that through its use of speculative place and time, McAdams's novel gives us such a space to do this, as it ensnares the reader into a productive knot of unknowing through its representation of a paradox of simultaneously grounded and traveling indigeneity. McAdams's novel disrupts the idea of simple settler-colonial sense of place through her use of diasporic Native nationalism. Neva is both in place as a Creek person in Atlanta and out of place in Coatapeque. However, over the course of the novel she begins to see the Indigenous land claim stretch across borders, uniting an Indian Country into a red state not dependent on U.S. political logics.

Of course, there are numerous other interpretive touchstones laced throughout McAdams's work. The title calls up Wallace Stevens's poem "Disillusionment of Ten o'clock," which ends with the lines, "Only, here and there, an old sailor, / Drunk and asleep in his boots, / Catches tigers, / In red weather" (70). This allusion evokes the displaced (but concretely timed) sailor and the dream of both conquest and discovery, gliding ever so subtly in his dreams on what we might imagine as Jace Weaver's Red Atlantic.[15] And then there is the idea of the "red" revolutions, the countercultural movements, and the Indigenous uprisings of the leftist and Indigenous people in Central America and the EZLN in Chiapas, which as fictionally rendered in McAdams's novels are also engaged in violence (though significantly not with the same motives as the oppressive governments they fight). In weaving together these threads we see an alternative red space from the conservative red states of the novel's opening. Instead, here we have perhaps a "red" of the Weather Underground turned on its head, where McAdams's novel shows us both the faulty logic of imagining the U.S. South as homogeneously white and conservative and the troubling idealism of the activist movement that continues to traffic in narratives of empire rather than reimagine the world through new speculative moments of (re)creation.[16]

McAdams's work accomplishes this through its moments of deep continuity where the narration imagines a hemispheric Indian Country born of different maps and other ways of seeing and knowing time. Toward the middle of the novel, Neva experiences her first tremor, and she makes notes of the fault lines that divide space and time, ruminating: "Here she lived in the present moment, no longer on the fault line between a past she did not know and a future she could not imagine. On a different fault line, though" (68). Here the difference marks her shift between the temporal and the spatial: the immediate present of Coatepeque—described elsewhere as "the land that time forgot"—and the realization of an embodied earthly fault line (91). The novel describes the shift from the temporal and spatial like this: "Until the ground buckled and the fault line opened up, between Atlanta and Coatepeque, running straight through the middle of Alabama, Indian Country—it was all Indian Country—but you had to look a little harder to see it in the South, in Alabama, the heart of Creek country. A map cracking open to reveal red earth beneath it, the way skin might part over the red flesh of the body. The war her parents fought in, she could see it was the same war fought in Coatepeque, where she stood on the sidelines, then as a child, now as an outsider" (69). This joining of South and South, of the temporal and spatial, leads us to the chronotope of the speculative, when we have to ask to what end do we imagine McAdams's speculative South? When the map cracks open, the connections of indigeneity are realized, but McAdams warns that Neva, the Creek character on the outside looking in at the revolution in Coatepeque, is on the fault line without yet fully understanding the ties that her transit makes possible. Thus, unlike Hogan's drawing together of Indigenous traditions into a speculative tribe, McAdams's novel reminds us of the danger of assuming a mobile indigeneity without realizing the sovereign lands, ideologies, and politics of other Native nations. In so doing, she allows us to complicate our approach to understanding both the possibilities and perils of the categories of the Native and global South.

Not until Neva experiences her own earthquake toward the end of the novel do we begin to see the way that tribalography works within the creation of the main character. This is not a Western coming-of-age story, nor is it a rebirth or resurrection. Rather, as the earth opens up, Neva emerges from it as a Creek person born into her own story for the first time. To get there, however, she has had to move back in time through the fictional Coatapeque into the time of Los Altos. She has had to unlearn the colonial narratives of Indian Removal, the Creek Wars, and Spanish colonialism, to emerge from a split earth of her own. Or as Neva realizes, instead of her obsessive cataloguing of the "before" and the "after": "Now there was nothing but the earthquake" (145). So unlike other approaches to reconstructing, reimagining, and recohering the U.S. South that according to Byrd render "Indians [. . .] caught within a struggle over the priority of the prior that sets them *before* settlers and arrivants to be adjudicated and dismissed, unearthed and reclaimed, in patternings that actively continue and maintain their removal from the past, present, and future of their own lands that became the South," McAdams's novel re-earths multiple Souths, calling attention to the alternate space-times that exist alongside the ones Neva imagines ("Return" 617).

This re-earthing is also a task of re-membering, both in the sense of memory construction and in opposition to the act of dis-membering South from South. Colonialism dis-membered the Indigenous Souths of Mexico and Central America from the Souths of the United States and the Caribbean. But *Red Weather* re-members these spaces through Indigenous readings. However, as the novel warns of memory, "What did she really remember and what had she filled in later? Who could say? Memory was a canny trickster, as full of mischief as Rabbit, who stole fire and nearly burned up the whole world. Remembering was like that. You had to be careful what embers you fanned to life; memories could rage out of control. They could leave your world bare" (89). This canny trickster asks that we speculate, but cautions that we do so carefully, lest we burn up what we chase. In other words, we cannot simply make one revolution stand for another. The Guatemalan Civil War is not the Zapatista uprising is not the Creek Red Stick War. The displacement of Mayan peoples in the days of the United Provinces of Central America is not the Removal of southeastern Native peoples. It is not a re-membering where one memory or limb might be substituted for another—the locality of struggle remains paramount. But to be sure: it *is* all Indian Country, and it *is* all the same war. This ongoing battle in turn allows us to reconfigure the state of loss that can at times overdetermine how Native and southern histories are told. By reconfiguring the concept of loss, we can examine the role of speculative histories and geographies for a reconsideration of various red state logics (e.g., conservative, Indigenous, Marxist) and the varied souths that they call on for their meanings.

McAdams's work splits open the easily colored demographic map, revealing a red earth just below the surface. Fault lines, her novel suggests, do not adhere to flat-mapped boundaries. Locating her work in a speculative no-state asks the reader to reexamine historical narrative trajectory by looking back to the ephemeral possibilities of when states and nation-states are created and dissolved. And indeed, colonial nation-states *are* speculative projects. Like speculative projects, they depend on imagination, and if enough people believe, they are incredibly powerful—not to mention profitable—entities. However, this is not to say that McAdams's work forwards an imaginary nationalism for southeastern Native peoples. Rather, it is through the very act of travel that McAdams is able to demonstrate the reality of the American hemisphere—all of it—as Indian Country. As the land splits open for Neva to emerge, we see that it is not her nostalgic sense of place that matters, but rather it is the land, in all its agency, that claims its own.

Past Petroculture: Resilience in *My Louisiana Love*

Unlike the fictional tribes and speculative settings of *Power* and *Red Weather*, Sharon Linezo Hong and Monique Verdin's 2012 documentary *My Louisiana Love* deals in events all too real for those living in the Gulf South. The film follows Verdin, a young Houma Indian woman who has returned to Louisiana to live with her father's family. The chronicle begins around 2004, and the film follows her and her family through Hurricanes Katrina and Rita as well as the BP oil spill. Over the course of the film, which chronicles six years, viewers learn about Houma tribal history and culture as revealed through conversations between Verdin and her grandmother Matine, and they witness the profound personal and collective losses of Bayou people as a result of the region's entanglement with the oil and gas industry. The losses of the film are almost too numerous to count. From the literally disappearing land to the destruction of homes in the storm, and from the losses deriving from mental illness to the physical sickness resulting from the exposure to leaked crude oil, the film may seem to deal only in loss. It is bleak, and it is difficult to determine what hope there might be in the drama of petroculture writ small onto one Native American community in the U.S. South.

Despite this amassed sense of loss, I argue that like Linda Hogan's *Power* and Janet McAdams's *Red Weather,* the film points toward a resilience through its construction of an Indigenous temporality. The film signals a distinct time signature against and behind the temporality of what might appear to be a lost cause of the "dying Delta." However, this is not the Lost Cause of the Confederate South. Rather, like the narrative of Omishto, it is a lost cause as conceived by Robert Warrior—one signaling the emancipation of future possibility that comes with having lived through one's own apocalypse. These causes do not deal in linear time, where one may look backward and forward down the line, but rather they appeal to currents of a spiralic looping where every end marks another beginning. Arguably, it is easy to construct other temporal structures within the world of a novel where fiction and speculation are the standard. Hong and Verdin, however, manage to build a nonfiction narrative based on Indigenous time through the use of film. They keep the pace of each shot slow in relation to the next, and the film links images from the end of the film to the beginning. Using numerous still photographs, the film holds the viewer's gaze on the static image and juxtaposes such stillness with the awareness of the incredibly fast pace of land loss for the Houma Nation.

The United Houma Nation of Louisiana represents a Native southern community where the temporality of the lost cause can be reexamined within a Native perspective rather than from an overdetermined Confederate southern one. As a tribe that has been denied federal recognition, repeatedly denied cultural recognition through the lingering effects of Jim Crow–era policies, and unduly affected by Louisiana's infamous "acre per hour" land loss, they may seem to be continually fighting losing battles.[17] As a tribal people that live connected by waterways and depend on coastal economies, they also represent a community that can teach the rest of the world about how to sustain through what may seem like points of finality. This, however, would require recognition—cultural, intellectual, and political. And it would also require recognition of alternate ways to conceive of time and region, and the losses that inform these concepts. The homelands of the Houma, the Gulf South, with its tides controlled by the temporality of planetary time, offers a potential space to think through sustainability—with its etymologically embedded temporal logic of the prolonged.

The film attempts to form a chain of recognition across these concepts through the autobiographical approach to Verdin's life. Working backward through her own personal history, Verdin comes to construct a narrative that queries the temporal pace of belonging for Indigenous peoples in Louisiana. About half an hour into the film, Verdin is finally able to return to her grandmother's home after Hurricane Katrina. The destruction is overwhelming with a visible flood line at approximately five feet high around each room. Photos and furniture are moldy, mildewed, torn, and tarnished. Verdin's boyfriend and artistic partner, Mark Krasnoff, turns the camera on Verdin and asks her what she will miss about the house. In response, she chronicles both the joys and small hardships from looking out the kitchen window to collecting water from the cistern. Each shot moves slowly from room to room and then back outside where Verdin surveys the land. At first there is no music, and the viewer only hears the buzzing insects who have managed to survive through the storm. A seemingly lone bird chirps while Verdin holds a ventilator mask to her face. At this moment, she points to something in a pile of wreckage and says, "An armadillo—it's right there," to which Krasnoff responds in pleasant surprise, "It's alive?! Yes. Oh my God. He made it." Verdin observes in response, "Because he's a dinosaur." The camera zooms in on the animal, and a slow banjo tune begins to play as Verdin takes photographs of the scene.

The pace of this scene, juxtaposing the movement of the visual and verbal survey of profound loss with the still frame of photography, leaves the viewer to contemplate growth and stasis. As the banjo picks a melody that slowly reverberates across the visual image, the viewer is invited to consider the natural processes of land healing alongside the man-made disaster of oil rigs that float off their bases. The collocation is made even more evident by the shot of the armadillo—"the dinosaur," as Verdin calls it—next to a ruined Yamaha motorbike. The armadillo serves as an apt metaphor for unlikely survival as the species belongs to the last remaining biological families in its order *Cingulata*. Its name in Nahuatl, *āyōtōchtli*, means "turtle-rabbit," thus signaling the possibility of a shift in temporal perspective between that which is at once very quick, even hopping when startled, but also armored to live and survive very slowly. Though the Houma language is closely related to Choctaw and not Nahuatl, as an embedded metaphor that carries significance, the armadillo's appearance in the visual image calls up multiple meanings across the Indigenous Americas. It is this very ability to shift in pace, to adjust the temporality, that can allow something to exist beyond its own supposed apocalypse or evolutionary extinction, and this is what the film demonstrates.

Toward the end of the film, after Verdin has experienced the suicide of her partner Krasnoff and the death of her father due to cancer, she travels through the swamp on a boat. Through voice-over narration, she offers, "Since losing my father and Kras, I can see how the illness of our land and waters breeds illness on our people." However, she continues, "our love ties us to this place and makes us feel responsible to care for it." The camera then follows her into a dark room as she explains, "It was by instinct that I first picked up a camera and began documenting my family." We watch her develop black-and-white film—a slow process to be sure in this age of digital photography—as she continues, "And now these images and stories bear witness to a disappearing Louisiana." However, her very act of documenting this way of life ensures at least some measure of its continuance, and her developing of the film literally renders the appearance of her community before the viewer's eyes. In recording the increasing absences, she flips the logic of archival presence for the colonial project, turning the lens against the imperial gaze even as she must participate in the trappings of its seductive culture. Significantly, the film then cuts to a scene of her grandmother Matine's ninety-sixth birthday party as she blows out candles on her cake. This scene is juxtaposed with a direct cut to the burning flames atop the tall stacks of a refinery, leaving the viewer with an uneasy realization of the stakes of life lived in the age and shadow of oil. Notably, after this scene the shot cuts to Verdin carrying plants for her grandmother's new garden, signaling to the viewer that an exclusive focus on perpetual loss serves no use for future growth.

Additionally, the Gulf South, as a space where the rapid rise of the geological age of petroculture crashes against the otherwise slow geological processes of tidal flux, erosion, and river flows, allows us to think through what is at stake in linking alternate temporalities and periodization to our regional studies. This rethinking of time from Indigenous methodologies gives us the space to think about the vexing questions not only pondered by literary historians but also confronting all of us in this age of ecological change. The film does not provide answers, and indeed these questions are big ones, not likely solved by a single literary or cultural text. However, our shift from privileging land-based regional histories to ones that examine waterways also allows us to shift from our literary histories of the region that privilege Old and New Souths as a priori categories. In thinking with this different temporal construction, the resulting assembled archive may look messy, incoherent, or even vaguely disjointed. However, this new construction may allow us to see new archives that emerge from the continually revised logics of the region we examine rather than from the inevitable story of their presupposed functions as pieces of national narrative-making. It asks that we forego the Lost Cause in favor of lost causes—postapocalyptic futures that, rather than breeding misplaced nostalgia, enliven some form of future possibility for the region.

There is resilience in *My Louisiana Love*, which closes with Verdin planting new crops with Matine and building her own home out of a repurposed shipping container. Not all is romantic hope, however. As Verdin does literally within her new home, we too live metaphorically inside the material conditions of our present-day container-shipping global economy of petroculture, and the change in our intellectual conceptions of time and region will affect little without large and small real-life actions.[18] Verdin does not simply offer a romantic remedy (Indigenous or otherwise) for the problems of what has been called the Anthropocene. Earlier in the film, she shows herself literally pumping gas as she and Krasnoff flee Hurricane Katrina, bound in escape to the very commodity they must resist. *My Louisiana Love* does not rewrite a romantic narrative about a nostalgic Houma identity; instead, it proposes Houma sovereignty as at least one concrete means of active legal protection for the Nation, its citizens, and the land. The issues of Native American national sovereignty should remain paramount, as these policy avenues offer at least some possibility of land protection even in the most vulnerable environments, but individual humans must also start the hard work of examining their own habits in the age of petroculture.

Despite the film's success in avoiding the representation of clichéd "Ecological Indians," it is also possible that some viewers might read it as squarely within the literary tradition of Robert T. Jackson's southern disaster complex.[19] For as Jackson explains, "this native Southern discourse has succeeded in imagining a history that becomes not just a resource for environmental protection, a political tool, a portentous spiritual and aesthetic wellspring, but a restorative environment in itself. Welcome to Dixie" (569). As the tone of his closing sentence suggests, such projects should be read skeptically for the old southern ideologies they uphold through embedded narratives of traditionalism. I think, though, that the difference between the lowercased "native" of Jackson's critique and the uppercase "Native" of the Native South *does* matter here. There must be a way to recognize exclusive Native rights to Indigenous lands without dismissing all critiques of settler-colonial structures and practices via the appeal to Indigenous knowledges, myths, and histories as "romanticizing." This is why political, material Indigenous land claim matters over and above a southern "sense of place." The possessive of the film's title, then, might be among the most important words of the film. The Indigenous land of the present-day U.S. South is not an abstract place. It is claimed by Native people, and at the risk of sounding romantic, I argue that likewise it claims them.

Causes over Losses

All three of the texts I examine in this chapter feature stories about surviving past the point of loss. In their exploration of their various tempests, they create stories about how to move forward, about what causes are worth pursuing into the future. Each constructs ways forward by repurposing and reanimating past stories into tales that might take them into the next world. To call these stories romantic renderings or compensatory fictions is as unimaginative as it is offensive. The precise power of stories is to build and create ways for humans to live. Indeed, stories have power, which is why we have to examine the causes behind the tales of loss. Does the story ask that people remain static in a state of loss? Does it only look backward? Or does it look ahead, ready to grow and adjust to the needs of a quickly changing world? This is just one way to understand the importance of Indigenous stories that grow and reconnect with origin stories in order to maintain land claim and provide people with strategies for moving forward. The tempests in these texts recast the idea of apocalypse within an Indigenous worldview where creation and destruction are not mutually exclusive categories and where spiralic time moves the journey forward while also managing to pass through old, productive moments of survival. In changing the temporal structures, they also manage to shift spatial conceptions. Each text reads the palimpsestic region of the U.S. South past the recently overlaid Confederate conceptions. As such, they adjust our conceptions of time, of place, of extinction, of survival. In short, they move us to a new red state. In this movement, they demonstrate that these narratives are not so much essentialist as they are essential.

It is hard to know what the future holds for the U.S. South, or for Native people, or for Native people from or in the U.S. South. As Choctaw critic Michael Wilson offers in his analysis of Ray Young Bear's *Black Eagle Child*, "the long story of indigenous peoples is not finished, and [...] we may yet have something to say about our destinies" (xxiii). And he asks: "Who knows what will happen if indigenous peoples crystalize their thoughts on independence in the next hundred years, among new generations of peoples from all backgrounds who will think about the world quite differently than we do today, and who may have a far different approach to the deep injustices of American history?" (xxiv). Such a question has provocative resonance for the U.S. South where, although we still have a long way to go, many may have found it impossible one hundred years ago to imagine the region we see today. At the same time, many in the U.S. South once again seem bent on the politics of racial and ethnic exclusion, imagining peoples from other Souths who should be removed from the region for the benefit of the "economy." Today, I see a U.S. South at a dubious crossroads with both the real potential for a dangerous regression into its worst impulses and at the same time a great potential to unite people from all backgrounds into a better future for a better world. It will depend on the stories that get told and the time we take to understand them.

Rights and Returns
A Coda

I would like to close with a consideration of the *return*. By way of conclusion and introduction (which within the project's own methodology might be thought of as similar moments), I offer a short set of readings of two Native authors who, in one way or another, have tackled the spatial, temporal, and phenomenological dynamics at work in the Native South: Jack D. Forbes and Craig Womack. These two writers are known for their frankness and humor as well as their equally compelling creative and critical outputs. Taken together, they offer a way to understand that Native people are reclaiming the territory in the region known today as the U.S. South. Forbes focuses on solidarity across the deep time of Indigenous memory, whereas Womack asks audiences to consider the stakes of sovereignty inherent in Native stories. Most significantly, they both work to challenge linear temporality, recognizing the returns of creation stories that have a lived material effect on the future of Native sovereignty in the U.S. South. These narratives ultimately disrupt the easy classification of red states as white spaces that exist solely in the U.S. South, and these writers' creative works theorize a red state for the future.

To begin, I offer a reading of Powhatan-Delaware/Lenape-Renape author Jack D. Forbes's short story "The Dream of Injun Joe: A Page from the Alcatraz Papers," originally published in the short story collection *Only Approved Indians Can Play* (1995) and revised for inclusion in the anthology *The People Who Stayed: Southeastern Indian Writing after Removal* (2010). The story recounts only a small snippet of time from the American Indian Movement's occupation of Alcatraz Island in the 1970s, a critical nexus in the Red Power movement. In outlining a vision of the future for Native empowerment, Forbes narrates the story of an Iroquois man named Joe as he considers issues of land greed, power, and the inability of non-Natives to acknowledge Native dreams for survival and new power structures. The speaker Joe begins to describe his dreams in the third person, calling himself "Injun Joe" (the name Mark

Twain uses for his Indian villain in *The Adventures of Tom Sawyer*) and imagining the days of the Seminole fighter Osceola. Forbes's Injun Joe imagines a Native southern military force of "Creeks, mixed-bloods, and freed slaves" (37), willing to begin a campaign for justice in the Southeast in the 1830s and 1840s, establishing freedom for nonwhites while not replicating the inherent problems of coercive colonial power. However, this is where Joe's dreams hit a snag—"what to do with white people" (39)? As Forbes writes, "Injun Joe had studied history enough to know that ultimately empires enslave the victors as much as the defeated" (40). Forbes's Injun Joe desires "a land full of mixed people but, and this was the big one, without the political oppression resulting from the uninterrupted economic and political power of white elites," and he recalls a moment when such a dream happened in some parts of the Native South when "Indians, blacks, whites, red-blacks, mulattoes, half-breeds, you name it [were] living together, intermarrying, sharing life, getting along, until the sacred treaties were broken and the white ruling class decided that brown people had no right to self government anywhere in the territory of Yankee-Dixi-Doo" (40, 41). Forbes realizes that power and sovereignty remain the deciding issues. Land economics drive the discussion, and the classification of people as phenotypically tied to their (lack of) freedom as humans results from a southern enslavement economy that is not confined to the south of the Mason-Dixon line. Rather, Dixie has invaded the very middle of Yankee-Doodle-Doo. But to reverse the dynamic of winner and loser is not enough for Forbes's Injun Joe. Rather, the issue of power must be addressed. This power is both material in its attachment to land and psychological in its relationship to narrative order and historical memory. The treaties in question are almost always about land claim, land sale compensation, and the preservation of sovereign territorial borders. This is not a dream about a "sense of place" but about the very real political issue of land claim inherent in the call for Red Power.

The corruption of power affects both Native and non-Native, and the results are apparent in the pieces of non-Native fiction that this book has examined. The non-Native South has had to atone little for its genocide against southeastern Indian people. As Forbes's Injun Joe notes, such enormous power not only affects the victims, but it also has lasting negative results for the perpetrators. Rather than acknowledge the living Native people in their midst, white people in the post–Civil War U.S. South have repeatedly returned to the narrative expectation that transforms their crimes against Native people into their own sense of defeat, their own Lost Cause. The white South is largely built on the narrative of Indian Removal as complete and the resulting loss as total—and this narrative is not confined to an easy periodization of southern literature. And the question remains: does Jack Forbes's Injun Joe have a place in this narrative of southern identity? If twenty-first-century audiences and critics still cannot separate a narrative of southern defeat from the narrative of Native loss, how can Joe's dreams be realized? As Forbes writes: "In Joe's dreams there was always a place for good people of all races. He realized, in fantasy as in real life, that the majority of white people were not bad, that they were also victims. He tried in his dreams to fantasize ways that Indians could somehow communicate with these silent white people. He never found a way" ("The Dream" 41). This impossible gulf between Native people and "good" white people, I argue, is in many ways due to the white settler southerner's continued preoccupation with a southern "sense of place." The difficulty in loving the land that inherently does not belong to them may be a challenge too big for the settler southerner to tackle. Even those well-meaning, progressive "blue dots" that reside in deeply red states still imagine *their home* as something worth fighting for. The catharsis of loss appeals equally to the need for progressive and conservative narratives of South-ness. They dream of an Injun Joe, removed or rescued, but they never pause to consider the narrative of land reclamation inherent in his dreams.

The majority of silent white people who cannot seem to speak across racial lines in order to find their commonality with Native or African American people have been the focus of much political punditry since the 2016 election. Who are the people in former "blue states" across Pennsylvania and the Midwest who preferred a regressive American dream to a progressive promise? Would a progressive "blue" America have any more respect for Native people and their status as sovereign nations? I opened the book with my recounting of Forbes's words following the 2009 inauguration where he cautioned my classmates and me to recognize the destruction "progressive" American fantasies have wrought on Native peoples in the past. Yet this latest turn in American politics has been particularly regressive in ways that likely promise danger for Native peoples, lands, and recognized sovereignty. As the case with the Dakota Access Pipeline appears in 2017, even when Native people stand against the forces of big oil greed, it seems a change of the political wind can undo the victories of hard-fought battles that protect not just themselves but all of us from the exploitation of the earth's resources for the gain of the few. If, as Forbes imagines, there are good, silent white people, then what will it take for them to speak up? What price will their silence cost all of us in the years to come? Historically speaking, what price have we already paid for their past silences?

One might demonstrate that Forbes's Injun Joe offers a dream just as apocryphal as his non-Native counterparts. He deals in fantasies of solidarity among "Indians, blacks, whites, red-blacks, mulattoes, half-breeds, you name it" in order to mount a resistance. However, these stories of resistance are incredibly important nodes in the continued fight for sovereignty. If the white U.S. South has continued to claim the land via story, as we have seen with narratives about the Lost Colony, the American Revolution, and Indian Removal, then why can't Native people make a reclamation of their territory with their own stories? As Womack asserts, "It is way too premature for Native scholars to deconstruct history when we haven't yet constructed it" (*Red on Red* 3). Womack works toward this construction in both his personal and academic writing. In "Howling at the Moon: The Queer but True Story of My Life as a Hank Williams Song," Womack writes: "Storytelling [...] is a vast terrain with many possibilities for getting lost, as well as for finding one's way, and not enough folks [are] talking about better maps that represent the real territory in question" (33). I am interested in these better maps. Though there is the potential to lose one's way, I argue that southern studies' engaging its investment in settler colonialism is worth the risk. I remain aware that Romine, among others, has demonstrated that "the real" is tricky terrain. However, and let me be clear, the Native nations of this continent have real and continued sovereign land claims—no scare quotes, no hedging, no postmodernly inclined deconstruction of "reality." There is real territory in question here. This is not a "sense" of sovereignty. It is an ongoing battle of five hundred years.

As Cutcha Risling Baldy explains, the sovereign stories that come with these claims are often read as metaphors. However, these tricksters and their lessons are not purely symbolic notions that require no action.[1] As Womack offers, "It may sound funny, but sometimes my life makes the most sense to me when I think of it as a narrative, kind of like a creation story, where you start with chaos, confusion, as in the Creek story where everyone is stumbling about in a thick fog, bumping into each other and getting hurt" ("Howling" 45). This narrative, though challenging, does offer a way forward. He continues: "But then, by the end of the story, the fog lifts, individuals have banded together with the animals they ran into and discovered their clans and their place among the people" (46). This eventual clarity, however, does not guarantee a permanent reprieve from chaos, especially if one remembers the temporal order of return. As Womack explains, "I think the story is like a circle; periodically, you end up back in the fog and chaos, but as you get further along, the darkness becomes more manageable, and you know eventually you will emerge out into the light of the broader landscape" (46). It is this light of the broader landscape, *all of it Indian Country* as Janet McAdams reminds us, that suggests the importance of how stories build the map to Indigenous people returning and reclaiming the territory. Womack's recognition of the circular form of this story suggests the importance in thinking with and through a spiralic time. The stories do come around again, and with each revolution they mean something different. Humans have the ability to shape the stories that come back around; humans have the agency to pull forward the narratives that lead to a better future.

I would like to close with a thought experiment that might offer some "real-world" potential for how one could redress the continued problems of what I have theorized as the red state: property taxes. Frequently, whenever Native nations propose moving land into trust as part of their federal recognition plans, non-Natives get uncomfortable. This anxiety seems to stem from the age-old question of how Native people could ever reasonably expect to "get their land back" when so many non-Natives own homes and businesses on what was surely once Native-owned land. For a moment, let us consider that all of those landowners pay state property tax. And let us also consider that in many cases, particularly in the Southeast, these states have this land precisely through theft, whether that comes in the way of not recognizing Indian treaties or ignoring Supreme Court orders. My question is: what if every single non-Native property holder was made aware of the provenance of their land's appearance on the state tax rolls? And what if instead of paying those property taxes to the state of Georgia for example, these property taxes were paid to the federally recognized tribes removed from that territory through fraudulent and/or shady treaty negotiations? Despite many popular misconceptions, most tribes do not have "casino money" rolling in, and the revenue from these property taxes would go a long way to sustaining the coffers of tribal nations who are badly in need of the money to support their citizenry and maintain their infrastructure. This act would also send a powerful reminder about land claim. While many U.S. citizens live under the myth of individual property ownership, everyone knows what will happen if they neglect to pay their property taxes. The land doesn't really *belong* to the inhabitant; fail to pay the taxes, and it belongs to the state. Even if the amount was small, the recognition of land claim might advance a great deal if the average American paid the appropriate Indigenous nation for their continued settlement on Native land. It might even make red states *Red* again.

This suggestion probably strikes some as hopelessly naïve and others as woefully insufficient to redress all the wrongs of colonial invasion. I don't disagree. I have lived and worked most of my life in one red state or another. I am as jaded as I am optimistic about the future of the region. However, one thing I remain confident about is the power of stories to change the future. Like many others, my grandmother called telling a lie "telling a story." To me, this has always been a nice euphemism. It allows us to believe that the lie is just that—a story. However, sometimes these stories take on power, and when they are based on a lie, then that can get dangerous. In a way, though, because history is selective and frequently based on power dynamics, it can become difficult to see how all stories are not, to a certain extent, lies, and how all lies, in a way, are nothing but stories. As this book has shown, whether the story is about loss or resilience, removal or resistance, such dynamics result frequently from the interactions between the storyteller and her audience.

However, despite being "dangerous" and "wondrous things," as Thomas King says, "The truth about stories is that that's all we are" (*Truth about Stories* 9, 2).

Throughout this book, I have attempted to show the spiralic time that stories chart as they return and pass through the individuals that receive them. When considering Native history, these tellings and retellings and re-retellings almost always deal in territorial claim. Indigenous peoples have origin stories that link them to a place and that do not begin with colonialism. These colonial process narratives continue to dominate much of one's everyday experience of the world, and they have long organized literary and historical pedagogy. To organize the admittedly broad contours of this project I have tried to think through the multivalent meanings of what "red states" might generate in several of its southern and Native iterations. Rather than simply examine the superficial convergences between Indigenous land claims and southern narratives of place, I have attempted to cast into relief the specific contextual histories and narrative forms that demonstrate the significant divergences between a settler-colonial South and Native sovereignty in the region. I have worked to push against an overdetermined narrative of loss or the Lost Cause in order to move the emergent scholarship of the Native South in line with some of the more nuanced and productive conversations happening in Native American studies. In addition to my hopes that this book might initiate some productive conversation between Native American and southern literary studies (even if it comes at my expense), I also desire that it might have at least some small ripple in how non-Native southerners imagine their adopted homes. If even one non-Native person pauses to consider how his or her "southern" identity remains dependent on settler-colonial fantasies of dispossession, then I will remain grateful for the opportunity to spill so much ink trying to right a wrong in which I myself am implicated. I know that the numerous violences of settler colonialism cannot be undone. These are not "losses," after all; they are thefts, murders, wars, and cover-ups. But even if it seems naïve, this is not a lost cause. Though it may take a long time, there are ways to make this right; there are ways to return the land. The real work is happening now.

NOTES

Red States: An Introduction

1. In many ways, my analytic framework mirrors a regionally inflected literary studies approach to Kevin Bruyneel's arguments in *The Third Space of Sovereignty: The Postcolonial Politics of U.S.-Indigenous Relations* (2007), where he outlines how the "spatial boundaries around territory and legal and political institutions and the temporal boundaries around the narratives of economic and political development, cultural progress, and modernity" (xiii) categorize the possibilities and exercise of sovereignty for present-day Native nations.

2. For a history of the Red Power movement and its enduring legacy, see Paul Chaat Smith and Robert Warrior's foundational *Like a Hurricane: The Indian Movement from Alcatraz to Wounded Knee* (1997), as well as Daniel Cobb and Loretta Fowler's *Beyond Red Power: American Indian Politics and Activism since 1900* (2007).

3. Wilson establishes his argument by countering William Blevis and extending previous work on Gerald Vizenor by Kimberly Blaeser. See *Writing Home: Indigenous Narratives of Resistance* (2008).

4. Both Leigh Anne Duck's *Nation's Region: Southern Modernism, Segregation, and U.S. Nationalism* (2009) and Jennifer Greeson's *Our South: Geographic Fantasy and the Rise of National Literature* (2010) explore facets of this phenomenon with precision.

5. This rule was updated on June 29, 2015, to designate "historical" as prior to 1900. See Bureau of Indian Affairs, 25 CFR Part 83, "Federal Acknowledgement of Indian Tribes."

6. For an example of one instance where Native people were literally forced into this construction, see "The Campaign for Racial Purity and the Erosion of Paternalism in Virginia, 1922–1930: 'Nominally White, Biologically Mixed, and Legally Negro'" by J. Douglas Smith. Also, it should be noted that two of the major anthologies of southern literature, W. W. Norton's *Literature of the American South* and *The Oxford Book of the American South*, include very little Native material in their contents.

7. Perdue, Green, and Kidwell have each published numerous foundational works in the field, including Perdue's *Cherokee Women: Gender and Culture Change, 1700–1835* (1999), Green's *The Politics of Indian Removal: Creek Government and Society in Crisis* (1985), and Kidwell's *Choctaws and Missionaries in Mississippi, 1818–1918* (1995).

8. See Malinda Maynor Lowery's *Lumbee Indians in the Jim Crow South: Race, Identity, and the Making of a Nation* (2010) and Christina Snyder's *Slavery in Indian Country: The Changing Face of Captivity in Early America* (2012).

9. See Claudio Saunt's *A New Order of Things: Property, Power, and the Transformation of the Creek Indians, 1733–1816* (1999).

10. For an overview of the breadth and depth of ethnohistorical work on the Native South, see Theda Purdue and Michael D. Green's *The Columbia Guide to the American Indians of the Southeast* (2001). Additionally, this project is also indebted to work by scholars such as Tiya Miles, Robbie Ethridge, and Patricia Galloway.

11. As John Lowe offers in *Calypso Magnolia: The Crosscurrents of Caribbean and Southern Literature* (2016), "narrative [...] cuts across maps that create artificial lines around peoples and cultures" (7).

12. See Dimock's formative *Through Other Continents: American Literature across Deep Time* (2006) for an analysis of several texts that challenge the space/time continuum as bound up with the formation of the colonial nation-state. As she notes, "In many parts of the non-Western world, a very different ontology of time prevails" (2). Also see the 2011 collection edited by Virginia Jackson, *On Periodization: Selected Essays from the English Institute* (2010).

13. Foucault marks this shift from the eighteenth century in "*Society Must Be Defended*" (1997), noting, "History thus becomes a knowledge of struggles that is deployed and that functions within a field of struggles; there is now a link between the political fight and historical knowledge" (171). He goes on to examine the uses of this type of power within both large-scale institutional forms (*Security, Territory, Population* [2004]) and within the discursive terrain called on in evoking the idea of the individual body (*The Birth of Biopolitics* [2004]). Additionally, as Trefzer states regarding the non-Native southern modernist authors she examines, "As they were digging deep into the past to trace the Native American history of their region, they discovered a history deeply entwined with national policy and international politics" (182).

14. See Raymond Williams, *Marxism and the Literature* (1977).

15. As I note above, there has been a critical dearth of seeing the Native American presence in southern literature, and though I hesitate to make the still obligatory gesture of recounting the ways that southern studies scholarship has overlooked Native history, it unfortunately remains necessary at this present moment. Although New Southern Studies offers distinct promise for a recognition of Native presences in the literature of the region, many critical works about the U.S. South fail to acknowledge the importance of Indigenous history and identity in the region. Michael Kreyling's otherwise excellent work *The South That Wasn't There* (2010) almost ironically renders its title true by making the Native South absent within the work. Likewise, Deborah Cohn's equally provocative *History and Memory in Two Souths* (1999) deftly analyzes the convergences between literature of the U.S. South and Spanish America, but Cohn only attends to Indigenous identity as a shadowy backdrop to the black/white racial binary of either region's plantation economy. Douglas Mitchell's *A Disturbing and Alien Memory: Southern Novelists Writing History* (2008) does a good job of demonstrating the continued use of history in imagining the region, but likewise, it rarely pays attention to the Native history that subtends numerous southern fictions.

16. Likewise, Huhndorf's *Mapping the Americas: The Transnational Politics of Contemporary Native Culture* (2009) offers an excellent analysis of how transnational study might help think through issues within contemporary Native studies scholarship. This approach also offers a way to consider periodization, as Fuchs argues, "Like any grand narrative, the literary histories that give us periodization require in-

terrogation and qualification, both of which are enabled by a transnational account" (326).

17. Also see chapter 5 of Trefzer's *Disturbing Indians*, Don Doyle's *Faulkner's County: The Historical Roots of Yoknapatawpha* (2001), and Robert Dale Parker's "Red Slippers and Cottonmouth Moccasins: White Anxieties in Faulkner's Indian Stories" for a discussion of Faulkner's use of themes from Native history. As Trefzer notes, "In studying Faulkner's representations of Indians, it is tempting to get caught up in questions of historical accuracy, ethnographic authenticity, and political correctness" and that he, like many other authors, perpetuates stereotypes of Native people by writing about "mythical Indians of [his] own imagination" (151–52). This echoes Parker, who notes that Faulkner's portrayals of southeastern Indian people amounts to "nonsense" ("Red Slippers" 81). However, as Trefzer points out, "A close examination of the Native American signifier in Faulkner's fiction shows us that Faulkner's Indian texts do not participate in a mimetic understanding of literature as simply reflecting a (historical) reality outside the text, but instead in the distortion and displacement of these 'historical realities'" (152). This project remains interested in the effects produced by these distortions in southern literature, and I look forward to the forthcoming volume from the University Press of Mississippi, *Faulkner and the Native South* (2018). Also see Phillip Carroll Morgan's *Riding Out the Storm: 19th Century Chickasaw Governors, Their Lives, and Intellectual Legacy* (2013) for a discussion of the historical contexts of Yakni Patafa as Chickasaw leader Cyrus Harris's family home.

18. See, for example, chapter 4, "'Been to the Nation Lord, but I Couldn't Stay There': Cherokee Freedmen, Internal Colonialism, and the Racialization of Citizenship" of Jodi Byrd's *The Transit of Empire*.

Chapter 1. Recovery

1. Green's papers in the Southern Historical Collection at the University of North Carolina at Chapel Hill include approximately three thousand items in more than a hundred folders related to *The Lost Colony*, with many of those devoted to correspondence and research about the source material. Additional research materials can be found in Samuel Selden's correspondence with Green and Green's daily diary entries from the year before the play's premiere.

2. For examples of this story and the subsequent interpretations of it, see Sandra Messinger Cypress's *La Malinche in Mexican Literature: From History to Myth* (1991), Paula Gunn Allen's *Pocahontas: Medicine Woman, Spy, Entrepreneur, Diplomat* (2003), and Frances Karttunen's *Between Worlds: Interpreters, Guides, and Survivors* (1994).

3. For a thorough understanding of White's watercolors see *A New World: England's First View of America* by Kim Sloan. The collection includes almost all of White's watercolors from the British Museum collection, and it includes numerous essays contextualizing White's works for his period.

4. Michael Harkin has several interesting readings of the Roanoke history and its latter-day renderings. I do not agree with all of his conclusions, but I follow his methodology of reading the archive alongside the repertoire in order to imagine how meaning has been made from this historical event. See Harkin's "The Floating Island:

Anachronism and Paradox in the Lost Colony," "Performing Paradox: Narrativity and the Lost Colony of Roanoke," and "Time's Arrow: Violence and Ethnohistorical Surrealism in the Lost Colony."

5. These include but are not limited to Jonathan Gil Harris, Stephen Greenblatt, Karen Kupperman, and Alden Vaughn.

6. See Diana Taylor's *The Archive and the Repertoire: Performing Cultural Memory in the Americas* (2003) for a discussion of how colonial memory is staged from and against the historical archive.

7. See Thomas Cartelli, "From First Encounter to 'Fiery Oven': The Effacement of the New England Indian in *Mourt's Relation* and the Histories of the Pequot War" in *Indography: Writing the "Indian" in Early Modern England* (2012).

8. Vizenor writes of White and De Bry's images in *Fugitive Poses* (1998), arguing that these images become the earliest form of *indians* as advertisements for the Americas as a place free from actual Native people and replaced with Europe's aesthetic vision of the Indian.

9. As Neil Whitehead argues concerning representation of British Guiana and the Amazon, such a positivistic production does more to produce for English audiences an epistemology of themselves rather than the people they encounter.

10. Throughout the chapter, I cite the version of Hakluyt's texts edited and collected by David Beers Quinn in the two-volume collection, *The Roanoke Voyages, 1584–1590: Documents to Illustrate the English Voyages to North America under the Patent Granted to Walter Raleigh in 1584* (1991). Most of the English-language papers we have regarding the Roanoke voyages come through Hakluyt's collection. Some documents are extant only in his editions, but in many cases, Quinn has worked to corroborate that an original source, even if now lost, preceded Hakluyt's printing. As Quinn notes, there are also numerous Spanish-language archival sources, which scholars are only just now beginning to read for clues to the circumstances surrounding early English colonization.

11. See Kim Sloan's *A New World: England's First View of America* (2007).

12. For varying, although representative, histories of the 1587 Lost Colony, see James Horn, *A Kingdom Strange: The Brief and Tragic History of the Lost Colony of Roanoke* (2010), Karen Ordahl Kupperman, *Roanoke: The Abandoned Colony* (1984), Lee Miller, *Roanoke: Solving the Mystery of the Lost Colony* (2002), and David Stick, *Roanoke Island: The Beginnings of English America* (1983). For an extended consideration of the Indigenous people of Roanoke and their role in the colonial efforts of the English in the late 1500s, see Michael Leroy Oberg, *The Head in Edward Nugent's Hand: Roanoke's Forgotten Indians* (2008). See Tony Horwitz's *A Voyage Long and Strange* (2008) for an overview for how U.S. popular cultural history reimagines the Lost Colony among other colonial expeditions. For a discussion of the ways in which early modern events are redeployed in the present-day United States, see the epilogue to Rebecca Bach's *Colonial Transformations: The Cultural Production of the New Atlantic World, 1580–1640* (2000), "Twentieth-Century Transformations: Pocahontas and Captain John Smith in Late-Twentieth-Century Jamestown."

13. See Stephen Greenblatt's formative work, "Invisible Bullets," in *Shakespearean Negotiations* (1988) for an analysis of how Harriot's work creates structures of relation between the Algonquian and English peoples.

14. It seems important to note here that the primary texts from the Roanoke voyages profoundly lack the term "Indian." Rather, "savages" operates as the common descriptor of the inhabitants of the newly christened "Virginian" coast. Only twice across the numerous written records of the voyages are the people of the Americas called "Indians." One instance appears in a rough draft of "Anonymous Notes for the Guidance of Raleigh and Cavendish," a text that David Beers Quinn posits to be a rough draft with difficult-to-corroborate accuracy or origins. The text catalogues necessary provisions and outlines a code of conduct for the voyagers: "First that no Souldier do violat any woman, 2 That no Souldier do take any mans goodes forcibly from hym. 3 That no Indian be forced to labor unwillingly. 4 That no Souldier shall defraud Her Majeste of her fyfte. 5 That no Souldier abbandon his ensegne without leave, of his Capten, 6 That non shall stryke or mysuse any Indian, 7 That non shall Enter any Indians howse without his leave" (qtd. in Quinn 138).

Quinn believes that these regulations as they pertain to the Indigenous inhabitants are likely original but that they are adapted from previous military codes of conduct, which may be adapted from Spanish sources. Thus, the term "Indian" comes to be applied to the people of Roanoke only through their connection to, and presumed needed protection from, English subjects. These codes would have likely applied not to the 1587 colony of planter families but instead to the earlier expeditions of male soldiers. This means that the women named would be Native women given that no other women would be present. Aside from this instance, nearly none of the materials from the voyages themselves make use of the term "Indian."

15. See chapter 2, "Bermuda's Ireland: Naming the Colonial World" in Bach's *Colonial Transformations* for a discussion of the significance of the act of naming people and places in early colonial contact.

16. For an extended discussion of the rhetoric of paradise, see Jonathan P. A. Sell, *Rhetoric and Wonder in English Travel Writing, 1560–1613* (2006).

17. Several scholars have discussed the missing silver cup at length, arguing that it constituted an early misunderstanding over the terms of commodity exchange in transatlantic contact. See Seth Mallios, *The Deadly Politics of Giving: Exchange and Violence at Ajacan, Roanoke, and Jamestown* (2006) and Cynthia Van Zandt, *Brothers among Nations: The Pursuit of Intercultural Alliances in Early America, 1580–1660* (2008).

18. Jace Weaver covers part of Manteo's history in *The Red Atlantic* (2014).

19. See Alden T. Vaughan, *Transatlantic Encounters: American Indians in Britain, 1500–1776* (2006) for a thorough overview of Manteo and Wanchese as cultural interpreters.

20. All dictionary references are to the *Oxford English Dictionary Online*, dictionary.oed.com.

21. In addition to this record, several historians point to the even more problematic concern over John White's identity. While some see his written record as consistent with that of a singular individual, others question if John White the painter was the same as John White the governor. Others still believe that the two Whites were one and the same, but they remain puzzled over his odd archival absence in any other dealings aside from those that directly concern Roanoke. For an overview of this debate see pages 40–47 of Quinn's *The Roanoke Voyages*.

22. The accounts of the performance I offer come from the summers of 2009 and 2011. In 2009 I attended *The Lost Colony* four nights, and I sat in a different location for each performance in order to consider the use of space as a central node to the audience's experience of the play. In 2011 and 2015, I revisited the play. Additionally, I discussed these performances with several 2009 participants. In each of these instances, questions arose regarding agency and intentionality when dealing with live performance. When I refer to the original manuscripts, I cite Green's own copies contained in the archives of the Southern Historical Collections at UNC-Chapel Hill or Lawrence Avery's 2001 edition of Green's *The Lost Colony* available from UNC Press. Throughout the chapter, I offer material from the play, relevant information from my conversations with those who are a part of these yearly productions, and my experiences as an audience member.

23. For instance, see Matthew Thompson's dissertation "Staging 'the Drama': The Continuing Importance of Cultural Tourism in the Gaming Era" (2009) and Gina Caison's interview with director Eddie Swimmer, "'We're Still Here': Eddie Swimmer on Cherokee History, Life, and Outdoor Drama in the Appalachian Mountains" (2010) in the *North Carolina Literary Review* about the relaunch of the Eastern Band of Cherokee Indians' outdoor drama *Unto These Hills*. Originally written by Kermit Hunter and under the direction of a largely non-Native Cherokee Historical Association, the play is now produced by the tribe.

24. Donald Pease made a similar point in remarks during his July 13, 2010, lecture, "Transnational Melancholia," given at the 2010 University College Dublin's Clinton Institute for American Studies Summer School. This line of argument, which mirrored my own early thoughts on the 2009 outdoor drama performances, and our brief conversation that followed spurred my thinking on this point, and I am indebted to his remarks on this topic.

25. For Green's perspective on this new theater form, see William Howard Rough's "'What the American Public Needs': A 'Theater of the People'" as well as Green's introductions to the 1946 and 1954 printed editions contained at the end of the presently available 2001 edition of the play edited by Laurence Avery. Cecelia Moore investigates the heavy involvement of the WPA in the creation of *The Lost Colony* in *The Federal Theatre Project in the American South: The Carolina Playmakers and the Quest for American Drama* (2017).

26. For instance, see Angela Pulley Hudson's *Real Native Genius: How an Ex-Slave and a White Mormon Became Famous Indians* (2015) and her interview on episode 13 of the *About South* podcast where she explains the local vectors informing the history of the performative Choctaw, Okah Tubbee.

27. See Laurence Avery's introduction to the 2001 edition of the play for an overview of the issues surrounding the RIHA's attempt to stage the initial performance in 1937.

28. Despite reaching a legitimate—and obvious—conclusion that racial performance functions rather disturbingly in these outdoor dramas, Zogry's analysis is problematic for its methods. Despite being published in 2011, he only draws from a single performance he saw in 2000, thus negating the importance of the dynamics of the continual revisions to the performance. Additionally, he offers quotes from "archival" sources, yet in his endnotes, it seems that he has not conducted any first-

person research in the archive, instead drawing his quotes from another single scholar's study and presenting those quotes as contextualized. While perhaps these methodological problems do not undermine his conclusions, they do lead him to make several mistakes in the specific details he analyzes to support his argument, including the trajectory of costuming in the play, and as noted above, the regional specificity needed to contextualize the mechanisms of power and history that the plays evoke.

29. The "wages of whiteness" linked to the material benefits of a white racial identity is discussed by David Roediger in his important text *The Wages of Whiteness: Race and the Making of the American Working Class* (1991), but importantly, he follows the logic of W. E. B. Du Bois's formative analysis of the use of race and labor in the Reconstruction-era U.S. South in *Black Reconstruction in America* (1935). I argue that historical narratives of Anglo-American land attachment, such as those found in these performances, may have been understood by some audiences as one more material asset in the historical shoring up of the benefits of being white in the U.S. South. However, this, like many of the wages of whiteness, works without actually offering any white people anything more than the feeling that they maintained a landed superiority in the region even if they did not own any land.

30. Of course, the disguise was not that thorough and the names are listed in the program as the same actor, yet every night I attended, the audience gasped in amazement when the on-stage transformation of this character occurred. One evening, the man next to me remarked, "I didn't realize that was the same man!" Brian Clowdus, who played this dual part in 2009, confirmed for me that repeatedly audience members noted their surprise to him. While he appreciated the audience's willing suspension of disbelief, he chuckled at their frequent surprise with the statement, "I mean, come on. How surprised can people be? I'm the only guy on stage with a pointy beard and a curly mustache."

31. Interestingly, but perhaps coincidentally, agona, DAӨ, is the Cherokee word for famine.

32. Dacia Dick, the actress who played Agona in the 2009 season, expressed her initial skepticism of the role and its portrayal of the Native woman as a slapstick figure. She said she felt caught between the audience's expectations of Agona as comic relief and her own desire to portray Agona as a more complex woman. Ultimately, she decided that she might play Agona as less of a slapstick role and more of a curious young woman who is genuinely interested in the newcomers and their odd ways. Representing Agona as outgoing and curious with a playful sense of humor rather than the object of a hurtful colonial joke helped her create a space where Agona could become more humanized while still allowing the audience to see her as a comedic character.

33. One need only examine the ironically named First Families of Virginia alongside the numerous people who trace their genealogy back to Pocahontas to understand how early interracial contact in the colonial South between Natives and Europeans is not necessarily a mark of racial danger to landholding legitimacy and southern racial nostalgia.

34. This phenomenon is most strongly represented in the group known as The Lost Colony Center for Science and Research, who conducts the Lost Colony DNA Project aiming to test people throughout the coastal region to establish a link between the

colonists and the local tribes. Additionally, even as recently as the summer of 2011, while I was conducting fieldwork at the newly designed historical center on Roanoke Island, I overheard docents telling visitors that the Lumbee were descended from the Lost Colony. This information was also offered by the cast members who led the backstage tour at the theater.

35. Since the 2013 season, *The Lost Colony* has employed a new director who restored the traditional Historian narrator (dressed in Indiana Jones–style archaeological wear), eliminated the curtain call, and employed several of the features of the mid-twentieth-century character interpretations, including the use of the offensive "tonto speak" for Native characters.

Chapter 2. Revolution

1. See "revolution" n. in the *Oxford English Dictionary*.

2. For a discussion of how the U.S. South worked as both legitimizing agent and disavowed presence in early American national narratives, see Jennifer Rae Greeson's *Our South: Geographic Fantasy and the Rise of National Literature* (2010). This chapter is also indebted to ideas from Bernard Bailyn's *The Ideological Origins of the American Revolution* (1976).

3. See "volute" n. in the *Oxford English Dictionary*.

4. See John Oliphant's *Peace and War on the Anglo-Cherokee Frontier 1756–63* (2001).

5. In what seems to be an eerie coincidence given its release in 2000, Gibson's character measures the chair at "9 pounds and 11 ounces—perfect," signaling much of Pease's later argument on the affective power of the film's afterlife to support the Patriot Act in a post-9/11 world.

6. See Scott Romine's discussion of Agrarian and chair industry logics in *The Real South: Southern Narratives in the Age of Reproduction*.

7. For example, see Joseph J. Ellis, *American Sphinx: The Character of Thomas Jefferson* (1998); Annette Gordon-Reed, *Thomas Jefferson and Sally Hemmings* (1998); Peter Onuf, *The Mind of Thomas Jefferson* (2007); and most recently John Meacham, *Thomas Jefferson: The Art of Power* (2013).

8. All materials from Jefferson come from the Library of America edition, *Thomas Jefferson: Writings* (1984).

9. See Robert Berkhoffer, *The White Man's Indian*; Anthony Wallace, *Jefferson and the Indians: The Tragic Fate of the First Americans* (1999); and Gordon Sayre, "Jefferson and Native Americans: Policy and Archive" in *The Cambridge Companion to Thomas Jefferson* (2009).

10. See Peter Onuf, *The Mind of Thomas Jefferson*.

11. See William McLoughlin, *Cherokee Renascence in the New Republic* (1992) as well as Justice, *Our Fires Survive the Storm*, for an overview and legacy of Dragging Canoe and the Chickamauga.

12. See Wallace's *Jefferson and the Indians* as well as Cynthia Cumfer's *Separate Peoples, One Land* (2007) and John Oliphant's *Peace and War on the Anglo-Cherokee Frontier, 1756–63*.

13. All materials from Washington come from the Library of America edition, *George Washington: Writings*.

14. All materials from Marshall come from the Library of America edition, *John Marshall: Writings* (2010).

15. See Busick's *A Sober Desire for History: William Gilmore Simms as Historian* (2001) and Nakamura's *Visions of Order in William Gilmore Simms: Southern Conservatism and the Other American Romance* (2009) for an overview and analysis of Simms's use of history.

16. See Guild's *Simms: A Literary Life* (1992) and Butterworth and Gibler's *William Gilmore Simms: A Reference Guide* (1980).

17. For instance, see Caroline Gilman, Review of *Mellichampe* in *The Southern Rose*. Excerpted in *William Gilmore Simms: A Reference Guide* (1980) and Arthur Hobson Quinn, *American Fiction: An Historical and Critical Survey* (1936).

18. See *An Early and Strong Sympathy: The Indian Writings of William Gilmore Simms* (2003).

19. See James Merril, *The Indians' New World: Catawbas and Their Neighbors from European Contact through the Era of Removal*; Charles Hudson, *The Catawba Nation* (2007); and Robin Beck, *Chiefdoms, Collapse, and Coalescence in the Early American South* (2013).

20. In addition to Gallay's *The Indian Slave Trade: The Rise of the English Empire in the American South, 1670–1717* (2002) and Snyder's *Slavery in Indian Country*, see Paul Kelton, *Epidemics and Enslavement: Biological Catastrophe in the Native Southeast, 1492–1715* (2007), and William Ramsey, *The Yamasee War: A Study of Culture, Economy, and Conflict in the Colonial South* (2010).

21. See Merril, *The Indians' New World*.

22. For an analysis of the history and critical reception of these archetypes, see chapter 2, "This Island's Mine: The Parallax Logic of Caliban's Cacophony" in Jodi Byrd's *Transit of Empire*.

23. Atakulla is based on the historical Attakullakulla. It is unclear why Hunter shortened the name.

24. For the historical backdrop of *HITW*'s action, see Cynthia Cumfer's *Separate Peoples, One Land*, John Oliphant's *Peace and War on the Anglo-Cherokee Frontier, 1756–63*, and John L. Nichols's "Alexander Cameron, British Agent among the Cherokee, 1764–1781." For a comprehensive biography of Daniel Boone along with the varying ways that his story has been told by different people throughout the years, see the biography *Boone* (2007) by Robert Morgan.

25. When I told my father, stepmother, and stepsister that the play was based primarily on fiction and that the Geof Stuart family never existed, they were upset. My father felt especially cheated since he thought the play worked hard to establish its "authenticity," while my sister concluded maybe the real events did not matter anyway and that the story—rather than the archive—might be "the thing."

26. It seems likely that two of Hunter's sources about the Stuart family were Philip M. Hamer's two essays, "John Stuart's Indian Policy during the Early Months of the American Revolution" and "Correspondence of Henry Stuart and Alexander with the Wataugans."

27. For example, Atakulla wears white, signifying his association with peace and diplomacy, while Dragging Canoe wears red to show his more militaristic standpoint. This might also signal their alliances with red and white towns within the Cherokee political organization. See Duane Champagne's *Social Order and Political Change* (1992) for an overview of Cherokee and other southeastern tribes' sociopolitical structures during this period.

28. At this point it seems productive to admit that I too felt the sense of expectation during the summer of 2011 when revisiting each of these dramas. While all of the performances were relatively the same, I felt tied to the dramatic interpretations I had seen in 2009 and found myself longing for the narratives I had grown attached to two years before.

29. See Perdue's *Cherokee Women* for a discussion of changing Cherokee gender roles during the period represented by the play.

30. For numerous examples of this phenomenon, see Bergland's *The National Uncanny*.

31. See *Brecht on Theatre* (1977) for a discussion of how performance can achieve alienation through the use of gestus. Brecht writes of the alienation affect, "the actor must invest what he has to show with a definite gest of showing. It is of course necessary to drop the assumption that there is a fourth wall cutting the audience off from the stage and the consequent illusion that the stage action is taking place in reality and without an audience" (136). While the action I identify here is indeed a movement of the hand, Brecht notes that gestus goes beyond this even when expressed in this way because beyond achieving a simplistic verisimilitude between actor and character, it "allows conclusions to be drawn about the social circumstances" (105).

32. See https://www.teaparty.org/about-us/.

33. See Matt Murray's "'Redskins Pride' social media campaign backfires" from today.com.

34. See Risling Baldy, "U.S. Patent and Trademark Office cancels trademark registrations for the Washington Racial Slur team! or In which I attempt to explain How did we get here? Where do we go from here? To Twitter we go! #NotYourMascot" or numerous posts by Adrienne Keene on her blog, *Native Appropriations*.

35. As this book was heading to press in December 2017, the Native group and D.C.-based nonprofit Rising Hearts Coalition staged a "culture jam" where for about three hours they convinced many people on the Internet that the team had changed the name to the Washington Redhawks.

Chapter 3. Removal

1. See William S. Maltby's *The Black Legend in England: The Development of Anti-Spanish Sentiment, 1558–1660* (1971).

2. For a biographical overview of Boudinot, see *Cherokee Editor: The Writings of Elias Boudinot* (1996), edited by Theda Perdue. For thorough publication details of the *Phoenix*, see Robert G. Martin's "The *Cherokee Phoenix*: Pioneer Indian Journalism." Though heavily dated, the article offers numerous statistical details about the publication and material history of the newspaper.

3. See Simms in the *Charleston City Gazette*, March 15, 1830, where he wrote, "The committee are well satisfied, that every humane and benevolent individual, who is anxious for the welfare of the great body of the Cherokees, and is correctly informed of their true condition, must feel desirous for their removal, provided it can be effected with their consent." The language of consent looms large here as one of the key points of conflict in Native land and resource management. The Native American Graves Protection and Repatriation Act includes the language of consultation, which several entities who wish to effect projects on Native land emphasize is not the same as "consent." To be clear, the law requires "consultation," a murky concept that leaves the door wide open for projects that Native nations and their allies actively protest, including the Dakota Access Pipeline, among others.

4. For more information about the Treaty Party and the Treaty of New Echota, see Thurman Wilkins's *Cherokee Tragedy: The Ridge Family and the Decimation of a People* (1970, 1989) and Julia Coates's *Trail of Tears* (2014).

5. See Daniel Heath Justice's excellent reading of the question of intentionality and legacy in chapter 2 of *Our Fires Survive the Storm*.

6. Again, see Perdue, *Cherokee Editor*. Also see Bethany Schneider's "Boudinot's Change: Boudinot, Emerson, and Ross on Cherokee Removal" for an outline of this shift.

7. See Guilds's edited collection *"Long Years of Neglect": The Writings of William Gilmore Simms* (1989) for an overview of this argument and the application of it by numerous Simms critics.

8. For examples of these debates, see Gavin Wright's *Slavery and American Economic Development* (2006) and Mark Smith's *Debating Slavery: Economy and Society in the Antebellum American South* (1998). For an older version of this logic in the twentieth century, see the recovered 1932 publication *The Plantation* by Edgar Tristram Thompson. For examples of analyses that nuance the plantation South by considering subregional development, see Daniel Usner's *Indians, Settlers, and Slaves in a Frontier Exchange Economy: The Lower Mississippi Valley before 1783* (1992) and Calvin Schermerhorn's *Money over Mastery, Family over Freedom: Slavery in the Antebellum Upper South* (2011).

9. For various Removal histories, tribally specific or otherwise, see Garrison as well as Theda Perdue and Michael D. Green's *The Cherokee Removal: A Brief History with Documents* (1995), Julia Coates's *Trail of Tears*, William McLoughlin's *Cherokee Renascence in the New Republic*, Michael D. Green's *The Politics of Indian Removal: Creek Government and Society in Crisis* (1985), Robbie Ethridge's *Creek Country: The Creek Indians and Their World* (2003), Clara Sue Kidwell's *Choctaws and Missionaries in Mississippi, 1818–1918* (1995), James Atkinson's *Splendid Land, Splendid People: The Chickasaw Indians to Removal* (2003), and Anthony Wallace's *The Long, Bitter Trail: Andrew Jackson and the Indians* (1993). For an overview of the long geographic and temporal scope of Removal with documents from numerous tribes and sites of Removal, see Heidler and Heidler's classroom-friendly casebook, *Indian Removal* (2006).

10. See George Wilson Pierson, *Tocqueville in America* (1938, rpt. 1996) for the ways in which Tocqueville wrote about and used the scene of Choctaw Removal in his writings.

11. See John and Mary Lou Missall's *The Seminole Wars: America's Longest Indian Conflict* (2004).

12. For a history of Cherokee Removal in particular, see Coates, Purdue, Green, and McLoughlin. For a literary history of the discourse surrounding Removal, see Justice. As noted earlier, Justice offers a compelling reading of the Treaty of New Echota itself in *Our Fires Survive the Storm*. For an overview of the Eastern Band of Cherokee Indians' particular history during the Removal period, see John Finger, *Eastern Band of Cherokees, 1819–1900* (1984).

13. See Coates's "'None of Us Is Supposed to Be Here': Ethnicity, Nationality, and the Production of Cherokee Histories."

14. See Schneider as well as chapter 5 of Philip Round's *Removable Type: Histories of the Book in Indian Country, 1663–1880* (2010) as an example of analyses that query this assumption. Also see Floyce Alexander's "Emerson and the Cherokee Removal."

15. See Foucault's *Security, Territory, Population*.

16. For a thorough discussion of infrastructure as it pertains to the Creeks, see Angela Pulley Hudson's *Creek Paths and Federal Roads: Indians, Settlers, and Slaves and the Making of the American South* (2010).

17. See Griffith's *McIntosh and Weatherford* (1998) as well as Frank's *Creeks and Southerners* (2005). Also, for an overview of Creek Removal, see Michael Green's *Politics of Indian Removal*.

18. As Hudson notes with an example taken from a *Georgia Journal* advertisement promoting a road constructed by McIntosh, "'There are good ferries and bridges so that travelers need not be apprehensive that they will be detained on the road by high waters. The accommodations on the road will be good; and as the Indians have made large crops, there is no doubt that corn may be purchased at any time on the road for less than one dollar per bushel.'" She continues: "the 'Indians' referred to in this newspaper notice were probably not the individual Creek men and women engaged in small-scale daily exchanges with travelers, but were instead the large-scale producers engaged in plantation-style agriculture" (139).

19. The fact that these are imagined in relation to other Souths of Mexico and Peru again complicates the registers of how print audiences could understand their relationship to a global South based on exploitative economies and Native land dispossession. Although one could think of the global South as an anachronistic category here, moments such as this one, as well as Moore's *Geographical Reader*, signal the ways that the global South is a concept that might apply if we reconceived of our ideas of period.

20. For a history of Dexter's personal motivations in speculation, his New England ties, and his work at facilitating Removal, see Jane Kamensky's cultural and biographical history, *The Exchange Artist: A Tale of High-Flying Speculation and America's First Banking Collapse* (2008).

21. William Apess's 1828 "Indian Nullification on the Unjust Laws of Massachusetts" represents an excellent contemporaneous example of how Removal debates occurred throughout the North and the South. See Apess's *On Our Own Ground* (1992) for his work as well as editor Barry O'Connell's analysis of the larger significance of this work in context of national debates about the Nullification Crisis.

22. Natalie Joy explores the intersections of the anti-Removal and abolition movements in her dissertation "Hydra's Head: Fighting Slavery and Indian Removal in Antebellum America" (2008). She follows the work of Mary Hershberger, who notes

in "Mobilizing Women, Anticipating Abolition: The Struggle against Indian Removal in the 1830s" that Indian Removal was one of the first major national debates in the United States in which women played a large part. Joy also examines the anti-Removal petition orchestrated by Catherine Beecher, and like Schneider, she examines the participation of the Emersons in this debate. As Joy notes of the Supreme Court controversy in 1832, "Once again, antiremovalists responded to the removal crisis with a massive petition campaign. This time, however, the antiremoval campaign began in the abolitionist press, not the missionary press, as before. Most missionaries had abandoned the antiremoval cause in 1832, but abolitionists continued to include Indian removal as a key component of their antislavery ideology" (122).

23. See Claudio Saunt's *A New Order of Things* regarding how critics read the plantation economy onto Native people rather than examining the ways that Native people negotiated the plantation economy through strategies that may not always fit the parameters of the association between race and capital in the region. Also see the debate in the journal *Ethnohistory* where Perdue outlines the problems of thinking of race as an overdetermined way to measure's one actions within the southern plantation economy in "Race and Culture: Writing the Ethnohistory of the Early South," and Saunt, Krauthamer, Miles, Naylor, and Sturm respond together in "Rethinking Race and Culture in the Early South," asserting that race was the determining factor for the region at this time. Perdue then responds to their response, noting that "One of the most pernicious features of American racism is that it comes in so many permutations. To focus on one is not to deny the existence of others—or the interconnectedness of them all" ("A Reply" 406).

24. See Gina Caison, "Claiming the Unclaimable: Forrest Carter, *The Education of Little Tree*, and Land Claim in the Native South."

25. See Paul A. Thomsen's *Rebel Chief: The Motley Life of Colonel William Holland Thomas, C.S.A.* (2004).

26. This situation seems analogous to the ongoing Dakota Access Pipeline protests; whereas the #NoDAPL movement has gained considerable public attention and support, other energy-related "improvement" projects have not been as widely covered, including the proposed Bayou Bridge Pipeline that would cut through the Atchafalaya Basin in Louisiana and affect the United Houma Nation.

27. See Chavez, "Eastern Band of Cherokees opposes energy substation near Kituwah"; Fionn-Bowman, "Duke Energy and Cherokee Indians friends again"; McKie, "Swain asses moratorium on Duke construction"; Murawski, "Duke Energy won't build near sacred Cherokee site"; and Thornton, "North Carolina Cherokees are in escalating legal battle with Duke Energy over sacred site."

28. See Alexandra Harmon's *Rich Indians: Native People and the Problem of Wealth in American History* (2010) for a discussion of how this rhetoric works to undo gains made by tribal nations under the casino economy.

29. See the series of articles written by Sue Sturgis for the Institute for Southern Studies' web publication *Facing South*, including "Wal-mart's history of destroying sacred sites," "Sacred Indian mound destroyed for sports complex in Alabama," and "Alabama city destroying ancient Indian mound for Sam's Club." Also see McCreless, "JSU Professor: American Indian site is gone."

30. These reviews and more mirroring these sentiments of detail can be found in the editorial and customer reviews of the novel on Amazon.

31. See LeAnne Howe's *Choctalking on Other Realities* for a discussion about the counterclockwise spiralic patterns of water and southeastern stomp dances.

32. Cutcha Risling Baldy has been chronicling the way that Donald Trump echoes Andrew Jackson in her blog *CutchaRislingBaldy.com*. Following Baldy, Adrienne Keene has also discussed the significance of Trump's elevating of Jackson's troubling legacy.

Chapter 4. Resistance

1. Although the Lumbee were not legally recognized by the state under the name "Lumbee" until the 1950s, for clarity's sake I will refer to them by this name throughout the chapter. When referencing the legal, sovereign entity of the Lumbee Tribe of North Carolina across the historical record, I frequently refer to them as the Tribe as a way of holding their sovereign national existence in view across the changes in their tribal name.

2. In this chapter, I would like to suspend the question of whether the Lumbee should be federally recognized and instead focus on the questions of why and how they have not. To state my bias, I support Lumbee recognition.

3. In addition, see Adolph Dial and David K. Eliades, *The Only Land I Know: A History of the Lumbee Indians* (1975) and W. McKee Evans, *To Die Game: The Story of the Lowry Band, Indian Guerrillas of Reconstruction* (1995).

4. In addition to Dial and Evans, see Christopher Oakley, "The Legend of Henry Berry Lowry: *Strike at the Wind!* and the Lumbee Indians of North Carolina," and R. W. Reising, "Literary Depictions of Henry Berry Lowry: Mythic, Romantic and Tragic" for thorough histories of the Henry Berry Lowry story in both its "historical" and "constructed" versions.

5. The U.S. Census Bureau reported that for 2009–13, 31.7 percent of Robeson County lives below the poverty line in comparison to 17.5 percent of the rest of North Carolina. See census.gov.

6. See John Stossel's "Freeloaders" segment from his March 25, 2011, show on Fox News. The entire segment clip can be found online in David Neiwart's April 4, 2011, column for *Crooks and Liars*.

7. In March 2017 Chavis was indicted on charges of money laundering and fraud in his application and use of federal monies for his school programs in Oakland, California. See *Arizona Daily Independent*, "UofA Grad Ben Chavis indicted in Oakland charter school scam," and *SF Gate*, "Former Oakland charter schools director charged with fraud."

8. Kevin Bruyneel outlines this phenomenon in *The Third Space of Sovereignty* (2007) as a rhetorical tool of boundary making that attempts to negate Indigenous resistance to the settler-colonial state.

9. For an overview of the recognition battles from a Lumbee tribal government perspective, see Lumbee Tribe of North Carolina, "Federal Recognition: The Lumbee Tribe's One Hundred Year Quest."

10. Indeed, the history of Lumbee federal recognition has produced considerable tension between the Lumbee and other southeastern tribes. Two of the largest groups opposed to Lumbee recognition are the Eastern Band of Cherokee Indians and the United South and Eastern Tribes, a coalition of twenty-six tribes along the Eastern Seaboard and Gulf Coast states. While these groups claim not to oppose recognition as such, they wish for the Lumbee to seek a (BIA) process for administrative recognition rather than recognition through an act of Congress. The Lumbee, if federally recognized, would be the largest federally recognized tribe east of the Mississippi River with more than 56,000 members. Many feel that this would necessarily strain an already short supply of needed resources for tribes in the U.S. while others point out that this "piece-of-the-pie" logic keeps the discourse of power operating as perceived conflicts among Native people rather than locating the true culprit at the federal level. In this debate over federal recognition, one of the most frequent appeals against the Lumbee's quest is that they have too often changed their "theory" of existence. To their opponents, this serves as evidence against their true indigeneity. To many, it proves that the Lumbee are merely opportunistic recognition seekers, looking for government support when they do not meet the criteria for being a federally recognized tribe. As they have been labeled with several names over the years, including Croatan, Cherokee, Siouan, and Cheraw, the Tribe's opponents dwell on these inconsistencies as attempts to take a piece of the federal pie by co-opting other groups' cultural legibility. Tribes who oppose the congressional recognition claim that this process is not clear or specific enough in its standard of historical tribal continuity. See Michell Hicks, "Statement of the Principal Chief of the Eastern Band of Cherokee Indians Regarding Federal Recognition of the Lumbee Tribe of North Carolina"; James T. Martin, "Statement of Enrolled Member, Poarch Band of Creek Indians and Executive Director of the United South and Eastern Tribes, Inc., Regarding Federal Recognition of the Lumbee Tribe of North Carolina." These tribes claim not to oppose Lumbee recognition so much as they oppose congressional recognition as a path to federal recognition. Because up until 2016, the 1956 Lumbee Act had been interpreted as both recognizing and terminizing the Tribe, many legal scholars agreed that the Lumbee were barred from seeking BIA recognition and instead must pursue recognition through the congressional path. The 2016 statement from the Department of the Interior regarding the Lumbee Act changes the landscape of this matter. Also see Dial and Eliades, *The Only Land I Know* (1975), Karen I. Blu's *The Lumbee Problem: The Making of an American Indian People* (1980), and Stanley Knick's "Because It Is Right," in *Native South*. Knick's impressive 2008 article argues that the archeological record confirms Robeson County as a pre-invasion and continual site of Indigenous meeting and trade. The most comprehensive study of Lumbee identity and recognition is Malinda Maynor Lowery's *Lumbee Indians in the Jim Crow South: Race, Identity, and the Making of a Nation* (2010). See also Christopher Oakley's *Keeping the Circle: American Indian Identity in Eastern North Carolina, 1885–2004* (2005).

11. As Vine Deloria Jr. and Clifford Lytle note regarding Allotment policy in *American Indians, American Justice* (1983): "In 1881 the first indication was given that allotments might become a national policy when President Chester A. Arthur, in de-

livering his first annual message to Congress proposed a plan by which Indians would be brought into the mainstream of American life. The solution to the nagging Indian problem, he felt, was simply 'to introduce among the Indians the customs and pursuits of civilized life and gradually absorb them into the mass of our citizens'" (8).

12. T. J. Morgan, the commissioner of Indian affairs, stated: "While I regret exceedingly that the provisions made by the State of North Carolina seem to be entirely inadequate, I find it quite impractical to render any assistance at this time. The Government is responsible for the education of something like 36,000 Indian children and has provision for less than half this number. So long as the immediate wards of the Government are so insufficiently provided for, I do not see how I can consistently render any assistance to the Croatans or any other civilized tribes" (qtd. in Dial and Eliades 93). The language here is telling. The Lumbee, due to their "civilized" status, have effectively already been terminated and relegated to the state's "care." Thus, the very logic that allowed for their "success" as Native people also denied their status as such.

13. See Maynor Lowery's *Lumbee Indians in the Jim Crow South*, chapter 3.

14. See chapter 2, "The Interstitial Indian: The Lumbee and Segregation's Middle Caste," in Leslie Bow's seminal study *Partly Colored: Asian Americans and Racial Anomaly in the Segregated South* (2010) for a discussion of how the dynamics of biracial rhetoric play out within the Lumbee community.

15. See Maynor Lowery, Sider, and Dial for various accounts of this history.

16. Less than ten years later, under the Indian Citizenship Act of 1924, the federal government enacted legislation to unilaterally confer U.S. citizenship on Indigenous people not previously recognized as citizens. This act was, in part, a response to Native service in World War I. Because the Lumbee were not at the time a recognized tribe, they were already U.S. citizens. However, this did not mean that the logic of unilateral citizenship and the antecedents that developed from it did not significantly inform their quest for federal recognition. In fact, the same logic that led to their recognition as Cherokee a few years earlier can be contextualized through the turmoil in North Carolina regarding the Eastern Band of Cherokee and the Indian Citizenship Act. In 1924 the Lumbee Tribe again went before the federal government, this time requesting recognition as the Cherokee Indians of Robeson County, but this designation requires a necessary context of the contemporaneous politics in North Carolina. Acting under the guidance of A. W. McLean, the Tribe sought funds for their schools and health programs. In a telling correlation, however, also in 1924, the state of North Carolina was in the process of establishing the Baker Roll for the Eastern Band of Cherokee. The Baker Roll remains a hotly contested document, and in many cases the state of North Carolina projected undue influence on the affairs of the Eastern Band regarding whom they might name as tribal members. A lot of this controversy seems to stem from concerns over voting in the state in the beginning of the century. The Democratic Party of North Carolina was anxious over a perceived loss of power as more and more minorities reached for the ballot. Due to this anxiety, they began contesting the citizenship of many Eastern Band members, and they campaigned to deny the validity of votes cast for Republican candidates by the Eastern Cherokee in 1920. In May 1924, just a month before the passage of the Indian Citizenship Act, a U.S. district court decided that "Eastern Cherokees were noncitizen federal wards

and therefore not entitled to vote" (Finger, *Cherokee Americans* 46). Even after the Citizenship Act passed, however, it "in no way infringed upon voting requirements set by individual states. Citizenship, then, did not automatically bring about enfranchisement as North Carolina Cherokees would discover" (ibid.). The situation in North Carolina surrounding the Indian Citizenship Act and Cherokee identity was hardly benign. Considering this contemporaneous issue with citizenship and the Eastern Band of Cherokee Indians, the North Carolina Democrat McLean's push to identify the Indians of Robeson County as Cherokee seems a bit suspicious. McLean served as a member of the North Carolina Democratic Committee in 1920, and he served as governor of the state from 1925 to 1929. There is virtually no way that McLean would not have been informed of, if not directly involved in, the disenfranchisement of North Carolina's Cherokee population. If the Democratic Party could umbrella the Indians of Robeson County under the disenfranchised Cherokee, it would virtually ensure their winning elections in the Robeson and Scotland counties. Fortunately or unfortunately, depending on one's perspective, the federal government denied recognition to the Cherokee Indians of Robeson County.

17. These twenty-two tribal members, known in the community as the "original 22," submitted a constitution to the BIA, but it was denied. Seven of the "original 22," along with their descendants, tried again in the 1970s to gain federal recognition, but they were again denied with the reasoning that the "Lumbee didn't exist" in the 1930s, so they could not possibly be recognized as Lumbee in the 1970s. Some of the group has worked to be identified as Tuscarora, which has led to contemporary divisions in the community. See chapter 6 of Lowery's *Lumbee Indians in the Jim Crow South* for a thorough analysis of the Siouan enrollment study. Also see Sider 133–36 and Blu 82–83.

18. Stanley Knick has argued recently that the name must be Native in origin and quite possibly historically correct as he charts its usage as far back as 1885 and Hamilton McMillan.

19. The history of Termination policy, also known as Public Law 83-280 and House Concurrent Resolution 108, is complex and multifaceted with numerous specific tribal and regional vectors. The fact that it remains commonly known as "Termination" demonstrates the ways in which the federal government, even in 1956, felt little compunction about naming their intention for Native people in the United States. For an overview of this legal era, see Donald Fixico, *Termination and Relocation: Federal Indian Policy, 1945–1960* (1986). For a tribal perspective of resistance to Termination, see Edward Valandra's *Not without Our Consent: Lakota Resistance to Termination, 1950–59* (2004).

20. In 1989 the associate solicitor for the Division of Indian Affairs stated in regard to the Lumbee Act: "I am constrained to advise you [Deputy to the Assistant Secretary, Indian Affairs] that the Act is legislation terminating or forbidding the Federal relationship and that, therefore, you are precluded from considering the application of the Lumbees for recognition." This statement has led to the Tribe continually seeking congressional recognition, something that the Eastern Band of Cherokee and USET strongly oppose. A related issue is the finding of *Maynor v. Morton* (1975), which found that the "original 22" of 1936 were not terminated by the 1956 act. For a complete discussion, again see Maynor Lowery. In 2016, this decision from 1989 was reversed. See United States Department of the Interior, "Reconsideration of the Lumbee Act of 1956."

21. See Oakley's "Legend of Henry Berry Lowry."

22. In a 2010 conversation with Maynor Lowery and her husband Willie French Lowery, she noted that while she sees a relationship between the economics of the play, the need to draw an audience, and larger issues of federal recognition, she isn't sure if other people see those ties as explicitly as they did at the play's inception in the 1970s.

23. See Amy Nelson's interview with Malinda Maynor Lowery, "*Strike at the Wind*: The struggle to sustain a culture," available on *NC Folk* from the North Carolina Folklife Institute.

24. Reba M. Lowry, "To Paul Green," 27 May 1970. For a history of Deloria's production, see Glenn Ellen Starr Stilling's online archive, "The Lumbee Indians: An Annotated Bibliography."

25. Because these plays were continually revised, it is important to remember that any given script does not indicate a static account of the play. Anecdotal evidence suggests that Umberger had removed these opening lines in the 1990s and 2000s.

26. Given the numerous number of Lumbee citizens who served in Vietnam, this reminder to the audience might take on a special resonance during the 1970s, and it links the viewing audience to a moment from the past. See Delano Cummings's *Moon Dash Warrior: The Story of an American Indian in Vietnam, a Marine from the Land of the Lumbee* (1998).

27. See Clyde Ellis, "'There's a Dance Every Weekend': Powwow Culture in Southeast North Carolina" in *Southern Heritage on Display: Public Ritual and Ethnic Diversity within Southern Regionalism* (2011).

28. For a discussion of the economic development that *Strike at the Wind!* could bring to the area, see Nelson, "*Strike at the Wind*."

29. For an overview of Willie French Lowery's life and work, see his website WillieFrenchLowery.wordpress.com, as well as the obituary by Ashley Melzer in *IndyWeek* and the profile of *Plant and See*'s rerelease in *Indian Country Today*.

30. See Jay Hansford C. Vest's "From Bobtail to Brer Rabbit: Native American Influences on Uncle Remus" and contributions by David Elton Gay, Sandra K. Baringer, and Sharon Holland in Jonathan Brennon's edited collection *When Brer Rabbit Meets Coyote: African-Native American Literature* (2003).

31. Indeed, Malinda Maynor Lowery and Willie French Lowery were married, and she has articulated that her thinking about Lumbee identity was influenced by Willie's artistic and political creations.

While Nunn's work deals most specifically within a black/white binary, I follow his lead that such issues were largely the result of academic folklorists and the cultural industry as each "worked to delimit the separate white and black musical spheres" (7).

32. Maynor Lowery, however, doesn't romanticize, continuing, "I don't want to make it sound like Willie suddenly became this family man, because he didn't. So it wasn't like there was this sudden shift in terms of his lifestyle, but in terms of his creative output, there was definitely a shift" (Melzer, "Unexpected Revival").

33. See "Making Christianity Sing: The Origins and Experience of Lumbee Indian and African-American Church Music" in *Confounding the Color Line: Indian-Black Relations in a Multidisciplinary Perspective*.

34. See the online archive for *Sounds of Faith*, created by Maynor Lowery and hosted by the University of North Carolina at Chapel Hill, as well as her documentary of the same name.

Chapter 5. Resilience

1. See the *OED* entry "hurricane" under etymology: "from the Carib word given by Oviedo as huracan, by Peter Martyr (as translated by R. Eden) as furacan."

2. See Delia Goetz and Sylvanus G. Morley's edition of Adrian Recinos's translation of *Popol Vuh: The Sacred Book of the Ancient Quiché Maya* (1991) as well as Dennis Tedlock's translation and 1996 edition of the *Popol Vuh* and Mary Ann Miller and Karl Taube, *An Illustrated Dictionary of the Gods and Symbols of Ancient Mexico and the Maya* (1997).

3. See Cutcha Risling Baldy's blog entry "On telling Native people to just 'get over it' or why I teach about *The Walking Dead* in my Native Studies classes," where she explains how the experience of Native people in the Americas is perhaps best understood as a zombie apocalypse.

4. For an excellent example of criticism that elucidates these connections, see Chadwick Allen's award-winning article "Serpentine Figures, Sinuous Relations: Thematic Geometry in Allison Hedge Coke's *Blood Run*."

5. For example, see Catherine Rainwater, "Who May Speak for the Animals? Deep Ecology in Linda Hogan's *Power* and A. A. Carr's *Eye Killers*"; Pascale McCullough Manning, "A Narrative of Motives: Solicitation and Confession in Linda Hogan's *Power*"; Yonka Krasteva, "Encounters across Time and Space: The Sacred, the Profane, and the Political in Linda Hogan's *Power*"; Lydia Cooper, "'Woman Chasing Her God': Ritual, Renewal, and Violence in Linda Hogan's *Power*."

6. Hardin's argument's central flaw remains in its complete refusal to read this Native text within a Native tradition. Statements such as "Hogan's critique of apocalyptic narrative requires that we trace the apocalypticism to its source, the Europeans" (137) completely negate Indigenous religious traditions and sacred stories, which have not as Hardin posits been entirely "suppressed or radically altered" (152n3). In this style of argument it seems that Hardin has engineered his own metaphorical apocalypse of Native worldviews in order to forward a reading of the work that only considers Western-based epistemologies. Furthermore, he fails to recognize that the coming of Europeans itself enacted apocalyptic events about which Native people created their own stories in order to incorporate the horrific events of colonial invasion into their persistent survival.

7. "Ohni." Durbin Feeling, *The Cherokee-English Dictionary* (1975).

8. Again, Hardin reads the name "Ama" within a Western colonial lens, noting that it means "landlady" or "housekeeper" in Spanish (146). Indeed, this meaning might be relevant, but I argue for a reading of the novel that stays closer to home in Hogan's Southeast.

9. I owe thanks to Cherokee linguist Ben Frey for helping me think through this difference and distinction as well as its implications.

10. Hogan notes in an interview with Barbara J. Cook that she believes that Indigenous knowledges "account for and hold scientific theory" and that "We understand

astronomy [...] We know agriculture and had to teach the European arrivals about planting" (13).

11. See Jane Lawrence, "The Indian Health Service and the Sterilization of Native American Women"; D. Marie Ralstin-Lewis, "The Continuing Struggle against Genocide: Indigenous Women's Reproductive Rights."

12. Much work has been done to demonstrate the linkages between the U.S. South and further Souths of the Caribbean, Mexico, and Central America. See Jessica Adams, Michael Bibler, and Cécile Accilien's *Just Below South: Intercultural Performance in the Caribbean and the U.S. South* (2007), Helen Regis's *Caribbean and Southern: Transnational Perspectives of the U.S. South* (2006), Jon Smith and Deborah Cohn's *Look Away! The U.S. South in New World Studies* (2004), and Deborah Cohn's *History and Memory in Two Souths: Recent Southern and Spanish American Fiction* (1999).

13. Neva and her friend Kira see the film *Baby Boom* (released in the United States in October 1987) in the theater in Coatepeque. This event places the novel squarely in the middle of the Salvadoran and Guatemalan "civil wars." Thus the novel predates the later EZLN uprising in 1994 in Chiapas, but the general history of leftist Indigenous uprisings informs the novel's larger plot. McAdams notes on her website, "I would have felt presumptuous using any one country's literal political history. I wanted to create a place in which my character Neva, a mixedblood Indigenous *North* American could understand her own complex political history by witnessing one that not only parallels but is deeply connected to her own." I would like to thank my exceptional undergraduate student Reese Cody for lining up several dates and events from the novel, including the *Baby Boom* moment.

14. See Hector Perez-Brignoli, *A Brief History of Central America* (1989), and Thomas L. Pearcy, *The History of Central America* (2007).

15. Jace Weaver, *Red Atlantic: American Indigenes and the Making of the Modern World* (2014).

16. See Ron Jacobs's *The Way the Wind Blew: A History of the Weather Underground* (1997).

17. See Mark Edwin Miller's chapter 5, "A Matter of Visibility: The United Houma Nation's Struggle for Federal Acknowledgment," in *Forgotten Tribes: Unrecognized Indians and the Federal Acknowledgment Process* (2004).

18. See Boris Vormann, *Global Port Cities in North America: Urbanization Processes and Global Production Networks* (2014), and Marc Levinson, *The Box: How the Shipping Container Made the World Smaller and the World Economy Bigger* (2006).

19. See Shepard Krech, *The Ecological Indian: Myth and History* (1999). Several scholars have critiqued Krech's work as reductive and short-sighted in its descriptions of Indigenous knowledges regarding ecological practices. See, for example, Michael Harkin and David Rich Lewis, eds., *Native Americans and the Environment: Perspectives on the Ecological Indian* (2007).

Rights and Returns: A Coda

1. See Risling Baldy, "Coyote Is Not a Metaphor: On Decolonizing, (Re)claiming and (Re)naming 'Coyote.'"

BIBLIOGRAPHY

Adams, Henry. *The Education of Henry Adams*. 1918. Ed. Ira B. Nadel. Oxford: Oxford University Press, 1999. Print.

Adams, Jessica, Michael P. Bibler, and Cécile Accilien, eds. *Just Below South: Intercultural Performance in the Caribbean and the U.S. South*. Charlottesville: University of Virginia Press, 2007. Print.

Alexander, Floyce. "Emerson and the Cherokee Removal." *ESQ: A Journal of the American Renaissance* 29.3 (1983): 127–37. Print.

Allen, Chadwick. "Serpentine Figures, Sinuous Relations: Thematic Geometry in Allison Hedge Coke's *Blood Run*." *American Literature* 82.4 (2010): 807–34. Print.

Allen, Paula Gunn. *Pocahontas: Medicine Woman, Spy, Entrepreneur, Diplomat*. New York: HarperCollins, 2003. Print.

Anderson, Eric Gary. "Literary and Textual Histories of the Native South." *The Oxford Handbook to the Literature of the U.S. South*. Ed. Fred Hobson and Barbara Ladd. New York: Oxford University Press, 2016. 17–32. Print.

———. "Native American Literature, Ecocriticism, and the South: The Inaccessible Worlds of Linda Hogan's *Power*." *South to a New Place: Region, Literature, Culture*. Ed. Suzanne W. Jones and Sharon Monteith. Baton Rouge: Louisiana State University Press, 2002. 165–83. Print.

———. "On Native Ground: Indigenous Presences and Countercolonial Strategies in Southern Narratives of Captivity, Removal, and Repossession." *Southern Spaces*, 9 August 2007. Web. 13 May 2010.

———. "The Presence of Early Native Studies: A Response to Stephanie Fitzgerald and Hilary E. Wyss." *Early American Literature* 22.2 (2010): 280–88. Print.

Anderson, Eric Gary, Taylor Hagood, and Daniel Cross Turner, eds. *Undead Souths: The Gothic and Beyond in Southern Literature and Culture*. Baton Rouge: Louisiana State University Press, 2015. Print.

Apess, William. *On Our Own Ground: The Complete Writings of William Apess, a Pequot*. Ed. Barry O'Connell. Amherst: University of Massachusetts Press, 1992. Print.

Atkinson, James. *Splendid Land, Splendid People: The Chickasaw Indians to Removal*. Tuscaloosa: University of Alabama Press, 2004. Print.

Avery, Laurence. "Introduction: At the Lost Colony." *The Lost Colony: A Symphonic Drama of American History*. Ed. Laurence G. Avery. Chapel Hill: University of North Carolina Press, 2001. 1–19. Print.

Bach, Rebecca Ann. *Colonial Transformations: The Cultural Production of the New Atlantic World, 1580–1640*. New York: Palgrave, 2000. Print.

Bailyn, Bernard. *The Ideological Origins of the American Revolution.* Enlarged ed. Boston: Belknap, 1992. Print.

Beck, Robin. *Chiefdoms, Collapse, and Coalescence in the Early American South.* New York: Cambridge University Press, 2013. Print.

Bergland, Renée L. *The National Uncanny: Indian Ghosts and American Subjects.* Hanover, N.H.: University Press of New England, 2000. Print.

Berkhofer Jr., Robert F. *The White Man's Indian: Images of the American Indian from Columbus to the Present.* New York: Vintage, 1978. Print.

Blackbourn, David. "'The Horologe of Time': Periodization in History." *PMLA* 127.2 (2012): 301–7. Print.

Blu, Karen I. *The Lumbee Problem: The Making of an American Indian People.* Cambridge: Cambridge University Press, 1980. Print.

Boles, John B. *A Companion to the American South.* Malden, Mass.: Wiley-Blackwell, 2002. Print.

Bone, Martyn. *The Postsouthern Sense of Place in Contemporary Fiction.* Baton Rouge: Louisiana State University Press, 2005. Print.

Boudinot, Elias. *Cherokee Editor: The Writings of Elias Boudinot.* Ed. Theda Perdue. Athens: University of Georgia Press, 1983. Print.

———. "From the Cherokee Phoenix (Continued from Last Issue)." *Augusta Chronicle and Georgia Advertiser*, 14 March 1828. American Antiquarian Society. Worcester, Mass.

Bow, Leslie. *Partly Colored: Asian Americans and Racial Anomaly in the Segregated South.* New York: New York University Press, 2010. Print.

Bowen-Mercer, Carrie. "Dancing the Chronotopes of Power: The Road to Survival in Linda Hogan's *Power.*" *From the Center of Tradition: Critical Perspectives on Linda Hogan.* Ed. Barbara J. Cook. Boulder: University Press of Colorado, 2003. 157–77. Print.

Brecht, Bertolt. *Brecht on Theatre: The Development of an Aesthetic.* Ed. and trans. John Willett. New York: Hill & Wang, 1977. Print.

Brennon, Jonathan, ed. *When Brer Rabbit Meets Coyote: African–Native American Literature.* Champaign: University of Illinois Press, 2003. Print.

Brooks, Lisa. "The Primacy of the Present, the Primacy of Place: Navigating the Spiral of History in the Digital World." *PMLA* 127.2 (2012): 308–16. Print.

Bruyneel, Kevin. *The Third Space of Sovereignty: The Postcolonial Politics of U.S.-Indigenous Relations.* Minneapolis: University of Minnesota Press, 2007. Print.

Busick, Sean R. *A Sober Desire for History: William Gilmore Simms as Historian.* Columbia: University of South Carolina Press, 2005. Print.

Butterworth, Keen, and James E. Kibler. *William Gilmore Simms: A Reference Guide.* Boston: Macmillan, 1980. Print.

Byrd, Jodi A. "A Return to the South." *American Quarterly* 66.3 (2014): 609–20. Print.

———. *The Transit of Empire: Indigenous Critiques of Colonialism.* Minneapolis: University of Minnesota Press, 2011. Print.

Caison, Gina. "Claiming the Unclaimable: Forrest Carter, *The Education of Little Tree*, and Land Claim in the Native South." *Mississippi Quarterly* 64 (2011): 585–607. Print.

———. "'We're Still Here': Eddie Swimmer on Cherokee History, Life, and Outdoor Drama in the Appalachian Mountains." *North Carolina Literary Review* 19 (2010): 46–59. Print.

Carson, James T., Robbie Ethridge, and Greg O'Brien. "A Line in the Sand." *Native South* 1 (2008): ix–xvi. Print.

Cartelli, Thomas. "From First Encounter to 'Fiery Oven': The Effacement of the New England Indian in *Mourt's Relation* and Histories of the Pequot War." *Indography: Writing the "Indian" in Early Modern England*. Ed. Jonathan Gil Harris. New York: Palgrave Macmillan, 2012. 57–60. Print.

Cartwright, Keith. "Tar-Baby, Terrapin, and Trojan Horse—A Face-the-Music Cosmo Song from the University's Hind Tit." *PMLA* 131.1 (2016): 174–78. Print.

Champagne, Duane. *Social Order and Political Change: Constitutional Governments among the Cherokee, the Choctaw, the Chickasaw, and the Creek*. Stanford, Calif.: Stanford University Press, 1992. Print.

"Change the Redskins Name to 'The Washington Tea Party!'" Constitutional Rights PAC. ConstitutionAlly. 2014. Web. 13 June 2014.

Chaplin, Joyce E. "Roanoke 'Counterfeited According to the Truth.'" *A New World: England's First View of America*. Ed. Kim Sloan. Chapel Hill: University of North Carolina Press, 2007. 51–63. Print.

Chavez, Will. "Eastern Band of Cherokees opposes energy substation near Kituwah." *Cherokee Phoenix*, 9 February 2010. Tahlequah, Okla. Web. 14 May 2014.

———. "EBCI council designates Kituwah mound 'sacred site.'" *Cherokee Phoenix*, 17 December 2013. Tahlequah, Okla. Web. 14 May 2014.

"Cherokee Indians—proceedings in Congress." *The Southron*, Washington, Georgia, 23 February 1828. American Antiquarian Society. Worcester, Mass.

Cherokee Phoenix and Indians Advocate. New Echota, Georgia. 31 May 1834. American Antiquarian Society. Worcester, Mass.

"Cherokees." *Augusta Chronicle and Georgia Advertiser*, 6 November 1827. American Antiquarian Society. Worcester, Mass.

Chiles, Katy L. *Transformable Race: Surprising Metamorphoses in the Literature of Early America*. New York: Oxford University Press, 2013. Print.

"Cis-Atlantic, Creek affairs." (Montgomery) *Alabama Journal*, 29 June 1827. American Antiquarian Society. Worcester, Mass.

"Civilized correspondence." *Cherokee Phoenix and Indians Advocate*, 12 August 1831. American Antiquarian Society. Worcester, Mass.

Clowdus, Brian. Personal interview. 5 September 2009.

Coates, Julia. "None of Us Is Supposed to Be Here: Ethnicity, Nationality, and the Production of Cherokee Histories." Diss. University of New Mexico, 2002. Print.

———. *Trail of Tears*. Santa Barbara: ABC-CLIO, LLC Greenwood, 2014. Print.

Cobb, Daniel M., and Loretta Fowler. *Beyond Red Power: American Indian Politics and Activism since 1900*. Santa Fe: School for Advanced Research Press, 2007. Print.

Cohn, Deborah. *History and Memory in Two Souths: Recent Southern and Spanish American Fiction*. Nashville: Vanderbilt University Press, 1999. Print.

"Concluding Roundtable." Postcolonial Theory, the U.S. South, and New World Studies Joint ALA/SSSL Symposium. December 2002. Puerto Vallarta, Mexico. Print.

Cook, Barbara J. "From the Center of Tradition: An Interview with Linda Hogan." *From the Center of Tradition: Critical Perspectives on Linda Hogan*. Ed. Barbara J. Cook. Boulder: University Press of Colorado, 2003. 11–16. Print.

Cooper, Lydia. "'Woman Chasing Her God': Ritual, Renewal, and Violence in Linda Hogan's *Power*." *ISLE* 18 (2011): 143–59. Print.

"Creek Territory and Creek Affairs." *Augusta Chronicle and Georgia Advertiser*, 18 January 1828. American Antiquarian Society. Worcester, Mass.

Cumfer, Cynthia. *Separate Peoples, One Land: The Minds of Cherokees, Blacks, and Whites on the Tennessee Frontier*. Chapel Hill: University of North Carolina Press, 2007. Print.

Cummings, Delano. *Moon Dash Warrior: The Story of an American Indian in Vietnam, a Marine from the Land of the Lumbee*. Livermore, Maine, and Rockbridge Baths, Va.: Signal Tree Publications, 1998.

Cypress, Sandra Messinger. *La Malinche in Mexican Literature: From History to Myth*. Austin: University of Texas Press, 1991. Print.

Deloria, Ella. *The Life Story of a People*. "The Modern Questor." 1941. Appalachian State University Special Collections. Record Number: DELO001.

Deloria, Philip J. *Indians in Unexpected Places*. Lawrence: University Press of Kansas, 2004. Print.

———. *Playing Indian*. New Haven, Conn.: Yale University Press, 1988. Print.

Deloria, Vine, Jr. *God Is Red: A Native View of Religion*. 30th anniversary ed. Golden, Colo.: Fulcrum, 2003. Print.

———. *Red Earth, White Lies: Native Americans and the Myth of Scientific Fact*. Golden, Colo.: Fulcrum, 1995. Print.

Deloria, Vine, Jr., and Clifford M. Lytle. *American Indians, American Justice*. Austin: University of Texas Press, 1983. Print.

Dexter, Andrew. "Letter to Mr. Baker." (Montgomery) *Alabama Journal*, 22 August 1828. American Antiquarian Society. Worcester, Mass.

Dial, Adolph L., and David K. Eliades. *The Only Land I Know: A History of the Lumbee Indians*. Syracuse, N.Y.: Syracuse University Press, 1975. Print.

Dick, Dacia. Personal interview. 15 August 2009.

Dimock, Wai Chee. *Through Other Continents: American Literature across Deep Time*. Princeton, N.J.: Princeton University Press, 2006. Print.

Doyle, Don H. *Faulkner's County: The Historical Roots of Yoknapatawpha*. Chapel Hill: University of North Carolina Press, 2001. Print.

Du Bois, W. E. B. *Black Reconstruction in America, 1860–1880*. 1935. New York: Free Press, 1998. Print.

Duck, Leigh Anne. *The Nation's Region: Southern Modernism, Segregation, and U.S. Nationalism*. Athens: University of Georgia Press, 2006. Print.

Eaton, John. "From the Phoenix." (Milledgeville) *Georgia Journal*, 13 November 1830. American Antiquarian Society. Worcester, Mass.

"Editorial Reviews." *Cold Mountain: A Novel* by Charles Frazier. Amazon.com, 2011. Web. 12 September 2011.

Ellis, Clyde. "'There's a Dance Every Weekend': Powwow Culture in Southeast North Carolina." *Southern Heritage on Display: Public Ritual and Ethnic Diversity within*

Southern Regionalism. Ed. Celeste Ray. Birmingham: University of Alabama Press, 2003. 79–105. Print.

Ellis, Joseph J. *American Sphinx: The Character of Thomas Jefferson*. New York: Vintage, 1998. Print.

Ethridge, Robbie. *Creek Country: The Creek Indians and Their World*. Chapel Hill: University of North Carolina Press, 2003. Print.

Evans, William McKee. *To Die Game: The Story of the Lowry Band, Indian Guerrillas of Reconstruction*. Baton Rouge: Louisiana State University Press, 1971; reprint, Syracuse, N.Y.: Syracuse University Press, 1995. Print.

"Executive Department, Milledgeville, Ga." *Augusta Chronicle and Georgia Advertiser*, 15 December 1830. American Antiquarian Society. Worcester, Mass.

Feeling, Durbin. *Cherokee-English Dictionary*. Tahlequah: Cherokee Nation of Oklahoma, 1975. Print.

Finger, John R. *Cherokee Americans: The Eastern Band of Cherokees in the Twentieth Century*. Lincoln: University of Nebraska Press, 1991. Print.

———. *The Eastern Band of Cherokees, 1819–1900*. Knoxville: University of Tennessee Press, 1984. Print.

Fionn-Bowman, Rhiannon. "Duke Energy and Cherokee Indians friends again." *Creative Loafing* Charlotte, 3 August 2010. Web. 1 September 2010.

Fixico, Donald L. *Termination and Relocation: Federal Indian Policy, 1945–1960*. Albuquerque: University of New Mexico Press, 1986. Print.

Forbes, Jack D. *Africans and Native Americans: The Language of Race and the Evolution of Red-Black Peoples*. 2nd ed. Urbana: University of Illinois Press, 1993. Print.

———. "The Dream of Injun Joe: A Page from the Alcatraz Seminars." *The People Who Stayed: Southeastern Indian Writing after Removal*. Eds. Geary Hobson, Janet McAdams, and Kathryn Walkiewicz. Norman: University of Oklahoma Press, 2010. 33–41. Print.

———. *Only Approved Indians Can Play*. Norman: University of Oklahoma Press, 1995. Print.

Foucault, Michel. *The Birth of Biopolitics: Lectures at the Collège de France, 1978–1979*. Trans. Graham Burchell. New York: Palgrave Macmillan, 2008. Print.

———. *Power/Knowledge*. Ed. Colin Gordon. New York: Pantheon, 1980. Print.

———. *Security, Territory, Population: Lectures at the Collège de France, 1977–1978*. Trans. Graham Burchell. New York: Palgrave Macmillan, 2007. Print.

———. *"Society Must Be Defended": Lectures at the Collège de France, 1975–1976*. Trans. David Macey. New York: Picador, 2003. Print.

Frank, Andrew. *Creeks and Southerners: Biculturalism on the Early American Frontier*. Lincoln: University of Nebraska Press, 2005. Print.

Frazier, Charles. *Cold Mountain*. New York: Grove, 1997. Print.

———. *Thirteen Moons*. New York: Random House, 2006. Print.

———. *Thirteen Moons: Removal*. Trans. Myrtle Driver Johnson. Cherokee, N.C.: Museum of the Cherokee Indian, 2009. Print.

Fuchs, Barbara. "Golden Ages and Golden Hinds; or, Periodizing Spain and England." *PMLA* 127.2 (2012): 321–27. Print.

Gallay, Alan. *The Indian Slave Trade: The Rise of the English Empire in the American South, 1670–1717*. New Haven, Conn.: Yale University Press, 2003. Print.

Garrison, Tim Alan. *The Legal Ideology of Removal: The Southern Judiciary and the Sovereignty of Native American Nations*. Athens: University of Georgia Press, 2009. Print.

Gaul, Theresa Strouth. "Introduction." *To Marry an Indian: The Marriage of Harriet Gold and Elias Boudinot in Letters, 1823–1839*. Ed. Theresa Strouth Gaul. Chapel Hill: University of North Carolina Press, 2005. 1–76. Print.

Gilman, Caroline. Review of *Mellichampe*. *The Southern Rose*. Excerpted in *William Gilmore Simms: A Reference Guide*. Eds. Keen Butterworth and James E. Kibler. Boston: Macmillan, 1980. 36–38. Print.

Gilmore, Ruth Wilson. "What Is to Be Done?" *American Quarterly* 63.2 (2011): 245–65. Print.

Goetz, Delia, and Sylvanus G. Morley. *Popol Vuh: The Sacred Book of the Ancient Quiche Maya*. Trans. Adrian Recinos. Norman: University of Oklahoma Press, 1991. Print.

Goodheart, Adam. "Trail of Tears." *New York Times*, 29 October 2006. Web. 15 September 2010.

Gordon-Reed, Annette. *Thomas Jefferson and Sally Hemings: An American Controversy*. Updated ed. Charlottesville: University of Virginia Press, 1998. Print.

Gray, James. "The Lost Colony." *American Motorist*, August 1937, Gettysburg, PA, excerpted in the *Daily Advance*, September 1937, Elizabeth City, N.C. Folder 3168, Paul Green Papers #03693, Southern Historical Collection, Louis Round Wilson Special Collections Library, University of North Carolina at Chapel Hill.

Gray, Richard. "Inventing Communities, Imagining Places: Some Thoughts on Southern Self-Fashioning." *South to a New Place: Region, Literature, Culture*. Eds. Suzanne W. Jones and Sharon Monteith. Baton Rouge: Louisiana State University Press, 2002. xiii–xxiii. Print.

Green, Michael D. *The Politics of Indian Removal: Creek Government and Society in Crisis*. Lincoln: University of Nebraska Press, 1985. Print.

Green, Paul. "Diary Entry." 29 March 1937. Folder 401, Paul Green Papers #03693, Southern Historical Collection, Louis Round Wilson Special Collections Library, University of North Carolina at Chapel Hill.

———. "A Farewell to the Civil War." 1961. MS for *We Dissent*. Folder 3926g, Paul Green Papers #03693, Southern Historical Collection, Louis Round Wilson Special Collections Library, University of North Carolina at Chapel Hill.

———. "Letter to Professor Burnett Hobgood." 19 February 1959. Folder 4478, Paul Green Papers #03693, Southern Historical Collection, Louis Round Wilson Special Collections Library, University of North Carolina at Chapel Hill.

———. *The Lost Colony: A Symphonic Drama of American History*. Ed. Laurence G. Avery. Chapel Hill: University of North Carolina Press, 2001. Print.

———. "Notes on Lumbee Indian Drama." Personal Correspondence. Folder 4598–9, Paul Green Papers #03693, Southern Historical Collection, Louis Round Wilson Special Collections Library, University of North Carolina at Chapel Hill.

———. "Paul Green to Gene Warren." Personal Correspondence. Folder 4600, Paul Green Papers #03693, Southern Historical Collection, Louis Round Wilson Special Collections Library, University of North Carolina at Chapel Hill.

Greenblatt, Stephen. *Shakespearean Negotiations: The Circulation of Social Energy in Renaissance England*. Berkeley: University of California Press, 1989. Print.

Greer, I. G. "The Southern Appalachian Historical Association, Inc." *Horn in the West: A Drama of the Southern Appalachian Highlands Souvenir Program*. Boone, N.C.: Southern Appalachian Historical Association, 1952. 17–18. Folder 136, Samuel Selden Papers #04378, Southern Historical Collection, Louis Round Wilson Special Collections Library, University of North Carolina at Chapel Hill.

Greeson, Jennifer Rae. *Our South: Geographic Fantasy and the Rise of National Literature*. Cambridge, Mass.: Harvard University Press, 2010. Print.

Griffith, Benjamin W. *McIntosh and Weatherford: Creek Indian Leaders*. Tuscaloosa: University of Alabama Press, 1998. Print.

Guilds, John Caldwell, ed. *Long Years of Neglect: The Work and Reputation of William Gilmore Simms*. Little Rock: University of Arkansas Press, 1989. Print.

———. *Simms: A Literary Life*. Little Rock: University of Arkansas Press, 1992.

Guilds, John Caldwell, and Charles Hudson, eds. *An Early and Strong Sympathy: The Indian Writings of William Gilmore Simms*. Columbia: University of South Carolina Press, 2003.

Hamer, Philip M. "Correspondence of Henry Stuart and Alexander Cameron with the Wataugans." *Mississippi Valley Historical Review* 17.3 (1930): 451–59. Print.

———. "John Stuart's Indian Policy during the Early Months of the American Revolution." *Mississippi Valley Historical Review* 17.3 (1930): 351–66. Print.

Hardin, Michael. "Standing Naked before the Storm: Linda Hogan's *Power* and the Critique of Apocalyptic Narrative." *From the Center of Tradition: Critical Perspectives on Linda Hogan*. Ed. Barbara J. Cook. Boulder: University Press of Colorado, 2003. 135–55. Print.

Harkin, Michael E. "The Floating Island: Anachronism and Paradox in the Lost Colony." *Small Worlds: Method, Meaning, and Narrative in Microhistory*. Eds. James F. Brooks, Christopher R. N. DeCorse, and John Walton. Santa Fe, N.M.: School for Advanced Research Press, 2007. 121–44. Print.

———. "Performing Paradox: Narrativity and the Lost Colony of Roanoke." *Myth and Memory: Stories of Indigenous-European Contact*. Ed. John Sutton Lutz. Vancouver: University of British Columbia Press, 2007. 103–17. Print.

———. "Time's Arrow: Violence and Ethnohistorical Surrealism in the Lost Colony." *Anthropology and Humanism* 34.1 (2009): 11–20. Print.

Harkin, Michael E., and David Rich Lewis, eds. *Native Americans and the Environment: Perspectives on the Ecological Indian*. Lincoln: University of Nebraska Press, 2007. Print.

Harlow, Barbara. *Resistance Literature*. New York: Routledge, 1987. Print.

Harmon, Alexandra. *Rich Indians: Native People and the Problem of Wealth in American History*. Chapel Hill: University of North Carolina Press, 2013. Print.

Harriot, Thomas. *A Briefe and True Report of the New Found Land of Virginia*. 1590. New York: Dover, 1972.

Hatley, Jeff. Personal interview. 7 August 2009.
Hatley, Shannon. Personal interview. 7 August 2009.
Hausman, Blake M. *Riding the Trail of Tears*. Lincoln: University of Nebraska Press, 2011. Print.
Heard, Abraham A. "The Cherokees." *Augusta Chronicle and Georgia Advertiser*, 21 April 1830. American Antiquarian Society. Worcester, Mass.
Hedge Coke, Allison Adelle. *Streaming*. Minneapolis: Coffee House Press, 2014. Print.
Heidler, David S., and Jeanne T. Heidler. *Indian Removal: Norton Documents Reader*. New York: W. W. Norton, 2006. Print.
Hershberger, Mary. "Mobilizing Women, Anticipating Abolition: The Struggle against Indian Removal in the 1830s." *Journal of American History* 86 (1999): 15–40. Print.
Hicks, Michell. "Statement of the Principal Chief of the Eastern Band of Cherokee Indians Regarding Federal Recognition of the Lumbee Tribe of North Carolina." 12 July 2006. Committee on Senate Indian Affairs. Washington, DC: Government Printing Office, 2006. Print.
Hobson, Fred, and Barbara Ladd, eds. *The Oxford Handbook of the Literature of the U.S. South*. New York: Oxford University Press, 2016. Print.
Hobson, Geary, Janet McAdams, and Kathryn Walkiewicz, eds. *The People Who Stayed: Southeastern Indian Writing after Removal*. Norman: University of Oklahoma Press, 2010. Print.
Hogan, Linda. *Power*. New York: W. W. Norton, 1999. Print.
Hoover, Bob. "'Thirteen Moons' by Charles Frazier." *Post-gazette.com*. 1 October 2006. Web. 5 September 2011.
Horn, James. *A Kingdom Strange: The Brief and Tragic History of the Lost Colony of Roanoke*. New York: Basic Books, 2010. Print.
Horn in the West: A Drama of the Southern Appalachian Highlands. By Kermit Hunter. Dir. Julia A. Richardson. Perf. Wes Martin and Andrew Dylan Ray. Southern Appalachian Historical Association. Daniel Boone Amphitheater. Boone, N.C. Summer 2009. Performance.
Horowitz, Tony. *A Voyage Long and Strange: On the Trail of Vikings, Conquistadors, Lost Colonists, and Other Adventurers in Early America*. New York: Picador, 2009. Print.
Howe, LeAnne. *Choctalking on Other Realities*. San Francisco: Aunt Lute Books, 2013. Print.
———. *Spiral of Fire*. Dir. Carol Cornsilk. Adanvdo Vision, Vision Maker, 2005.
Howe, LeAnne, and Kirstin Squint. "Choctawan Aesthetics, Spirituality, and Gender Relations: An Interview with LeAnne Howe." *MELUS* 35 (2010): 211–45. Print.
Hudson, Angela Pulley. *Creek Paths and Federal Roads: Indians, Settlers, and Slaves and the Making of the American South*. Chapel Hill: University of North Carolina Press, 2010. Print.
———. "'Forked Justice': Elias Boudinot, the U.S. Constitution, and Cherokee Removal." *American Indian Rhetorics of Survivance*. Pittsburgh: University of Pittsburgh Press, 2006. 50–66. Print.
———. *Real Native Genius: How an Ex-Slave and White Mormon Became Famous Indians*. Chapel Hill: University of North Carolina Press, 2015. Print.

Hudson, Charles. *The Catawba Nation*. Reissued ed. Athens: University of Georgia Press, 2007. Print.

Huhndorf, Shari M. *Going Native: Indians in the American Cultural Imagination*. Ithaca, N.Y.: Cornell University Press, 2001. Print.

———. *Mapping the Americas: The Transnational Politics of Contemporary Native Culture*. Ithaca, N.Y.: Cornell University Press, 2009. Print.

Hunter, Kermit. *Horn in the West: A Drama of the Southern Appalachian Highlands*. Boone, N.C.: Unpublished, 1952. Folder 31, Miscellaneous Scripts, 1930–1977 and undated #04862, Southern Historical Collection, Louis Round Wilson Special Collections Library, University of North Carolina at Chapel Hill.

"Indian Spring Reserve." *Augusta Chronicle and Georgia Advertiser*, 18 March 1828. Advertisement. American Antiquarian Society. Worcester, Mass.

Jackson, Robert. "The Southern Disaster Complex." *Mississippi Quarterly* 63.3/4 (2010): 555–70. Print.

Jackson, Virginia, ed. *On Periodization: Selected Essays from the English Institute*. ACLS Humanities e-book. American Council of Learned Societies. 2010. Web. 24 February 2012.

Jacobs, Ron. *The Way the Wind Blew: A History of the Weather Underground*. London: Verso, 1997. Print.

Jefferson, Thomas. *Writings*. Ed. Merrill D. Peterson. New York: Library of America, 1984.

Joy, Natalie Irene. "Hydra's Head: Fighting Slavery and Indian Removal in Antebellum America." Diss. University of California, Los Angeles, 2008. Print.

Justice, Daniel Heath. *Our Fires Survive the Storm: A Cherokee Literary History*. Minneapolis: University of Minnesota Press, 2006. Print.

Kamensky, Jane. *The Exchange Artist: A Tale of High-Flying Speculation and American's First Banking Collapse*. New York: Penguin, 2008. Print.

Karttunen, Frances. *Between Worlds: Interpreters, Guides, and Survivors*. New Brunswick, N.J.: Rutgers University Press, 1994. Print.

Kelton, Paul. *Epidemics and Enslavement: Biological Catastrophe in the Native Southeast, 1492–1715*. Lincoln: University of Nebraska Press, 2009. Print.

Kidwell, Clara Sue. *Choctaws and Missionaries in Mississippi, 1818–1918*. Norman: University of Oklahoma Press, 1995. Print.

Kim, Sue. *On Anger: Race, Cognition, Narrative*. Austin: University of Texas Press, 2013. Print.

King, Thomas. *The Inconvenient Indian: A Curious Account of Native People in North America*. Minneapolis: University of Minnesota Press, 2013. Print.

———. *The Truth about Stories: A Native Narrative*. Minneapolis: University of Minnesota Press, 2003. Print.

Knick, Stanley. "Because It Is Right." *Native South* 1.1 (2008): 80–89. Print.

Krasteva, Yonka. "Encounters across Time and Space: The Sacred, the Profane, and the Political in Linda Hogan's *Power*." *Transatlantic Voices: Interpretations of Native North American Literatures*. Ed. Elvira Pulitano. 206–24. Lincoln: University of Nebraska Press, 2007. Print.

Krech III, Shepard. *The Ecological Indian: Myth and History*. New York: W. W. Norton, 1999. Print.

Kreyling, Michael. *The South That Wasn't There: Postsouthern Memory and History.* Baton Rouge: Louisiana State University Press, 2010. Print.

Kupperman, Karen Ordahl. *Roanoke: The Abandoned Colony.* 2nd ed. London: Rowman & Littlefield, 2007. Print.

Langbauer, Laurie. "Early British Travelers to the U.S. South." *Southern Literary Journal* 40.1 (2007): 1–18. Print.

Lawrence, Jane. "The Indian Health Service and the Sterilization of Native American Women." *American Indian Quarterly* 24 (2000): 400–419. Print.

Levinson, Marc. *The Box: How the Shipping Container Made the World Smaller and the World Economy Bigger.* Princeton, N.J.: Princeton University Press, 2008. Print.

The Literature of the American South. Eds. William Andrews, Minrose C. Gwin, Trudier Harris, and Fred Hobson. New York: W. W. Norton, 1997. Print.

The Lost Colony. By Paul Green. Dir. Robert Richmond. Perf. Brian Clowdus, Dacia Dick. Roanoke Island Historical Association, Manteo, N.C. Summer 2009. Performance.

The Lost Colony Center for Science and Research. 2007. Web. 12 May 2012.

"The Lost Colony Lives Again." *Raleigh News and Observer*, July 1938. Raleigh, N.C. Print. Folder 3168, Paul Green Papers #03693, Southern Historical Collection, Louis Round Wilson Special Collections Library, University of North Carolina at Chapel Hill.

"Lost Colony Sequel Planned at Pembroke." *Raleigh News and Observer*, August 2, 1970. Raleigh, N.C. Folder 4600, Paul Green Papers #03693, Southern Historical Collection, Louis Round Wilson Special Collections Library, University of North Carolina at Chapel Hill.

Lowe, John Wharton. *Calypso Magnolia: The Crosscurrents of Caribbean and Southern Literature.* Chapel Hill: University of North Carolina Press, 2016. Print.

Lowery, Malinda Maynor. *Lumbee Indians in the Jim Crow South: Race, Identity, and the Making of a Nation.* Chapel Hill: University of North Carolina Press, 2010. Print.

———. "Making Christianity Sing: The Origins and Experience of Lumbee Indian and African-American Church Music." *Confounding the Color Line: Indian-Black Experience in a Multidisciplinary Perspective.* Ed. James F. Brooks. Lincoln: University of Nebraska Press, 2002. Print.

———. *Sounds of Faith.* 1999. University of North Carolina, Chapel Hill. Web. 13 April 2013.

Lowery, Malinda Maynor, and Willie French Lowery. Personal interview. 8 February 2011.

Lowery, Reba. "To Paul Green." Folder 4601, Paul Green Papers #03693, Southern Historical Collection, Louis Round Wilson Special Collections Library, University of North Carolina at Chapel Hill.

Lowery, Willie French. *Plant and See.* 1969. Paradise of Bachelors, 2014. MP3.

———. *Proud to Be a Lumbee.* 1976. Paradise of Bachelors, 2004. MP3.

———. *Willie French Lowery.* 19 July 2010. Web. 29 January 2015.

The Lumbee Tribe of North Carolina. "Federal Recognition: The Lumbee Tribe's One Hundred Year Quest." The Lumbee Tribe of North Carolina, 23 January 2009. Web. 1 March 2009.

Mallios, Seth. *The Deadly Politics of Giving: Exchange and Violence at Ajacan, Roanoke, and Jamestown.* Tuscaloosa: University of Alabama Press, 2006. Print.

Maltby, William. *The Black Legend in England: The Development of Anti-Spanish Sentiment, 1558–1660.* Durham, N.C.: Duke University Press, 1971.

Manning, Pascale McCullough. "A Narrative of Motives: Solicitation and Confession in Linda Hogan's *Power*." *Studies in American Indian Literatures* 20.2 (2008): 1–21. Print.

Marshall, John. *Writings.* New York: Library of America, 2010.

Martin, James T. "Statement of Enrolled Member, Poarch Band of Creek Indians and Executive Director United South and Eastern Tribes, Inc. Regarding Federal Recognition of the Lumbee Tribe of North Carolina." 1 April 2004. House Resources Committee. Washington, DC: Government Printing Office, 2004. Print.

Martin, Robert G., Jr. "*Cherokee Phoenix*: Pioneer Indian Journalism." *Chronicles of Oklahoma* 25 (1947): 102–18. Print.

McAdams, Janet. *Red Weather.* Tucson: University of Arizona Press, 2012. Print.

McCray, Mike. "Press play: Lumbee musician Willie French Lowery's legacy." *Fayobserver.com*, 5 July 2012. Web. 13 May 2014.

McCreless, Patrick. "JSU professor: American Indian site is gone." *Anniston Star*, 21 January 2010. Web. 1 May 2011.

McKie, Scott. "Swain passes moratorium on Duke construction." *Cherokee One Feather*, 9 March 2010. Web. 23 March 2012.

McLoughlin, William G. *Cherokee Renascence in the New Republic.* Princeton, N.J.: Princeton University Press, 1986. Print.

McMillan, Hamilton. *Sir Walter Raleigh's Lost Colony: An Historical Sketch of the Attempts of Sir Walter Raleigh to Establish a Colony in Virginia, with the Traditions of an Indian Tribe in North Carolina, Indicating the Fate of the Colony of Englishman Left on Roanoke Island in 1587.* Wilson, N.C.: Advance, 1888. Print.

Meachum, Jon. *Thomas Jefferson: The Art of Power.* Reprint ed. New York: Random House, 2013.

Means, Russell. "'I Am Not a Leader': Russell Means' 1980 Mother Jones cover story." *MotherJones.com*, 22 October 2012. Web. 15 December 2015.

Melzer, Ashley. "The unexpected revival of Lumbee rock 'n' roll." *IndyWeek.com*, 4 July 2012. Web. 13 May 2015.

Merrell, James. *The Indians' New World: Catawbas and Their Neighbors from European Contact through the Era of Removal.* New York: W. W. Norton, 1991. Print.

Metcalf, Stephen. "Yokely-Dokely America: The disgracefulness of Charles Frazier." *Slate.com*, 12 October 2006. Web. 12 September 2011.

Miles, Tiya. *The House on Diamond Hill: A Cherokee Plantation Story.* Chapel Hill: University of North Carolina Press, 2010.

———. *Ties That Bind: The Story of an Afro-Cherokee Family in Slavery and Freedom.* Berkeley: University of California Press, 2006. Print.

Miller, Lee. *Roanoke: Solving the Mystery of the Lost Colony.* New York: Penguin, 2000. Print.

Miller, Mark Edwin. *Forgotten Tribes: Unrecognized Indians and the Federal Acknowledgment Process.* Lincoln: University of Nebraska Press, 2006. Print.

Miller, Mary Ann, and Karl Taube. *An Illustrated Dictionary of the Gods and Symbols of Ancient Mexico and the Maya*. London: Thames & Hudson, 1997. Print.

Missall, John, and Mary Lou Missall. *The Seminole Wars: America's Longest Indian Conflict*. Gainesville: University Press of Florida, 2004. Print.

Mitchell, Douglas. *A Disturbing and Alien Memory: Southern Novelists Writing History*. Baton Rouge: Louisiana State University Press, 2008. Print.

Moore, Cecelia. *The Federal Theatre Project in the American South: The Carolina Playmakers and the Quest for American Drama*. Lanham, Md.: Lexington Books, 2017.

Moore, Marinda Branson. *The Geographical Reader, for the Dixie Children*. Raleigh, N.C.: Branson, Farrar, 1863. American Antiquarian Society. Worcester, Mass.

Moretti, Franco. *Atlas of the European Novel, 1800–1900*. London: Verso, 1998. Print.

Morgan, Phillip Carroll. *Riding Out the Storm: 19th Century Chickasaw Governors, Their Lives, and Intellectual Legacy*. Ada, Okla.: Chickasaw Press, 2013. Print.

Morgan, Robert. *Boone: A Biography*. Chapel Hill, N.C.: Algonquian Books of Chapel Hill, 2008. Print.

Murawski, John. "Duke Energy won't build near sacred Cherokee site." *NewsObserver.com*, 2 August 2010. Web. 1 September 2010.

Murphey, James E., and Sharon M. Murphey. *Let My People Know: American Indian Journalism, 1828–1978*. Norman: University of Oklahoma Press, 1981. Print.

Murphy, Ryan, and Brad Falchuck, creators. *American Horror Story: Roanoke*. FX, 2016.

Murray, Matt. "'Redskins Pride' social media campaign backfires." today.com, 30 May 2014. Web. 1 July 2014.

My Louisiana Love. Dir. Sharon Linezo Hong. Perf. Monique Verdin, Mark Krasnoff. Within A Sense, LLC. 23 April 2012. Web. 10 February 2013.

Nakamura, Masahiro. *Visions of Order in William Gilmore Simms: Southern Conservatism and the Other American Romance*. Columbia: University of South Carolina Press, 2009. Print.

Neiwart, David. "John Stossel's racist attack on tribes as 'freeloaders': A farrago of ignorance and lies." *CrooksandLiars.com*, 4 April 2011. Web. 11 April 2011.

Nelson, Amy. "Strike at the Wind: The struggle to sustain a culture." An interview with Malinda Maynor Lowery. *NC Folk*. North Carolina Folklife Institute. 29 May 2010. Web. 1 February 2011.

"New York Indians." *Georgia Journal*, 23 January 1830. American Antiquarian Society. Worcester, Mass.

"News from the Cherokees." *Augusta Chronicle and Georgia Advertiser*, 12 July 1826. American Antiquarian Society. Worcester, Mass.

Nichols, John L. "Alexander Cameron, British Agent among the Cherokee." *South Carolina Historical Magazine* 97.2 (1996): 94–114. Print.

Nunn, Erich. *Sounding the Color Line: Music and Race in the Southern Imagination*. Athens: University of Georgia Press, 2015. Print.

Oakley, Christopher Arris. *Keeping the Circle: American Indian Identity in Eastern North Carolina, 1885–2004*. Lincoln: University of Nebraska Press, 2007. Print.

———. "The Legend of Henry Berry Lowry: *Strike at the Wind!* and the Lumbee Indians of North Carolina." *Mississippi Quarterly* 60.1 (2007): 59–80. Print.

Oberg, Michael Leroy. *The Head in Edward Nugent's Hand: Roanoke's Forgotten Indians*. Philadelphia: University of Pennsylvania Press, 2008. Print.

Oliphant, John. *Peace and War on the Anglo-Cherokee Frontier, 1756–63*. Baton Rouge: Louisiana State University Press, 2001. Print.

Onuf, Peter S. *The Mind of Thomas Jefferson*. Charlottesville: University of Virginia Press, 2007. Print.

Opothle Yoholo, John Stidham, Mad Wolf, Menawee, Yoholo Micco, Tuskeekee Tustenuggee, et al. "Letter to Col. Thomas L. McKenney." Reprinted from the *National Journal*, 3 March 1826. *Augusta Chronicle and Georgia Advertiser*, 7 July 1826. American Antiquarian Society. Worcester, Mass.

Oxford English Dictionary Online. dictionary.oed.com. Web.

Parker, Robert Dale. *Changing Is Not Vanishing: A Collection of American Indian Poetry to 1930*. Philadelphia: University of Pennsylvania Press, 2011. Print.

———. "Red Slippers and Cottonmouth Moccasins: White Anxieties in Faulkner's Indian Stories." *Faulkner Journal* 18.1–2 (2003): 81–100. Print.

The Patriot. Dir. Ronald Emmerich. Perf. Mel Gibson, Heath Ledger, Joely Richardson. Columbia Pictures, 2000. DVD.

Pearcy, Thomas L. *The History of Central America*. New York: Palgrave Macmillian, 2006. Print.

Pease, Donald E. *The New American Exceptionalism*. Minneapolis: University of Minnesota Press, 2009. Print.

———. "Transnational Melancholia." University College Dublin Clinton Institute for American Studies Summer School. Dublin, Ireland. July 2010. Presentation.

Perdue, Theda. *Cherokee Women: Gender and Culture Change, 1700–1835*. Lincoln: University of Nebraska Press, 1998. Print.

———. "Introduction." *Cherokee Editor: The Writings of Elias Boudinot*. Ed. Theda Perdue. Athens: University of Georgia Press, 1983. 3–38. Print.

———. "Race and Culture: Writing the Ethnohistory of the Early South." *Ethnohistory* 51.4 (2004): 701–23. Print.

———. "A Reply to Saunt et al." *Ethnohistory* 53.2 (2006): 406. Print.

Perdue, Theda, and Michael D. Green. *The Cherokee Removal: A Brief History with Documents*. 2nd ed. Boston: Bedford/St. Martin's, 2005. Print.

———. *The Columbia Guide to American Indians of the Southeast*. New York: Columbia University Press, 2011. Print.

Perez-Brignoli, Hector. *A Brief History of Central America*. Berkeley: University of California Press, 1989. Print.

"Perspectives." *Raleigh News and Observer*, 11 July 1971. Section 4. Folder 4600, Paul Green Papers #03693, Southern Historical Collection, Louis Round Wilson Special Collections Library, University of North Carolina at Chapel Hill.

Pierson, George Wilson. *Tocqueville in America*. 1938. Reprint ed. Baltimore: Johns Hopkins University Press, 1996. Print.

Quayson, Ato. "Periods versus Concepts: Space Making and the Question of Postcolonial Literary History." *PMLA* 127.2 (2012): 342–48. Print.

Quinn, Arthur Hobson. *American Fiction: An Historical and Critical Survey*. New York: D. Appleton-Century, 1936. Print.

Quinn, David Beers, ed. *The Roanoke Voyages, 1584–1590: Volumes I and II*. New York: Dover, 1991. Print.

Rainwater, Catherine. "Who May Speak for the Animals? Deep Ecology in Linda Hogan's *Power* and A. A. Carr's *Eye Killers*." *Figuring Animals: Essays on Animal Images in Art, Literature, Philosophy, and Popular Culture*. Ed. Mary S. Pollack and Catherine Rainwater. New York: Palgrave Macmillan, 2005. 261–80. Print.

Ralstin-Lewis, D. Marie. "The Continuing Struggle against Genocide: Indigenous Women's Reproductive Rights." *Wicazo Sa Review* 20 (2005): 71–95. Print.

Ramsey, William L. *The Yamasee War: A Study of Culture, Economy, and Conflict in the Colonial South*. Lincoln: University of Nebraska Press, 2010. Print.

"Real Early South." Perf. Angela Pulley Hudson. *About South Podcast*. 9 September 2016. Web.

"*Red Weather* Historical Contexts." Janetmcadams.org. 2012. Web. 10 December 2017.

Regis, Helen. *Caribbean and Southern: Transnational Perspectives of the U.S. South*. Athens: University of Georgia Press, 2006. Print.

Reising, R. W. "Literary Depictions of Henry Berry Lowry: Mythic, Romantic, and Tragic." *MELUS* 17 (1991–92): 87–103. Print.

Ridge, John, and David Vann. "Letter." Reprinted from the *National Journal*, 3 March 1826. *Augusta Chronicle and Georgia Advertiser*, 7 July 1826. American Antiquarian Society. Worcester, Mass.

Rifkin, Mark. *Beyond Settler Time: Temporal Sovereignty and Indigenous Self-Determination*. Durham, N.C.: Duke University Press, 2017. Print.

Risling Baldy, Cutcha. "Coyote Is Not a Metaphor: On Decolonizing, (Re)claiming and (Re)naming 'Coyote.'" *Decolonization: Indigeneity, Education and Society* 4.1 (2015): 1–20. Web. 10 December 2015.

———. "On telling Native people to just 'get over it' or why I teach about The Walking Dead in my Native Studies classes." *CutchaRislingBaldy.com*. 11 December 2013. Web. 11 December 2013.

———. "U.S. Patent and Trademark Office cancels trademark registrations for the Washington Racial Slur team! or In which I attempt to explain How did we get here? Where do we go from here? To Twitter we go! #NotYourMascot." *Cutcha RislingBaldy.com*. 18 June 2014. Web. 20 June 2014.

Roach, Joseph. *Cities of the Dead: Circum-Atlantic Performances*. New York: Columbia University Press, 1996. Print.

Roediger, David R. *The Wages of Whiteness: Race and the Making of the American Working Class*. London: Verso, 1991. Print.

Romine, Scott. *The Real South: Southern Narrative in the Age of Cultural Reproduction*. Baton Rouge: Louisiana State University Press, 2008. Print.

Rough, William Howard. "'(What) the American Public Need': A 'Theater of the People', an Interview with Paul Green." *North Carolina Literary Review* 18 (2009): 8–21. Print.

Round, Phillip. *Removable Type: Histories of the Book in Indian Country, 1663–1880*. Chapel Hill: University of North Carolina Press, 2010. Print.

Rumble: The Indians Who Rocked the World. Dir. Catherine Bainbridge and Alfonso Maiorana. ARTE GEIE and Rezolution Pictures, 2017.

Sarris, Greg. *Keeping Slug Woman Alive: A Holistic Approach to American Indian Texts*. Berkeley: University of California Press, 1993. Print.

Saunt, Claudio. *A New Order of Things: Property, Power, and the Transformation of the Creek Indians, 1733–1816*. Cambridge: Cambridge University Press, 1999. Print.

Saunt, Claudio, Barbara Krauthamer, Tiya Miles, Celia E. Naylor, and Circe Sturm. "Rethinking Race and Culture in the Early South." *Ethnohistory* 53.2 (2006): 399–405. Print.

Sayre, Gordon. "Jefferson and Native Americans: Policy and Archive." *The Cambridge Companion to Thomas Jefferson*. Ed. Frank Shuffelton. New York: Cambridge University Press, 2008. 61–72. Print.

Schermerhorn, Calvin. *Money over Mastery, Family over Freedom: Slavery in the Antebellum Upper South*. Baltimore: Johns Hopkins University Press, 2011. Print.

Schmidt, Rob. "Fox special on Indian 'freeloaders.'" NewspaperRock. *BlueCorn Comics.com*. 25 March 2011. Web. 11 April 2011.

Schneider, Bethany. "Boudinot's Change: Boudinot, Emerson, and Ross on Cherokee Removal." *ELH: English Literary History* 75 (2008): 151–77. Print.

Scruggs, Ralph. Letter. *Cherokee Phoenix*. New Echota. 12 August 1831. American Antiquarian Society. Worcester, Mass.

Selden, Samuel. "American Drama in the Open Air." *Horn in the West: A Drama of the Southern Appalachian Highlands Souvenir Program*. Boone, N.C.: Southern Historical Appalachian Association, 1952. 7–8, 28–29. Folder 136, Samuel Selden Papers #04378, Southern Historical Collection, Louis Round Wilson Special Collections Library, University of North Carolina at Chapel Hill.

Sell, Jonathan P. A. *Rhetoric and Wonder in English Travel Writing, 1560–1613*. Burlington, Vt.: Ashgate, 2006. Print.

Shakespeare, William. *The Tempest*. New York: W. W. Norton, 2003. Print.

Sider, Gerald. *Living Indian Histories: Lumbee and Tuscarora People in North Carolina*. Chapel Hill: University of North Carolina Press, 2003. Print.

Simmons, Matthew. "Introduction." *The Life of Francis Marion*. The Simms Initiative. University of South Carolina. 2011. Web. 15 October 2011.

Simms, William Gilmore. "The Broken Arrow." *An Early and Strong Sympathy: The Indian Writings of William Gilmore Simms*. Eds. John Caldwell Guilds and Charles Hudson. Columbia: University of South Carolina Press, 2003. 81–98. Print.

———. From *The Charleston City Gazette*. March 15, 1830.

———. *The Geography of South Carolina: Being a Companion to the History of That State*. Charleston: Babcock & Co., 1844. Print.

———. *Mellichampe, a Legend of the Santee*. New York: Harper & Brothers, 1836. Print.

———. "North American Indians." *An Early and Strong Sympathy: The Indian Writings of William Gilmore Simms*. Eds. John Caldwell Guilds and Charles Hudson. Columbia: University of South Carolina Press, 2003. 7–19. Print.

———. *The Partisan: A Tale of the Revolution*. New York: Harper & Brothers, 1835. Print.

Skinner, Nell. "To Paul Green." 31 May 1970. Folder 4600, Paul Green Papers #03693, Southern Historical Collection, Louis Round Wilson Special Collections Library, University of North Carolina at Chapel Hill.

Sloan, Kim. *A New World: England's First View of America*. Chapel Hill: University of North Carolina Press, 2007. Print.

Smith, J. Douglas. "The Campaign for Racial Purity and the Erosion of Paternalism in Virginia, 1922–1930: 'Nominally White, Biologically Mixed, and Legally Negro.'" *Journal of Southern History* 68.1 (2002): 65–106. Print.

Smith, Jon. *Finding Purple America: The South and the Future of American Cultural Studies*. Athens: University of Georgia Press, 2013.

Smith, Jon, and Deborah Cohn. "Introduction: Uncanny Hybridities." *Look Away! The U.S. South in New World Studies*. Eds. Jon Smith and Deborah Cohn. Durham, N.C.: Duke University Press, 2004. 1–19. Print.

Smith, Mark. *Debating Slavery: Economy and Society in the Antebellum American South*. London: Cambridge University Press, 1998. Print.

Smith, Paul Chaat, and Robert Warrior. *Like a Hurricane: The Indian Movement from Alcatraz to Wounded Knee*. New York: New Press, 1997. Print.

Snyder, Christina. *Slavery in Indian Country: The Changing Face of Captivity in Early America*. Cambridge, Mass.: Harvard University Press, 2010. Print.

Steele, Ian. *Warpaths: Invasions of North America*. Oxford: Oxford University Press, 1995. Print.

Stevens, Scott. "Letter to the Editor." Unpublished manuscript. 2010.

Stevens, Wallace. *The Collected Poems: The Corrected Edition*. New York: Vintage, 2015. Print.

Stewart, Kathleen. *Ordinary Affects*. Durham, N.C.: Duke University Press, 2007. Print.

Stick, David. *Roanoke Island: The Beginnings of English America*. Chapel Hill: University of North Carolina Press, 1983. Print.

Stilling, Glenn Ellen Starr. "The Lumbee Indians: An Annotated Bibliography." Appalachian State University. 2012. Web. 15 April 2011.

Stossel, John. "Freeloading doesn't help the freeloaders." FOXBusiness.com, 4 April 2011. Web. 11 April 2011.

Sturgis, Sue. "Alabama city destroying ancient Indian mound for Sam's Club." *Facing South*. The Institute for Southern Studies, 4 August 2009. Web. 1 May 2011.

———. "Sacred Indian mound destroyed for sports complex in Alabama." *Facing South*. The Institute for Southern Studies, 1 January 2010. Web. 1 May 2011.

———. "Wal-mart's history of destroying sacred sites." *Facing South*. The Institute for Southern Studies, 3 September 2009. Web. 1 May 2011.

Tamarkin, Elisa. "Losing Perspective in the Age of News." *PMLA* 125 (2010): 192–200. Print.

Taylor, Diana. *The Archive and the Repertoire: Performing Cultural Memory in the Americas*. Durham, N.C.: Duke University Press, 2003. Print.

Taylor, Melanie Benson. "In Deep." *south: a scholarly journal* 48 (2015): 68–73. Print.

———. *Reconstructing the Native South: American Indian Literature and the Lost Cause*. Athens: University of Georgia Press, 2011. Print.

Taylor, Michael C. "Hello, America: The Life and Work of Willie French Lowery." An Interview. *Southern Cultures* 16.3 (2010): 79–101. Print.

TeaParty.Org. "About Us." Web. 1 July 2015.

Tedlock, Dennis, ed. and trans. *Popol Vuh: The Definitive Edition of the Mayan Book of the Dawn of Life and the Glories of Gods and Kings*. New York: Touchstone, 1996.

Thompson, Edgar Tristram. *The Plantation*. 1932. Eds. Sidney Mintz and Georgia Baca. Columbia: University of South Carolina Press, 2010. Print.

Thompson, Matthew. "Staging 'the Drama': The Continuing Importance of Cultural Tourism in the Gaming Era." Diss. University of North Carolina, 2009. Print.

Thomsen, Paul A. *Rebel Chief: The Motley Life of Colonel William Holland Thomas, C.S.A*. New York: Tom Doherty & Associates, 2004. Print.

Thornton, Richard. "North Carolina Cherokees are in escalating legal battle with Duke Energy over sacred site." Examiner.com, 25 July 2010. Web. 1 September 2010.

Timber, Alex, and Michael Friedman. *Bloody Bloody Andrew Jackson*. 2006.

Townsend, Alfred. *The Swamp Outlaws, or the North Carolina Bandits*. New York: R. M. DeWitt, 1872. Print.

Tracy, Susan. *In the Master's Eye: Representations of Women, Blacks, and Poor Whites in Antebellum Southern Literature*. Amherst: University of Massachusetts Press, 1995. Print.

Trefzer, Annette. *Disturbing Indians: The Archaeology of Southern Fiction*. Tuscaloosa: University of Alabama Press, 2007. Print.

Trumpener, Katie. "In the Grid: Period and Experience." *PMLA* 127.2 (2012): 349–56. Print.

"TYRANNY UPDATE: Obama strips Washington Redskins of their trademark." TeaParty.org. Web. 1 June 2014.

Umberger, Randy. "Randy Umberger to Hector MacLean." Folder 4600, Paul Green Papers #03693, Southern Historical Collection, Louis Round Wilson Special Collections Library, University of North Carolina at Chapel Hill.

———. "Randy Umberger to Paul Green." Folder 4600, Paul Green Papers #03693, Southern Historical Collection, Louis Round Wilson Special Collections Library, University of North Carolina at Chapel Hill.

———. *Strike at the Wind!* Unpublished, 1971. Folder 4601–3, Paul Green Papers #03693, Southern Historical Collection, Louis Round Wilson Special Collections Library, University of North Carolina at Chapel Hill.

United States Census. "State and County Quick Facts: Robeson County." 2 December 2015. Web. 10 January 2016.

United States of America. Department of the Interior. Bureau of Indian Affairs. Federal Acknowledgment of American Indian Tribes 25 CFR Part 83. 29 June 2015. Washington, DC: Government Printing Office, 2015. Print.

United States of America. Department of the Interior. Office of the Solicitor. Memorandum M-37040: Reconsideration of the Lumbee Act of 1956. 26 December 2016. Washington, DC: Government Printing Office, 2016. Print.

"University of Alabama report on Oxford stone mound; City councilwoman: Company told workers not to remove mound." Reprinted in *Anniston Star*, 9 July 2009. Web. 1 May 2011.

Usner, Daniel. *Indians, Settlers, and Slaves in a Frontier Exchange Economy: The Lower Mississippi Valley before 1783*. Chapel Hill: University of North Carolina Press, 1992. Print.

Valandra, Edward. *Not without Our Consent: Lakota Resistance to Termination, 1950–59*. Urbana: University of Illinois Press, 2006. Print.

Van Zandt, Cynthia. *Brothers among Nations: The Pursuit of Intercultural Alliances in Early America, 1580–1660*. London: Oxford University Press, 2008. Print.

Vaughan, Alden T. *Transatlantic Encounters: American Indians in Britain, 1500–1776*. New York: Cambridge University Press, 2008. Print.

Vaughan, Alden T., and Virginia Mason Vaughan. *Shakespeare's Caliban: A Cultural History*. New York: Cambridge University Press, 1993. Print.

Vest, Jay Hansford C. "From Bobtail to Brer Rabbit: Native American Influences on Uncle Remus." *American Indian Quarterly* 24 (2000): 19–43. Print.

Vizenor, Gerald. *Fugitive Poses: Native American Indian Scenes of Absence and Presence*. Lincoln: University of Nebraska Press, 1998. Print.

———. *Manifest Manners: Postindian Warriors of Survivance*. Hanover, N.H.: Wesleyan University Press, 1994. Print.

Vormann, Boris. *Global Port Cities in North America: Urbanization Processes and Global Production Networks*. New York: Routledge, 2014. Print.

Wallace, Anthony. *Jefferson and the Indians: The Tragic Fate of the First Americans*. Cambridge, Mass.: Harvard University Press, 1999. Print.

———. *The Long, Bitter Trail: Andrew Jackson and the Indians*. New York: Hill & Wang, 1993. Print.

Warrior, Robert Allen. "Native Critics in the World: Edward Said and Nationalism." *American Indian Literary Nationalism*. Eds. Jace Weaver, Craig S. Womack, and Robert Allen Warrior. Albuquerque: University of New Mexico Press, 2006. 179–223. Print.

Washington, George. *Writings*. New York: Library of America, 1997. Print.

Weaver, Jace. *The Red Atlantic: American Indigenes and the Making of the Modern World, 1000–1927*. Chapel Hill: University of North Carolina Press, 2014. Print.

———. "Splitting the Earth: First Utterances and Pluralist Separatism." *American Indian Literary Nationalism*. Eds. Jace Weaver, Craig S. Womack, and Robert Allen Warrior. Albuquerque: University of New Mexico Press, 2006. 1–89. Print.

Whisenhunt, Dan. "Crowd braves dreary weather to bless site of mound in Oxford." *Anniston Star*, 31 August 2009. Web. 1 May 2011.

———. "Heflin man brings stories, photos back from 'mound.'" *Anniston Star*, 12 July 2009. Web. 1 May 2011.

———. "Smith says controversial mound was put at top of hill by natural forces." *Anniston Star*, 29 June 2009. Web. 1 May 2011.

White, Richard. *The Middle Ground: Indians, Empires, and Republics in the Great Lakes Region, 1650–1815*. Cambridge: Cambridge University Press, 1991. Print.

Whitehead, Neil L. "South America/Amazonia: The Forest of Marvels." *The Cambridge Companion to Travel Writing*. Eds. Peter Hume and Tim Young. Cambridge: Cambridge University Press, 2002. 122–38. Print.

Wilkins, David E. "Henry Berry Lowry: Champion of the Dispossessed." *Race, Gender and Class* 3.2 (1996): 97–111. Print.

Wilkins, David E., and Anne Merline McCulloch. "'Constructing' Nations within States: The Quest for Federal Recognition by the Catawba and Lumbee Tribes." *AIQ: American Indian Quarterly* 19 (1995): 361–88. Print.

Wilkins, Thurman. *Cherokee Tragedy: The Ridge Family and the Decimation of a People*. 2nd ed. Norman: University of Oklahoma Press, 1989. Print.

Williams, Raymond. *Marxism and Literature*. Oxford: Oxford University Press, 1977. Print.

"Willie French Lowery's *Plant and See* Released Today." Indian Country Today, 4 July 2012. Web. 26 December 2017.

Wilson, Charles Reagan. *Baptized in Blood: The Religion of the Lost Cause, 1865–1920*. Athens: University of Georgia Press, 1983. Print.

Wilson, Michael D. *Writing Home: Indigenous Narratives of Resistance*. East Lansing: Michigan State University Press, 2008. Print.

Wimsatt, Mary Ann. *The Major Fiction of William Gilmore Simms: Cultural Traditions and Literary Form*. Baton Rouge: Louisiana State University Press, 1989. Print.

Womack, Craig S. "Howling at the Moon: The Queer but True Story of My Life as a Hank Williams Song." *As We Are Now: Mixblood Essays on Race and Identity*. Ed. William S. Penn. Berkeley: University of California Press, 1998. 28–49. Print.

———. *Red on Red: Native American Literary Separatism*. Minneapolis: University of Minnesota Press, 1999. Print.

Wright, Gavin. *Slavery and American Economic Development*. Baton Rouge: Louisiana State University Press, 2006. Print.

Zogry, Michael J. "Lost in Conflation: Visual Culture and Constructions of the Category of Religion." *AIQ: American Indian Quarterly* 35.1 (2011): 1–55. Print.

INDEX

NOTE: Page numbers in *italics* indicate illustrations.

absence of Native people: in archive, 32, 33–34, 38, 39, 42–45, 227n21; as simulation, 32, 33, 36–37, 38, 226nn8–9; in southern studies scholarship, 17–18, 224n15. *See also* loss, narratives of; presence of Native people

Accilien, Cécile, 9

Adams, Henry, 75

Adams, Jessica, 9

Adams, John Quincy, 117, 118

Adventures of Tom Sawyer, The (Twain), 217–18

aesthetic victimry, 36, 44, 226n8

affective history: land claim and audience desire for, 138–39; outdoor dramas and, 46

African American literatures, 20–22

African Americans: distinguished as nonsettlers, 20; Native identity and, 19–20; "one-drop" rules and, 20. *See also* plantation economy; racial binary; racism; slavery; white supremacists and white supremacy

Alabama: Creek people and, 207; Creek Removal from, 118, 128; sacred mounds in, destruction of, 145

Alabama Journal, 120–21, 128

Alabama people, as terminated (and reinstated), 171

Alamance, Battle of, 93, 94, 102

Alcatraz Island, occupation of, 217

Algonquian people: archival absences and, 44–45; early modern narratives of loss and, 33, 38; as "going English," 42; horror of Roanoke story and, 30–31, 63; lost items as justification for imperial violence against, 39–40, 227n17; Lumbee Tribe and, 171–72, 192; referred to as "Virginians," 38, 227n14; Roanoke as profound "win" for, 44; terms of reference for, 38, 227n14; white claims of Indigenous ancestors and, 54, 61–62; as "white Moors," 41

Allotment, 237–38n11; Dawes Act (1887), 166, 168, 169–70; Jefferson and, 77–78; Lumbee–Lost Colony theory and, 168; Lumbee Tribe quest for federal recognition as correlating with, 166, 168–70, 238n12

Amadas, Philip, 37, 39–40, 42

American Horror Story, 29–31

American Indian Movement (AIM), occupation of Alcatraz Island, 217

American Indians, as term, xiii

American Revolution narratives, 24–25, 65–66; "bad" Indian converted to "good" and, 90–91; Confederate States of America and, 70; exceptionalism of U.S. South in, 67–68; indigenization of whiteness and, 65, 69–70, 85–86, 88–89, 91–93, 95, 102, 103–5; Native weaponry and, 86–87, 89; place naming and, 84–85; political claims as legitimized by, 66, 70–72, 79; poor white southerners interacting with Native people in, 70–71, 80, 84; sovereignty of Native American nations and, 66; spiralic temporality and, 65–66, 84, 102; U.S. South seen as inheritor of, in escape from "tyranny" of U.S. North, 80, 103; white land tenure in, legitimization of, 91–93. *See also* revolution

Anderson, Eric Gary, 6, 10–11, 14, 17, 52, 111, 164, 201

Anglo-Cherokee War (1758–61), 69

apocalypse(s): destructive and regenerative power of, 200–206, 208, 215–16, 241n8; disaster as nature and (un)nurture

263

apocalypse(s) (*continued*)
and, 195; distinguished from European biblical referents, 195, 200–201, 241n6; Native American survival of, 195, 241n3; "natural" vs. "man-made" disasters and, 194, 195; periodization and, 197–98; as tribalography, 196, 210. *See also* resilience; survival of Native Americans; violence, colonial

archive: absence in, 32, 33–34, 38, 39, 42–45, 227n21; as myth, 62

Arthur, Chester A., 237–38n11

Attakullakulla, 97; as character (Atakulla), 93–94, 97, 97–98, 231n23, 232n27

audience. *See* reception

Augusta Chronicle and Georgia Advertiser, 121–23, 124–25, 128–30, 208

authenticity: audience reception and, 15–16, 81; construction of, 7–8, 15, 18, 224n13; as function of desire, 16; historical detail and, 148; measurement of, and removal of Native people, 19; Native people serving as markers of, 96; perceived, versus sovereign identity, 192

Avatar (film), 90

Avery, Laurence, 50, 57, 60

Baker Roll, 238–39n16
Bakhtin, Mikhail, 49
Baldy, Cutcha Risling, 105, 108, 220
Bamnett, Timpoochy, 109
Barlowe, Arthur, 37, 39–40, 41
Bears Ears National Monument, 157
Beecher, Catharine, 234–35n22
Beloved Path, 71, 98–99
Bergland, Reneé, 69, 90
Berkhofer, Robert, 73, 96
Berry, Henry, 169
Bibler, Michael, 9
Blackbourn, David, 19
Black Eagle Child (Young Bear), 216
Black Legend, logic of, 110
Bloody Bloody Andrew Jackson (Timber and Friedman), 26, 111, 136, 155–58
Boles, John, 115
Bone, Martyn, 111
Boone, Daniel, as character in *Horn of the West*, 93, 94, 95, 103, 104, 150
Boone, N.C., 71, 94–95, 104

Bost, Suzanne, 18
Boston Tea Party, 105–6
Boudinot, Elias, 111–12, 120; ousted as editor of *Phoenix*, 131; reception of, 113, 114–16; against Removal, 112, 113, 123–24, 130–31, 133; in Treaty Party for Removal, and treason of, 112–13, 119
Bowen-Mercer, Carrie, 201
BP oil spill, 26–27, 195, 211
Bradford, William, 54
Bradley, Regina, 20
Brecht, Bertolt, 104, 232n31
Brendt, John, 147–48
"Broken Arrow, The" (Simms), 25, 111, 112, 132, 133–35
Brooks, Lisa, 13–14, 22, 27, 144–45, 197. *See also* spiralic temporality
Bruyneel, Keven, 223n1, 236n8
Buffon, Count (Georges-Louis Leclerc), 73, 74
Bureau of Indian Affairs (BIA). *See* federal recognition of tribes
Busick, Sean, 81
Butler, Pierce, 207
Butterworth, Keen, 90
Byrd, Jodi, 7, 10–11, 207, 208, 210

Caldwell, Erskine, 90
Caribbean Indigenous peoples: spiralic temporality and, 23; worldview of, in Hogan's *Power*, 200–201, 241n6
Carib people, 194, 207
Carney, Virginia, 99
Carrington, Edward, 72
Cartelli, Thomas, 34, 40
Carter, Asa/Forrest, 135, 137
Cartwright, Keith, 20, 197
"casino tribes," attempts to divide against, 144
Cassique of Kiawah, The (Simms), 80, 89
Catawba people, 81–82; absence of, from considerations of Native South, 82–83; as allies of Revolutionary cause, 86; authenticity of, questioned, 82–83; as federally recognized tribe, 82; as landlord to European settlers and dispossession, 82; reservation of, 82; Simms character based on, 80–81, 83–91; survival and persistence in place of, failure to recognize, 83; as terminated (and reinstated), 171

Central America, spiralic temporality and, 23
Chaplin, Joyce E., 33
Charleston City Gazette, 112, 233n3
Chastellux, Marquis de (François Jean de Beauvoir), 74
Chavis, Ben, 165, 236n7
Cheraw people, as one-time Lumbee Tribe name, 171–72, 237n10
"Cherokee," as one-time Lumbee Tribe name, 170, 172, 173, 237n10, 238–39n16
Cherokee Indians, Eastern Band. *See* Eastern Band of Cherokee Indians
Cherokee Indians of Robeson County, 170, 238–39n16. *See also* Lumbee Tribe of North Carolina
Cherokee Nation: accused of having corrupt economy, 125, 129–30, 234n19; accused of having hierarchical government, 125; Beloved Path of, 71, 98–99; Chickamauga Consciousness, 71, 76, 99; conflict of, and American Revolution, 71, 76; government of, as threat to white land claim, 121–24, 128–30; Kituwah Mound conflict, 142–45, 150, 236n26; Native American studies as method and, 11–12; sacred earth and, protection of, 142–46, 150; spiralic temporality and, 22; worldview and language of, in Hogan's *Power*, 199, 200, 203–4, 207. *See also* Cherokee people, Removal of; *Horn in the West*
Cherokee Nation v. Georgia (1831), 117, 118–19
Cherokee people, Removal of (Trail of Tears): as exceptional narrative, 117; focus of histories of, 116, 117; government of Cherokee people as threat to white land claim, 121–24, 128–30; historical fiction and construction of narrative history, 136–42, 146–50; lost cause narrative and, rejection of, 131–32; mixedblood/fullblood binary of, 119; print cultures, Cherokee involvement in, 120–21; "progressive" versus "revisionist" histories of, 119; resistance to, 113, 118–20, 131–32; *Riding the Trail of Tears* narrative of, spiralic temporality and, 150–55; Supreme Court decisions in, 117, 118–19; Treaty Party resulting in, 112–13, 119, 124; white southern identity and, 128–29. *See also* Indian Removal

Cherokee Phoenix (newspaper), 25, 112, 113, 120–21, 123–25, *126–27*, 130–32
Chiapas, Mexico, 208, 209
Chickamauga Consciousness, 71, 76, 99
Chickasaw people: Faulkner and, 18–19; Native American studies as method and, 11–12; Removal of, 118
Chiles, Katy, 73
Choctaw people: Faulkner and, 18–19; Removal of, 118; spiralic temporality and, 22
citizenship (Indian Citizenship Act, 1924), 166, 238–39n16
Civilian Conservation Corps, 54
civil rights movement, 12
Civil War: Indian Removal viewed as sin precipitating, 109–10, 116, 158; Lumbee Tribe resistance in, 161–62; as next predictable event in long series, 78, 115; Reconstruction period following, 163; Simms and context of, 79–80, 83, 113–14, 115; southern (white) identity and, 111; as white apocalypse, 154. *See also* Lost Cause narrative, Confederate; plantation economy; secession
Clowdus, Brian, 52, *59*
Coates, Julia, 119, 135, 152
Cohen, Felix, 172
Cohn, Deborah, 9, 224n15
Coke Act (1883), 168
Cold Mountain (Frazier), 111, 146, 147–49
Colley, Brook, 35, 105
Collier, John, 172
colonialism. *See* settler colonialism; violence, colonial
Columbus, Christopher, 200
Confederate States of America: American Revolution narratives and, 70; as linked to global South, 110, 124–25; sovereignty of, as never recognized, 7. *See also* Civil War; Lost Cause narrative, Confederate; secession
Conroy, Frank, 147
Cook, Barbara J., 200, 241–42n10
Cornnels, Charles, 109
counterclockwise movement, 196, 197
counternational movement and sentiment: Indian figure as stand in for treason and, 106–7; Indian Removal as, 71; indigenization of whiteness and Native history as,

INDEX   265

counternational movement and sentiment (*continued*) 102, 158; in Lumbee cultural productions, 181; secession as, 71. *See also* northern states, southern identity and "tyranny" of; southern identity

creation stories. *See* origin stories

Creek people: creation stories of, 207, 208, 220; Native American studies as method and, 11–12; Removal of, 25, 117–18, 120–21, 123–24, 128–29, 208; resistance to Removal, 118; worldview/universe of, and McAdams's *Red Weather*, 206–11. *See also* McIntosh, William; Womack, Craig

Croatan people: Lumbee–Lost Colony theory and, 167, 168; as one-time Lumbee Tribe name, 169, 170, 237n10, 238n12

Croatoan, Roanoke Island inscriptions of, 37, 43

Dakota Access Pipeline, 157, 219, 233n3, 235n26

Dare, Virginia, 37

Davis, LaRose, 20

Dawes Allotment Act (1887), 166, 168, 169–70

De Bry, Theodore, 37, 226n8

deep time, 23

Deloria, Ella, 177–78

Deloria, Philip, 49, 51, 60, 106, 107

Deloria, Vine, Jr., 4–5, 237–38n11

Democratic Party of North Caroline, 238–39n16

Derrida, Jacques, 36

de Soto, Hernando, 81, 84

Dexter, Andrew, 128

Dial, Adolph, 162, 164, 177

Dick, Dacia, 229n32

Dimock, Wai Chee, 13, 23, 224n12

"Disillusionment of Ten o'clock" (W. Stevens), 209

Dragging Canoe, 76, 97; as character, 71, 93–94, 96, 98, 232n27

"Dream of Injun Joe, The" (Forbes), 217–19

Du Bois, W. E. B., 229n29

Duke Energy / Kituwah Mound, 142–45, 150, 235n26

Eastern Band of Cherokee Indians: Baker Roll of, 238–39n16; formation and reservation/land purchases of, 119, 136–37; Indian Citizenship Act (1924) and, 238–39n16; Kituwah Mound conflict, 142–45, 150, 236n26; Lumbee Tribe named as Cherokees, 170, 172; opposition to federal recognition of Lumbee Tribe, 237n10, 239n20; *Unto These Hills* outdoor drama, 47, 104, 228n23; Yonaguska Literature Initiative, 150

Eaton, John, 125

"Ecological Indians," 215, 242n19

economy and economics: capitalism and Lumbee Tribe, 160, 165–66; commissioning of *The Lost Colony* and, 50; race and, as issues in Native American studies, 10; of *Strike at the Wind!* outdoor drama, 174, 183, 240n22. *See also* plantation economy; poor white southerners

Education of Henry Adams, The (Adams), 75

Education of Little Tree, The (Carter), 135, 137, 148

Elizabeth I: as character, 32, 180; "Virginia" and, 38–39

Emmerich, Ronald, 67, 68, 70; *The Patriot*, 66–70, 87, 147, 230n5

empire: transit of, 207; victors as victims in, 218, 219

English colonization, Black Legend logic of, 110. *See also* settler colonialism

ethnohistory, 10, 17–18

exceptionalism of U.S. South: Cherokee Trail of Tears and, 117; disjoining of sense of place from material land claim and, 111; *The Lost Colony* and, 31; Lumbee Tribe of North Carolina as challenging, 161, 163, 164, 170, 174; objections to *The Patriot* film and, 67–68; outdoor dramas and, 49. *See also* Lost Cause narrative, Confederate

"Farewell to the Civil War" (Green), 53

Faulkner, William, 17–18, 90, 225n17

federal recognition of tribes: historical narrative prior to 1900, requirement for, 7, 171, 173, 223n5, 237n10, 239n17; Indian Reorganization Act and, 172; physical examinations to determine status, 172; right-wing co-optation of struggle for, 165–66. *See also* Lumbee Tribe of North Carolina: federal recognition of

266 INDEX

—lack of: destruction of sacred sites and, 145; in Georgia, 34–35; United Houma Nation and, 212

Federal Theatre Project, 54

Fernando, Simon, as character, 32

First Families of Virginia, 229n33

Fitzgerald, Carol, 185, 189

"Five Civilized Tribes," 81

Florida. *See* Seminole people

Forbes, Jack D., 1–2, 20, 217, 219; "The Dream of Injun Joe," 217–19

Foucault, Michel, 15, 47, 96, 122, 156, 224n13

Frank, Andrew, 132

Frazier, Charles: *Cold Mountain*, 111, 146, 147–49; *Thirteen Moons*, 25–26, 111, 136–42, 145–48, 149–50

Friedman, Michael, 111. See also *Bloody Bloody Andrew Jackson*

Fuchs, Barbara, 224–25n16

Fulford, Forris, 185

Gallay, Alan, 82

Garrison, Tim Alan, 117

Gaul, Theresa Strouth, 113

Geographical Reader, for the Dixie Children (Moore), 109–10, 135, 234n19

Geography of South Carolina, The (Simms), 85

George II, 169

Georgia: gold in, 124–25, *126–27*; Indian Removal and, 113, 117, 118–19, 123, 124, 128–30, 131; lack of federally recognized tribes in, 34–35; place names in, 153. *See also* Cherokee Nation; Indian Removal

Georgia Journal, 125, *126–27*, 129, 234n18

gestus (Brechtian), 104, 232n31

Gilman, Caroline, 90

Gilmore, Ruth Wilson, 15

global South: Confederate States of America linked to, 110, 124–25; movement from U.S. South to, 207–11; U.S. South linked to, 124–25, 234n19

Goetz, Delia, 206

Goodheart, Adam, 138–39, 147

Gorman, John C., 164

Gray, James, 53–54

Gray, Richard, 16–17

Great Depression, 50

Greaves, Brendan, 185–86, 187

Green, Michael D., 10

Green, Paul: as father of outdoor drama, 32, 50; as opponent of segregation and white supremacy, 52–53, 60; on southern fiction, 53; on spectacle, 52; *Strike at the Wind!* and, 175–79, 183

—works: "Farewell to the Civil War," 53; *Last of the Lowries*, 178. See also *Lost Colony, The*

Greeson, Jennifer Rae, 68, 72, 106

Griffith, Benjamin, 132, 133

Guatemala, 208

Guilds, John Caldwell, 80–81, 90, 113–14, 132, 135

Hagood, Taylor, 164

Hakluyt, Richard, 37, 39, 40, 42, 43, 44, 226n10

Hardin, Michael, 200–201, 202, 241n6, 241n8

Harjo, Joy, 22

Harkin, Michael, 33, 56, 225–26n4

Harlow, Barbara, 14, 187

Harriot, Thomas, 37, 44

Harris, Drew, 60

Harris, James Brantly, 162

Harris, Trudier, 20

Harrison, William Henry, 77–78

Hatley, Jeff, 97–98, 100–101

Hatley, Shannon, 100–101

Hausman, Blake, 26; *Riding the Trail of Tears*, 26, 111, 136, 150–55

Heard, Abraham A., 125

Heath, R. Scott, 20

Hedge Coke, Allison Adelle, 22; "In the Year 513 PC," 197–98, 199; "We Were in a World," 194

Helm, Levon, 190

Hemmings, Sally, 72

Hershberger, Mary, 234–35n22

Hicks, Elijah, 131

historical fiction: construction of narrative history and, 136–42, 146–50; methodology of Native American studies and, 99–100

Hobson, Geary, 8, 21

Hogan, Linda: *People of the Whale*, 199; *Power*, 26, 198–206, 207, 210; regional creations of, 199–200; *Solar Storms*, 199

Holland, Sharon, 20

Hong, Sharon Linezo, 26–27, 211–15

Hoover, Bob, 146

Hopie, Nahetlue, 109
Horn in the West (Hunter), 25, 47, 71–72, 91–93; as ahistorical, 94–97, 103–5, 231n25; audience and reception of, 94–95, 96–97, 98–99, 149; audience response to Native characters, 100–102; geography of performance and, 104; historical accuracy, attempts to increase, 97–98, 102, 232n28; as legitimizing white land claim, 91–93, 95, 103–5; long staging history of, 91, 98; Native characters based on archival sources, static identities and, 94–97, 98–100, 101–2, 105; *The Patriot* and, 70; plot of, 93–94, 103–4
Houma Nation, United, 26–27, 211–15, 235n26
Howe, LeAnne, 21, 22, 151, 196; *Mico Kings*, 196
"Howling at the Moon" (Womack), 220
Hudson, Angela Pulley, 10, 51–52, 117–18, 122, 123, 234n18
Hudson, Charles, 80–81, 132, 135
Huhndorf, Shari M., 103, 224–25n16
Humphrey, Josephine, 161
Hunter, Kermit, 25, 50; *Unto These Hills*, 47, 104, 228n23. See also *Horn in the West*
Huracán (K'iche Mayan God): destruction of past world to create anew, 194, 195, 198, 199, 201–4, 205–6; etymology of "hurricane," 194, 195, 200, 241n1
Hurricane Katrina, 197–98, 213, 215
hurricanes: etymology of term, 194, 195, 200, 241n1; as natural versus man-made disasters, 194, 195; as tribalography, 196. See also apocalypse(s); Huracán; Hurricane Katrina
Hurston, Zora Neale, 198–99
hybridity, 9, 19

identity. See Native identity; southern identity
Inca people, 110
indian, as European invention, 36, 226n8
"Indian," as term, in Roanoke primary texts, 38–39, 227n14
Indian Citizenship Act (1924), 166, 238–39n16
Indian Country: hemispheric, 208, 209–10, 211; tribal specificity versus homogeneous ideas of, 27
Indian Removal, 8, 25–26, 116–17; absence in archive as presaging, 34, 44–45; American Revolution and plans for, 76, 77–78, 89–91; Catawba people waiting out, 82; complexity of, as commonly downplayed, 116–17, 135; constriction of Native past and future and, 77–78; as counternational moment, 71; death and destruction caused by, 118, 119; as human rights abuse, 113, 117; identity of Natives undermined by, 142; impoverishment of Natives and, 77; land tenure, white, and, 111, 154; as loss, litany of, 119, 136; Native land claims forgotten during, 86; as next predictable event in long series, 78, 115; ongoing Native presence as undermining narratives of, 8; periodization and, 116, 128, 136; plantation economy and, 117, 122–24, 124–25, 129–30, 132–35; pressure by states for, 117–18; as sin precipitating Civil War, 109–10, 116, 158; southern (white) identity and, 110–11, 128–29, 218; states' rights and, 121, 128; temporal range of, 116–17; women and debates on, 234–35n22
—narratives of: audience and, 136; *Bloody Bloody Andrew Jackson* as failed satire of, 155–58; conflation of, with Lost Cause narrative, 111, 124–25, *126–27*, 135–36, 150, 218–19; conflation of "poor white" and "Native" as, 87–89; death of Natives and, 89–91; historical fiction and construction of narrative history, 136–42, 146–50; non-Native consumption of, 151; as obscuring survival and persistence in place, 83; spiralic temporality and, 150–55; "tragically defeated Native" and, 124
—resistance to: by Cherokee people, 113, 118–20, 131–32; historical fiction about, and construction of narrative history, 136–42, 146–50; intertribal assistance with, 118; land purchases / establishment of reservation (Eastern Band of Cherokee Indians), 136–37, 142–46; Seminole military battles in, 118, 124, 218; survival and persistence as, 16, 135–36, 152–53; women and abolitionist press and, 234–35n22
Indian Removal Act (1830), 118
Indian Reorganization Act (1934), 166, 172
Indians of Robeson County. See Lumbee Tribe of North Carolina

indigeneity: challenges posed by, 208–9; federal interest in relationship between land claim and, 171; logics of, in formation of U.S. South, 13; long loss and, 31

indigenization of whiteness: "aboriginal impulse" of attachment to land and, 16–17; American Revolution narratives and, 65, 69–70, 85–86, 88–89, 91–93, 95, 102, 103–5; appeal to Native history as rebellious and counternational, 102, 158; by claiming affiliation to Indian figure while dispossessing Native peoples, 19–20, 75, 77–78, 86, 136; claims to Native identity and, 17, 54, 60–62, 229–30nn33–34; Lumbee–Lost Colony origin story and, 61–62, 177, 229–30n34. *See also* Indian Removal; place, non-Native southerners and sense of

Indigenous inhabitants of North America, as term, xiii

Indigenous land claim. *See* land claim, Indigenous

Indigenous temporalities. *See* spiralic temporality

Institute of Outdoor Drama, 174, 178

internal borders, 141

"In the Year 513 PC" (Hedge Coke), 197–98, 199

Iroquoian-speaking people, 171

Jackson, Andrew, 79, 116, 117, 118, 119, 125, 158. *See also Bloody Bloody Andrew Jackson*

Jackson, Robert T., 215

Jamestown colony, 40

Jamison, David Flavel, 114

Jefferson, Thomas, 25, 71; ambivalence and doublethink of, 72, 84; on character traits of Natives, 74, 76; on character traits of southerners, 73–75, 107; environmental/climatic determinism and, 73, 74, 75; land speculation by, 76; on Native as existing in idealized state without state interference, 72–73, 76, 77, 78, 170; Native policy/Removal and, 62, 75–76, 77–78, 106, 117; *Notes on the State of Virginia*, 74; slavery and, 72; on "tyranny" of northern states and secession, 76–77; white land tenure and, 72, 75–76, 77–78

Jim Crow system: as calcifying racial prejudice, 163; "Cro" as colloquialism for Lumbee Tribe, 170; Indians and pressures of, 163; interracial nature of Lumbee Tribe and resistance to, 163; lack of federal recognition and, 212. *See also* racism; white supremacists and white supremacy

Johnson, Myrtle Driver, 150

Justice, Daniel Heath, 11, 71–72, 99, 113, 119–20, 196–97

Kaddipah River, 84–85

Katapa peoples. *See* Catawba people

Katherine Walton (Simms), 70, 80

Kibler, James, 90

Kidwell, Clara Sue, 10

Kim, Sue, 187

King, Thomas, 106–7, 222

Kituwah Mound conflict, 142–45, 150, 236n26

Knick, Stanley, 237n10, 239n18

Krasnoff, Mark, 213, 215

Krech, Shepard, 242n19

Kreyling, Michael, 224n15

land claim, Indigenous: audience desire for affective history and, 138–39; definition of, 3; as epistemological, 163–64, 191; Lumbee resistance and, 163–64, 167; mixed-blood peoples and, perceived lack of authenticity of, 20, 86; as musical subject, 190–91; persistence of Native presence and, 16; property tax proposal as redress for violations of, 221; protecting land, 142–46, 150, 198, 199, 215, 219; racism and, 163; as real territory, 220; red state as intersection of narrative order and, 2–4, 223n1. *See also* sovereignty of Native American tribes and nations

land tenure, white: American Revolution narratives and, 91–93; Cherokee government perceived as threat to, 121–24, 128–30; emotional excess as shoring up narratives of, 63–64; Indian Removal and, 111, 154; Jefferson and, 72, 75–76, 77–78; *The Lost Colony* and, 60–61, 229n29. *See also* Indian Removal; indigenization of whiteness; place, non-Native southerners and sense of; settler colonialism

Langbauer, Laurie, 56

Last of the Lowries (Green), 178

Lawson, John, 82

Ledagee, 109

Life-Story of a People, The (E. Deloria), 177–78

Lily and the Totem, The (Simms), 80

linear temporality: as keeping institutions of planters and founders central, 197; lost causes and, 36; red state and, 65; stepping out of, 14. *See also* spiralic temporality

literary studies, and construction of U.S. South through (hi)stories, 10–11

Little Prince, 120

Locklear, Herbert, 160, 181

Los Altos, state of United Provinces of Central America (UPCA), 208, 210, 211

loss: as enforcing idea of Native responsibility for white theft and suppression, 35; survival of apocalypse and, 196; as term in southern studies, 36. *See also* loss, narratives of

loss, narratives of: American Revolution narratives and, 103; archival absence and, 38; authenticity of Native history as measured by, 81; creation of, 39–40; framing of, 34; as justifying imperial violence, 36–37, 45, 226nn8–9; protection of sacred sites despite, 145–46; Roanoke Colony discourse as pervaded by, 24, 37–38, 43–45, 55. *See also* absence of Native people; lost causes

—as predating Confederate Lost Cause narrative, 9, 12–13, 36; American Revolution and, 71, 78; colonialism justified via, 56; Indian Removal and, 116, 128; Lost Colony (Roanoke) and, 36, 38, 55–57

Lost Cause narrative, Confederate: Indian Removal narratives conflated with, 111, 124–25, *126–27*, 135–36, 150, 218–19; Lost Colony, conflation with, 55–57; Lumbee resistance to, 164, 191; *The Patriot* and, 68, 70; scholarly recovery and, caution on, 34–35, 64; southern Gothic and, 164; southern rock and, 189–90; undeadness and, marks of, 164. *See also* Confederate States of America; loss, narratives of: as predating Confederate Lost Cause narrative; lost causes

lost causes: archival absence of Natives and narratives of, 36; Cherokee rejection of narrative of, 131–32; convergence and, 35, 56, 147; hope and, 35–36; linear tempo-

rality and, 36; saving land as, 146; United Houma Nation and, 211–15. *See also* Lost Cause narrative, Confederate

Lost Colony. See *Lost Colony, The*; Roanoke Colony

Lost Colony, The (Green), 24, 50; archival absences and, 32, 44–45; authenticity and, 29, 62–63; backstage tours by actors in, 61–62, 229–30n34; colonial critique and, 53–54, 58, 60, 63–64; commissioning of, and political climate, 50; curtain call controversy, 45, 64; exceptionalism of U.S. South and, 31; fictive genealogies and, 54; foundational colonial narrative and, 54–55, 102; geography of performance, 104; Historian/Narrator/Sir Walter Raleigh character in, 52, 54, 57–58, *59*, 62–63, 229n30, 230n35; historical accuracy and, 54, 57; historical retellings, change over time of, 52, 55–58, 61–64, *63*, 230n35; land attachment and, 60–61, 229n29; loss and, 31, 32, 33, 55–57; Lost Cause narrative, conflation with, 55–57; "middle ground" of colonialism and, 61; Native character "Agona," 32, 44–45, 60–61, 229nn31–32; as ongoing outdoor drama, 31–32, 182; race and, 56–57, 228–29n28; racial mixing and, trope of, 32, 54, 60–61, 229nn33–34; reception of, 50, 54; religion and, 55; research by author of, 32, 225n1; as "symphonic drama," 50; white southern loss conflated with Native losses, 24, 103

Lost Colony DNA Project, 229–30n34

Louisiana: land loss and, 212; *My Louisiana Love*, 26–27, 211–15; pipeline projects, 235n26; United Houma Nation, 26–27, 211–15, 235n26

Lowe, John, 10–11, 224n11

Lowery, D. F., 170

Lowery, George, 120

Lowery, Malinda Maynor, 10, 151, 161, 163, 166, 167–68, 177–78, 184, 185, 191–92, 240n31; on Willie French Lowery's music, 188, 240n32; *Sounds of Faith* (documentary), 188–89; *Strike at the Wind!* and, 174, 240n22

Lowery, Willie French: homecoming of, 188, 190, 240n32; rerelease of works of, 185, 186

—musical sound of: as "ahead of its time"/ Indigenous time, 186; as confounding racial assumptions, 183–87, 189–90; cross-cultural vocal harmonies in, 185, 188–89, 192; future-looking ethos of, 189–90; homecoming as theme of, 187–88, 190, 240n32; Henry Berry Lowry as subject in, 190–91; as "Lumbee" sound, 184; national anthem of Lumbee, 191; place and politics as considerations in, 189–90; as resistant sound, 187; sovereign identity and, 190–92

—works: *Overdose*, 184, 186; *Plant and See*, 26, 161, 183–84, 184, 185, *186*, 187–90; *Proud to Be a Lumbee*, 26, 161, 183–84, 190–92; *Strike at the Wind!* (score), 159, 167, 182, 184

Lowrie, James, 169

Lowry, Allen, 162, 163, 180

Lowry, Henry Berry: as character, 178, 180–81; conscription into Civil War service, resistance to, 161–62; disappearance of, and "will never die" refrain, 162, 164–65; as "Indian Robin Hood," 162; interracial nature of Lumbee band and pluralistic alliances of, 163, 185; land claim ("the only land I know") and, 163–64, 179, 191; "Lowry Wars" and, 162; narrative shifts of Lumbee history and, 166–67; as subject of music, 190–91. See also *Strike at the Wind!*

Lowry, Reba M., 177

Lowry, Rhoda, as character, 180–81

Lowry, William, 162

Lowry wars, 26, 162, 178, 179

Lumbee (band). *See* Lowery, Willie French

Lumbee Act (1956), 173, 237n10, 239n20

Lumbee Tribe of North Carolina, 8; capitalistic nationalism and, 160, 165–66; as "civilized," 168–69, 238n12; as "free persons of color," 161; Indian Normal School of, 168, 170, 171, 183; interracial nature of, 163, 168, 175, 184, 185; as justification for federal policies, 166, 168–70, 238n12; land claim/ownership and, 163–64, 167, 168, 169, 171, 176; *The Life-Story of a People*, 177–78; political points made using, 165–66; as term, 236n1. *See also* Lowery, Willie French: musical sound of; *Strike at the Wind!*

—federal recognition of, 161, 166, 236n2; congressional recognition sought, 237n10, 239n20; history of quest for, as correlating with shifts of federal Native policy, 166, 168–70, 172–73, 238–39n16, 239nn19–20; land claim and, 168; Lost Colony origin theory and, 168–69, 176; "original 22," 172, 239n17, 239n20; outdoor drama *Strike at the Wind!* and quest for, 173–74, 176, 183, 240n22; physical examination to determine status, 172; repeated changes of tribal names and origin theories in effort to secure, 166, 170–73, 237n10, 239nn17–18; right-wing co-optation of struggle for, 165–66; state recognition of, 169, 173, 238n12; tribes opposed to, 237n10, 239n20

—identity of: as complicated, 175; as constructed, 177–78; divisions among Tribe and, 170, 177; national, 166–67, 176, 184, 185

—as Lost Colony descendants: origin story theory, 61–62, 167–70, 176, 192, 229–30n34; pressure to create outdoor drama depicting, 175–77

—resistance by, 26, 160–61; Civil War and conscription into service, 161–62; land claim and, 163–64, 167; "Lowry Wars," narratives of, 162–63; music as, 190–92; retelling stories and, 162; southern exceptionalism based on white supremacy and biracial classifications, challenges to, 161, 163, 164, 170, 174; sovereignty and, 167; spiralic temporality and, 161; as unexceptional, 161; U.S. nationalism, refusal to be co-opted into, 160–61. See also *Strike at the Wind!*

Lytle, Clifford, 237–38n11

MacLean, Hector, 179

Madison, James, 72–73, 74

Mad Wolf, 109

Manteo, 41–44; as character, 32, 57, 63

Manteo, N.C., 45, 54, *63*

mapping, 137, 140–42, 148, 149–50

Marion, Francis, 80, 85

Marshall, John, 79

Marxist literary studies, 12–13

Mayan people, 194, 195, 199, 201–4, 205–6, 207

Maynor Lowery, Malinda. *See* Lowery, Malinda Maynor

Maynor v. Morton, 239n20

McAdams, Janet, 8, 21, 22, 220, 242n13; *Red Weather*, 26, 206–11, 242n13

McInnis, Jarvis, 20

McIntosh, Chilly, 120

McIntosh, William, 25, 111, 117, 118, 121, 123–24, 234n18; Simms's narrative about ("Broken Arrow"), 25, 111, 112, 132, 133–35

McLean, A. W., 170, 171, 238–39n16

McMillan, Hamilton, 239n18; *Sir Walter Raleigh's Lost Colony*, 167–70

Means, Russell, 65

Mellichampe (Simms), 25, 70, 71; absence of Blonay character in Simms scholarship, 80, 81, 83; "bad" Indian converted to "good" and, 90–91; conflation of poor whites with Natives and, 87–89; guilt about Native death and, 89–90; indigenization of whiteness and, 85–86, 88–89; mixedblood Catawba character Blonay, 80–81, 83–91; place naming and, 84–85, 141; reception of, 83–84, 88–89, 90

memory: McAdams's *Red Weather* and, 20–21, 210–11; outdoor dramas and, 49, 51

Menawee, 109

Merrell, James, 86

Metcalf, Stephen, 147

Mexico: fictionally rendered, 208, 209; Spanish colonization of, 110, 210; spiralic temporality and, 23; U.S. South linked to, 124–25, 234n19

Micco, Yoholo, 109, 120

Mico Kings (Howe), 196

Miles, Tiya, 20

Miller, Lee, 40

Mississippi, Removal of Choctaw Nation from, 118

Mississippian people, worldview of, in Hogan's *Power*, 200

Mitchell, Douglas, 224n15

Mitchell, Margaret, 16–17

mixedblood characters: Simms's portrayal of, and absence in Simms scholarship, 80, 81, 83; viewed as not "counting" as Indian, 81. *See also* racial mixing, trope of

mixedblood peoples: binary with fullblood, Cherokee Removal and, 119; broken treaties as destruction of sovereignty of, 218; Indigenous land claims decreased via imagined lack of "authenticity" of, 20, 86; New World identity of, 61

Moore, Marinda Branson, 116, 158; *Geographical Reader, for the Dixie Children*, 109–10, 135, 234n19

Moretti, Franco, 141

Morgan, T. J., 238n12

Morley, Sylvanus G., 206

Murawski, John, 144

Muscogee Creek people: McAdams's *Red Weather* and, 206–7, 208; worldview of, in Hogan's *Power*, 200

music, 184–85, 187, 188–90, 192, 240n31. *See also* Lowery, Willie French: musical sound of

My Louisiana Love (Hong and Verdin film), 26–27, 211–15

Nakamura, Masahiro, 84

narrative: nature of, 12–13, 224n11; power dynamics of, 221–22; returns of creation stories, 217, 220

narrative order: definition of, 3; red state as intersection between Indigenous land claims and, 2–4, 223n1; spiralic temporality and critique of, 22–23. *See also* periodization and reperiodization; spiralic temporality

nation-states, as speculative, 211

Native American, as term, xiii

Native American Graves Protection and Repatriation Act, 233n3

Native American literatures, 10–11; African American literatures and, 20–21; emerging, 21; geographic birth and, accident of, 21–22; Native literary critics of, 11–12; spiralic temporality and, 22; survival of apocalypse and, 195; thinking hemispherically and, 208, 209

Native American studies: as epistemological framework versus object-focused discipline, 11–12, 28, 149; geographic birth and, accident of, 21–22; progressive fantasy versus regressive movement, 1–2, 219; race and economy as issues in, 10; spiralic temporality and, 196–97; tribal specificity and, 27. *See also* spiralic temporality

—methodology of, 11–12, 21, 27–28, 197; alternate temporalities and, 154–55; each ending as potential beginning, 195; historical fiction and, 99–100

Native history: authenticity of, as measured by representation of loss, 81; construction of, and Native policy, 7–8; historic sites, preservation of, 12; as pervasive in southern literature, 2, 16, 17–19, 225n17; "recovery" efforts of, as attempted mitigation of racism, 12; Simms's use of, 80

Native identity: African Americans and, 19–20; claiming of "red," 4–5; complexity of, in U.S. Southeast, 175; Indian Removal as undermining, 142; non-Native expectations of and effects on, 182; "playing Indian" by Natives, 177–78, 182; "playing Indian" by non-Natives, 19–20, 49, 105–8; state involvement in, 238–39n16; static, and Native characters based on archival sources, 94–97, 98–100, 101–2, 105; white view of, 172. *See also* federal recognition of tribes; Lumbee Tribe of North Carolina: identity of; *Red* state as Indigenous space

Native South: authenticity of representations of, 17–18; internal border between U.S. South and, 141; "pre" and "post" markers of, 111; Removal narratives perceived as defining experience of, 83; scholarly recovery of, caution on, 34–35, 64; as term, xiii

Native South (journal), 8

New Orleans, and Hurricane Katrina, 197–98

New Southern Studies, 9–10, 27, 224n15

New World: (dis)location of U.S. South in, 9–10; *Lost Colony* and, 58; mixedblood peoples' identity of, 61; settler colonialism and staging of, 34

New York (state), 129, 171

"Night They Drove Ole Dixie Down, The" (Robertson), 190

North Carolina: author's origins in, 27; Catawba Nation proposed siting in, 82; Cherokee Removal from, 119; Civil War and, 161–62; individualized land claims by Cherokee people in, 119; Kituwah Mound–Duke Energy conflict, 142–45, 150, 235n26; outdoor drama tradition in, 50; recognition of Lumbee Tribe, 169, 173, 238n12; as underfunding Indian schooling, 171, 238n12. *See also* Eastern Band of Cherokee Indians; *Horn in the West*; Lumbee Tribe of North Carolina; Robeson County, N.C.

northern states, southern identity and "tyranny" of: *Bloody Bloody Andrew Jackson* musical and, 157–58; Indian Removal and, 129, 158; Jefferson on, 72, 76–77, 78; uncanny hybridity of U.S. South and, 9; U.S. South as inheritors of American Revolutionary cause, 80, 103. *See also* southern identity

Nowhere Else on Earth (Humphrey), 161

Nunn, Erich, 185, 240n31

Oakley, Christopher Arris, 166–67

Obama, Barack, 1–2, 165–66

O'Connor, Flannery, 90

Oglala Lakota Pine Ridge reservation, 165

Old/New Souths: as a priori categories, shift from, 214; Indigenous temporal framework not addressed by, 13, 153, 154; spiralic temporality as troubling distinction of, 22–23

Onuf, Peter, 73

"ordinary affects," 138, 140

origin stories: apocalypse, regenerative power of, 207, 208; as pre-colonial, 222; returns of, 217, 220. *See also* Lumbee Tribe of North Carolina: federal recognition of

Ortiz, Simon, 8

Osage people, and Native American studies as method, 11–12

Osceola, 218

outdoor dramas, 45–46; affective history and, 46; audience perception of actors, 45; as compensatory fiction, 183; competing sovereign claims and, 49–50; as "essence" of history, 50–51; fictive genealogies and, 52, 54; Foucauldian power and, 47; Paul Green as father of, 32, 50; historical retellings, change over time of, 46, 50–52, 55–58; knowledge-making and, 51–52; land claim and, 52, 56, 229n29; long staging histories of, 31–32, 47–48, 71, 91, 98; memory and, 49, 51; Native control of participation in, 46, 47, 228n23; periodi-

outdoor dramas (*continued*)
zation and, 47–48; production changes, audience response to, 52; racial politics and, 52–54, 56, 56–57, 228–29n28, 229n29; reception traditions of, 50; spectacle and, 52; strategic dehistoricization and, 48–49; structures of feeling as maintaining structures of power and, 46, 48, 56–57, 60–61, 63–64. See also *Horn in the West*; *Lost Colony, The*; *Strike at the Wind!*

Overdose (W. F. Lowery), 184, 186

Owens, Louis, 21

pan-Indianism, 199–200
Parker, Robert Dale, 21, 225n17
Partisan, The (Simms), 70, 80, 83, 84, 85–86
Patriot, The (Emmerich film), 66–70, 87, 147, 230n5
Patriot Act, 230n5
Pease, Donald, 66–69, 70, 228n24, 230n5
Pee Dee people, 172
Pembroke, University of North Carolina at, 183
Pendleton, Edmund, 76
People of the Whale (Hogan), 199
Perdue, Theda, 10, 98, 235n23
Perez-Brignoli, Hector, 208
performance studies, 7
periodization and reperiodization, 13–14; alternate temporal frameworks to, 13–14; American Revolution narratives and, 71; apocalypses survived by Native Americans and, 195, 197–98; audience and, 14–15; authenticity and, 19; colonial enterprise and, 13, 224n12; Indian Removal and, 116, 128, 136; outdoor dramas and, 47–48; policy and, 171; postcolonial literary studies and, 13, 224n13; region and, 13–14; resilience and, 195, 196, 197–98; sense of place and, 111; simultaneity and, 19; spiralic temporality and, 13–14, 23, 27, 197; transnational study and, 224–25n16. See also spiralic temporality
Peru, 110, 124–25, 234n19
Pierce, C. F., 171
pipeline projects, 157, 219, 233n3, 235n26
place, non-Native southerners and sense of: versus diasporic Native nationalism, 209; versus landed Indigenous sovereignty, 5–7, 164, 179–80; reperiodization and, 111; silence of "good" white people and, 219. See also indigenization of whiteness; settler colonialism

place names: land claims and, 84–85, 141, 218; Lumbee Tribe name and, 173; naming rights, 141; spiralic temporality and, 153

Plant and See (W. F. Lowery), 26, 161, 183–84, 184, 185, *186*, 187–90

plantation economy: anxiety about, and myths of indigeneity, 116; as dominating considerations of region, 13; expansion of workforce via "one drop" rules, 20; Indian Removal to facilitate, 117, 122–24, 124–25, 129–30, 132–35; Native people as beneficiaries of, 124, 132–33, 235n23; paternalism of, 134; profitability as measure of, 115; sovereignty of Native Nations as threat to, 122–24, 218; unsustainability of, displaced onto Native nations, 115, 132–33. See also economy and economics; racial binary

Plymouth Rock, 54
Pocahontas, 229n33
Pocahontas (Disney film), 90
Poe, Edgar Allan, 90
political claims, legitimization of, with American Revolution narratives, 66, 70–72, 79
poor white southerners: interactions with Native people, and narratives of the American Revolution, 70–71, 80, 84; *The Patriot* and examination of, 67, 68–69. See also southern identity
Popol Vuh, 23, 195, 205–6
postcolonial literary studies, periodization and, 13
postmodernism, 195
poverty: rates of, in Robeson County, N.C., 165, 236n5; right wing as blaming federal recognition of tribes for, 165–66. See also poor white southerners
Power (Hogan), 26, 198–206, 207, 210
Powhatan, Jamestown war with, 40
presence of Native people: how audiences see or fail to see, 16; persistence of, 8, 16, 83, 135–36, 152–53, 237n10. See also resilience; survival of Native Americans
print cultures, 110–11; audience and, 114–15, 120–21, 124, 125, 234n19; chaotic mach-

inations as backdrop to, 120; *Cherokee Phoenix* excerpts in non-Native southern papers, 121, 123–25, *126–27*; coplacement of selected news items and, 114–15, 123–25, *126–27*; critical reception and, 113, 115–16; divided Native nations and, exploitation of, 123–24; linkage of power, print, and infrastructure of Cherokee people, 121–22; William McIntosh / Creek controversy and, 123; as staged, 114–15

property tax, modest proposal regarding, 221

Proud to Be a Lumbee (W. F. Lowery), 26, 161, 183–84, 190–92

Public Law 280 and House Concurrent Resolution 108 (1956), 166, 172–73, 239n19

Quayson, Ato, 13

Quinn, Arthur Hobson, 83, 90

Quinn, David Beers, 39, 41, 42, 43, 226n10, 227n14

R*dsk*ns trademark, 107–8, 232n35

race: construction of, 10, 218; environmental determinism, Jefferson and, 73, 74, 75; freedom and, 71; Willie French Lowery's music as confounding assumptions of, 183–87, 189–90; protoracial markers, 37–38, 41; racial determinism, 84–85. *See also* racial binary; racial mixing, trope of; racism; whiteness

racial binary (black/white): Lumbee cultural productions and rejection of, 174; music and, 240n31; Native South effaced in, 8, 224n15. *See also* mixedblood peoples; plantation economy; slavery

racial determinism, Simm's mixedblood character and, 84–85

racial mixing, trope of, 32, 54, 60–61, 229n33. *See also* mixedblood characters

racism: of *Bloody Bloody Andrew Jackson*, 155–58; land ownership by nonwhite persons and, 163, 180; Lumbee–Lost Colony theory and, 168; outdoor dramas and, 52–54, 56, 56–57, 228–29n28, 229n29; of physical examination to determine Tribal status, 172; reading reprehensible authors for understanding of, 114; "recovery" efforts of Native history as attempted mitigation of, 12; of Simms, 113–14; as structure of feeling that informs structures of power, 56–57. *See also* Jim Crow system; white supremacists and white supremacy

Raleigh, Sir Walter, 41, 42, 43–44, 54, 167; as character, 32, 57–58, 62–63, 229n30. *See also* Roanoke Colony

reception, 13, 14–15, 19; alternatives to periodization and, 14–15; authenticity and, 15–16, 81; *Bloody Bloody Andrew Jackson* and, 155, 156, 157–58; of Boudinot, 113, 114–16; Frazier's *Cold Mountain* and, 147–49; Frazier's *Thirteen Moons* and, 137–40, 147; Green's *Lost Colony* and, 50, 54; Hunter's *Horn in the West* and, 94–95, 96–97, 98–99, 100–102, 149; Indian Removal narratives and, 136; land claim and desire for affective history, 138–39; Lumbee production *Strike at the Wind!* and, 174–75, 178, 179, 181, 182–83; meaning for political material world and, 4, 15–16, 224n13; presence of Native people, seen or not seen, 16; print cultures and, 113–16, 120–21, 124, 125, 234n19; of Simms, 113–16; Simms's Blonay character and, 83–84; Simms's *Mellichampe* and, 83–84, 88–89, 90; sympathy and, 81. *See also* authenticity; periodization and reperiodization

— outdoor dramas: location of, 174; perception of actors, 45; production changes to, 52; traditions of, 50

Reconstruction, 163

recovery, 24; of Native history as attempted mitigation of racism, 12; scholarly, caution about, 34–35, 64. *See also Lost Colony, The*; outdoor dramas; Roanoke colony

Red Power movement: Alcatraz Island occupation and, 217; battle against Native mascots and, 108; land claim and, 217, 218; Lumbee history and identity and, 160, 174; McAdams's *Red Weather* and, 207; Red state as Indigenous space and, 3–5

red state(s): American Revolution narratives and, 86, 89, 102; *Bloody Bloody Andrew Jackson* as apology for, 157–58; counternational framework of, 106–7, 158; historical razing of fact and, 94; as intersection of Indigenous land claims (space)

red state(s) (*continued*)
and narrative order (time), 2–4, 223n1; Jefferson and emergence of, 72, 75, 77; linear time and, 65; Lumbee Tribe and, 166, 167; morals and, fantasy of, 134; outdoor dramas and construction of, 56–57; progressive fantasies versus regressive movement and, 1–2, 219; spiralic temporality and, 65–66. *See also* Indian Removal; recovery; *Red* state as Indigenous space; resilience; resistance of Native nations in U.S. South; revolution

Red state as Indigenous space: continuous Indigenous resistance and, 181; definition of, 3–4, 159; land claim and, 179–80, 221; Red Power movement and, 3–5; resilience and, 195, 196, 197, 207, 208, 209, 216; returns of origin stories and, 217; tribally specific cultural productions and creation of, 165, 167, 192–93. *See also* resilience; resistance of Native nations in U.S. South

Red States, as title of text, 1–2

Red Stick War, 117

Red Weather (McAdams), 26, 206–11, 242n13

region and regionalism: belonging and, 3–4, 159, 179–80; collaborative regional geography, 199–200, 203–4, 207–8, 241–42n10, 242n13; histories and, 54–55, 106; machinations of power and, 5; periodization and, 13–14; spiralic temporality and, 197; tribal specificity and, 27

Reid, Harry, 107

Reising, R. W., 166

religion: apocalypse, European biblical referents versus Indigenous religious traditions, 195, 200–201, 202, 241n6; "going English" and, 42; *The Lost Colony* and, 55; music of, Native peoples and, 188–89; sin of Indian Removal as precipitating Civil War, 109–10, 116, 158

Removal. *See* Indian Removal

reperiodization. *See* periodization and reperiodization

representation: as illuminating non-Native views, 17; by Native people, 17–18

resilience, 26–27, 194–95, 215–16; periodization and, 195, 196, 197–98; *Red* state as Indigenous space and, 195, 196, 197, 207, 208, 209, 216. *See also* apocalypse(s); resilience: narratives of; survival of Native Americans

—narratives of: destruction and, regenerative power of, 194, 195, 199, 200–206, 208, 215–16, 241n8; movement South and, 207–8; romanticization as minimal in, 196; sovereignty and, 196–97; spiralic temporality and, 195, 196–97, 212; tribalography and, 196, 210

resistance literature: alternate temporal frameworks and, 14; anger and, 187; as continuing to "write home," 5; as narrative and indictment, 187

resistance of Native nations in U.S. South, 25–27, 159–60; claiming of "red," 4–5; as continuous, 181; narratives of, as constructions, 160, 219–20; retelling of stories to survive, 159–60; tribal specificity and, 27. *See also* Indian Removal: resistance to; Lumbee Tribe of North Carolina: resistance by; resilience

returns of creation stories, 217, 220. *See also* spiralic temporality

revolution, 24–25; definitions of, 65–66; as heuristic, 24; Indigenous uprisings, 208, 209–11, 242n13; as metaphor for understanding red state, 65–66; spiralic temporality and, 66, 154. *See also* American Revolution narratives

Revolutionary Regulators, 93–94

Richardson, Riché, 20

Richmond, Robert, 45, 57, 64

Ridge, John, 21, 109, 112, 118, 119, 120, 121, 133

Riding the Trail of Tears (Hausman), 26, 111, 136, 150–55

Rifkin, Mark, 23

Riggs, Lynn, 21

Rising Hearts Coalition, 232n35

Roach, Joseph, 49

Roanoke colony (Lost Colony): "CRO" and "Croatoan" inscriptions on trees, 37, 43; as earliest act of settler colonialism, 30, 54; as English defeat, 38, 44, 56–57; as horror story, 30–31, 63; loss as pervading discourse of, 24, 37–38, 43–45, 55; loss of silver cup, Secotan people and, 39–40, 227n17; Lost Cause narrative, conflation with, 36, 38, 55–57; Lumbee–Lost Colony theory, 61–62, 167–70, 176, 192, 229–30n34; Lumbee–Lost Colony theory, pressure to create outdoor drama focused on, 175–77; narrative of intrigue and chaos and, 37; prelapsarian space and, status of, 38–40, 42, 44; simulated absences in archive of, 36–37, 226n8. *See also Lost Colony, The*

Roanoke Island Historical Association (RIHA), 54–55, 104

Robertson, Robbie, 190

Robeson County, N.C.: archeological record showing pre-invasion continual Indigenous presence, 237n10; location of, and tourism/audience, 174; poverty rates in, 165, 236n5; *Strike at the Wind!* as economic benefit to, 174. *See also* Lumbee Tribe of North Carolina

Robeson County Historical Drama, Inc. (RCHD), 176–77, 178–79

Rockefeller Foundation, 54

Rodat, Robert, 70

Romine, Scott, 15–16, 69, 92–93, 99, 220

Roosevelt, Franklin, 50

Ross, John, 112, 113

Said, Edward, 35–36

Sarris, Greg, 12, 48

Saunt, Claudio, 10, 235n23

Schmidt, Rob, 165

Scruggs, Ralph, 131

Searchers, The (film), 60

secession: as background to Simms's work, 78–79, 83; as counternational movement, 71; Jefferson on potential for, 76–77; as next predictable event in long series, 78

Secotan at Aquascococke, and missing silver cup, 39–40, 227n17

Seiger, Ronald, 185

Selden, Samuel, 50–51, 52, 95–96, 101, 225n1

Selocta, 109

Seminole people: Hogan's *Power* and, 200, 204, 207; Removal attempts (Seminole Wars), 118, 124, 218

settler colonialism: absence of Native people and, as narrative, 31; African Americans distinguished as not being settlers, 20; American Revolution as asserting nationhood of, 66; apocalypse, destructive and regenerative power of, 202–3; Black Legend logic of English versus Spanish colonization, 110; definition of, 3; as foregone conclusion, assumption of, 44; as horror story, 30–31, 64; Indigenous origin stories as predating, 222; investment/divestment of southern studies of narratives of, 9, 12, 27–28, 220, 222; Lumbee–Lost Colony theory and, 168; as man-made disaster, 195; "middle ground" of, 61; property tax proposal as redress for wrongs of, 221; as speculative projects, 211; staging of Americas as "New World" and, 34; transit of empire, 207. *See also* apocalypse(s); Indian Removal; land claim, Indigenous; land tenure, white; narrative order; plantation economy; Roanoke colony; slavery; violence, colonial

Sevier, John, 94, 95

Shakespeare, William, 90–91

Sherman, William Tecumseh, 79

Sider, Gerald, 171

Simmons, W. Matthew, 79, 171

Simms, William Gilmore, 25, 78–79, 111–12; audience and, 114–15; Confederacy and, 79–80, 83, 113–14, 115; context of, 78–80, 83; critical reception of, 113, 115–16; focus on American Revolution, 80; on Indian Removal, 112, 233n3; as influence on *The Patriot*, 70; Native histories employed by, 80; Native people portrayed by, 80–81, 83–91; print culture and, 112; production of narrative history and, 79–80; racism of, 113–14

—works: "The Broken Arrow," 25, 111, 112, 132, 133–35; *The Cassique of Kiawah*, 80, 89; *The Geography of South Carolina*, 85; *Katherine Walton*, 70, 80; *The Lily and the Totem*, 80; *The Partisan*, 70, 80, 83, 84, 85–86; *The Yemassee*, 80, 89. See also *Mellichampe*

Siouan people, as one-time Lumbee Tribe name, 171–72, 237n10

Sir Walter Raleigh's Lost Colony (McMillan), 167–70

Skinner, Nell, 176–77

slavery: African Americans as not being settlers, 20; economics of American Revolution and, 68; Indian slave trade, 82;

slavery (*continued*)
    white supremacy and, 20. *See also* plantation economy; racial binary; racism
Smith, Jon, 9, 67–68, 69, 70, 147
Smith, Paul Chaat, 196
Snyder, Christina, 10, 82
Solar Storms (Hogan), 199
Sontag, Susan, 156
Sounds of Faith (M. M. Lowery documentary), 188–89
South, as term, xiii
South Carolina: Civil War and, 113–14; confederacy movement as led by, 79; as front in American Revolution, 68; nullification by, 69, 71, 79, 83, 84–85. *See also* Catawba people; *Patriot, The*; Simms, William Gilmore
Southern Appalachian Historical Association, 91–92, 96, 104
southern disaster complex, 215
southern feelings, Native sovereignty as undermined by, 16. *See also* structures of feeling, as maintaining structures of power
southern Gothic: Lost Cause ideology and, 164; Simm's Blonay character and, 84; undeadness and, 164
southern identity (white): Civil War and, 111; conflation of, with Native, 75, 87–89, 103; as contingent and performative, 9; Indian Removal and, 110–11, 128–29, 218; Jefferson on, 72, 73–75; "playing Indian" and, 19–20, 49, 105–8; pre–Civil War narratives of freedom and land tenure and, 78; print cultures and, 115. *See also* indigenization of whiteness; Lost Cause narrative, Confederate; northern states, southern identity and "tyranny" of; place, non-Native southerners and sense of; poor white southerners; settler colonialism
southern literature: Native history as pervasive in, 2, 16, 17–19, 225n17; thinking hemispherically about, 208, 209
southern rock, 184–85, 187, 189–90
southern studies: African American literatures and, 20–21; as "container" that might overflow, 18; as effacing Indigenous people and politics, 6, 10–11; investment/ divestment of settler-colonial narratives from, 9, 12, 27–28, 220, 222; "loss," emptying cache of term, 36; Native American studies methodology and, 27–28, 197; Native history as absent in, 17–18, 224n15; progressive fantasy versus regressive movement, 1–2, 219; recovery, caution on, 34–35, 64; "red" as term and, 4–5; undisciplined knowledge and, 197. *See also* Native American studies
Southron, The, 129
sovereignty of Native American tribes and nations: American Revolution and, 66; Bruyneel's "third space" of, 223n1; Indian Removal and, 122, 136; as inherent, 7, 220; Jefferson as ignoring complexity of governments of, 73, 76; Jefferson's perception of lack of government of, 72–73, 76, 77, 78, 170; of Lumbee Tribe, 167; music and, 190–92; print cultures and concern with, 122; recognition by other sovereign nation-states, 7; recognition by southern studies as problematic, 18; recognition by U.S. Supreme Court, 119; recognition of other tribes, 7; resilience narratives and, 196–97; retelling stories and, 150, 160, 220; right wing as convoluting, 165, 236n8; saving land and, 215; versus sense of place of non-Native southerners, 5–7, 164, 179–80; southern feelings as undermining, 16; spiralic temporality and, 145, 196–97, 220; state courts and, 117; in *Strike at the Wind!*, 181–82; terms used in text and, xiii; as threat to plantation economy, 122–24, 218; as threat to white land claim, 121–24, 128–30; tribal specificity and, 27; as value, 165. *See also Red* state as Indigenous space
Spanish Armada, 37
Spanish colonization, 110, 194, 202
spectacle, 52
spiralic temporality: American Revolution narratives and, 65–66, 84, 102; critique of narrative order, 22–23; definition of, 22; "double threading" and, 23; film and, 212–13; Indian Removal narratives and, 150–55; Lumbee resistance and, 161; Native American literature and, 22; new moments of, 66; as nonuniversal, 23–24;

pattern versus exceptionality, 23; periodization and, 13–14, 23, 27, 197; recurrence beyond "history repeating itself," 22; red state and, 65–66; resilience and, 195, 196–97, 212; resistance and, 14, 192; as return, 222; revolution and, 66, 154; settler-colonial distinction of Old and New Souths and, 22–23; sovereignty of Native nations and, 145, 196–97, 220; synchronic/diachronic analysis and, 14

split earth, 18–19

Squint, Kirstin, 10–11, 21

states' rights, and Indian Removal, 121, 128

Steele, Ian, 44

Stevens, Scott Manning, 155–56, 157

Stevens, Wallace, 206–7; "Disillusionment of Ten o'clock," 209

Stewart, Kathleen, 138

Stidham, John, 109

Story, Joseph, 79

Stossel, John, 165–66

Strike at the Wind! (W. F. Lowery score), 159, 167, 182, 184

Strike at the Wind! (Umberger play), 26, 47, 161, 173–74; audience and, 174–75, 178, 179, 181, 182–83; as compensatory fiction, 183; as critique of southern racism and pathos, 175, 178, 180–82; federal recognition and, quest for, 173–74, 176, 183, 240n22; identity and, 181–83; land claim, 179–82; lost causes and, 178, 180, 181–82, 183; "Lost Colony sequel" and, pressure to create, 175–77; Willie French Lowery and, 159, 167, 182, 184; as Lumbee cultural text, 179, 183; Lumbee Tribe national identity and, 166–67; racial complexity/Indigenous nationalism and, 175; as resistance narrative, 180–81, 183; revisions and changes to, 240n25; sovereignty and, 181–82; staging of, struggles to maintain, 174–75, 182–83, 240n22; survival of people as focus of, 178; violence in, 178–79. *See also* Lumbee Tribe of North Carolina

structures of feeling, as maintaining structures of power, 46, 48, 56–57, 60–61, 63–64

Stuart, David, 79

Stuart, Henry, 95

Supreme Court, U.S.: *Cherokee Nation v. Georgia*, 117, 118–19; utility companies and sovereignty of Indian Tribes, 143–44; *Worcester v. Georgia*, 79, 119

survival of Native Americans: of apocalypses, 195, 241n3; armadillo as metaphor for, 213; as focus of *Strike at the Wind!*, 178; Indian Removal, resistance to, 16, 135–36, 152–53; Indian Removal as obscuring, 83; retelling of stories and, 159–60. *See also* apocalypse(s); resilience

Swamp Outlaws, The (Townsend), 161

Swanton, John R., 171–72

Tamarkin, Elisa, 114–15

Tarleton, Banastre, 80

Taylor, Diana, 51

Taylor, John, 76–77

Taylor, Melanie Benson, 10–11, 12–13, 18, 21, 34–36, 55, 103, 136, 139

Taylor, Michael, 182, 184

Tea Party, 107; American Revolution narratives and, 70; *Bloody Bloody Andrew Jackson* as commentary on, 155, 157; racist attacks by, 165; right-wing co-optation of Lumbee story and, 165–66; U.S. South at crossroads, 216; Washington R*dsk*ns trademark and, 107–8

Tempest, The (Shakespeare), 90–91

Termination, 239n19; Catawba persistence during, 82; Jefferson and, 77–78; Lumbee Tribe federal recognition and, 171, 237n10, 239n20; Lumbee Tribe requests for federal recognition and correlation with, 166, 172–73

Their Eyes Were Watching God (Hurston), 198–99

Thirteen Moons (Frazier), 25–26, 111, 136–42, 145–48, 149–50

Thomas, William Holland, 136

Thornton, Richard, 143–44

Timber, Alex, 111. *See also Bloody Bloody Andrew Jackson*

time: deep time, 23; as plural temporalities, 14–15, 23; of settler colonialism, 23–24. *See also* linear temporality; spiralic temporality

Tocqueville, Alexis de, 118

Tompkins, Hillary, 173

Townsend, George Alfred, 161

Tracy, Susan, 88, 89

INDEX 279

Trail of Tears. *See* Cherokee people, Removal of
transit of empire, 207
"Travels in the South" (Ortiz), 8
treaties, broken: as corruption of power, 218; as general outcome, 82
Treaty of Cusseta (1832), 118
Treaty of Dancing Rabbit Creek (1830), 118
Treaty of Fort Jackson (1814), 117
Treaty of Indian Springs (first), 117
Treaty of Indian Springs (second), 117–18, 120–21, 123, 124, 134
Treaty of Nation Ford (1840), 82
Treaty of New Echota (1835), 112–13, 119
Trefzer, Annette, 10–11, 18, 224n13, 225n17
tribalography, 195, 196, 210
tribal specificity, 27
Troup, George, 117, 123
Trump, Donald, 1, 116, 157, 158
Trumpener, Katie, 14–15, 17
Tryon, William, 94, 95
Tsali, 138, 140
Turner, David Cross, 164
Tuscarora people, 172, 239n17
Tustenuggee, Apauli, 109
Tustenuggee, Coosa, 109
Tustenuggee, Tuskeekee, 109
Twain, Mark, 217–18

Umberger, Randy, 167, 174, 175, 176–77, 178–79, 240n25. See also *Strike at the Wind!*
United Keetoowah Band of Cherokee Indians, 143
United Provinces of Central America (UPCA), 208, 210, 211
United South and Eastern Tribes, 237n10, 239n20
University of North Carolina at Pembroke, 183
Unto These Hills (Hunter), 47, 104, 228n23
U.S. South: as abjected and repressed from national imaginary, 30; at crossroads, 216; construction of, through (hi)stories, 10–11; (dis)location in New World paradigm, 9–10; questioning borders of, resilience and, 207–8, 209; uncanny hybridity of, 9. *See also* Confederate States of America; counternational movement and sentiment; exceptionalism of U.S. South; global South; loss, narratives of; Native identity; southern identity; white people

Vann, David, 109, 118, 121, 131
Verdin, Monique, 26–27, 211–15
Vietnam war and veterans, 240n26
violence, colonial, 222; American Revolution narratives and, 68; creation of loss and justification of, 39–40; lack of atonement for, 218; resilience narratives of destruction and renewal and, 202; retelling of stories to justify, 159; simulated absence of Native Americans as justification of, 36–37, 45, 226nn8–9. *See also* apocalypse(s); Indian Removal; racism; slavery
Virginia: confederacy movement as led by, 79; Jefferson non-South and, 72; loss and absence narratives and, 36; as prelapsarian space, 38–40, 42, 44. *See also* Roanoke Colony
Vizenor, Gerald, 32, 36–37, 39, 44, 226n8
von Wedel, Lupold, 41, 42

Waccamaw people, 172
Walker, Alice, 17
Walkiewicz, Kathryn, 8, 21
Wallace, Anthony, 73, 76
Wanchese, 41–42; as character, 32, 57, 63
Ward, Nancy (Nanye'hi), 97, 98; as Beloved Woman, 98–99; as character, 71, 93–94, 96, 98, 99–100, 101–2, 103, 105
Warren, Gene, 175–76
Warrior, Robert, 11, 35, 196, 212
Washington, George, 79
Washington R*dsk*ns trademark, 107–8, 232n35
Watuagan people, 76
Wayne, John, 60
Weaver, Jace, 10–11, 18–19, 209
Welburn, Ron, 20
Welty, Eudora, 17
"We Were in a World" (Hedge Coke), 194
White, John: archival absence of, 36–37, 44, 227n21; attempt to find Roanoke Colony, 37, 38, 42–44, 57; as character, 32; identity of, 227n21; simulation of absence by, 36–37, 226n8; watercolors and drawings of, 32, 33, 37, 44
White, Richard, 61

Whitehead, Neil, 226n9
whiteness: as beleaguered, 71, 158; phenotypic register of, and Native people, 41, 218; "wages of," 56, 229n29. *See also* indigenization of whiteness
white people: "good," 219; nativism of, conservative ideology and, 57; silence of, 219. *See also* empire; Indian Removal; land tenure, white; poor white southerners; red state(s); settler colonialism; southern identity; Tea Party; Trump, Donald; whiteness; white supremacists and white supremacy
white space, 142, 148, 217
white supremacists and white supremacy: American Revolution narratives and, 70; emotive excess as shoring up narratives of, 63–64; Native policy in support of, 166; Native sovereignty, aggressions against, 20; systemic racism against black citizens, 20; Tea Party attacks on minorities as trial balloon for, 165. *See also* Jim Crow system; racism

Wilkins, David, 163
Williams, Raymond, 17, 46
Wilson, Charles Reagan, 55
Wilson, Michael, 5, 216
Wimsatt, Mary Ann, 84, 90
Wingina, 32, 41
Wishart, Davis, 13
Womack, Craig, 6–7, 10–11, 21, 207, 217, 220; "Howling at the Moon," 220
women, and Indian Removal debates, 234–35n22
Worcester, Samuel, 119
Worcester v. Georgia (1832), 79, 119

Yemassee, The (Simms), 80, 89
Yemassee War (1715), 82
Yoholo, Opothle, 109
Yonaguska (Drowning Bear), 139, 150
Young Bear, Ray, 216

Zogry, Michael, 55, 228–29n28

The New Southern Studies

The Nation's Region: Southern Modernism, Segregation, and U.S. Nationalism
    by Leigh Anne Duck
Black Masculinity and the U.S. South: From Uncle Tom to Gangsta
    by Riché Richardson
Grounded Globalism: How the U.S. South Embraces the World
    by James L. Peacock
*Disturbing Calculations: The Economics of Identity in
Postcolonial Southern Literature, 1912–2002*
    by Melanie R. Benson
American Cinema and the Southern Imaginary
    edited by Deborah E. Barker and Kathryn McKee
Southern Civil Religions: Imagining the Good Society in the Post-Reconstruction Era
    by Arthur Remillard
Reconstructing the Native South: American Indian Literature and the Lost Cause
    by Melanie Benson Taylor
Apples and Ashes: Literature, Nationalism, and the Confederate States of America
    by Coleman Hutchison
Reading for the Body: The Recalcitrant Materiality of Southern Fiction, 1893–1985
    by Jay Watson
Latining America: Black-Brown Passages and the Coloring of Latino/a Studies
    by Claudia Milian
Finding Purple America: The South and the Future of American Cultural Studies
    by Jon Smith
The Signifying Eye: Seeing Faulkner's Art
    by Candace Waid
*Sacral Grooves, Limbo Gateways: Travels in Deep Southern Time,
Circum-Caribbean Space, Afro-creole Authority*
    by Keith Cartwright
Jim Crow, Literature, and the Legacy of Sutton E. Griggs
    edited by Tess Chakkalakal and Kenneth W. Warren
Sounding the Color Line: Music and Race in the Southern Imagination
    by Erich Nunn
Borges's Poe: The Influence and Reinvention of Edgar Allan Poe in Spanish America
    by Emron Esplin
Eudora Welty's Fiction and Photography: The Body of the Other Woman
    by Harriet Pollack
Keywords for Southern Studies
    edited by Scott Romine and Jennifer Rae Greeson
Navigating Souths: Transdisciplinary Explorations of a U.S. Region
    edited by Michele Grigsby Coffey and Jodi Skipper
The Southern Hospitality Myth: Ethics, Politics, Race, and American Memory
    by Anthony Szczesiul

Where the New World Is: Literature about the U.S. South at Global Scales
    by Martyn Bone
Red States: Indigeneity, Settler Colonialism, and Southern Studies
    by Gina Caison
The Whole Machinery: The Rural Modern in Cultures of the U.S. South, 1890–1946
    by Benjamin S. Child

CPSIA information can be obtained
at www.ICGtesting.com
Printed in the USA
LVHW091827291122
734230LV00005B/515

9 780820 358796